- Get into the tub only after washing all suds off your body. Never get soap in the bath. That means not taking your hand towel into the bath, either.
- Get out and wash more thoroughly if you like—ears, hair, and teeth. Get your neighbor to scrub your back.
- Go back for another soak.

EVENING

- Return to your room. Dinner will be ready soon.
- Do you want beer? Do you want saké during the meal? Ask for it.
- At dinner, eat each course as it is presented. Rice, soup, and pickles are served last. Stop drinking beer and saké when the rice arrives.
- If the meal was served in your room, you will be disturbed shortly after dinner by someone whose job it is to take out the *futon* from the cupboards and make the beds. Stay in the room, go and have another bath, check out the bars/reading rooms in your inn, or go for a walk in town. Walking in the streets in *yukata* is acceptable in hot spring towns. Use the wooden clogs (geta) provided by your inn.
- Go to bed, still in your *yukata* if you like.

MORNING

- In the morning, answer your wake-up call. Have breakfast in your *yukata* or street clothes. Only the highest-class inns serve breakfast in the room these days.
- Pay the bill. Say goodbye.
- Do not steal the family heirlooms before you go, or the moss from the garden as somebody did in Kyoto. A souvenir *yukata* can usually be bought.

CLASSIC
JAPANESE
INNS
& COUNTRY GETAWAYS

C L A S S I C
JAPANESE
INNS
& COUNTRY GETAWAYS

Margaret Price

KODANSHA INTERNATIONAL
Tokyo • New York • London

Maps by Tadamitsu Omori
Line drawings by the author

Published by Kodansha International Ltd., 17–14 Otowa 1-chome, Bunkyo-ku, Tokyo 112–8652, and Kodansha America, Inc.

Distributed in the United States by Kodansha America, Inc., 575 Lexington Avenue, New York, New York 10022, and in the United Kingdom and continental Europe by Kodansha Europe Ltd., 95 Aldwych, London WC2B 4JF.

Copyright © 1999 Margaret Price and Kodansha International Ltd.
All rights reserved.
Printed in Japan.
First edition, 1999

2 3 4 5 6 7 8 9   02 01 00

ISBN 4–7700–1873–8

CONTENTS

Introduction 7

The Evolution of the Japanese Inn 17

Architecture and Gardens 20

The Inn Experience 25
   A Word About Meals 27

Using This Book 29

D E S T I N A T I O N S

1. Tokyo   35
   Quick Getaways from Tokyo   37
2. Kamakura, Kanagawa Prefecture   41
3. Tochigi Prefecture   46
4. Gumma Prefecture   51
5. Hakone, Kanagawa Prefecture   56
6. Izu Peninsula, Shizuoka Prefecture   62
7. Masuho-cho, Yamanashi Prefecture   71
8. Lake Suwa and Takato, Nagano Prefecture   74
9. Matsumoto, Nagano Prefecture   79
10. Nakasendo, Nagano Prefecture   83
11. Zenkoji Temple, Nagano Prefecture   89
12. Nozawa Onsen, Nagano Prefecture   97
13. Hida-Takayama, Gifu Prefecture   101
14. Shirakawa-go and Gokayama, Gifu/Toyama Prefectures   108
15. Mino, Gifu Prefecture   113
   In Praise of Japanese Paper   116

16. Ise and Tokaido, Mie/Aichi Prefectures 118
17. Niigata Prefecture 128
18. Aizu Wakamatsu, Fukushima Prefecture 136
19. Yamagata Prefecture 143
20. North Tohoku, Iwate/Akita/Aomori Prefectures 149
21. Kanazawa, Ishikawa Prefecture 156
22. Noto Peninsula, Ishikawa Prefecture 164
   In Praise of Wajima Lacquerware 166
23. Kyoto 170
24. Nara 181
25. Kii Peninsula, Wakayama Prefecture 187
26. Arima Onsen, Hyogo Prefecture 193
27. Kinosaki Onsen, Hyogo Prefecture 197
28. Miyama-cho, Ama-no-Hashidate and Obama,
   Kyoto/Fukui Prefectures 201
29. Kurashiki, Okayama Prefecture 208
30. Fukiya, Okayama Prefecture 213
31. Hiroshima and Iwakuni, Hiroshima/Yamaguchi Prefectures 217
32. Hagi, Yamaguchi Prefecture 223
33. Matsuyama, Ehime Prefecture 230
34. Yufuin and Beppu, Oita Prefecture 235
35. Karatsu and Arita, Saga Prefecture 242

APPENDICES

Alternative Inns 248

Classic Hotels 262

Alphabetical List of Inns 265

Checklist of Inns 269

Favorite Inns 275

Ryokan-style Accommodation in Tokyo under ¥8,000 276

Helpful Japanese Phrases 278

Glossary 281

Acknowledgments 287

INTRODUCTION

In 1985, in the midst of a nostalgia boom for the young Emperor Showa (previously known as Emperor Hirohito; 1901–89), two large-format guidebooks came out almost simultaneously, each overflowing with glossy photographs of inns where the emperor had stayed while on tours of duty around the country to encourage the nation in the postwar reconstruction years. These inns were the best ones the provinces could manage. For the royal visit, old establishments added on new rooms in the finest timbers or renovated whole wings. The guidebooks show where His Majesty slept, where He bathed, and the foods He was fed. His modestly clad figure is seen stepping from black cars onto red welcome carpets. The emperor had been pronounced no longer a god. But he was still a god out there. A Japanese journalist once told me that when the emperor took his first trips into the provinces, even his droppings were scooped up from the sawdust of the thunder boxes and kept in jars. The legend was alive.

For the emperor, these trips outside Tokyo were an adventure. Cloistered in the curtained rooms of his hybrid Western-Japanese palace, eating porridge for breakfast and sleeping on a bed, he did not know how the other half lived. Thus it was that chamberlains had to give lessons to the emperor of Japan on how to sleep in a *futon* before he stayed in his first public inn—the Murao inn at Kaminoyama, Yamagata, on August 16, 1947. He is said to have confided to one of his attendants later: "These places called inns are certainly well fitted out for one's convenience."

For me, the emperor's inns glowed in the pages of those guidebooks. They were oases in the architectural catastrophe that had become postwar urban Japan. It was reassuring to know that there was some beauty left; it turned out that these pockets of old Japan were in every city and hot spring town, preserving a great tradition of innkeeping.

The guides added fuel to a smoldering longing for the good stuff of Japan that was slowly rekindled by similar books with such titles as *Nihon no Meiryokan* (The Great Inns of Japan), *Rekishi to Bungaku no Yado* (Inns of History and Literature), and *Nihon Rashisa no Yado* (Inns That Speak of Japan). I bought every publication on the subject I could find and my collection now exceeds seventy volumes.

After I discovered Japanese inns, I became a different sort of traveler. I stopped searching for sights and focused on beautiful inns—and then I found that where there were good inns, the best sights were not far away.

Many of the emperor's inns let me down. Being the poshest and richest they had also been the first to cleave concrete additions, jungle baths, video-game rooms, and velvet-upholstered karaoke bars when economic times turned up. They had package deals for company trips, banquet rooms for two hundred, and refectories for breakfast en masse. It took a brave innkeeper in the 1960s and 1970s to stay small, for the pressure was on to lure the large groups. A lot of the inns that expanded then are now struggling as the tide has turned again and Japan has rediscovered the "small inn." Group trips are out; yuppie, luxury, and family travel are in. And we individual travelers profit as more and more people renovate handsome old family homes and serve them up as places to stay. Meanwhile 1990s inns built with inflated 1980s assets are sumptuous monuments to modern indulgence.

Had my agenda been to search for "the inn that has everything," I could have filled this book with ¥40,000–70,000-a-night nouveau riche palaces where "the best" could be taken for granted. The Izu Peninsula will one day sink under their weight. No, my challenge was to find the inns with atmosphere, good taste, and innkeepers who care.

In this book, I have concentrated on two types of inn: structures that have managed to hang on more or less as they were in the Edo period (1600–1868)—their elegance intact, if at times fading—and new ones built and managed with integrity. They might be old, they might be new. Not all of them have beautiful gardens, good food, luxurious hot spring baths. Many don't even have a toilet in the room. But almost all of them have that special something that comes with being in a lovely building or having well-crafted fittings or hand-picked tableware. In my explorations I have been fortunate to unearth quite a few best-kept secrets that only emerge by word of mouth. And just when I think I know all the best inns in a town, I learn of another gem, and so the search goes on.

Margaret Price
Tokyo

The curtained entrance conceals a hidden world of luxury and discreet service. Iwa-no-Yu, page 91.

A lush garden and a new perspective on the world from floor level. Tawara-ya, page 173. →

A welcome of whisked green tea and sweets. Takashima-ya, page 133.

Traditional structures in a classic garden.
Historical section, Matsuda-ya, page 228.

Exhilarating hot spring bathing with an ocean view. Hashiri-yu bath, Horai, page 64.

Contemporary indulgence in a bath. O-an, page 58.

A Kyoto-style kaiseki *feast for the summer; the courses come one after another. O-an, page 58.*

Delicately sliced blowfish sashimi, the ultimate wintertime treat. Tomoe, page 227.

EVOLUTION OF THE JAPANESE INN

In the seventeenth century, the Tokugawa shogunate instituted an ingenious system to control the nation of 250 domains it had recently unified. Divided by high mountains, these domains were virtually autonomous kingdoms and a clever plan was needed to keep local lords from rising up. The shogunate's solution called for the lords of every domain to travel to the capital of Edo (now Tokyo) every second year to pay their respects to the shogun. Upon taking their leave, the *daimyo*, as the lords were called, were required to leave their wives, children, or close relations behind as hostages to ensure good behavior in their home province.

The trips to Edo were massive undertakings, involving hundreds or even thousands of people in a single retinue. In the case of the Kaga domain (present-day Ishikawa Prefecture), a long procession of up to three thousand announced its approach with ranks of men marching with spears and standards, preceded by foot soldiers with brooms and dustpans.

To make these compulsory trips feasible, the shogunate invested in the upkeep of five major official highways, and instituted a system of post towns, where domainal retinues could get refreshments, lodgings, fresh horses, and couriers.

Daimyo and their closest retainers stayed at officially designated inns in these post towns. Called *honjin*, they were grandiose establishments with regal gates, classical gardens, and ornate *shoin*-style rooms with tatami-covered daises for the lord. Under the *honjin* were *waki-honjin* and *hatago*, the official lodgings for middle-ranked samurai, lower-ranked samurai, and servants.

As the new military capital of Edo grew in size and importance, merchants, peddlers, pilgrims, and tourists began frequenting the highways and other inns sprang up to cater to them. Any inn that was not a *hatago* was called a *kichin yado*. "*Kichin*" literally means "fee for firewood," so here travelers were expected to fend for themselves, while presumably paying little more than a fee for the charcoal they burned. They went into town for meals and entertainment, often involving liaisons with post town women.

But this did not last long. In one of its rather frequent purges against excess, and especially against prostitution, the Tokugawa shogunate pronounced that all inns must serve dinner, which in effect denied men the excuse of going out on the town. To circumvent this new proclamation, female entertainers began coming to the inns. And the rather unusual system of supplying evening meals as well as breakfast (*makanai-tsuki*) became a mainstay of the Japanese inn, a custom that continues to this day.

When a traveler slid open the door and stepped into the entrance, he would first come to the inn's *choba*, where the money changed hands. The master of the house or an attendant would ask the traveler what he wanted to spend and if negotiations led to an agreement on price, he would be shown his room, given tea, and offered a bath before the evening meal. The meal would be taken in the room and after the dishes were cleared away, a maid would lay out a mattress for sleeping. In the morning the guest would be woken for breakfast, which was again eaten in his room.

Among the items that travelers carried in those days were portable pillows made of wood, with compartments for carrying valuables such as personal seals and money. The traveler would also have an inkstone and brushes, a lantern, candles, and toiletries, but very little else, for most people traveled on foot. The luxury of a palanquin was reserved for the *daimyo* and his women, and there were no wheeled carriages on Japanese roads.

A meal at an inn consisted of rice, soup, and pickles, with perhaps some grilled fish and boiled vegetables. Raw fish is the first thing that appears in a meal nowadays, but records from the Edo period (1600–1868) don't even mention sashimi. Until refrigeration became widely used in modern times, raw fish was confined to the fast-food category, sold in Edo at food stalls.

The people of the Edo period were great travelers of the armchair variety. This is attested to by the immense popularity of landscape prints. Two of the most favored collections of "pictorial travel guides" were *Fifty-three Stations of the Tokaido* and *Scenes of the Kiso Highway*, both by woodblock artist Ando Hiroshige (1797–1858). *Fifty-three Stations* sold twenty thousand copies in the 1830s and became a major best-seller. Humorous tales about travel on the Tokaido formed another genre. The best-read of these was the comic novel *Shank's Mare* (*Tokaido-chu Hizakurige*) by Jippensha Ikku (1765–1831), which related the misadventures of a couple of buffoons called Yaji and Kita along Japan's principal thoroughfare. Practical guides on highway travel, how to avoid pickpockets, and what to do if you fell sick also saw publication.

As more and more people took to the roads, inns sprang up in places other than the post towns—at scenic spots, near pilgrimage temples, at hot springs, in prosperous merchant towns. And innkeeping became more and more of an art. Exotic bathhouses were added, cotton robes supplied, and whisked green tea and famous local sweets fed to guests when they arrived. Around the inns, souvenir shops and bars supplied pre- and post-dinner amusement. Every tourist spot had its own souvenir sweets, crackers, pickles, and handicrafts—as they do today.

So what remains of these early, eighteenth- to twentieth-century inns? Lodges in their pure Edo-period form are rare. Many early structures fell pray to postwar fire department regulations on buildings of wood, or to the even more irrepressible social pressures to pull down those "old-fashioned eyesores" to make way for modern concrete monoliths the nation could be proud of. In the decades-long rush to develop Japan's economy, few inns were rebuilt with integrity. The result is that those spots that should have the greatest scenic beauty are now the ones you would put first on your list of places to avoid.

But today's travelers still have treasures to unearth. Japan may be a small country for the urban dweller, but it is a huge frontier for the adventurer. This is due to the extremely mountainous terrain, which once divided the land into so many miniature culturally autonomous kingdoms. Modern trains and highways have overcome the barriers that once kept these pockets of culture unique, and at one stage it seemed that local cultures might be churned into homogenized ignominity. But now, after a fifty-year love affair with the West, people are reevaluating their traditions and dusting off the better ones.

You can find old post town inns in such pockets as Narai, Magome, and Tsumago on the former Nakasendo highway (see Destination 10), where things haven't changed much from the Edo period. There is one original inn on the old Tokaido road as well—the Ohashi-ya (Destination 16).

Hot spring inns have been reasonably strong survivors and a handful of precious three- and four-story wooden inns of the type in vogue around the early 1900s are still to be found. Among those listed in this book are the Rinsen-kaku in Shibu Onsen (Destination 11), the Myoga ya Honkan in Nasu (Destination 3), and the Noto-ya Ryokan in Ginzan Onsen (see Alternative Inns). The Sekizen-kan in Gumma (Destination 4) has the oldest extant hot spring building in Japan, dating to 1690.

Aside from these relics you can also find converted farmhouses, storehouses, and townhouses. But the majority of intimate inns today are 1900s constructions in the *sukiya* style. Let's examine the *sukiya* and other common architectural styles found at these inns, then look at the inn experience itself.

ARCHITECTURE AND GARDENS

The Japanese Room

If you can imagine a Japanese temple hall—a dark sea of floorboards without interior walls, punctuated only by pillars—you have some idea of where Japanese interior styles had their beginnings. Somehow those big empty spaces had to be divided up for comfortable living, so *tsuitate* (standing partitions), *byobu* (folding screens), and *fusuma* (removable sliding screens) entered the Japanese interior. Those cavernous halls also craved light so with the invention of paper came *shoji*, window screens covered in translucent paper. Meanwhile, in temples, Buddhist priests were hanging sacred pictures on walls and placing offerings of flowers and incense before them. These wall spaces developed into recesses dedicated to hanging scrolls, eventually evolving into the *tokonoma* alcove, another feature of the Japanese room.

These three devices—removable partitions, *shoji*, and the *tokonoma*—came to be fundamental to all Japanese interiors and can still be found in today's traditional inns.

Also fundamental to Japanese architecture is its reverence for wood, a material that Japanese carpenters found close at hand and easier to put up and pull down than brick or stone. Japanese architecture developed to accommodate the peculiarities of the country's climate: wide eaves to protect from the monsoonal rains, and a multitude of devices to let in breezes—raised floors, floor-level openings, and open-worked transoms—because the humid summer months were the hardest of all to bear.

Tatami mats were a relatively late addition to the Japanese room, not coming into common use until the seventeenth century. Though they may appear to be simple flat floor coverings, these mats are actually several centimeters thick and packed with straw. The surface is a covering of reeds stitched together and bound at the edges with cloth. When one side becomes worn it is flipped over and used for another year.

Shoin, *Sukiya*, and *Minka*

In this book you will frequently come across the terms *sukiya* and *shoin*. These refer to the two main architectural styles in vogue in the Edo period (1600–1868), when a prosperous merchant culture emerged. Pure and hybrid forms of *sukiya* and *shoin* are what you will encounter most frequently at Japanese inns.

The *shoin* style, which was favored by lords and high-ranking samurai, had pompous entrances with ornate tiled roofs, and fancy reception rooms with a large alcove next to a space containing staggered shelves and cupboards and a *shoji* screen with decorative latticework adjoining a hall. The sliding doors (*fusuma*) may have been covered in murals, and the ceilings were often coffered. The reception room would also look out on a carefully cultivated garden with a venerable pine and gnarled plum trees. After the modern era, it became fashionable to attach a token Western-style guest room with stuffed velvet chairs and antimacassars.

The *sukiya* style grew up at around the same time as the *shoin*, but was inspired by tea-ceremony architecture with its lightweight wooden structures, cedar-tiled roofs, fragile bamboo gates, and mossy gardens like mountain paths.

Solid, symmetrical, and heavy typify *shoin* features; fluid, delicate, and light epitomize *sukiya* style. Newly built Japanese inns often mix the two. A room may exhibit the delicate use of timber typical of the *sukiya*, but have such *shoin* touches as an extra alcove with staggered shelves and a decorative *shoji* screen adjoining the hall. They work together well.

Not all of the inns in this book are of the refined *sukiya* or *shoin* styles; many of the cheaper *minshuku* are old farmhouses or townhouses that once belonged to artisans or tradesmen. These are referred to as *minka* and they share the more robust features of the common people's architecture: heavy exposed beams, plaster or packed-earth interior walls, and in the farmhouses a sunken hearth around which guests gather for meals.

The *Tokonoma* and Staggered Shelves

The *tokonoma* is traditionally the first place a guest would approach in a Japanese home. Kneeling in front of this recessed area, he would place his hands on the tatami in front of him and observe the scroll and other decorations, asking the host to explain their meanings and origins.

The tradition of placing art in the *tokonoma* is carried on at inns. In better establishments, a scroll with calligraphy, an ink painting, or a humorously illustrated poem appropriate to the season or occasion will be hung in the *tokonoma*, complemented by a simple arrangement of flowers from the field and perhaps an incense container—all legacies of the tea ceremony. In lower-class establishments, these may fall victim to cheap framed art, plastic flowers, a television, a safe, or, perhaps, a carved statue of a bear. But if you are staying in a small inn where obvious care is taken in the choice of the *tokonoma* art, by all means ask the meaning of the scroll. If your inn has *shoin*-type features such as a recess with staggered shelves, you may find a writing box or incense container displayed there, and adjoining it an intricately carpentered *shoji* screen on an interior bay window, letting light in from the hall. This *shoji*-lit recess has its origins in early Buddhist temples, as a place where priests performed their studies.

The best piece of timber in the room can usually be found in the main *tokonoma* pillar, called the *tokobashira*. It was once customary to use precious indigenous woods—horse chestnut, camphor, or mulberry—from trees two hundred years old or more, and for the *tokobashira* to be cut square. This changed from the end of the 1800s when exotic foreign woods such as ebony were imported, and unusual gnarled or knotted timbers came into vogue. You may be able to judge the vintage of your room from this feature. One of the most popular timbers for the *tokobashira* now is the *Kitayama sugi*, a straight cypress trunk that is stripped of bark and polished until it is smooth and cream-colored, with an attractive grooved texture.

The *tokonoma* may have a tatami-covered or a wood-covered surface, and it may be raised or not. Originally it was raised. One of the theories has it that the evolution of the *tokonoma* comes from the tea-ceremony room, where it had been the custom for lordly personages to be seated on a raised tatami-covered dais. But the Zen-inspired tea masters who perfected the tea ceremony decided it more appropriate to put precious utensils up on the dais and relegate all men to being equals down on the floor, their thinking being that powerful men perish while great art lives on.

God Shelves and Altars

In agricultural and fishing communities, where religious observances were a vital part of everyday life, the *kamidana* ("god shelf") and *butsudan* (Buddhist family altar) had pride of place in the home, and in farmhouse inns you will not be able to miss them. In large Niigata farmhouse inns, for example, I have seen huge *kamidana* in the shape of elaborate miniature shrines erected high up near the rafters, and *butsudan* that reached from floor to ceiling with richly gilded interiors.

Walls

In their original forms, Japanese structures were of wattle and daub, consisting of a woven frame of vines packed with rice straw and earth. The earth was smoothed on interior walls. In some old inns, or very expensive new ones, you might encounter these earthen walls, and you might even discover a small decorative window crisscrossed with vines in the wall next to the *tokonoma*, a part of the wattle and daub skeleton deliberately exposed in an aesthetic device used in teahouses. In newly built inns, however, it is more likely that you will find earth-texture wallpaper resembling a fine-grained sandpaper. You can judge the quality of a new inn by whether it has real earthen walls or wall paper.

Ceilings

The first thing you see when you wake up and the last thing you see before you go to sleep is the ceiling, and Japanese architects have long made a feature of this often-neglected area of a room. It may be covered in a matting of woven strips of wood or bamboo, or planks of generously grained timber held in place with *saobuchi*, strips of bamboo, or other woods. In rooms designed for tea cere-mony, there may be three levels of ceiling, each with a different timber or bam-boo covering. The staggered levels were originally incorporated to lend the illusion of space to small spaces.

Your room may have carvings or delicate latticework on the transoms above the room-dividing sliding screens. If so, take a moment to enjoy the play of light through the openwork. Some transoms may be elaborately carved to reveal different designs on each side. Others may have geometric patterns. The Yoshida Sanso in Kyoto has stained glass.

Screens

The sliding doors in your rooms are actually removable sliding screens, which allow for flexibility in creating spaces. It was on sliding screens in castles and lordly mansions that some of Japan's greatest paintings were executed. The con-cept of framing pictures and hanging them on the walls did not exist. These days, the paper coverings on sliding doors are decorated mostly with stencil or woodblock designs. Notice the doorpulls, too, and their range of shapes, from geometric to plant and animal shapes.

Shoji screens covered in translucent paper now serve mostly as window cover-ings to mute the light. But, originally, *shoji* did the job of keeping out the weather as well. People who have lived in houses with only *shoji* for window coverings insist that they keep a house warmer than glass. Heavier wooden shutters secured the exterior on cold or rainy days.

Does your room have a garden? You might find that the *shoji* are a special variety called *yukimi shoji* ("snow-viewing *shoji*"), which has a lower section that can be raised to view the garden from a seated position at floor level.

Gardens

Typical of the inns in the older sections of towns is the *tsubo-niwa*, or courtyard garden, a small contemplative space containing a few well-placed rocks, a tree, some shrubs, a stone lantern, and a bit of mossy ground. Kyoto inns such as the Kinmata provide especially exquisite examples. They are miniature versions of the stone gardens at Zen temples, which represent the universe in a small space and are meant for meditation.

Larger estates, especially those constructed in the *shoin* style, might have elaborately designed gardens adjoining corner rooms, with venerable pine and plum trees (two symbols of longevity), red and green *momiji* maples, and impressive rocks bordered by azaleas and ferns. Examples of such gardens are at the Fukuki in Obama, the Kyo-tei in Saitama, the Mukaitaki in Aizu Waka-matsu, and the Takashima-ya in Iwamuro Onsen.

You may occasionally encounter gardens that are large enough to be described as stroll gardens, such as the lovely glade at the Okasen in Mino, or the pine gardens found at the Chigasaki-kan in Chigasaki, the Yoyo-kaku in

Karatsu, or the Monju-so Shoro-tei in Ama-no-hashidate. Such gardens will also have stone lanterns, and stone washbasins approached via stepping stones embedded in a mossy path. The washbasin is where you rinse your hands and mouth before entering a tearoom, but in an inn garden it is mainly for appearance. It may have a bamboo spout that clacks against a stone after emptying its water load—originally a device that farmers set up in their fields to scare off deer.

The *daimyo*-style stroll garden, which presents new and stunning vistas at every turn of the path, is rare for an inn, but there is one inn with this type of garden in this book—the Hakkei-tei in Hikone.

And, finally, one inn deserves particular mention for the eloquent way it erases the barrier between outside and inside in the traditional Japanese mode: the Tawara-ya in Kyoto has gardens that really do feel like they are part of your room.

THE INN EXPERIENCE

The Entrance

The entrance to an inn is similar to a traditional Japanese home, except for the addition of a modest sign and perhaps a split curtain out front indicating the place is open for business. Like high-class traditional restaurants, both the pathway leading to the inn and the stone or concrete landing inside the door are supposed to be sprinkled with water as a sign of welcome. Slide the door open, and the *banto* (chief attendant), maid, or *okami* (madam of the house) will appear to greet you. You will be offered the house slippers while a maid takes your bags.

The Room

At the entrance to your room, you must take off the slippers, which are for walking in the inn's public places (but never on tatami) and enter in bare or preferably stockinged feet. (The tatami floor has been swept and wiped with a dry cloth on hands and knees and does not take too kindly to sweaty soles.)

Take a seat on one of the flat cushions at the low table. The maid will join you, pour some tea, and ask you to fill out a registration form. She will also ask what time you prefer your bath and dinner. Unless it is late, you would normally take a bath before eating and ask for the meal any time from about 6:00 P.M. to 8:00 P.M. The maid will then leave you to absorb the calm of your sparsely furnished room.

Bathing

Either in the cupboard or on the floor in a corner of the room, you will find a rectangular box called a *midare-bako* (box for loose items) that holds a *yukata* (a light cotton kimono) and, in cooler months, a woolen jacket for warmth. A Japanese guest will change into the *yukata* as soon as he or she arrives and head immediately for the bath. The *yukata* is what you are expected to wear while within the inn's walls.

There will also be a small rectangular towel and a toothbrush in your *midare-bako*, while some higher-class establishments provide complimentary *tabi* (split-toed socks) and bathing aides such as loofahs and pumice stones.

Many newer inns now have private baths in the rooms, but quite a number of the older establishments in this book do not. In either case, there will be a communal bath, and it remains one of the great indulgences of the *ryokan* experience to soak in the inn's large tub. A hot spring inn will frequently have several baths—an indoor one, an outdoor one, and maybe a *kazoku-buro* (private baths for family use). There may be unusual tubs, perhaps one carved out of a single block of stone, or your own private cauldron. In times past, the biggest and most luxurious baths were reserved for males, but today the gender designation is often rotated on a daily basis so guests may try out each different facility.

Bathing is a drawn-out affair, in which people will wash once quickly before the first dip in the tub, then get out for a thorough, leisurely scrub. After rinsing, they will then relax in the tub for a longer time, often getting in and out several times.

Bathing etiquette requires you to wash once before getting into the tub, and to avoid getting soap in the water, so rinse off well and do not take washcloths or small towels in with you.

Hot tea—and perhaps free beer—is sometimes laid out in the resting area outside the bath for post-soak refreshment. If there are several baths, the more enthusiastic guests will sample a different one before and after dinner and again before breakfast.

Dining and After

Traditionally, the evening meal was brought to the guests' rooms, but today fewer and fewer inns are providing this service. However, there is no greater luxury than having a magnificently prepared feast served course by course in your own quarters, and the great inns perpetuate this excellent custom.

Whether you dine in your room or a large hall, dishes are brought separately, or in spurts, depending on the class of inn. If you want beer or saké with your meal, order them at the outset. You will usually be expected to dish out your own rice and tea when you are ready. Rice, miso soup, and pickles are an important finale to the meal, so leave room for them. And they will not be served until you say you are ready to end the meal. This means you must also finish drinking. If you want to continue drinking, stop for the rice and soup and carry on later.

An inn that takes pride in its cooking will use only the freshest seasonal foods, and choose tableware that compliments each item in color, shape, and texture. The true art of Japanese cooking is said to be in obtaining the freshest possible ingredients in season and doing as little as possible to them, then creating a feast that is as visually enticing as it is appealing to the palate.

After dinner you may bathe again or stroll the streets of the local town—in your robes and wearing the inn's *geta* (wooden clogs). While you are out (or even if you remain in the room), inn staff will lay out the futons for your night's sleep. If you are staying at a *minshuku* or some of the more inexpensive inns, you will be expected to lay out your own futon and put it away in the morning.

A word on tipping: at an inn where dinner is served in your room, it is customary for a Japanese guest to tip the maid ¥1,000 to ¥2,000. This is placed in a small envelope, or folded inside a piece of white paper, and handed over discreetly at the start of your stay or when the dishes start to arrive at dinner. Be careful not to give the tip to the *okami* (madam of the house). It should only be given to the maid attending your room. The maids will generally pool their tips and redistribute them evenly among themselves.

Breakfast and the Bill

Only a few inns now serve breakfast in the guests' rooms. Even good inns consider it more genteel to guide you to fresh quarters for the morning meal while the mundane tasks of putting away your futon and tidying the room are completed. You may go to breakfast in your cotton robe, even though it may be crumpled from sleep, and get dressed for the day perhaps after a morning soak in the communal bath.

Pay your bill as you are about to leave. On top of the room charge and incidentals, your account will probably also include consumption tax and a regional tax (at this writing five percent and three percent, respectively). Hot spring inns sometimes charge a small fee for bathing (around ¥100 per person).

When the bill is paid and your footwear is retrieved, the maids who attended you and the madam or master of the establishment will see you off with a bow.

A Word About Meals

There are four basic types of meals you will encounter at a Japanese inn:

● *Kyo-kaiseki* (Kyoto-style *kaiseki*)—This refers to the king of formal cuisines, and it is usually presented in about eight courses. Most inns serve variations on *Kyo-kaiseki*, with different degrees of success. The meal might begin with an aperitif of plum wine served with hors d'oeuvres. This is followed by *sashimi* (dip the slices of raw seafood in the small dish of soy sauce seasoned to taste with the green horseradish), clear soup, a grilled food (*yakimono*), a steamed food (*mushimono*), a simmered food (*nimono*), and a saladlike food with dressing (*uemono*). The meal is brought to a close with rice, miso soup, pickles, and fruit or jelly for dessert.

● Country Fare—Common country fare often features whole grilled river fish, especially *ayu* (sweetfish) and *yamame* (Japanese trout) in summer; carp *sashimi* year-round; *sansai* (wild mountain vegetables such as fern fronds and butterbur) served boiled and lightly flavored or as tempura; nourishing vegetable broths; and small hot-pots of pork, chicken, beef, or even wild boar, often cooked at the table. In the country, white rice was a luxury, while oats, barley, millet, and buckwheat were poor-man's foods, eaten much more frequently than rice. There has been a revival of interest in these grains, and many country establishments now make a point of serving handmade buckwheat noodles or sticky potato (*tororo-imo*) poured over rice mixed with barley.

● **Home-style Meal**—At the family-run bed and breakfasts known as *minshuku*, (such as the ones at Shirakawago, Gokayama, Nakasendo, and Tono), you will experience the typical home-cooked meal. In its most basic form this might be something like grilled fish, *chawan mushi* (baked savory egg custard), rice, miso soup, and pickles, but depending on the district you might also be served *sansai* (wild mountain vegetables) and other local delicacies in season.

● **Breakfast**—The basis of the traditional breakfast is rice, miso soup, grilled fish, and pickles. These are usually supplemented with a salty plum (which alkalizes the system) and sheets of *nori* seaweed to eat with your rice. (Lay a sheet of *nori* on the rice and scissor the ends together with your chopsticks to trap rice inside; dip the *nori* into soy sauce first unless it is the soy-sauce flavored variety.) Other possible breakfast foods are *natto* (sticky fermented beans), an acquired taste, and raw egg (add a dash of soy sauce and beat it with your chopsticks, then pour over hot rice). At most places, you can request a fried egg as a replacement. In inns that take pride in their seafood, you should expect superb sun-dried fish called *himono*, which is grilled. Hida-Takayama has its own famous breakfast food called *hoba miso*. In this dish, miso seasoned with chopped leeks and other condiments is set on a large magnolia leaf and grilled at your table over a small charcoal brazier.

A Word of Caution

I recommend all visitors to Japan to stay at least one night at a good inn. Everything fine and genteel that one associates with the Japan of old is encapsulated there. But take it slowly. What with the etiquette of the bath, having food served in your room, and maids coming and going to make your beds, there is little time for private reverie. Without a bed or chairs, your room may not provide the comfort you expect, and your food will have flavors and textures that are mostly unfamiliar. If you crave privacy and are not a fan of futons and soy sauce, the novelty may soon wear thin.

Even for me, Japanese inns are best taken in small doses. If you are planning an extended trip around Japan, give yourself a break at a Western-style hotel every couple of nights. Or choose some inns where you can stay without meals (*sudomari*). But don't try this in remote places, as finding a steak and fries in the hinterlands may not be easy.

With these cautions in mind, set out to enjoy yourself. There are many surprises and much to be gained from the inn experience.

USING THIS BOOK

Choosing a Destination and Getting There

Should you select a destination because it is home to an intriguing inn, or choose an inn because of its appealing location? The answer is either, depending on your purpose or mood. This book works both ways.

My own inclination leans toward the former, but in the case of the latter I focus on destinations with cultural or historic interest (rather than those known solely for their scenic beauty). I am drawn to forgotten towns with streets of old houses—the more neglected the better—because the overlooked places tend to have more surprises. Having said that, I am also drawn to the mountain-and-rice-field settings of the Japanese countryside.

The next decision involves transportation. Do you go by car, train, or plane? A car is not a practical or even an enjoyable option in densely populated areas such as Kamakura or the Kyoto-Nara region, but in the countryside I have found that having your own transportation adds immeasurably to the enjoyment of the trip so I have recommended one for some destinations. Don't be afraid to strike out on your own, even at the risk of getting lost. Taking a wrong turn on the back roads has led to some of the most rewarding experiences I have ever had. But even if you plan to stick to the straight and narrow, allow time for mistakes because road signs can be misleading and local people are generally inept at giving directions.

When traveling long distances and pressed for time, I usually take a plane or a fast train, then hire a car. At the end of the stay I may use the *norisute* option of dropping off the car at a different location.

How the Inns Were Chosen

For a country with such a small amount of habitable land, the volume and variety of accommodation in Japan is astonishing. The big ferroconcrete hotels, the "pensions," and the *minshuku* guesthouses all have their advantages, but I have steered clear of just about all of them in this guide to concentrate on small inns with character. I have not worried about whether there is a bath and lavatory in each room since some of the loveliest old buildings have only communal amenities and this is often reflected in lower prices. I have focused on the quality and ambience of the rooms, avoiding places with cheap furnishings and fittings.

I have pardoned this to a degree if the building itself is noteworthy, or if the rates are reasonable enough to overcome the drawbacks.

The inns I have chosen range from ¥2,500 per person per night to ¥60,000. Most are in the ¥15,000 to ¥25,000 range, and provide meals. Each was selected because it was inspiring in some way and is the kind of place you could proudly take a visitor for a one-off *ryokan* experience. But read the description before choosing. If you are out for an elegant evening, you don't want to stay in a fend-for-yourself farmhouse-style *minshuku*.

And for the budget traveler, though there are several lower-priced inns and *minshuku* in this guide, please take note that the "inn experience" rather than cheap accommodations has been my focus. For guidelines to more inexpensive lodgings, consult "Choosing an Inn When Left to Your Own Devices" and "On a Budget" in this section.

Specifications

Each inn description begins with a listing of specifications. These include:

● **Rates:** The posted price is per person (except for some of the classic hotels listed on pages 262 to 264). Prices for staying without meals, with breakfast only, or with both dinner and breakfast are listed if offered. When booking, say *"Sudomari onegai itashimasu"* if you want no meals, and *"Choshoku nomi onegai itashimasu"* if you just want breakfast; otherwise it will be assumed that you want both meals. But please do not ask for no meals or just one meal unless you are sure this option is available. Study the specifications for each inn. Many inns rely on income from the food to make ends meet. Also note the price quoted per person may go up or down according to the number of people in one room. You will be charged more for single-person use. Prices do not include tax unless stated. Expect to be charged up to an extra eight percent in taxes (at this writing), plus your incidentals. At hot spring inns, there may also be a charge and a tax for bathing, but this only amounts to a few hundred yen. Finally, always confirm the price before booking.

● **Rooms:** This entry gives you an idea of the type of sleeping quarters. Most of the inns listed are wooden structures, or unobtrusive concrete with wooden interior features. They are generally one- or two-story structures with no more than forty rooms. Japanese-style rooms will have tatami, futon bedding, and other traditional features. The designation "Western style" generally means beds have been installed in a Western-type room, which may have a few Japanese touches such as *shoji* screens. Where relevant I have tried to specify the better rooms, but things may have changed since my visit. When in doubt, ask what rooms are available at what price and state your preference.

● **Bath and toilet:** High prices at a good-looking inn used to be an indication of private bath/toilet facilities in the room, but this is no longer the case. The number of rooms with a private bath and toilet is indicated in the *Room* entry of each inn. Older accommodations may have only Japanese-style squat toilets.

● Communal bathing: All inns have at least one communal bath regardless of whether there are baths in the rooms or the inn has access to hot spring water. The specifications list the type of communal baths available. If you are seeking hot spring waters, scan the main text in each entry. A lot of people seem to equate *ryokan* with hot springs, but please note that quite a few of the inns listed are not in hot spring resorts. The designation "alternating" means there are separate hours for men and women for the same bathing facility.

● Language: Do not expect English to be spoken with great fluency, even at places listed as having "some English." The designation "English spoken" indicates that at least one person associated with the inn speaks English with confidence, but keep in mind that he or she may not be on hand at all hours. Try to make your initial booking in Japanese or with the help of a Japanese friend. There should be no problems after you arrive—as long as you familiarize yourself with the rules listed in "Inn Etiquette—A Quick Reference Guide" in the endpapers.

Alternative Inns

Some alternatives to the main inns are listed in the Appendices. These fall into two categories: second choices in the same area, or excellent inns located near but outside the scope of a Destination. A third type of inn of lesser caliber has been mentioned in the main text if it provides overnight lodging in a town or village introduced in the chapter but not covered by the other inns. In these instances, I have simply listed a phone number in the text.

Local Tourist Information

For places where there is already plenty of tourist information available (Tokyo, Kamakura, Kyoto, Hakone, the Izu Peninsula, and Kanazawa), I have been brief in my area descriptions. As a companion to this volume, I recommend that the serious traveler obtain a copy of the travel bible *Gateway to Japan* (Kodansha International).

I would also suggest availing yourself of the local tourist information office, usually found in or near the main station. Almost without exception, the staff will be able to supply you with maps and pamphlets, and often point out the more interesting sights. The maps, though mostly in Japanese, will give you a clear idea of the main tourist spots. For detailed travel advice before setting out, the Japan National Tourist Organization (JNTO) has a Tourist Information Center in the Yurakucho area of Tokyo (☎ 03–3201–3331) and in Kyoto (☎ 075–371–5649) in front of Kyoto Station. While on the road, make use of JNTO's travel-phone service at ☎ 0088–22–4800 or 0120–44–4800, both toll free. For drivers, a bilingual map book such as *Road Atlas Japan* (Shobunsha) will be essential.

Choosing an Inn When Left to Your Own Devices

As far as I know, apart from the TBS television network award, there is no independent rating organization for inns in this country. And it is hard to trust the majority of guidebooks because they are either written by the publishing arms of tour operators with a vested interest in the inns, or by companies that only include inns willing to pay for a listing. The result is that many precious inns are not mentioned in Japanese guidebooks at all.

So if you are looking for inns in places not covered by this guide, take note of the following: As a rule of thumb, I have found that anything around or over ¥25,000 per person (including meals) is an almost certain guarantee of quality food, service, accommodation, and style. That may seem expensive, but staying at a top-ranked Japanese inn is a special occasion. The better international hotels often charge this much, and they do not throw in two meals. At ¥18,000 to ¥20,000, you are straddling a borderline—it could be superb, or it could prove disastrous. But the most dangerous price level of all is around ¥15,000. You may find yourself paying for depressing sleeping quarters and a dollied-up meal offering such overworked dishes as spiny lobster with a cold French sauce. Notable exceptions are the Sakamoto in Suzu and Eiraku-ya in Nozawa Onsen. Anything under ¥10,000 is pot luck. And if you don't need luxury, there are some fun inn experiences in this book for ¥2,500 to ¥10,000.

On a Budget

I have not always listed a cheaper inn at a destination, so the budget traveler should also be aware of the network of inexpensive Japanese inns recommended by the Japan National Tourist Organization (JNTO) at the Welcome Inn Reservation Center (☎ 03–3211–4201, fax: 03–3211–9009). These accommodations range in price from about ¥3,500 a night (per person, two people sharing) without meals and unlike some of the inns here, they are used to accommodating foreign guests. See page 276 for details on reserving a room.

Minshuku (private homes serving as bed and breakfasts) and *penshon* (the European version of a *minshuku*) are the other budget alternatives. *Minshuku* can be booked through various *minshuku* associations. Call the JNTO's TICs for further details (☎ 03–3201–3331).

Cheap Tricks—Tips on Getting the Best Inn Deals

● **Go in the off-season:** This is a much more pleasant way to travel in Japan anyway (see "Good Times to Travel").

● **Cut out meals:** If you do not particularly like Japanese food and the inn offers a no-meal option (*"sudomari"*), ask for it and dig up your own meals in town.

● **Have lunch instead:** If you are on a budget but want to experience the atmosphere of a beautiful inn, book for lunch at the expensive inn but stay at its cheaper neighbor. First check to see if the inn offers lunch. Hot spring inns sometimes offer a lunch-and-bath combination.

● **Choose a room without a bathroom**· The prices for rooms without lavatories are usually much lower, and such rooms exist in some of the loveliest inns, especially converted older homes. A lack of private bathrooms does not guarantee a lower price however. Witness the lovely Ryokan Kurashiki.

Good Times to Travel

Some of the best times to travel are the week after Golden Week (from around May 6, when you can benefit from gorgeous spring weather), the tail end of the summer holidays (the last week of August, first week of September), and the week after New Year (to be safe, after January 9). Winter is the off-season for many places, and unless you visit snow country you might find the scenery on the dreary side. But some places—like Kyoto—offer travel bargains at this time of year.

The rainy season in mid-June to mid-July is often ignored, but it has its own charm, not the least of which is fewer travelers on the road. Finally, no matter what the season, it is easier all around if you can arrange to be on the move during the week rather than on weekends.

Peak Seasons to Avoid

● Almost all spring weekends (except the week after Golden Week).

● Almost all autumn weekends (except for a couple of weeks after the summer holidays).

● Golden Week (the last week of April and first week of May), a period packed with public holidays. Many people take a few extra days off and make this one long holiday.

● *O-bon*, the Japanese All Souls Festival (up to ten days on either side of August 15). Many Japanese leave the city and head back to their hometown to visit family and friends, or take a vacation. However, the period from July to the end of August, while hot and busy, is filled with local festivals, which are best seen in the smaller country towns.

● *O-shogatsu*, the year end (from about December 28 to January 9). Again, there is a mass exodus from the cities to the countryside to visit family and friends. The most crowded times on roads and trains are December 28 to January 3. On January 1, however, most roads and inns will be empty and peaceful.

TOKYO

Tokyo at night, Tokyo Tower in foreground

ATTRACTIONS

Tokyo is a cozier place than you might expect. Essentially it is made up of hundreds of little village-like communities. Most people still depend on the neighborhood fishmonger, tofu maker, and dry cleaner found in shopping alleys leading away from the local station. Then there are the more sophisticated quarters of the city—Ginza, Shibuya, Shinjuku, and Ikebukuro. You can lose yourself in art galleries or department stores at any one of these major hubs, each a browser's paradise. And when you have had enough of concrete and crowds, you can withdraw to one of the quiet country lodgings just an hour or two from the city.

If you have only a few days in Japan, say two or three, I recommend spending all of your time in Tokyo and following suggestions in any of the various Tokyo city guides available, including Rick Kennedy's *Little Adventures in Tokyo*, Susan Pompain's *Tokyo for Free*, and Sumiko Embutsu's *Old Tokyo*. The Internet site

Tokyo Q (www.tokyoq.com) provides up-to-date listings of what's going on in the city. Having a special interest or goal in mind will make your navigation of the city more productive. For example, an acquaintance of mine with an obsession for cars filled his free time in Tokyo going to car showrooms, while another friend in search of indigo clothing spent her two days looking at folk art and Issey Miyake boutiques.

The following are some of my choices for the best of Tokyo: Enjoy the night lights of **Shinjuku**, from the street by walking around the entertainment district of **Kabukicho**, or from above by dining at the **New York Grill** (☎ 03–5323–3458) in the Park Hyatt Hotel, which has the best view of the city. If you cannot manage dinner, do try to get there for an equally impressive lunch with a view. In Ginza, have *yakitori* dinner at **Atari-ya** (☎ 03–3564–0045 at the rear of the street directly opposite Matsuya Department Store), followed by a stroll around the backstreets between Ginza and Shimbashi stations at about 10–11 P.M. as the glamorous madams of hundreds of bars see their customers to black limousines (weekdays only). Eat a dinner of breaded deep-fried delicacies on skewers at **Kushinobo** (☎ 03–3581–5056) on the third floor of the Akasaka Tokyu Building in **Akasaka**, and then cross the street and venture into the lanes full of high-class drinking establishments.

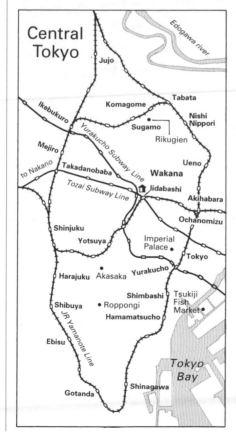

Go shopping in **Harajuku** and window-shopping at the designer **fashion houses** on the street that leads from Omotesando Avenue to the Nezu Museum.

In **Roppongi**, a fun place to eat is the elegant Japanese-style pub **Shunju** (☎ 03–3583–2611), perhaps after some shopping in the **Axis Building** (don't miss the tasteful textiles and the contemporary ceramics at Nuno and Savoir Vivre).

A bit further from the center of town is the beautiful garden **Rikugien,** near Komagome Station. Long underwear, household gadgets, and some amusing trinkets are for sale in stalls that line the street leading to **Toge-nuki Jizo** near Sugamo Station (also known as *Obaa-san no Harajuku*—Harajuku for grannies) on the fourth, fourteenth, and twenty-fourth of every month.

Indulge in a peaceful stroll around streets of old temples in the **Yanaka area** (see *Old Tokyo*).

It is fun to visit the **kitchenware markets in Kappabashi**; and an early-morning visit to the **Tsukiji fish markets** is an eye-opener on seafood, though camera-toting tourists are not given much patience.

There are **flea markets and antique fairs** around the city every weekend. My favorite is **Arai Yakushi** in Nakano on the first Sunday of the month (get off at Arai Yakushi-mae on the Seibu Shinjuku Line). And there is always something interesting happening at the **main art galleries** (see *Gateway to Japan* or *Tokyo for Free* for listings). If you want to avoid the admission fees of the better museums and still see quality art, try the **art salons** on the upper floors of most big department stores. The most venerable of the department stores is Mitsukoshi in Nihombashi; the trendiest are Isetan in Shinjuku, Matsuya in Ginza, and Seibu in Shibuya and Ikebukuro. While in the department store, the **food basements** are always good value. And at least once, try to get to the main entrance of a department store just before 10 A.M. so you can experience the daily opening ritual.

Quick Getaways from Tokyo

This depends on your idea of a quick trip. You can reach many wonderful parts of Niigata Prefecture in two hours by bullet train and Kyoto is only a two-and-a-half-hour ride. Compare this with an hour or so to reach Hakone, and up to three hours to get to some of the more isolated parts of the Izu Peninsula. While Izu and Hakone are much closer to Tokyo than Niigata and Kyoto, it may take you just as long to get there, and being closer to Tokyo they are more built up and attract larger crowds. This does not mean that there are not many wonderful places in Hakone and Izu. Just keep your options open. Other places within commuting distance of Tokyo may be found in the nearby prefectures of Saitama, Gumma, Tochigi, and Yamanashi and some of the more rural corners of Tokyo itself, including the mountainous Tama district. Specific information on some of these areas, as well as the more familiar Kanagawa Prefecture (Kamakura and Hakone) and Shizuoka Prefecture (Izu Peninsula), is contained in the following pages.

Favorite Overnight Escapes from Tokyo in the ¥10,000 to ¥20,000 Range:

DESTINATION 3: Honke Bankyu Bankyu Ryokan, Yunishigawa Onsen, Tochigi Pref. (2 hr 30 min to Yunishigawa Onsen on Tobu Line, 20 min by car).

DESTINATION 3: Myoga-ya Honkan, Shiobara, Tochigi Pref. (1 hr to Nasu Shiobara on Tohoku *shinkansen*, 50 min to Shiobara Onsen by bus).

DESTINATION 4: Sekizen-kan Honkan, Shima Onsen, Gumma Pref. (2 hr to Nakanojo on Agatsuma Line, 40 min to Shima Onsen by car or bus).

DESTINATION 4: Choju-kan, Hoshi Onsen, Gumma Pref. (70 min to Jomo Kogen on Joetsu *shinkansen*, 40 min to Hoshi Onsen by car).

DESTINATION 5: Fukuzumi-ro, Hakone, Kanagawa Pref. (1 hr by Tokaido *shinkansen* or Odakyu Line Romance Car to Odawara, 15 min by Hakone Tozan Railway to Hakone-Yumoto).

DESTINATION 6: Osawa Onsen Hotel, Osawa Onsen, Izu Peninsula, Shizuoka Pref. 2 hr to Shimoda, 45 min to Matsuzaki by bus).

DESTINATION 7: Villa Oka-no-Ie, Masuho-cho, Yamanashi Pref. (90 min by JR Chuo Main Line to Kofu, 40 min by Minobu Line to Kajikazawa, 20 min by taxi).

DESTINATION 11: Hana-ya inn, Bessho Onsen, Nagano Pref. (90 min to Ueda on Nagano *shinkansen*, 30 min to Bessho Onsen on Bessho Line). See Alternative Inns.

DESTINATION 16: Hazuki or Hazu Bekkan, Yuya Onsen, Aichi Pref. (1 hr 40 min by Tokaido *shinkansen* to Toyohashi, 50 min by Iida Line to Yuya Onsen).

DESTINATION 17: Osawa-kan, Osawa Onsen, Niigata Pref. (75 min by Joetsu *shinkansen* to Echigo Yuzawa, 12 min by Joetsu Line to Osawa, 5 min by inn pickup).

DESTINATION 17: Dairo-an, Niitsu, Niigata Pref. (2 hr by Joetsu *shinkansen* to Niigata City, 20 min by Shin'etsu Line to Niitsu, 10 min by taxi).

WAKANA 和可菜

LOCATION: Iidabashi Station

An old writers' retreat in a romantic part of Tokyo.

RATE: ¥12,000 w/breakfast, ¥10,000 w/o meals. **CREDIT CARDS:** Not accepted. **ROOMS:** 5 Japanese style (w/o bath). **COMMUNAL BATH:** 1—alternating. **CHECK-IN:** 15:00. **CHECK-OUT:** 10:00. **LANGUAGE:** No English, reservations in Japanese.

☎ 03–3260–3769 Fax: 03–3260–3769
4–7 Kagurazaka, Shinjuku-ku, Tokyo 162–0825
〒162–0825　東京都新宿区神楽坂4–7

■ ACCESS
BY TRAIN: 5 min on foot from Kagurazaka Stn (Subway Tozai Line) or 5 min on foot from Iidabashi Stn (Exit B3).
BY CAR: 500 m from Iidabashi Ramp (Shuto Expressway No. 5).

Kagurazaka alleyway

Tokyo overflows with towering Western-style hotels, but there are few traditional inns left. Of the few, the Wakana stands out for its colorful location—in the old geisha town of Kagurazaka—and its intriguing history, as the chosen working retreat of several novelists and script writers who have made Japanese screen history.

Kagurazaka was totally leveled in the air raids of World War II. The building that is the Wakana was raised from the ashes when the old geisha quarter began struggling back to life. The family of silver screen heartthrob Michiyo Kogure (1918–) purchased the building and in 1954 Kogure's beautiful younger sister, Toshiko Wada, opened it as an inn.

Wada san recalls that there were three hundred geisha in Kagurazaka in its heyday, and many of their houses lined the intriguing cobblestone alleys where the Wakana now stands. When a street fire alarmed neighborhood residents at 4 A.M., Wada remembers stepping out in her pajamas only to observe one geisha after another emerging fully dressed in kimono, their elaborate hairdos wrapped in cotton turbans. "Those Kagurazaka geisha had such pride," she says. Disregarding the potential danger, the astounded young innkeeper ran back inside wondering what kimono to drape herself in before fleeing for safer grounds.

There are no more than a dozen or so geisha in Kagurazaka today, and Wada suspects she is the longest-surviving resident in the old backstreet area. Indeed, the modern coffee shops, boutiques, and bars now lining Kagurazaka's sidewalks belie the existence of a historic institution like the Wakana.

Wada says she never made a conscious decision to run the Wakana exclusively for writers. "They just started using the place because of my connections with the film world." But the non-intrusive way in which Wada ran the inn most certainly drew writers too: total privacy was provided when it was needed, there were no set times for dinner, and breakfast was available at lunchtime if it was desired. "The writers usually stayed out late drinking and then sat up all night writing, so the last thing they wanted was to be dragged out of bed to have breakfast at eight," she explains. This was a revolutionary way to run an inn in the fifties and sixties, and no doubt the reason so many writers called it home.

For each room, Wada supplied manual pencil sharpeners (the electric ones chewed up too much of the pencil), family-sized boxes of matches (because all writers smoked), and large wastepaper baskets. A Kagurazaka stationery shop

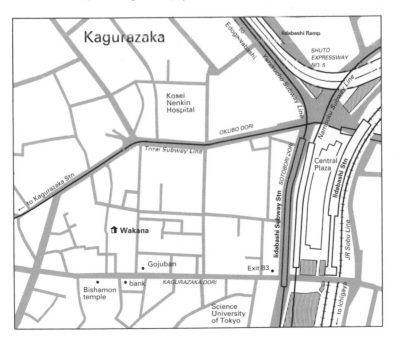

which sold manuscript paper that could be printed with writers' personal monograms was within walking distance of the inn.

Yoji Yamada (1931–), screenwriter and director of the world's longest-running movie series, *Otoko wa Tsurai Yo*, affectionately known as *Tora-san*, wrote all forty-eight installments of the series at the Wakana until leading actor Kiyoshi Atsumi (1928–1996) died in 1996. Yamada still drops by the Wakana, though instead of a pencil he brings a laptop. He is one of the few writers who still works at the Wakana. "They all prefer modern hotels and word processors now," says Wada. Which is one of the reasons that she has opened her doors to a wider range of clientele.

The inn is ideal for foreign travelers to Tokyo. No evening meals are provided, so you are free to choose from any of many cheap ethnic restaurants or pubs in the area.

The Wakana's accommodations are basic, but the place is spotless and the entryway and interior are sedate yet charming. The low tables on the tatami have sunken pits below them to dangle your legs in, perfect for the visitor not used to sitting cross-legged on the floor. Toilets and bath are shared. But the best part about the Wakana is its location. Even if you never stay there, do take a detour to this part of Kagurazaka just to sample a part of Tokyo that progress has left behind.

Other *Ryokan*-style Accommodation in Tokyo under ¥8,000.

At the back of the book is a list of *ryokan*-style lodgings in Tokyo registered with the Welcome Inn program. They range in quality according to their price: from ¥3,500 to ¥8,000 per person (double occupancy), no meals included. Please note that while the definition of "*ryokan* style" indicates you will sleep on a *futon* in a tatami room, the quality of the quarters or service may suffer when compared with some of the more elegant hand-picked inns in this book. Nevertheless, for the budget-minded traveler, these traditional-type inns are obviously an alternative worth considering. A large number are located in Taiko-ku, home to Asakusa and Yanaka, two districts redolent of old Tokyo. There are also inns conveniently located near Tokyo, Shibuya, Shinagawa, and Ikebukuro stations, which are major transportation hubs. For telephone numbers and further details, refer to the list on page 276.

2

KAMAKURA

Daibutsu

ATTRACTIONS

The seat of the first samurai government in twelfth- and thirteenth-century Japan, Kamakura is still home to ancient temples and other relics of a distinguished past, including many splendid private residences.

Kamakura is an easy day trip from Tokyo, but if you want to see its quiet temple precincts and gardens in the solitude in which they were meant to be viewed, avoid going on a weekend or public holiday. Kamakura's roads were built purposely narrow and mazelike to defend the fledgling shogunate from invaders on foot or horseback, and even today these narrow roads manage to hinder traffic. Walking them with hoards of other visitors is no fun, but on a quiet day Kamakura is an oasis.

Highlights include **Ajisaidera** near Kita-Kamakura Station, known for its hydrangeas in June; **Hokokuji** (also known as Takedera, the "bamboo temple"), which is set in a magnificent, manicured bamboo forest; and nearby **Sugimotodera. Komyoji** has a gorgeous garden (the waterlilies are spectacular in summer), and **Engakuji** is a sternly handsome Zen temple. Add **Kenchoji**, **Kakuonji**, and **Zuisenji** if you have an extra day. The most famous

Hokokuji

spot in Kamakura is the **Hachimangu**, the shrine of the Minamoto clan, the first shoguns of Japan, and most people start their tour of Kamakura here. The road leading to it is crowded with shops. Buy a *shuin* book from Hachimangu, and have it stamped or signed at each of the temples you visit. The **Daibutsu** (Great Buddha) is another Kamakura landmark.

KAIHIN-SO かいひん荘 鎌倉

LOCATION:
Kamakura

Stay in a former aristocrat's residence in a plush residential neighborhood, where expensive pine trees peer discreetly above high fences.

RATE: From ¥20,000 w/2 meals, from ¥12,000 w/o meals, children 30–70% off. **CREDIT CARDS:** AMEX, DC, VISA. **ROOMS:** 12 Japanese style, 1 Western style, 1 semi-Japanese—all w/bath. **COMMUNAL BATHS:** 2—men's, women's. **CHECK-IN:** 15:00. **CHECK-OUT:** 10:00. **LANGUAGE:** Some English.

☎ 0467–22–0960 Fax: 0467–25–6324
4–8–14 Yuigahama, Kamakura-shi, Kanagawa 248–0014
〒248–0014　神奈川県鎌倉市由比ヶ浜4–8–14

■ ACCESS
BY TRAIN: 5 min by car from Kamakura Stn (JR Yokosuka Line) or 5 min on foot from Yuigahama Stn (Enoden Line).
BY CAR: 5 km via Route 204 (Kanazawa/Kamakura Line) from Asahina IC (Yokohama/Yokosuka Doro).

Western-style parlor, Kaihin-so

This exclusive Kamakura neighborhood near the beach first become popular in the 1930s when the wealthy began building their summer residences here. Today it is home to many successful Tokyo businessmen, writers, and artists, who choose to live here year round.

The Kaihin-so combines Japanese and Western architecture of a manner that was popular in the 1920s, when it was first built by a baron. It was purchased by the current owners in the early 1940s and operated as a small inn catering to thirty guests at a time until 1982, when extensions and renovations increased its capacity. The original Western-style wing now houses a deluxe suite with bay windows and large twin beds. Three other rooms offer beds, but a tatami area for eating. The rest are traditional tatami rooms.

The inn's food is noteworthy for its seafood and vegetables in copious portions. The sashimi is delicious, as is the cooked fish at breakfast. In summer the Kaihin-so opens up the garden for barbecuing.

Nearby
From the inn it is a two-minute walk to the seaside and a fifteen- to twenty-minute walk to the popular sight-seeing area of Hase and the Great Buddha.

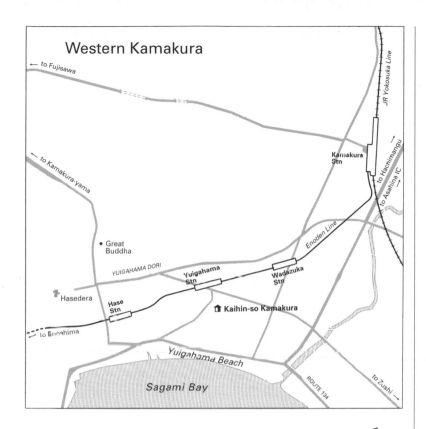

Western Kamakura

← to Fujisawa

← to Kamakura-yama

JR Yokosuka Line

to Hachimangu
to Asahina IC

Kamakura Stn

Enoden Line

• Great Buddha

YUIGAHAMA DORI

Yuigahama Stn

Wadazuka Stn

Hasedera

Hase Stn

☗ Kaihin-so Kamakura

to Enoshima

Yuigahama Beach

Sagami Bay

ROUTE 134

to Zushi →

CHIGASAKI-KAN 茅ヶ崎館

*The inn where move director Yasujiro Ozu
(1903–63) wrote several of his classics, including* Tokyo Story.

RATE: From ¥11,000 w/2 meals, from ¥7,500 w/breakfast, from ¥6,500 w/o meals, children from ¥5,500. **CREDIT CARDS:** Not accepted. **ROOMS:** 12 Japanese style (1 w/bath). **COMMUNAL BATHS:** 3 men's, women's, private (*kazoku-buro*). **CHECK-IN:** 15:00. **CHECK-OUT:** 10:00. **LANGUAGE:** Some English.

☎ 0467–82–2003 Fax: 0467–82–3133
3–8–5 Naka-kaigan, Chigasaki-shi, Kanagawa 253–0055
〒253–0055　神奈川県茅ヶ崎市中海岸3–8–5

■ ACCESS
BY TRAIN: 5 min by car from Chigasaki Stn (JR Tokaido Main Line).
BY CAR:　40 min (20 km) via Route 129 from Atsugi IC (Tomei Expressway) or 2 km via Route 134 from Chigasaki Kaigan Ramp (Shin Shonan Bypass).

Wickerwork hallway ceiling, Chigasaki-kan

We arrived at the Chigasaki-kan about 8 P.M. after a long day in tourist-swelled Kamakura. The Chigasaki-kan was the only "wooden inn" we could find close to Kamakura that had vacancies on a long weekend. The inn's unassuming *okami* guided us along wooden corridors to a simple corner room, and we asked if she would order us some sushi as we had heard that the inn did not provide dinner. She smiled and wondered if we would like a drink as well, and as she left to get us a beer she casually said, "This was the room that Ozu used."

I knew that the famous filmmaker had frequented the inn, but it wasn't until later, after reading *The Chigasaki-kan and Ozu Yasujiro*, a book on Ozu's relationship with this inn, that I found out Ozu had made the Chigasaki-kan his home for the better part of ten years after the war, when he returned from Singapore. Here he wrote *Late Spring (Banshun)* and *Tokyo Story (Tokyo*

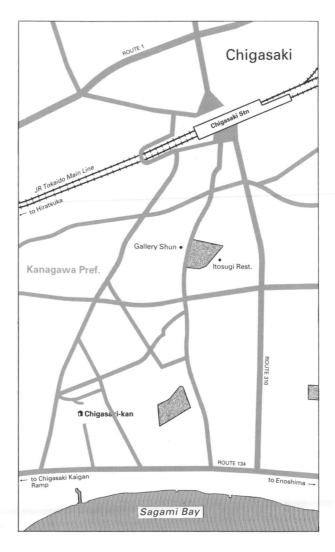

Monogatari)—his two great masterpieces. Now it turned out that we would be sleeping in the room he had made home—Number 2, on the corner.

Ozu's old quarters have the time-darkened wood and the high ceilings of an earlier time, but apart from that is unadorned, with just an alcove, a low table, and cushions on the floor. It occurred to us that Ozu's use of low camera angles might have come from his lengthy stay in rooms such as this.

Though the outside is now enclosed in sliding aluminum window shutters, the inn is still the same wooden building that Ozu loved, with a large pine garden and grassy paths. And in a nod toward Kamakura's oceanside location, the oldest surfboard in Japan has found new life as a garden bench under some pines just outside the room.

Breakfast was simple, with excellent grilled sun-dried fish served with rice, a tasty miso soup, good cod roe, a couple of small sausages, salad, and a cold fried egg. The owners have eliminated dinner from the tariff to allow guests to avail themselves of the local cafés, but should you wish you can order an evening meal.

Nearby

The town of Chigasaki is less inviting than it once was, with its black-sand beach and clutter of tourist, fishing, and surfing shops along the highway. Today, it is hard to imagine one of the world's greatest movie directors writing any sort of masterpiece here, but in Ozu's time the ocean and Mount Fuji were visible from the inn, and the view was unhindered by tall concrete structures. If you take a moment to imagine waves of traditional wooden houses with tiled roofs, a more convivial Chigasaki will emerge. The area around the *ryokan* is still quiet, and closer to the station you will find some interesting modern galleries and shops, among them Gallery Space Shun (☎ 046/–88–2553) and the chic, contemporary Japanese restaurant Itosugi (☎ 0467–88–3060).

3

TOCHIGI PREFECTURE

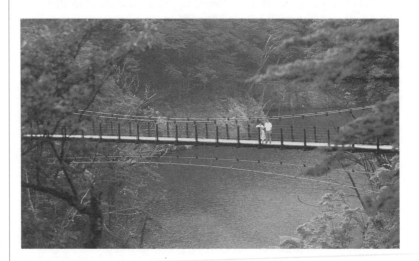

Shiobara Ravine

ATTRACTIONS

*In Tochigi, you will find two of the most popular tourist attractions close to Tokyo—Nikko, with its magnificent trees and elaborate shogun's mausoleum, and Mashiko, home of **mingei-style** pottery. Also nearby is the fascinating merchant's town of Tochigi City and the stone quarries of Oya.*

With good cause, most people going to Tochigi Prefecture head straight for **Nikko**, to see the first Tokugawa shogun's ornate mausoleum, or to **Mashiko**, the pottery town, which was home to the late Living National Treasure Hamada Shoji (1894–1978). While I have yet to discover an inspiring inn in either of these places, there are good Western-style hotels, particularly the splendid Nikko Kanaya Hotel, which is on a par with the Fuji-ya Hotel in Hakone for funkiness. My inns of choice for Tochigi are located in Nasu and Yunishigawa Onsen.

While in Tochigi, I recommend the much-overlooked **Tochigi City**, which is surprisingly close to Tokyo and doing much to preserve and re-create the classic *kura* architecture of the area with its handsome white plaster and black tiles. These *kura* exist from the time when Tochigi City was a major river port for trade with Edo, the old name for Tokyo. Now the post office, the phone boxes, and even the public lavatories are in *kura* style. A central public lavatory on the main street has been rebuilt in the more refined *sukiya* style, with a round window and stone basin, and is as impressive as some teahouses.

As if that were not enough, Tochigi has also taken to **suikin-kutsu**, a water-basin device that feeds trickling water into a large inverted pot concealed underground, where the dripping water elicits bell-like sounds. Almost every one of Tochigi's tourist attractions seems to have *suikin-kutsu* and provide bamboo earphones to listen to the crystalline sounds.

Information on these and other sights is available from the local tourist information center. Do not miss the handsome old **miso maker**, **Abuden**.

Tochigi is not far from the fascinating **old stone quarries of Oya**. The warm-looking, brown-flecked stone that came from the quarries can be seen in buildings and walls throughout the area. Visiting a quarry may not seem like an exciting thing to do, but the parts of the old quarries that allow tours are stunning in their grandeur. One stone cave has been turned into a temple—Oyaji—containing a mysterious Buddhist relief said to have been carved by the holy man Kukai (also known as Kobo-daishi; 774–835) in the Heian period (794–1185).

For more detailed information on Tochigi and Oya see *Weekend Adventures Outside Tokyo* by Tae Moriyama (Shufunotomo)

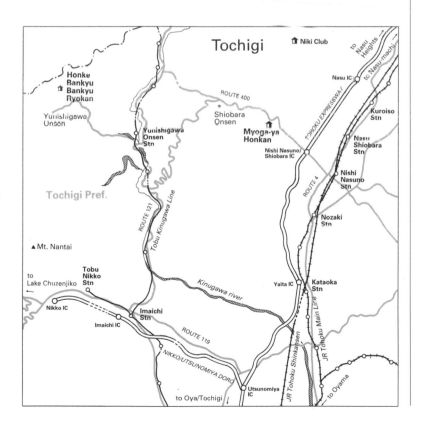

HONKE BANKYU BANKYU RYOKAN
本家伴久萬久旅館

A taste of harsher times—without the hardship—in an unusual rustic establishment with riverside hot spring pools.

RATE: ¥18,000–25,000 w/2 meals, children 30–50% off. **CREDIT CARDS:** AMEX, DC, MC, VISA. **ROOMS:** 45 Japanese style (11 w/bath). **COMMUNAL BATHS:** 7—2 men's, 2 women's, 3 outdoor (men's, women's, mixed). **CHECK-IN:** 15:00. **CHECK-OUT:** 10:00. **LANGUAGE:** Some English.

☎ 0288–98–0011 Fax: 0288–98–0666
749 Yunishigawa, Kuriyama-mura, Shioya-gun, Tochigi 321–2601
〒321–2601　栃木県塩谷郡栗山村湯西川749

■ ACCESS
BY TRAIN: 20 min by car from Yunishigawa Onsen Stn (Tobu Kinugawa Line).
BY CAR:　40 km via Route 121 from Imaichi IC (Tohoku Expressway to Nikko/ Utsunomiya Doro).

Open hearth in rustic lobby, Honke Bankyu Bankyu Ryokan

In the eleventh century, before warriors had organized into the elite ruling class known as the samurai, two clans fought for power—the Taira (also known as the Heike) and the Minamoto (also known as the Genji). The Minamoto won and their leader became Japan's first shogun. The defeated Heike fled to distant regions and made themselves scarce.

Long after the danger had passed, it was finally discovered where they had run. Their hidden settlements—which inevitably conjure up images of remote, concealed valleys and lives of hardship and deprivation—have since come to be known as *Heike mura*, the Heike villages.

The Heike family that fled to this particular valley was fortunate in that they had hot springs to ease the pain of exile. When peace returned to the region, it was the perfect place for an inn, and the first such accommodation to spring up 380 years ago was Honke Bankyu Bankyu. Successive sons kept up the inn, and it continues to be the most venerable of all the inns that subsequently nudged their way into this secluded region.

The inn rewards visitors adventurous enough to brave its remoteness with a surprisingly generous dose of comfort, excellent hot spring pools, and a fascinating Heike-style meal around an open hearth.

I cannot vouch for the newer annex, but in the original wing all the rooms face the river, no two are alike, and all are spacious and reflect a tasteful use of choice timbers. The best room, Aioi, has its own bath, but Honke Bankyu Bankyu's communal indoor and outdoor hot spring pools are the attraction for most visitors. In this sort of scenic snow country, there is something magical about soaking outdoors in a steamy rock pool.

Dinner is served in the riverside Heike Kakure-kan ("Hidden Heike Hall") around individual open hearths. The intriguing menu—wild mountain vegetablcs, fish from mountain streams, and game such as deer and wild fowl—attempts to give guests an idea of what the original Heike inhabitants ate to survive in this remote area. The house specialty is *issho-bera*, wild fowl dumplings flavored with miso and Japanese pepper and grilled on skewers over the coals. If you like your saké hot, freshly-cut long, green bamboo tubes will be filled and sunk into the ash alongside the skewers to heat. A cruder *nigori-zake* (cloudy saké) is served in the more conventional way. More familiar items on the menu are whole potatoes and tempura made with wild mountain vegetables.

Breakfast is a smorgasbord of Heike food with a choice of such staples as rice cooked with millet and topped with the sticky *tororo* potato, or plain white rice gruel, plus the inevitable mountain vegetables, and even dessert.

Nearby

Stop in and see the re-creation of a Heike settlement called
Heike no Sato, where you can inspect their primitive dwellings.
The site also has a shrine that dates back to Heike times.

MYOGA-YA HONKAN 明賀屋本館

LOCATION:
Shiyonoyu
Onsen,
Shiobara

Charming four-story wooden inn of faded grandeur set on the edge of a deep, lush valley with riverside hot spring pools.

RATE: From ¥13,000 w/2 meals. CREDIT CARDS: VISA. ROOMS: 43 Japanese style (17 w/bath). COMMUNAL BATHS: 5—1 men's, 1 women's, 3 outdoor (1 mixed, 2 private [*kazoku-buro*]). CHECK-IN: 14:00. CHECK-OUT: 10:00. LANGUAGE: Some English.

(☎) 0287-32-2831 Fax: 0287-32-2008
353 Shimo Shiobara, Shiobara cho, Nasu-gun, Tochigi 329–2921
〒329–2921　栃木県那須郡塩原町下塩原353

■ ACCESS
BY TRAIN: 50 min by bus from Nasu Shiobara Stn (JR Tohoku *shinkansen*).
BY CAR:　15 km via Route 400 from Nishi Nasuno/Shiobara IC (Tohoku Expressway).

Once a grand establishment complete with an imposing stone Frank Lloyd Wright–style hall (the Taiko-kan, now closed), the Myoga-ya is showing its age and more than a little shaky in parts. One is reluctant to lean too hard on the thin railings three or four stories above the steep Shiobara Ravine.

Fading grandeur aside, however, the Myoga-ya's sixty-year-old wooden building, four stories high in parts and highly unusual for this fact alone, is a treasure: the view overlooking the deep valley is spectacular, and the hike down to the riverside hot spring pools is an adventure not to be missed. While the descent to Myoga-ya's baths is far from scenic, and on the long, steep return climb one

*Riverside baths,
Myoga-ya Honkan*

promptly builds up a sweat worthy of another bath, the tubs carved out of the rock face along the lovely river are a little piece of heaven. Mixed bathing is the rule most of the time, but between the hours of 6:00 and 8:00 A.M. bathing is reserved for women only. For the less adventurous, there are three indoor baths that are more accessible: one for men, one for women, and one private *kazoku-buro* that can be reserved for families or large groups.

When I visited, the food at the Myoga-ya relied on wild greens, river fish, and a hot-pot of duck with vegetables, all nourishing and excellent value for the reasonable tariff. Dinner is served in your room on individual standing trays.

Nearby

With a car you can combine a stay at the Myoga-ya Honkan
with a day trip to the Oya stone quarries and Tochigi City.
You will need an extra day to cover Nikko and/or Mashiko.

4

GUMMA PREFECTURE

Choju-kan

ATTRACTIONS

Home to more hot springs than any other prefecture.

Gumma is regarded by many as the hot spring capital of Japan; it also has its share of rustic inns. But given my criteria for inclusion in *Classic Inns*, most of them are either too rough and ready, too ordinary, or too expensive. Only three Gumma inns are described here—the legendary Choju-kan; the Sekizen-kan, because it is home to the oldest extant inn building in the country; and the Kaya-no-Ie for its laid-back atmosphere.

The so-called *yokozuna* ("grand champion" in sumo terminology) of outdoor hot spring baths is **Takaragawa Onsen**. It is quite accessible from Tokyo, but a stay is unwarranted because the inn's new wing is unforgivably ugly. Nevertheless, if you are a hot spring lover, a dip in Takaragawa's outdoor baths, set by a fast-flowing stream, is unbeatable.

The historic spa town of **Kusatsu** may also be of interest for its daily demonstrations of the beating and stirring of the scalding waters of one of the old baths, and its *yubatake*, racks of mineral sediment harvested from the hot spring water and sold in bags for private use. Kusatsu has some atmospheric old inns in the town center, including the Yamamoto-kan (℡ 0279–88–3244) and the Osaka-ya (☎ 0279–88–2411), but the best Japanese guides all recommend the upmarket Tsutsuji-tei (☎ 0279–88–9321) for contemporary luxury.

Ikaho, another Gumma hot spring area on a refreshing mountain plateau, has the luxurious Fukuichi (☎ 0279–20–3000).

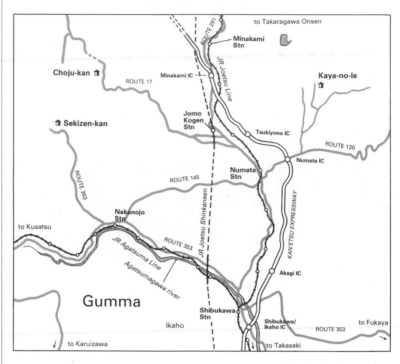

CHOJU-KAN 長寿館(法師温泉)

Isolated old country inn with a famous bathhouse.

RATE: ¥13,000–22,000 w/2 meals, 20% off w/breakfast only, children 30% off. **CREDIT CARDS:** AMEX, DC, VISA. **ROOMS:** 39 Japanese style (3 w/bath). **COMMUNAL BATHS:** 2—mixed, women's. **CHECK-IN:** 15:00. **CHECK-OUT:** 10:30. **LANGUAGE:** Some English.

☎ 0278–66–0005 Fax: 0278–66–0003
650 Nagai, Niiharu-mura, Tone-gun, Gumma 379–1401
〒379–1401　群馬県利根郡新治村永井650

■ ACCESS
BY TRAIN: 40 min by taxi from Jomo Kogen Stn (JR Joetsu *shinkansen*).
BY CAR: 25 km via Route 17 from Tsukiyono IC (Kan'etsu Expressway).

Mixed baths, Choju-kan

The Choju-kan is a seemingly lonely inn in the wilderness of Gumma that has become a legend in its own time. The holy man Kukai (also known as Kobo-daishi; 774–835) is said to have discovered the hot spring there twelve hundred years ago, but eleven centuries passed before an inn was built to accommodate overnight visitors. However, it is not the inn so much as its bathhouse that has made the Choju-kan famous. Images of this bath appeared in a series of travel advertisements in the 1980s and it has since become the most photographed bath in Japan.

With baths that were built before the turn of the nineteenth century, the bath-house is a big barn of a building with elegantly arched windows. An ethereal light filters through the windows, turning the interior into a splendid wooden cathedral—a holy place for bathing. Soaking at 43°C (110°F) takes place in four enormous sunken chestnut-wood tubs, each divided in half by logs. Rest your head on a log while massaging your feet on the pebble floor and enjoying the hot water bubbling up from below. It doesn't get much better than this.

Bathing is mixed at the Choju-kan—the only detraction from an otherwise perfect opportunity for solitude. But the bathhouse interior is so dim and steamy that you can go about your ablutions almost unnoticed.

The food is nourishing country-style fare. Your meal at the Choju-kan may include turtle soup in addition to such inland hot spring inn staples as carp sashimi and wild mountain greens.

For an inn so rustic and remote, the accommodations in both the old and new wings are of a consistently good quality. However, for atmosphere, try to book the original wing, the *honkan* (built in 1920). Hoshi Onsen is said to be at its best when the world is transformed by the silent whiteness of winter. You will need chains on your tires.

KAYA-NO-IE 萱の家

LOCATION: Kawaba-mura

A new two-story wooden lodge with big hot spring baths and vegetarian meals in the quiet countryside.

RATE: ¥15,000–18,000 w/2 meals, from ¥9,000 w/breakfast, children from ¥9,000 (w/2 meals). **CREDIT CARDS:** Not accepted. **ROOMS:** 6 Japanese style (1 w/bath). **COMMUNAL BATHS:** 2—men's, women's. **CHECK-IN:** 15:00. **CHECK-OUT:** 11:00. **LANGUAGE:** No English, reservations in Japanese.

☎ 0278–52–2220 Fax: 0278–52–2234

2077–1 Kawaba Yuhara, Kawaba-mura, Tone-gun, Gumma 378–0102
〒378–0102　群馬県利根郡川場村川場湯原2077–1

Entrance, Kaya-no-Ie

■ ACCESS
BY TRAIN: 30 min from Jomo Kogen Stn (JR Joetsu *shinkansen*).
BY CAR: 15 min (15 km) from Numata IC (Kan'etsu Expressway).

Kawaba-mura is a charming rural community about fifteen minutes from Numata (on the Kan'etsu Expressway) and thus highly accessible from Tokyo by car. It offers pastoral scenery; scenic half-day, full-day, and two-day walking courses sprinkled with old stone statues; and excellent milk and yogurt products from the local dairy.

Entrance hall adjoining open hearth

A good base from which to explore Kawaba-mura is the Kaya-no-Ie. A cluster of new, thatched-roof accommodations originally built so that students of a Takasaki technical college could experience country life, Kaya-no-Ie is now run as a nonprofit *ryokan*. It is not luxurious, but it has a certain style about it. The cypress baths are spacious, with mountain views. The food is vegetarian. Breakfast might consist of brown rice gruel, tofu, and slices of *daikon* (giant white radish). There are no televisions or karaoke equipment. Rather, guests gather around a sunken hearth for long chats into the night. In short, Kaya-no-Ie offers a perfect escape for overburdened Tokyoites seeking fresh air and a casual, relaxing getaway.

Nearby

The local produce center, a sparkling new building in the middle of nowhere on the way to the Kaya-no-Ie from Numata, has tourist information and local produce, including the excellent yogurt drinks. Ask there about hiking courses. If you are traveling by car, note that from Numata Route 120 takes you through mountainous country to Nikko in Tochigi Prefecture.

SEKIZEN-KAN HONKAN　積善館本館

LOCATION: Shima Onsen

Japan's oldest hot spring inn building and a 1930s Romanesque bathhouse.

RATE: From ¥7,500 w/2 meals, children 30% off. **CREDIT CARDS:** DC, MC, VISA. **ROOMS:** 23 Japanese style. **COMMUNAL BATHS:** 9–3 men's, 3 women's, 1 mixed, 2 outdoor (men's, women's). **CHECK-IN:** 14:00. **CHECK-OUT:** 10:00. **LANGUAGE:** No English, reservations in Japanese.

☽ 0279–64–2772 Fax: 0279–64–2369
INTERNET: sekizenkan.co.jp/
E-MAIL: info@sekizenkan.co.jp
Shima Onsen, Nakanojo-machi, Agatsuma-gun, Gumma 377–0601
〒377–0601　群馬県吾妻郡中之条町四万温泉

■ ACCESS
BY TRAIN: 40 min by bus from Nakanojo Stn (JR Agatsuma Line).
BY CAR:　1 hr (39 km) via Route 353 from Shibukawa/Ikaho IC (Kan'etsu Expressway).

An antiquated notice on the wall of the Sekizen-kan Honkan dating back to the forty-fourth year of the Meiji period (1912) proclaims that the price of an overnight stay shall be one sen for Japanese and five sen for foreigners. Foreigners, it was thought, could not survive without such Western-type foods as bread, butter, and meat, and these provisions had to be carted in at great expense. It is astonishing to think that even in the early 1900s a remote country inn was willing to go to the trouble of bringing in Western delicacies for a few guests. More astonishing is the thought that foreigners of the time were venturing that deep into the wilds. Even today, the trip takes over two hours by car.

The rocky dirt track leading to Shima Onsen must have been well worn even back then, for Japanese travelers have been visiting this hot spring for four hundred years. The Sekizen-kan Honkan is one of the oldest inns in Japan. The lobby building was constructed in 1691, which makes it the oldest standing hot-spring-inn structure in the land. Gumma Prefecture has designated it an important cultural asset. Guests stay in newer structures that have been added on, but you are free to walk around and admire the old pillars and beams and the modest display of historical odds and ends.

1930s bathhouse,
Sekizen-kan

However, the main attraction at Sekizen-kan is its 1930s bathhouse with tiled floors, arched windows, and five symmetrically placed stone bathtubs (in each of the men's and women's bathrooms). Enter from the outside pathway and you can see straight into the bathing area. Anyone with a passion for hot springs will no doubt have visited Choju-kan (also listed in this section) for its amazing wooden bathhouse. Sekizen-kan's bathhouse is a stone-and-white-granite version of the legendary Choju-kan bath. I enjoyed it even more since it is segregated and has such delightful touches—in the ladies' bath, at least—as a petite goldfish tank built into the rear wall, and a couple of amazing 1930s steam baths, which you reach by crawling through dwarf-size arched doors. Once inside, you lie on a tiled couch while the steam works to open your pores.

The Sekizen-kan has added a modern and more expensive section called the Kasho-tei Sekizen, but if you don't mind roughing it a little bit (taking out and putting away your own *futon*, sharing a rather sparse *bento*-type meal in a big tatami dining room, and putting up with no air conditioning), you'll find a stay in the 1930s rooms of the *honkan* older building much more rewarding. And the modest price (half that of the new section) includes two meals and access to both the 1930s bathhouse and the sparkling modern baths (with *rotemburo*) found in the new section.

Nearby

The name Shima literally means "Forty Thousand" and reflects the belief that the local hot spring waters cure forty thousand ills. The small enclave of Shima Onsen offers little in the way of sight-seeing, however, other than a sprinkling of inns and shops, which house some of the oldest pachinko machines I have ever seen. The Tamura inn up the road from the Sekizen-kan has an attractive thatch-roofed entryway, and a modest market lining the approach to the hot spring town comes alive every morning, offering local produce and rustic crafts. Ten minutes by car from Shima Onsen on the way back to Nakanojo is the Oketsu Mure, a series of beautiful rock pools sculpted by the Shimagawa river over thousands of years. It's worth taking the short walk down into the ravine for a look.

5

HAKONE

Fujiya Hotel

ATTRACTIONS

Tokyo's traditional hot spring playground, with outdoor "hells," access to Lake Ashinoko, and views of Mount Fuji.

Hakone is the most popular sight-seeing spot near Tokyo; literally reams of information are produced on what to do there. My recommendations would be, first, to take the **Hakone Tozan Railway** single-track railway from Odawara or Hakone-Yumoto. Get off at **Miyanoshita** for pie à la mode in the garden-side café at the historic **Fujiya Hotel**, followed by a stroll around the antique shops. Get on the Tozan Railway for Gora and its **Hakone Bijutsu-kan** (Hakone Art Museum), as much to walk through its stunning stroll garden of maples as to see its excellent collection of ancient pottery. Also visit **Owaku-dani**, "The Greater Boiling" (thermal pools). Get a good view of **Mount Fuji** from Komagatake, and take a cruise on **Lake Ashinoko**. If you just want a day of hot spring bathing, the **Tenzan** (☎ 0460–6–4126) in Oku-Yumoto offers a variety of baths and places to eat and drink. Pay the extra ¥1,000 on top of the set entrance fee for the deluxe bath. Get a taxi from Yumoto Station.

Recommended trips including Hakone

Because of its proximity to Tokyo, most people just come here for an overnight stay. But you could make it the first stop on a trip further down the Tokaido highway. See Destination 16 for one suggestion.

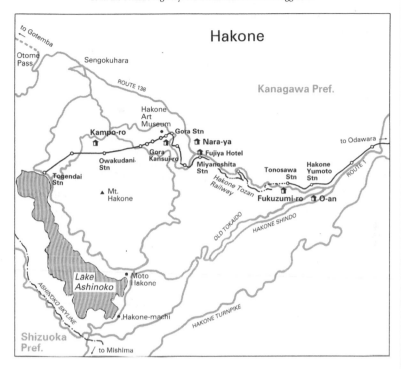

FUKUZUMI-RO 福住楼

Mazelike, antiquated inn with pretty details and charming indoor baths.

LOCATION: Tonosawa, Hakone

RATE: From ¥20,000 w/2 meals, ¥12,000 w/breakfast, from ¥10,000 w/o meals, children 30–50% off. **CREDIT CARDS:** AMEX, DC, VISA. **ROOMS:** 20 Japanese style (1 w/bath). **COMMUNAL BATHS:** 5–2 men's, 1 women's, 2 private (*kazoku-buro*). **CHECK-IN:** 14:00. **CHECK-OUT:** 10:00. **LANGUAGE:** No English, reservations in Japanese.

☎ 0460–5–5301 Fax: 0460–5–5911

74 Tonosawa, Hakone-machi, Ashigarashimo-gun, Kanagawa 250–0404

〒250–0315　神奈川県足柄下郡箱根町塔ノ沢74

■ ACCESS
BY TRAIN: 5 min by car from Hakone Yumoto Stn (Hakone Tozan Railway).
BY CAR: 10 min (7 km) via Route 1 from Odawara Nishi IC (Odawara/Atsugi Doro) via Tomei Expressway (Atsugi IC).

Women's bath, Fukuzumi-ro

"Ours is a non-extravagant, simple household and has been from our father's time and our father's father's time. We serve only such simple dishes as are in keeping with this, but should one of our distinguished guests wish us to prepare something more luxurious we shall be happy to do our best."

This advertising copy for the Fukuzumi-ro was distributed in Japanese shortly after it opened a century ago. The copywriter was Yukichi Fukuzawa (1839–1901), founder of Keio University, and a hero of the Meiji period (1868–1912). His face appears on the ten-thousand-yen note.

Fukuzawa played a large role in opening up Hakone for tourism. It is not certain what relationship Mr. Fukuzawa had to the Fukuzumi-ro inn, but it is true that the inn was a favorite of many intellectuals, among them the novelist Soseki Natsume (1867–1916)—who appears on the one-thousand-yen note.

Built in 1891, the present Fukuzumi-ro is a Meiji-period building and a survivor of the great Tokyo earthquake of 1923. Forgotten while Japan swamped itself in Western culture after the war, it was rediscovered in the 1980s by a new generation of visitors who came to appreciate its classic wooden structure, 1920s tiled roof, and charming art deco touches. Kazuyoshi Miyamoto (1941–), a noted architectural commentator and photographer, says in his book *Wafu Ryokan Kenchiku no Bi* that the Fukuzumi-ro is worthy of designation as a cultural asset.

Like many inns of its era, the Fukuzumi-ro added on new wings as it needed them in whatever crevice of land was left, and joined them together with corridors. The result is a fusion of styles in a wandering structure, so complex you almost need a map to navigate it. Its various *sukiya-*, *sanso-*, and *shoin*-style rooms are a showcase of precious cypress, cedar, zelkova, and pine, an extravagance made possible by the inn's location close to Hakone's famous forests.

The *sukiya*-style rooms are large and their nightingale-colored walls are soft on the eyes, with big windows that look out on the Hakone greenery.

The loveliest feature of all is the inn's main baths, which are round and fed by long bamboo pipes from outside. The baths, one for men and one for women, are made from the hollowed trunks of large pines, edged in copper with slatted wooden floors.

The many-course meal, with lots of fresh Sagami Bay seafood, is served in your room.

O-AN 桜庵

LOCATION: Hakone-Yumoto

Secluded super-deluxe inn in a contemporary style.

RATE: From ¥40,000 w/2 meals, children 30% off. **CREDIT CARDS:** AMEX, DC, VISA. **ROOMS:** 24 Japanese style, 8 Western style—all rooms w/bath. **COMMUNAL BATHS:** 2—men's, women's, both half outdoor. **CHECK-IN:** 15:00. **CHECK-OUT:** 11:00. **LANGUAGE:** English spoken.

☎ 0460–5–8222 Fax: 0460–5–8223
230 Yumoto-chaya, Hakone-machi, Ashigarashimo-gun, Kanagawa 250–0312
〒250–0312　神奈川県足柄下郡箱根町湯本茶屋230

■ ACCESS

BY TRAIN: 5 min by car, from Hakone Yumoto Stn (Hakone Tozan Railway).
BY CAR: 5 km via Route 1 from Odawara Nishi IC (Odawara/Atsugi Doro), via Tomei Expressway (Atsugi IC).

O-an means "cherry hermitage," but what a hermitage it is. Built for the set whose money buys mega-luxury and privacy, it combines the best of Japanese inn comfort with Western-style hotel facilities. In addition to twenty-four Japanese-style and eight Western-style rooms, it has an indoor swimming pool, a state-of-the-art conference room, and a teahouse modeled on a famous rustic teahut of the Omote-senke tea school.

When it was built in 1987 at the height of the "bubble" economy, the designers and carpenters had a field day. They gave to each of the twenty-four Japanese rooms a unique interior and to the eight Western-style rooms a Japanese ambience. Each room is suite sized; entrance is via its own small bridge from the main walkway. The chrome and carpet lounge bar is overdone in a nouveau riche sort of way, but the big cypress baths with marble walls and modern fixtures are a very special luxury.

O-an provides Kyoto-style *kaiseki* for guests in its Japanese rooms, and a restaurant meal for guests in the Western-style rooms.

Indoor swimming pool, O-an

KAMPO-RO　冠峰楼

LOCATION: Sengokubara, Hakone

Elegant resort-style inn.

RATE: From ¥35,000 w/2 meals, 20% off w/breakfast only, 30% off w/o meals, children 30% off. **CREDIT CARDS:** AMEX, DC, VISA. **ROOMS:** 18 Japanese style, 1 semi-Japanese style—all rooms w/bath. **COMMUNAL BATHS:** 4—men's, women's, 2 outdoor (men's, women's). **CHECK-IN:** 14:00. **CHECK-OUT:** 10:00. **LANGUAGE:** English spoken.

☎ 0460–4–8551 Fax: 0460–4–7600
1251 Sengokuhara, Hakone-machi, Ashigara-shimo-gun, Kanagawa 250–0631
〒250–0631　神奈川県足柄下郡箱根町仙石原1251

■ ACCESS

BY TRAIN: 35 min by car from Odawara Stn (JR Tokaido Line).
BY CAR: 18 km via Route 1 from Odawara Nishi IC (Odawara/Atsugi Doro) via Tomei Expressway (Atsugi IC).

Ever since a Japanese doctor confided in me that any health benefits from soaking in a hot spring were purely in the mind, I have ignored claims of cures for warts and infertility and taken the hot spring for what it is—a good hot bath. But, at the Kampo-ro, I began questioning the doctor's advice. My half-hour soak in its bath sent me into a sleep so deep that I awoke reborn. I still remember it as the best sleep of my life.

The Kampo-ro is hidden high in the hills about a twenty-minute drive from Hakone, on the hilly, sulfur-smelling road to Owakudani ("The Greater Boiling"). It commands an exclusive view of the Sengokubara Plains and the surrounding peaks. The minimum room charge gets you unusually spacious rooms in the ten-year-old main wing. For an additional charge you can stay in one of six original *hanare*, perhaps even the one where the empress stayed when she was still Princess Michiko.

The new wing seems almost too slick, but there is a graciousness and glow to the service at the Kampo-ro that immediately puts you at ease. I have not felt quality like this at many other inns. Similarly expensive establishments have the "service" down to a tee, but what I felt at the Kampo-ro was more akin to care.

The mark of a top inn is having two large rooms to each suite, one for eating and one for sleeping. The Kampo-ro is one of those. All meals are served in your room, and this inn's classic *kaiseki* is worth the price.

View from the tea-house garden, Kampo-ro

Kampo-ro

NARA-YA　奈良屋旅館

LOCATION: Miyanoshita, Hakone

Venerable old Hakone ryokan in atmospheric Miyanoshita.

RATE: From ¥25,000 w/2 meals, 20% off w/breakfast only, children 30% off. **CREDIT CARDS:** AMEX, VISA. **ROOMS:** 20 Japanese style, 4 *hanare* cottages—all rooms w/bath. **COMMUNAL BATHS:** 3—2 men's, 1 women's. **CHECK-IN:** 15:00. **CHECK-OUT:** 10:00. **LANGUAGE:** English spoken.

☏ 0460–2–2411 Fax: 0460–7–6231
162 Miyanoshita, Hakone-machi, Ashigara-shimo-gun, Kanagawa 250–0404
〒250–0404　神奈川県足柄下郡箱根町宮ノ下162

■ ACCESS
BY TRAIN: 3 min on foot from Miyanoshita Stn (Hakone Tozan Railway), or 15 min by car from Hakone Yumoto Stn (Hakone Tozan Railway).

BY CAR: 15 min (10 km) via Route 1 from Odawara Nishi IC (Odawara/Atsugi Doro) via Tomei Expressway (Atsugi IC).

The Nara-ya was my first Japanese inn experience; it was also the first place I ever saw snow. I have a picture of myself standing in the garden in my *yukata*, smiling while minute flakes of snow fall around me. I had no idea on that day in 1975 that I was staying at one of Hakone's most famous inns.

The Nara-ya was built about the time of the fifth Tokugawa shogun, Tsunayoshi (1646–1709). It started life as a *honjin*—an inn designated for the *daimyo* nobility traveling on the Old Tokaido Highway. In 1873 the Meiji emperor (1852–1912) stayed here while his villa was under repair, and members of the imperial household used it frequently in 1896.

The original Nara-ya was burned down in 1876, and again in 1885. It once had a Western-style hall so unusual that it was recorded in a book called *The Famous Places of Japan*, but the hall too fell prey to fire in 1889.

Although most of the buildings at Nara-ya now date back only to the turn of the century, they have many spectacular architectural features. Intricately carved gables in the bathroom of the *honkan* have a playfulness of design that you cannot find in modern architecture.

Nara-ya

The four *hanare* are the pick of the rooms.

Nearby

The Nara-ya is right across the road from the fantastic Fujiya Hotel, whose earliest buildings date to 1880. Do go in and have a drink in their garden-side coffee corner and check out the pictures of the moustache contest in the halls leading to the guest rooms. Also read the list in the reading room of overseas VIPs who have stayed at the Fujiya. You might also consider having lunch in the lovely dining room with its complicated coffered ceiling. Call ahead for reservations. Miyanoshita also has two expensive antique shops and several souvenir traps.

IZU PENINSULA

Mount Fuji from West Izu coast

ATTRACTIONS

Encompassing the scenic Izu Peninsula, Shizuoka Prefecture is packed with hot spring inns and built-up tourist meccas but has some spectacular scenery and hidden enclaves.

Along with Hakone, the Izu Peninsula has been Tokyo's playground since the capital was known as Edo. Like Hakone, it is full of hot springs, and such a large number of inns have sprouted up to cash in on them that one day the whole peninsula might cave in under the weight. In the meantime, enjoy what scenery is left, especially that on the west coast and the interior of the peninsula. I would suggest heading straight for the **Osawa Onsen Hotel**. You can do this via **Shimoda**—site of America's first consulate in Japan after it was forced to open up to relations with the West.

The town of Shimoda is built up, but some of its beaches are very pleasant, especially the white-sand Shirahama. An impressive bus trip can be taken between Shimoda and Matsuzaki on the scenic **Margaret Line**, a mountain-top drive. It takes two hours and twenty minutes, more than an hour longer than by ordinary roads.

Ten minutes from the Osawa Onsen Hotel is the town of **Matsuzaki**, which has well-preserved buildings in the distinctive black-and-white-tiled *namako-kabe* architecture.

Cherry-blossom season is a marvelous time to visit Osawa Onsen and Matsuzaki because of the cherry-lined river that meanders between them. The Osawa Onsen area also produces eighty percent of the cherry leaves used to wrap the famous *sakura-mochi*, a steamed red-bean paste sweet. The special variety of cherry trees grown here are trimmed to waist height and do not produce flowers.

From Matsuzaki, I recommend returning via the **west coast** of the Izu Peninsula. A ferry leaves five times a day from Matsuzaki to the port of Numazu, skirting pine-clad islands. Alternatively, the regular bus from Matsuzaki to Shuzenji shows some spectacular coastal scenery, especially around **Dogashima**. Then get a local train for a thirty-minute ride to Mishima, which is on the Tokaido *shinkansen* line.

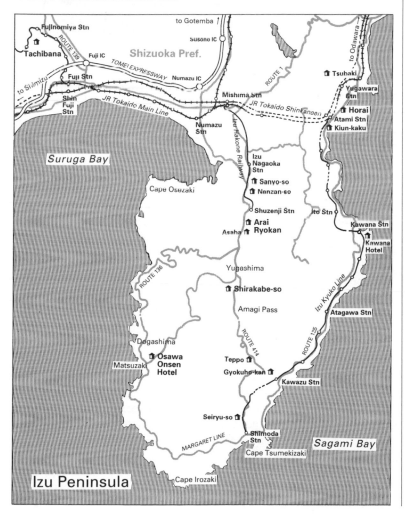

Somewhat more accessible to Tokyo are **Atami**, which has the deservedly popular Horai inn and the impressive **MOA Museum**; and **Shuzenji**, which has several inns of note, including the Asaba with its Noh stage.

Another place to consider staying at is the **Tachibana** *ryokan*, in the spectacular tea-growing area near Mount Fuji at Fuji City. A half-hour drive from there, the austere and beautifully kept Rinzai Zen temple **Seikenji** has an unusual landscape garden at the back of the main hall.

Recommended trips including the Izu Peninsula

Because of its proximity to Tokyo, Izu is just an overnight stay for most people. But you could make it the first stop an a trip further down the Tokaido highway. See Destination 16 for one suggestion.

HORAI 蓬莱

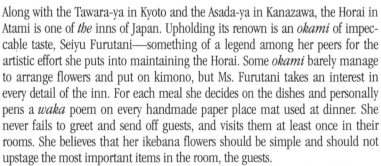

LOCATION:
Atami

Small, quiet inn with a sea view and a top reputation.

RATE: From ¥40,000 w/2 meals, from ¥30,000 w/breakfast, children 30–50% off. **CREDIT CARDS:** AMEX, DC, VISA. **ROOMS:** 16 Japanese style (w/bath). **COMMUNAL BATH:** 1—half-outdoor bath; alternating. **CHECK-IN:** 14:00. **CHECK-OUT:** 11:00. **LANGUAGE:** English spoken.

☎ 0557–80–5151 Fax: 0557–80–0205
750–6 Izusan, Atami-shi, Shizuoka 413–0002
〒413–0002　静岡県熱海市伊豆山750–6

■ ACCESS
BY TRAIN: 5 min by car from Atami Stn (JR Tokaido Main Line or *shinkansen*).
BY CAR:　22 km via Route 135 from Odawara Nishi IC (Odawara/Atsugi Doro) or 3 km via Route 135 from Atami City.

Hashiri-yu bath, Horai

Along with the Tawara-ya in Kyoto and the Asada-ya in Kanazawa, the Horai in Atami is one of *the* inns of Japan. Upholding its renown is an *okami* of impeccable taste, Seiyu Furutani—something of a legend among her peers for the artistic effort she puts into maintaining the Horai. Some *okami* barely manage to arrange flowers and put on kimono, but Ms. Furutani takes an interest in every detail of the inn. For each meal she decides on the dishes and personally pens a *waka* poem on every handmade paper place mat used at dinner. She never fails to greet and send off guests, and visits them at least once in their rooms. She believes that her ikebana flowers should be simple and should not upstage the most important items in the room, the guests.

The Horai's sixteen *sukiya*-style guest rooms each comprise a twelve-mat room and an eight-mat room, and a cypress bath. Do not forgo the big bath experience at the Horai, though. Put on your *yukata* and geta and totter down the long, steep, lantern-lit path to the Hashiri-yu. This is the ultimate Horai experience: its big wooden tub is protected from rain by a wide-eaved roof but is open to an exhilarating view of Sagami Bay. It is a special luxury to soak here in the mornings, watching the play of distant boats or, at nights, their flickering lights.

The food at the Horai is understated and perfect. The flavors have confidence and don't need ostentatious display. The ingredients are the best locally available, and they are prepared with the philosophy that the less done to them, the better. The special dish at the Horai is *Horai-mochi*, a fried cake of pounded rice containing chopped ginkgo nuts, *kikurage* (cloud-ear fungus), minced duck, and egg. Breakfast comes with the best horse mackerel *himono* (sun-dried fish) I have ever tasted.

ARAI RYOKAN 新井旅館

LOCATION: Shuzenji

Romantic old inn embodying a Japan of yesteryear, in a quiet hot spring resort.

RATE: From ¥23,000 w/2 meals, from ¥18,000 w/breakfast, ¥15,000 w/o meals, children 30% off. **CREDIT CARDS:** AMEX, MC, VISA. **ROOMS:** 41 Japanese style (19 w/bath). **COMMUNAL BATHS:** 6—men's, women's, outdoor (alternating), 3 private (*kazoku-buro*). **CHECK-IN:** 15:00. **CHECK-OUT:** 11:00. **LANGUAGE:** English spoken.

☎ 0558–72–2007 Fax: 0558–72–5119
970 Shuzenji, Shuzenji machi Tagata-gun, Shizuoka 410–2416
〒410–2416　静岡県田方郡修善寺町修善寺970

■ ACCESS
BY TRAIN: 10 min by car from Shuzenji Stn (Izu Hakone Railway)
BY CAR:　25 km via Routes 136 & 414 from Numazu IC (Tomei Expressway).

When this inn was built in 1872, the rest of Japan was going crazy over bustles, balustrades, and ballrooms. But the owners of the Arai wanted their inn to embody everything that was the pride of Japan—gardens, simple tatami rooms, and fine woodwork.

The maples, cherries, and other seedlings planted then are now gorgeous full-grown specimens. The original structure, with its cool corridors and curved wooden bridge leading to the rooms, is as elegant as it was when it was built. Undo the old brass locks of your wood-framed windows to look out on the view, which will be either over the Katsuragawa river or onto the inn's own courtyard garden, with its big pond lapping at the pillars, full of greedy red, white, and golden carp.

Hot water from the Shuzenji spring, discovered 1,200 years ago by the wandering priest Kukai (also known as Kobo-daishi; 774–835) supplies the inn's cavelike bathhouse, the Tempyo Daiyokudo (Tempyo Big Bath Hall). The

Tempyo Daiyokudo bath, Arai Ryokan

bathhouse, completed in 1933, took three years to build: the thick cypress pillars were imported from Taiwan because timber of this size could not be obtained in Japan, and twenty people worked tirelessly to move the massive rocks fifteen centimeters (six inches) a day to fashion its impressive pools.

Some of the country's great novelists, among them Nobel-prize winner Yasunari Kawabata (1899–1972), frequented the Arai. It was the setting for the famous novel *Shuzenji Monogatari* written in 1911 by Kido Okamoto (1872–1939).

A Kyoto-style *kaiseki* meal adds to the Arai's classic-Japan experience; the only thing that jars is the velvet-cushioned karaoke bar.

Nearby

Ask for directions to the inn's own teahouse, Soko Sanso (fifteen minutes by foot). It has a view of Mount Fuji and is set in a garden of three thousand red, white, and pink plum trees. You may not be able to see inside the tearoom, but the settingmakes the trip worthwhile. There is little else to see in the modest hot spring town of Shuzenji, apart from a hot spring pool that rises in the middle of the Katsuragawa river—where you may bathe in full view of passing motorists.

SHIRAKABE-SO　白壁荘

LOCATION:
Yugashima
Onsen, Amagi

An old haunt for writers, now a luxury inn with unusual baths.

RATE: From ¥15,000 w/2 meals, children 30–50% off. **CREDIT CARDS:** AMEX, DC, VISA. **ROOMS:** 28 Japanese style, 2 Western style—all rooms w/o bath. **COMMUNAL BATHS:** 6—men's, women's, 2 outdoor (men's, women's), 2 half outdoor (alternating). **CHECK-IN:** 15:00. **CHECK-OUT:** 10:00. **LANGUAGE:** No English, reservations in Japanese.

☎ 0558–85–0100　Fax: 0558–85–0726

1594 Yugashima, Amagi Yugashima-cho, Tagata-gun, Shizuoka 410–3206

〒410–3206　静岡県田方郡天城湯ヶ島町湯ヶ島1594

■ ACCESS
BY TRAIN: 20 min from Shuzenji Stn (Izu Hakone Railway).
BY CAR:　40 km via Routes 136 & 414 from Numazu IC (Tomei Expressway).

Broad tiled roofs, white plaster interior walls, and black pillars and beams epitomize what is known as *mingei* architecture. And this inn at Amagi Yugashima, in the center of the Izu Peninsula, is a fine example of the genre. The name, in fact, means "white walls."

The Shirakabe-so was renovated in 1988, but long before that it was a haunt of such literary greats as Yasushi Inoue (1907–91). His favorite room was the Amanjuku. It has a large square *irori* (fire pit), which makes it rather like being in your very own cottage. The inn is also proud of its Sensei-no-Heya (Great Writer's Room), which has its own study with a large desk and bookshelves of art books and encyclopedias.

Each of the rooms has a different shape and style, and bears the name of an Izu folk tale. This stems partly from the fact that inns in the area used to entertain travelers with storytelling, but it is also because one of Japan's foremost playwrights, Junji Kinoshita (1914–), who took his subjects from Japanese folklore, used to frequent this inn. All the names are from his Izu folk stories.

Here at the Shirakabe-so are two very special baths. The Big Rock Bath is carved from a fifty-three-ton rock unearthed when the inn was last renovated in 1988. It can hold ten thin people at a time. The Big Tree Bath is a rectangular tub made from a 1,200-year-old rosewood trunk from Gabon.

Rock bath, Shirakabe-so

Both of these unusual baths are semi-open air with male and female bathing hours. There are also segregated indoor and outdoor baths; one is called the Kotori-no-Yu (Little Bird Bath) after a novel by Yasunari Kawabata (1899–1972).

It is a great luxury to follow a bath or two with a ten-course Shirakabe-so meal. In winter the meal involves fewer courses but includes a wild boar hot-pot (the Izu mountains are a favorite of wild boar hunters). Since this area is only an hour from Shimoda on the sea, the sashimi is excellent, too. The *wasabi* (horse radish) will also be the real thing, because of the proximity to the Izu *wasabi* streams. *Wasabi* grows only in the cleanest running water. You might see clumps of it cultivated in steplike constructions down a watercourse.

Hot-pot at the hearth Shirakabe-so

OSAWA ONSEN HOTEL　大沢温泉ホテル

LOCATION:
Osawa Onsen,
near Matsuzaki

Inn built around dramatic namako-kabe tiled buildings with modern hot spring bathing and excellent food.

RATE: From ¥23,000 w/2 meals, 20% off w/breakfast only, 30% off w/o meals, children 30% off. **CREDIT CARDS:** AMEX, VISA. **ROOMS:** 15 Japanese style, 10 semi-Japanese style—all rooms w/o bath. **COMMUNAL BATHS:** 3—men's, women's, outdoor (alternating). **CHECK-IN:** 14:00. **CHECK-OUT:** 10:30. **LANGUAGE:** Some English.

☎ 0558–43–0121　Fax: 0558–43–0123
153 Osawa, Matsuzaki-cho, Kamo-gun, Shizuoka 410–3604
〒410–3604　静岡県加茂郡松崎町大沢153

■ ACCESS
BY TRAIN: 30 min by car from Shimoda Stn (Izu Kyuko Line).
BY CAR:　2 hr via Route 136 from Numazu IC (Tomei Expressway).

This is an atmospheric inn that has been deservedly well patronized by overseas

Osawa Onsen Hotel

visitors for more than two decades. Though not an easy place to reach, the port of Matsuzaki, which is the closest town to Osawa Onsen Hotel, is quiet and scenic, featuring fine examples of the handsome houses with black-and-white tiled exteriors called *namako-kabe*. The Osawa Onsen Hotel itself is one of the most dramatic examples of *namako-kabe* you will see anywhere on the Izu Peninsula, where the tiled walls afforded protection against the salty sea winds.

Some of these buildings date back four hundreds years, when they belonged to the estate of a village headman. Most accommodation is in a newer, concrete wing, which nonetheless has comfortable Japanese-style rooms that look out over a stunning sea of *namako-kabe* buildings surrounding a lush courtyard garden at the core of the inn.

The large cypress hot spring baths, one with an outdoor section, are welcome concessions to the tastes of modern *onsen* lovers.

Nearby

The inn sits across the road from a cherry tree–lined river that wends its way to Matsuzaki. Pick up an English map of Matsuzaki at the inn and take a bus there to spend a pleasant couple of hours strolling around the town's quiet streets. Enjoy the old houses and the *kote-e* art works of Edo period–artist Irie Chohachi (1815–1889) on display. Chohachi, who spent his early and later years in Matsuzaki, made delicate frescoes in plaster relief to decorate many buildings and one temple (the Jokanji) in the town. Matsuzaki is a good departure point for the historic port of Shimoda (about forty minutes by car), where the first American Consulate was set up after American Commodore Matthew Perry (1794–1858) arrived in Edo with his "black ships" demanding that Japan open up to the West after over two hundred years of seclusion.

TACHIBANA たちばな

LOCATION: Fujinomiya

A ryokan in lush tea country, with a panorama of Mount Fuji.

RATE: From ¥20,000 w/2 meals, from ¥11,000 w/breakfast, children 30–50% off. **CREDIT CARDS:** AMEX, VISA. **ROOMS:** 17 Japanese style, 2 Western style—9 rooms w/bath. **COMMUNAL BATHS:** 3—men's, women's, outdoor (alternating). **CHECK-IN:** 15:00. **CHECK-OUT:** 10:00. **LANGUAGE:** Some English.

☎ 0544–27–7000 Fax: 0544–24–0104
1085–4 Nonaka, Fujinomiya-shi, Shizuoka 418–0034
〒418–0034　静岡県富士宮市野中1085–4

■ ACCESS
BY TRAIN: 25 min by car from Fuji Stn (JR Tokaido *shinkansen*).
BY CAR:　10 km via Route 139 from Fuji IC (Tomei Expressway).

You can add immeasurably to your traveling pleasure in this area of Japan by doing it in May. Shizuoka Prefecture is Japan's supreme tea-producing area and the new tea leaves are bright and green in the fifth month—the hills of Shizuoka are a picture of terraced fields, with rows of tidily clipped hedges.

May is also picking season for what is called *ichiban-cha*, the first tea of the season. There are up to four pickings, but the first has the most chlorophyll, the highest concentration of vitamin C, and the best flavor. But do not believe the pictures you see of quaintly costumed maidens in sun bonnets plucking tea leaves: it is mostly done by machine now.

The best way to drink good green tea is by not pouring on boiling water, but using water cooked to about 70°C (160°F) and letting the tea steep for at least a minute, or up to three minutes for the higher grades. Drink it in small doses in small cups, and savor it like a liqueur. I questioned a local tea producer about rumors that tea these days contains MSG. He said no such practices are permitted in Shizuoka, where producers and packagers have taken an oath not to do anything that would harm the reputation of their industry.

You may have to make do with the tea bushes and forget about seeing Mount Fuji, as she is such a difficult lady to catch, especially in the spring. Clouds and fog often hide much of her, allowing only brief glimpses of the peak or one flank.

Like the Mona Lisa, Fuji-san must be one of the most overworked images in the world. But for me there was a big difference—when I went to the Louvre and saw the Mona Lisa, it was no big thrill; when I first saw Mount Fuji, the sight took my breath away. Nothing quite prepares you for Mount Fuji's presence, especially when you are in a city right at her feet, like Mishima, Fuji City, or Fujinomiya, where the mountain just looms above you.

You might think that the locals take the volcano for granted, seeing her, as they ostensibly do, every day. But they don't see her every day. She is there one day, gone the next, and her costume is ever-changing—snow, clouds, sunshine, the gloom of an overcast day draping her in ever-changing seasonal finery. She holds immense power over people's lives. Their conversations are full of her; their houses face her; and when she doesn't come out for guests, they make excuses for her. If this is the case for ordinary citizens living around Mount Fuji, imagine how great the pressure is for an inn that makes a living by her presence.

The Tachibana is on a picturesque hill in a quiet, high-class suburb of Fujinomiya, set among luxurious private homes and well-tended gardens. One of the lovelier gardens in the street belongs, in fact, to the Tachibana's old wing.

Mount Fuji from the banquet hall

More modern rooms, each with its own bathroom, toilet, and private view of Mount Fuji, are in the new wing across the road. The new wing also accommodates two big banquet halls, where the mighty mountain fills the floor-to-ceiling windows. Guests who stay in the old wing go to the new one for their meals.

The inn's maid told me that the majority of the Tachibana's guests are golfers who play at any of the half-dozen golf courses in the area. The accouterments are not luxurious and one of the rooms in the old wing, I noticed, was equipped with a mah-jongg table.

In the new wing there is an open-air hot spring bath, which has separate hours for male and female bathing. The bath looks out over a tea field and there are a number of houses within shouting distance. You feel a bit exposed stripping off in full view of all these private houses, but I suppose they have seen it all by now.

I should mention that the locals feel that the view of Mount Fuji from the Shizuoka side is the most beautiful. People living in Yamanashi will, of course, tell you differently.

The Tachibana claims to be an inn with high-class cuisine, but I found the *kaiseki* meals to be average. Come here mainly for the view.

7

MASUHO-CHO

Masuho climbing kiln

ATTRACTIONS

Superb rural scenery with Mount Fuji views.

Kofu, Yamanashi's capital, is a pleasant city with some historic sites related to warlord Takeda Shingen (1521–73), but my destination is always **Hirabayashi** in **Masuho-cho**, a place deep in the mountains with a lovely shrine, farms all around, and a view of Mount Fuji. Drop in at **Noa-no-Hakobune** (Noah's Ark, ☎ 0556–22–0299) in the town of Masuho-cho for a meal in stylish surroundings before heading up to the Villa Oka-no-Ie pension.

Try to time your trip to Yamanashi to coincide with the peach blossom season in March. The hills in parts of Yamanashi, especially on the way to Suwa (Destination 8), are awash in peach bloom.

Recommended trips including Yamanashi

There is easy access from Kofu, to Lake Suwa in Nagano, and then deeper into Nagano Prefecture.

● Masuho-cho (1 night)—Lake Suwa (1 night, Destination 8)—Matsumoto (day trip, Destination 9)

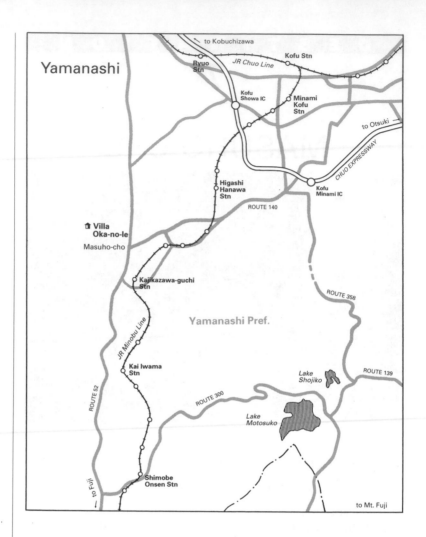

VILLA OKA-NO-IE　ヴィラ丘の家

Above-average pension in a farming community with a view of Mount Fuji.

RATE: From ¥8,500 w/2 meals. **CREDIT CARDS:** AMEX, VISA. **ROOMS:** 1 Japanese style, 6 Western style—all rooms w/bath. **COMMUNAL BATHS:** 1—alternating. **CHECK-IN:** 15:00. **CHECK-OUT:** 10:00. **LANGUAGE:** No English, reservations in Japanese.

☎ 0556–22–8700 Fax: 0556–22–8710

2155 Hirabayashi, Masuho-cho, Minami Koma-gun, Yamanashi 400–0514

〒400–0514　山梨県南巨摩郡増穂町平林2155

A *penshon* is the Japanese idea of a European "pension." In most cases it takes the form of a log house or Swiss chalet with window boxes, lace curtains, and croissants for breakfast. Although this book focuses on traditional Japanese-style accommodation, Villa Oka-no-Ie is one of the few exceptions. It is more "Japanese" than most *penshon* and also happens to be the sole accommodation in a stunning location. The high-ceilinged dining room looks out onto Mount Fuji and is surrounded by terraced rice paddies and vegetable fields—without a shop or vending machine in sight.

The Villa Oka-no-Ie was built in this rather out-of-the-way place thanks to a pottery kiln complex (the Masuho Noborigama) a five-minute walk up the road. Amateur potters from many parts of Japan come here to fire their pots in one of the wood-fired or other kilns available. Until the Villa was established, the closest lodgings were in a shabby inn fifteen minutes away.

The pension's owner is a potter himself and, for a little extra money, he will pull out some clay and show you how to make a pot of your own.

There is not much else to do up here—and that is the beauty of the place. The Masuho Kiln Art Shop on the kiln site is open to the public. From there, take a thirty-minute walk to the top of the slope and you will find the Himuro shrine, with its five hundred ancient stone steps (take them slowly) and magnificent old trees. Head down the mountain and you find yourself in farm country. Both walks can be magic for the jaded city-dweller. If you have ever wondered why the Japanese make such a fuss about their country's natural beauty, this place provides some of the answers.

The Villa Oka-no-Ie is spotless and tasteful, if a little too precious. The furnishings are European antique, but the feel is Japanese folk-style. There are two tatami guest rooms; the rest have beds. The baths and toilets are shared. The food is a French-Japanese hybrid and fair enough for the price. A herb garden languishes at the back.

Villa Oka-no-Ie

8

LAKE SUWAKO and TAKATO

Japan Alps and cherry blossoms, Takato

ATTRACTIONS

Hot spring zone, the castle town of Takato, and the farming valleys of Ina.

Given its relative proximity to Tokyo, the Lake Suwako area is a good first-night stop on the way from the capital to deeper Nagano.

In **Kami Suwa** (Upper Suwa) I recommend a wade in the big public baths at the **Katakura-kan** (☎ 0266–52–0604), a German-style brick structure originally built by the Katakura conglomerate for the hundreds of young female workers in its weaving and spinning factories of the 1920s to 1940s.

It is in **Shimo Suwa** (Lower Suwa), however, that the best inns and tourist attractions are to be found. Head for Shimosha, the lower section of the Grand Shrine of Suwa. Shimosha is known for its suicidal Ombashira Festival held every six years (in the Years of the Monkey and Tiger), during which dozens of men carry or "ride" massive fir trunks down a very steep mountainside. Men have been crushed to death by the hurtling trunks, but the trunks themselves

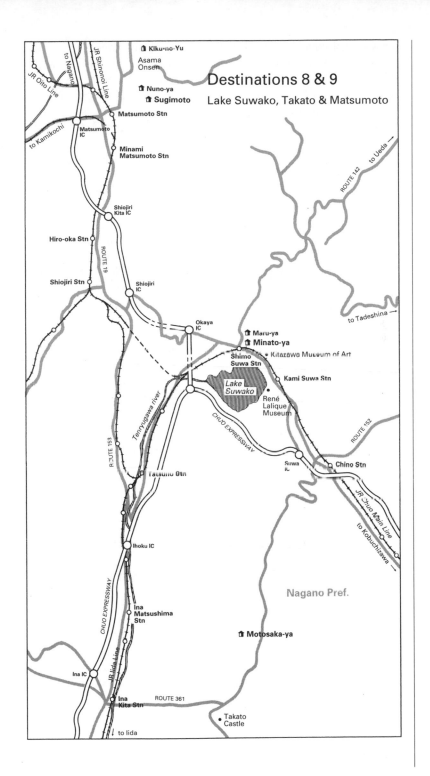

Destinations 8 & 9

Lake Suwako, Takato & Matsumoto

Kiku-no-Yu

Asama Onsen

Nuno-ya

Sugimoto

Matsumoto Stn

Matsumoto IC

Minami Matsumoto Stn

Shiojiri Kita IC

Hiro-oka Stn

Shiojiri Stn

Shiojiri IC

Okaya IC

Maru-ya

Minato-ya

Kitazawa Museum of Art

Shimo Suwa Stn

Kami Suwa Stn

Lake Suwako

René Lalique Museum

Tatsuno Stn

Suwa IC

Chino Stn

Ihoku IC

Nagano Pref.

Ina Matsushima Stn

Motosaka-ya

Ina IC

Ina Kita Stn

ROUTE 361

Takato Castle

to Iida

to Nagano

JR Shinonoi Line

JR Oito Line

to Kamikochi

ROUTE 19

ROUTE 142

to Ueda

to Tadeshina

CHUO EXPRESSWAY

Tenryugawa river

ROUTE 153

ROUTE 152

JR Chuo Main Line

to Kobuchizawa

CHUO EXPRESSWAY

JR Iida Line

survive as replacement pillars at both the upper and lower shrines.

After the festivities, sleepy Shimo Suwa reclaims its tranquility. Yet there is still plenty of interest: a museum with relics from the time Suwa was an Edo-period (1600–1868) post town, and a former inn where *daimyo* used to stay, the **Honjin Iwanami-ke**. In the Lake Suwako area two museums are devoted, oddly enough, to European glass: the **Kitazawa Museum of Art** (☎ 0266–58–6000), which has a collection of nineteenth-century Art Nouveau glassware by Émile Gallé (1846–1904) and others, and the **René Lalique Museum** of Art Nouveau glass (☎ 0266–57–2000).

The small castle town of **Takato** is also worth visiting, especially around April 18–20 when the cherry blossoms of the former castle grounds are in full bloom. This is one of Japan's great cherry blossom experiences, the blossoms here being of a sensuous, deep pink variety. Of course, timing a visit to see the cherry blossoms with a blue sky is like trying to see Mount Fuji on a clear day. But it is most decidedly worth the effort, as the trees in full bloom virtually block out the sky, against the backdrop of the snow-capped Japanese Alps.

If you are traveling by car, get to the **Takato Castle grounds** before 8 A.M. or you will never find a parking place. Take a picnic and share it with all the other crazy people under the trees.

Next to the castle grounds is the handsome **Shinshu Takato Bijutsu-kan** (Takato Museum of Art), a contemporary art museum where you can have a restful cup of coffee. Other attractions in the area include the modest house where an exiled shogunal concubine, Ejima, lived after an affair with a Kabuki actor.

Recommended trips including Lake Suwako

Combine Lake Suwako with Takato or make it the first-night stop on a longer trip to Nagano Prefecture.

- Lake Suwako (1 night)—Takato (day trip or 1 night)
- Lake Suwako (1 night)—Matsumoto (day trip, Destination 9)—Narai (1 night, Destination 10)

LOCATION:
Shimo-Suwa

MINATO-YA　みなとや旅館

Eccentric Edo-period inn with a fascinating meal and an unusual bath.

RATE: ¥18,000 (tax, service fee included) w/2 meals, 30% off w/breakfast only, 40% off w/o meals. **CREDIT CARDS:** Not accepted. **ROOMS:** 5 Japanese style (w/o bath). **COMMUNAL BATH:** 1 outdoor (alternating). **CHECK-IN:** 16:00. **CHECK-OUT:** 10:00. **LANGUAGE:** Some English.

☎ 0266–27–8144 Fax: 0266–27–8144
3532 Tatsu-machi, Shimosuwa-machi, Suwa-gun, Nagano 393–0015
〒393–0015　長野県諏訪郡下諏訪町立町3532

■ **ACCESS**
BY TRAIN: 3 min by car from Shimo Suwa Stn (JR Chuo Main Line).
BY CAR: 6 km from Okaya IC (Chuo Expressway).

The Minato-ya dates back ten generations to when Shimo Suwa, at the junction of the Nakasendo and Koshu Dochu highways, was named an official station town. The inn building is unremarkable, its five rooms low on luxury, and its service matter-of-fact; but its outdoor hot spring bath is a treat and its food a legend.

Pebble-floored outdoor bath, Minato-ya

Dinner is served in a tatami dining area on the first floor. Beforehand, you are invited to use the lovely outdoor bath, which is diligently emptied and washed twice a day, and carefully supervised so that each group of guests has total privacy. Pebbles cover the bottom of the bath—bliss for the soles.

The first course of dinner is a neat platter of thinly sliced, raw horse meat, which is eaten after being dipped in soy sauce with grated ginger. Arranged around the horse meat is a constellation of antique blue-and-white dishes, each bearing a small portion of something either unrecognizable or indescribable.

The unrecognizable things are mountain vegetables, such as fern fronds, butterbur, *azami* (thistle), and *kogomi* (ostrich fern). The indescribable things are crickets, baby bees, and *zazamushi* (the larva of another type of insect), cooked in salt and soy sauce. Eating insects is a Nagano tradition and old-timers smack their lips in delight when describing lightly salted baby bees grilled over hot coals.

I have enjoyed more than my share of wild vegetables in Japan, most of it bland or bitter, but these mountain vegetables are prepared with sensitivity to the integrity of each plant, seasoned with the right amount of the perfect condiment to release the intrinsic flavors.

The main course proffers a hot-pot of meat and leeks flavored with sweet, dark miso and eaten on top of white rice. This dish is so good that you want more and more. Unfortunately, the Minato-ya's spartan service does not stretch to seconds, and the local *yakitori* shop does a good business from still-hungry guests.

Breakfast at the Minato-ya is no less unusual than the evening meal, with a new selection of mountain vegetables and a small hot-pot of whole buckwheat in a mild pheasant stock sprinkled with *seri* (Japanese parsley).

My notes from my first stay ten years ago showed that the meal was identical—right down to the frozen persimmon and buckwheat gruel for breakfast.

Nearby

The lower shrine of the Suwa Taisha (Grand Shrine of Suwa) is a short stroll away. At the gates is the Shimotsuru sweet shop with excellent *shio-yokan*, a delicate salty bean-paste jelly. Next door to the Minato-ya is a local history museum with relics and pictures related to Edo-period (1600–1868) highway travel. Around the corner is Honjin Iwanami-ke, a former *honjin* inn for *daimyo*. Its glories have faded, but it does have a lovely corner room overlooking a three hundred-year-old Kyoto-style garden. Once one of the famed gardens on the Nakasendo highway, it features gnarled old pines and plums, a pond shaped in the character for *kokoro* (heart), and special rocks from all over Japan. The *honjin* is open to the public for a small fee and has clean, new, Japanese-style accommodations in the adjoining Kame-ya (☎ 0266–27–8023).

MOTOSAKA-YA 元酒屋

*Homey accommodations in old
saké brewer's residence.*

RATE: From ¥7,500 w/2 meals, from ¥4,500 w/breakfast, children 20–30% off. **CREDIT CARDS:** Not accepted. **ROOMS:** 5 Japanese style (w/o bath). **COMMUNAL BATH:** 1—alternating. **CHECK-IN:** 15:00. **CHECK-OUT:** 10:00. **LANGUAGE:** No English, reservations in Japanese.

☎ 0265–96–2021 Fax: 0265–96–2510
Osafuji Kurita, Takato-machi, Kami Ina-gun, Nagano 396–0305
〒396–0305　長野県上伊那郡高遠町長藤栗田

■ ACCESS
BY TRAIN: 40 min by car from Chino Stn (JR Chuo Main Line) or 15 min by car from Ina-shi Stn (JR Iida Line).
BY CAR: 40 min via Route 152 from Suwa IC (Chuo Expressway).

Motosaka-ya

Tsuetsuki Toge ("Walking-Staff Pass") is a mountain pass linking Chino and Suwa, in the Suwa Basin, with the Ina Valley. It is glorious in the cold months when distant sawtooth peaks are thick with snow against a blue sky. The road also goes to Takato, a downhill stretch through pastoral scenes dotted with white *kura* storehouses.

The Motosaka-ya is about halfway to Takato, not far from the Kurita bus stop. The inn's name—"former saké brewer"—reflects its previous incarnation. The brewery started business 250 years ago, when Kurita was a small post station, and while the building's function has changed the structure itself remains pretty much as it was. The five rooms in the upper level are for guests. Instead of brewing saké, the family now tends the inn and engages in a bit of farming on the side.

Farming and village life surround you at the Motosaka-ya. If you go walking in the village, you might spot a number of *koshinzuka* (stone posts) engraved with symbols for preventing fire and other disasters, or promoting jovial matrimonial relations. These are relics of a past when folklore ruled people's lives, and for some, perhaps, it is not much different now.

Meals at the inn are shared in an eighteen-mat, high-ceilinged room downstairs, and include river fish, beef sashimi, grilled beef, *chawan mushi* (egg custard), tempura, sweet chestnuts, and mountain vegetables.

Nearby

The castle town of Takato is best seen during the cherry blossom season, but remains a pleasant, if subdued, destination at other times.

9

MATSUMOTO

Matsumoto Castle

ATTRACTIONS

A former provincial capital and later castle town, Matsumoto features one of Japan's most handsome castles and a splendid street of craft shops that reflect a strong folkcraft tradition.

The sophisticated castle town of Matsumoto is so accessible from Tokyo that if you plan well, you could manage a day trip there. If you arrive early and leave after dusk, you will have time to see the four-hundred-year old **Matsumoto Castle** (Japan's oldest with original castle keep); the *nakamachi* **district**, which has the best craft and folk art shops in provincial Japan; the splendid **Matsumoto Mingei-kan** (Matsumoto Folkcraft Museum); and maybe lunch or dinner at the French restaurant Taiman, a Matsumoto institution. But as you've come all this way, why not stay the night in one of the inns listed or travel on to Narai on the old Nakasendo highway?

The **Chuo Mingei** showroom in the *nakamachi* holds about three hundred examples of Japanese- and Western-inspired Matsumoto furniture. All items are made of local timber and constructed without nails. The **Hakari Shiryo-kan**, or weights and measures museum, also in the *nakamachi*, has all imag-

Matsumoto Mingei-kan

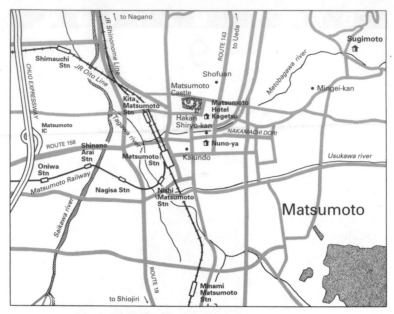

Note: See also area map in Destination 8.

inable devices for weighing everything from rice to silkworm cocoons. Three shops worth visiting are the long-standing **Chikiri-ya** folkcraft shop, selling folk art and toys from all over Japan and some from Southeast Asia; the **Hongo** craft shop, whose main specialty is hand-woven silk and other assorted crafts; and **Tohemboku**, for excellent contemporary ceramics, mainly Karatsu, Hagi, and Agano. There are also several shops specializing in Japanese or Asian antiques.

The **Taiman French restaurant** with its cathedral-like interiors, excellent art, and Matsumoto furniture, is easy walking distance from Nakamachi. The **Marumo coffee shop**, just off the main Nakamachi street, is another good place to stop for a breather. Its warm atmosphere is enhanced by Matsumoto furniture, delicious coffee, and classical music.

In the vicinity of the castle is the elegant and restful tea shop, **Shofu-an** (closed Tuesdays, no smoking). The Shofu-an serves green tea and their own Japanese sweets and is a branch of the refined Meiji-period (1868–1912) **Kaiundo** sweet shop in the middle of the city.

For such a charming castle town there is a surprising lack of Japanese-style accommodation. I have only the Sugimoto inn on the outskirts of the city to recommend or the Kiku-no-Yu in Asama Onsen (see Alternative Inns). If you prefer to stay in the city, I suggest a small Western-style hotel, the Matsumoto Hotel Kagetsu (✆ 0263–32–0114), built at the turn of the nineteenth century), or the inexpensive Ryokan Nuno-ya, right in the middle of the *nakamachi*.

Folk toys from Chikiri-ya, ceramics from Tohemboku, *oyaki* (grilled buns with savory fillings).

Recommended trips including Matsumoto

Use Matsumoto as a jumping-off point for a trip via Kiso Fukushima to Narai, on the ancient Nakasendo highway, or even to Takayama, which is only two or three hours away via the spectacularly empty, serenely beautiful Kaida Kogen at the base of holy Mount Ontake (see Destination 10).

An hour away from Matsumoto in the other direction is Nagano City, with the temple "town" of Zenkoji on its outskirts. Not far from Nagano are the well-planned town of Obuse, famous for its chestnut products and the Hokusai Museum, and Suzaka (see Destination 11).

Another alternative is to travel from Matsumoto toward the Sea of Japan coast to Kanazawa (Destination 21) and the Noto Peninsula (Destination 22).

- Matsumoto (1–2 nights)—Narai/Kaida Kogen (1 night in each or either, Destination 10)—Hida-Takayama (1–2 nights, Destination 13). Note that the trip from Matsumoto to Hida-Takayama via Kaida Kogen is only possible by car or bus.

- Matsumoto (1–2 nights)—Zenkoji (Nagano City)/Togakushi Shrine (1 night in each or either)—Suzaka Obuse (no accommodation of note in either Suzaka or Obuse, but Iwanoyu is close to both. Also highly recommendable is Hana-ya at Bessho Onsen, near Ueda. See Alternative Inns).

SUGIMOTO 旅館すぎもと

LOCATION: Utsukushi-ga-hara Onsen, Matsumoto

Reasonably priced contemporary ryokan in a semi-deserted hot spring town. Adventurous cuisine is served restaurant style.

RATE: From ¥15,000 w/2 meals, 30% off w/breakfast, 45% off w/o meals, children 30–50% off. **CREDIT CARDS:** AMEX. **ROOMS:** 18 Japanese style (8 w/bath). **COMMUNAL BATHS:** 3—men's, women's (each connect to outdoor bath), 1 private (*kazoku-buro*). **CHECK-IN:** 15: 00. **CHECK-OUT:** 10:00. **LANGUAGE:** No English, reservations in Japanese.

☎ 0263–32–3379 Fax: 0263–33–5830
451–7 Satoyamabe, Matsumoto-shi, Nagano 390–0221
〒390–0221 長野県松本市里山辺451–7

■ ACCESS
BY TRAIN: 15 min from Matsumoto Stn (JR Chuo Main Line).
BY CAR: 30 min via Route 158 from Matsumoto IC (Chuo Expressway).

Sugimoto is situated on the outskirts of Matsumoto, offering good service and value for money.Utsukushi-ga-hara Onsen was not always this quiet. It was the hot spring favored by the lord of Matsumoto Castle in the Edo period (1600–1868) and where he had his second house. The Sugimoto is the oldest of

*Raked stone court-
yard, Sugimoto*

all the inns and is found at the hot spring's source. The most recent owners have undertaken major renovations, and the inn is now decorated in the folk-art style, albeit without the patina of age.

Utsukushi-ga-hara Onsen is just a ten-minute drive from central Matsumoto. The well-drilled staff of the Sugimoto greet their guests at their car and this attention is maintained throughout the stay. At meals, an army of local youngsters pronounce the contents of your meal in loud, clear voices and then serve it with precision. This takes place in an impressive big-beamed old section of the former inn, which has been laid out so that each party of diners has a semi-private alcove.

The food is a feature of the inn, and it appears that even local people come for the novelty and theatrics of such specialties as steak brought to your table sizzling on a hot rock and a small stew cooked in a cone of paper over fire. In spite of the carnival atmosphere, the food was very good, confining itself entirely to local produce and wild vegetables.

Nearby

The excellent Matsumoto Mingei-kan (Matsumoto Folkcraft Museum) is fifteen minutes away by taxi. This museum was opened in 1962 by Taro Maruyama, a folkcraft lover and friend of the late Mingei Movement leader, Soetsu Yanagi (1889–1961). Displays of all sorts of Japanese folkcraft from Okinawan to Ainu (and some foreign) are housed in this elegant building.

10

NAKASENDO

Tsumago street

ATTRACTIONS

This historic highway dates from the Edo period (1600–1868), linking Tokyo (then called Edo) with Kyoto via Nagano. It has three well-preserved station towns.

In spite of several treacherously steep mountain passes, the **Nakasendo** was a well-trodden highway in the Edo period. It is well-worn today too, but for different reasons. In the old days, travelers were *daimyo* (provincial lords) and their samurai attendants, plus assorted merchants, peddlers, and couriers; today's travelers are hikers and tourists coming to discover the ancient highway and the well-preserved old station towns of Narai, Tsumago, and Magome.

There were sixty-nine stations on the Nakasendo in the 1700s. To give an idea of the distances involved, the Kiso stretch was ninety-two kilometers (fifty-seven miles) with eleven stations, and it was said to take three days on foot. Narai was the busiest station, supporting a thousand inns at its peak.

Narai is still the biggest and most interesting of the three towns, although **Tsumago** is the most beautifully preserved. **Magome** is also picturesque. They are all a little touristy, but a visit to one or all of these station towns—preferably with a night in an old Edo inn—is one of the best ways to experience a Japan of old.

For hikers, the walk between Magome and Tsumago, a journey of three and a half hours, is especially scenic and, although longer, it does not have as many steep sections as the other two hiking courses on the Nakasendo.

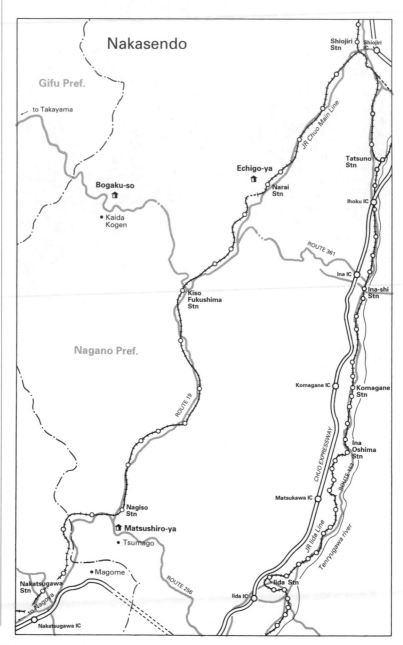

If you are interested in visiting Narai, I would also suggest combining it with a drive through the **Kaida Kogen** (Kaida Plateau), one of Japan's best-kept secrets. Spectacularly untarnished and serenely beautiful, the Kaida Kogen lies at the base of holy Mount Ontake. It links the interesting cities of Takayama and Matsumoto.

Recommended buys

Throughout this area you can find *gohei-mochi*, a delicious snack of skewered rice cake patties topped with miso or sesame paste and grilled. The area also has a thriving lacquerware tradition, fed by the abundant timbers of the Kiso Valley.

Recommended trips including the Nakasendo

Visiting each of the three station towns and spending time in each constitutes a full trip. But since Narai is separated from the other two by quite a distance, it could be combined with Matsumoto instead. From there you could even travel to Takayama. The Bogaku-so inn on the Kaida Kogen is not in any of the three towns, but between Matsumoto and Takayama.

- Matsumoto (1–2 nights, Destination 9)—Narai/Kaida Kogen (1 night in each or either)—Hida-Takayama (1–2 nights, Destination 13)

ECHIGO-YA 越後屋旅館

LOCATION: Narai

The best-appointed old inn on the Nakasendo.

RATE: From ¥13,000 w/2 meals. **CREDIT CARDS:** Not accepted. **ROOMS:** 5 Japanese style (w/o bath). **COMMUNAL BATH:** 1— alternating. **CHECK-IN:** 15:00. **CHECK-OUT:** 10:00. **CLOSED:** Obon in Aug and New Year holidays. **LANGUAGE:** No English, reservations in Japanese.

☎ 0264–34–3011
496 Narai, Narakawa mura, Kiso-gun, Nagano 399–6303
〒399–6303　長野県木曽郡楢川村奈良井493

■ ACCESS
BY TRAIN: 10 min on foot from Narai Stn (JR Chuo Main Line).
BY CAR: 30 km via Route 19 from Shiojiri IC (Chuo Expressway).

Of the three famous old station towns on the Nakasendo, Narai has not adhered to the same strict standards of authenticity as Magome and Tsumago—there are power lines overhead and cars drive freely down even the most traditional streets. But of the three, it has the most to see. It also has the most elegant inn on the Nakasendo, the Echigo-ya.

This inn was not a *honjin* (inn designated for the *daimyo* nobility), but a place where merchants and traveling salesmen stayed. Business started here in the late 1700s, and the patina of its dark pillars and floorboards, rubbed smooth by two hundred years of wear and daily polishing, shows the inn has been well cared for.

Echigo-ya

Paper umbrellas, oil lamps, a shop sign from the time when the inn once sold medicines, and many other antique objects attest to the inn's long history and make the Echigo-ya something of a living museum. Unlike most of the other lodgings on the Nakasendo, which are fairly spartan, the Echigo-ya's appointments and the quality of its hanging scrolls and flower arrangements put this inn in a class of its own.

All meals are served in your room. There will probably be carp sashimi, grilled river fish, and five to ten different mountain vegetables cooked according to grandmother's recipes, subtle and wholesome. The aging couple who run the Echigo-ya will usually only accept two parties at a time so they can ensure the best service.

The bath is small, but it is a lovely cypress one.

Nearby

The Echigo-ya alone makes a visit to Narai worthwhile, but you can spend a good half-day here inspecting the Tokuriya Kyodo-kan and Kamidon-ya Shiryo-kan museums and browsing in the high-quality gift and lacquerware shops. Take a drink from one of several wells that have supplied travelers with spring water since the Edo period. One temple in Narai, the Daihoji, has a headless stone statue that appears to be Buddhist, but is actually the Virgin Mary. It dates from the time of Christian persecutions in the sixteenth century, when many Christian relics were hidden or disguised. All the sights are marked on local tourist leaflets. There is a hiking course along part of the old Nakasendo—from Narai to Yabuhara—that takes about one hour and twenty minutes.

MATSUSHIRO-YA 松代屋旅館

LOCATION: Tsumago

The oldest ryokan *in Nakasendo's most pristinely preserved post town.*

RATE: From ¥10,000 w/2 meals, from ¥7,000 w/breakfast, from ¥5,000 w/o meals. **CREDIT CARDS:** Not accepted. **ROOMS:** 8 Japanese style (w/o bath). **COMMUNAL BATHS:** 2—men's, women's. **CHECK-IN:** 15:00. **CHECK-OUT:** 10:00. **CLOSED:** Wed. **LANGUAGE:** Some English.

☏ 0264–57–3022 Fax: 0264–57–3386
Tsumago, Nagiso-machi, Kiso-gun, Nagano 399–5302
〒399–5302　長野県木曽郡南木曽町妻籠

■ ACCESS
BY TRAIN: 5 min by car from Nagiso Stn (JR Chuo Main Line).
BY CAR: 24 km via Route 19 from Nakatsugawa IC (Chuo Expressway).

Three adjoining rooms, Matsushiro-ya

The old station town of Tsumago was an all-but-deserted backwater in 1965. But instead of luring industry here, the townspeople drafted laws to protect what they had, banning overhead power lines, cars in the older streets, and modern renovations without permission from the council—and the town now provides a proud example of historic preservation at its best. Tsumago's effort subsequently inspired other towns and cities struggling to keep progress at arm's length.

The Matsushiro-ya has the distinction of being the oldest of thirty lodges in the area, having weathered almost two hundred years of icy Nagano winds. The dirt road leading to it is a rarity in Japan. Its sharp curve is a deliberate Edo-period (1600–1868) device intended to foil, or at least slow, marauders with murderous intent.

If you can avoid traveling in summer and autumn, when swarms of tourists flood the town, you will get more out of a visit to Tsumago. But whatever season you travel in, things are quiet after dark. There are no cars and, at the Matsu-shiro-ya, not even the sounds of television disturb the deep mountain silence.

The best room is the detached *hanare* connected to the front rooms by a corridor. Meals invariably comprise carp sashimi, grilled river fish, *koya-dofu* (freeze-dried tofu), and healthy *tororo* soba (soba noodles with a sticky grated-yam topping).

There are two cypress baths, one for men and one for women.

Original road in front of Matsushiro-ya

Nearby

A favorite hiking trail leads from Tsumago to Magome

BOGAKU-SO 望嶽荘

LOCATION: Kaida-mura

Set on the exhilarating Kaida Plateau, this is a simple four-room inn with excellent country food.

RATE: From ¥9,000 w/2 meals, ¥5000 w/breakfast, ¥4,000 w/o meals, children 20% off. **CREDIT CARDS:** Not accepted. **ROOMS:** 7 Japanese style (w/o bath). **COMMUNAL BATHS:** 2—men's, women's. **CHECK-IN:** 15:00. **CHECK-OUT:** 10:00. **LANGUAGE:** No English, reservations in Japanese.

☎ 0264–42–3005

2806 Suekawa, Kaida-mura, Kiso-gun, Nagano 397–0301

〒397–0301　長野県木曽郡開田村末川2806

■ ACCESS

BY TRAIN: 40 min by bus (30 min by car) from Kiso Fukushima Stn (JR Chuo Main Line).
BY CAR: 60 km via Routes 19 & 361 from Shiojiri IC (Chuo Expressway).

The owner of the Bogaku-so, Mr. Teruo Nakamura, is the honorary president of the All Japan Reed Blowers Society. If you stay for dinner at his inn, you may find a little pile reeds or grasses alongside your chopsticks and, instead of saying grace, you get a lesson in blowing on them. After you have produced some embarrassing noises, Mr. Nakamura will show you how it is really done with a medley of melodic evergreens, proving that even grasses have other uses.

I doubt if Mr. Nakamura gives his recital every night, as he is a very busy man. He is also the chairman of the All Shinshu Reed Blowers Society; an official of the Hoeschs Lion Club; an advisor to the Prince Lakewood Golf Club; and counsel to the local Self-Defense Forces on outdoor survival, his field of expertise here being mushrooms, toadstools, and other edible and inedible fungi.

Thanks to Mr. Nakamura's knowledge of the wild, an interesting variety of fresh mountain flora is offered at mealtimes, all prepared and served with sophistication by Mr. Nakamura's daughter, Yumiko. She is the mainstay of the inn and takes care of its day-to-day business.

Originally, the Bogaku-so was an old country home, so its rooms were not intended for guests. The best room is upstairs, but for those who invariably rise in the middle of the night I suggest a downstairs room because the facilities are all on the lower floor.

The countryside around this inn belongs to one of Japan's lost paradises. The area is known as the Kaida Kogen, a place whose beautiful country roads have been deserted every time I've traveled them. Mount Ontake in the distance seems to cast its holy influence over the area, further enhancing the undisturbed aura of the place.

The Kaida Kogen is also worth knowing about as it links two of Japan's most well-preserved historic provincial centers, the castle towns of Matsumoto and Hida-Takayama. I recommend it as a route for traveling to either or both places, with a stop at Narai on the way.

Nearby

When I stayed at the Bogaku-so one May, Mount Ontake was still capped in snow and the area around the Bogaku-so was covered with banks of flowering forget-me-nots. The old school next door to the inn with its stream and water wheel—a genuine relic of days gone by—are worth exploring, as is the farming community across the road from the inn. The pastoral ways of today haven't changed much from those of the community's forebears. Japan's natural beauty is still very much in evidence here. The horiculturally inclined will find many treasures among the trees and down the stream. Further along the old back road are stone statues of the guardian of travelers.

If you like hot springs and are visiting by car, you might care to take the extra twenty to thirty minutes to drive to Ontake Myojin Onsen (☎ 0264–44–2346), a hot spring discovered in 1990. The outdoor rock baths here are spacious and rewarding. The indoor baths look out on Mount Ontake. There is no overnight accommodation, however.

Along the Kaida Kogen, there is a farm that breeds the sturdy little *Kiso-uma*, one of Japan's original horses. Mr. Nakamura tells the following story about how it was saved from extinction:

In the Meiji period (1868–1912) the modernizing government decided that Kiso horses, with their dumpy little bodies and short legs, were not suited for empire building. So all the Kiso horses were rounded up and bred with tall long-legged Western-style horses, until there were no more pure-bred Kiso horses left in Japan. Or so everyone thought. But two had survived the government initiative, a mare and an aging stallion that was thought to be sterile. However, it turned out to be a simple case of malnutrition. At the expense of his own family's less-than-ample food budget, the stallion's owner fed his horse the best food in the house until it grew strong again and gave the mare a foal.

11

ZENKOJI TEMPLE

Zenkoji

ATTRACTIONS

A lively old temple town. Nearby are two other interesting towns, Suzaka and Obuse, plus the serene Togakushi shrine, and Shibu Onsen, a hot spring town right out of the 1920s.

Zenkoji temple on the edge of Nagano City is a rare non-denominational Buddhist temple that attracted a huge following in the Edo period (1600–1868), spawning a whole town at its gates. Zenkoji opened its arms to people of all sects and promised salvation to anyone who made a pilgrimage there to rub the "**key to paradise.**" The actual key is still to be found in a pitch-black tunnel under the floor of the main hall.

While many temples around the country are losing patronage, Zenkoji's popularity remains high. Beautification projects associated with the 1998 Winter Olympics have given the street leading to the temple a fastidious sophistication (although detractors claim such projects have destroyed much of the charm of the old city). Nevertheless, allow at least a half-day to find the key to paradise and explore the shops on the road to the temple. There aren't many, but the store specializing in the Nagano blend of seven mixed ground peppers (*shichimi togarashi*) deserves an award for shop and packaging design.

The best alternative to staying near Zenkoji is to head for Togakushi, whose shrine, **Togakushi jinja**, set in pristine natural surroundings, has a mysteriously pacifying atmosphere. About an hour from Nagano by bus or car, the town of Togakushi comes alive in summer, when hoards converge on it to escape the heat, and in winter, when other hoards arrive to ski. In the off-seasons it is blissfully calm.

Suzaka City, almost a suburb of Nagano City, started taking an interest in its heritage in the 1990s and has now funded the preservation of a scattering of old houses around town. A special example of this is the **Suzaka Kurashikku Bijutsu-kan** (Suzaka Classic Museum). The city purchased this former abode of a kimono dealer to house an unusual and stunning array of kimonos from the Taisho period (1912–26). There is also the **Tanaka-ke** (Tanaka Family Mansion), which has regularly changing displays of this rich family's treasures.

Half an hour from Suzaka is the town of **Obuse**, a pioneer in civic beautification. Several decades of thoughtful planning have gone into building further tourist potential around its most famous asset, the **Hokusai-kan** (Hokusai Museum), which holds prints and some rare paintings by the great artist Katsushika Hokusai (1760–1849). The mainstays of the town's beautification efforts are the town's two major chestnut-sweet makers: **Obusedo**, which has a superb contemporary restaurant, and **Chikufudo**, which has one specializing in chestnut-studded rice. Also at Chikufudo is the interesting **Akari no Hakubutsu-kan** (Japanese Lamp Museum). The streets of Obuse are paved with blocks of chestnut wood.

The monkeys' bath, Jigokudani

Togari/Nozawa Onsen Stn

Eiraku-ya
Sumiyoshi-ya

ROUTE 202

ROUTE 117

Myoko Kogen Stn

Myoko Kogen IC

Iiyama Stn

Nagano Pref.

Lake Nojiriko

Shinano IC

JOSHIN'ETSU EXPRESSWAY

ROUTE 18

Toyoda/ Iiyama IC

JR Iiyama Line

Togakushi Heights

Yudanaka Stn

Nakatani

Togakushi shrine

Shinshu Nakano Stn

Rinsen-kaku
Kanagu-ya

JR Shin'etsu Line

Shinshu Nakano IC

Shibu Onsen

Shiga Heights

Toyoda Stn

TOGAKUSHI BIRD LINE

ROUTE 292

Obuse Stn

ROUTE 406

Gohonjin Fujiya

Hokusai Museum

to Takasaki

JR Nagano Shinkansen

Chikumagawa river

Zenkoji temple

Suzaka Stn

ROUTE 19

Nagano Stn

Iwa-no-Yu

Senni Onsen

Nagano Railway

Suzaka/ Nagano Higashi IC

Destinations 11 & 12
Nagano City & Environs

to Matsumoto

Nagano IC

ROUTE 406

to Karuizawa

Of course, Nagano is a skier's mecca and there is spectacular mountain country around **Shiga Kogen** (Shiga Heights). On the way to Shiga Heights and only thirty minutes from Nagano City is the rickety, pocket-size hot spring town of **Shibu Onsen**. Staying here at one of the old wooden inns—like the Rinsen-kaku or the Kanagu-ya—is close to experiencing what it must have been like to visit a hot spring town at the turn of the century. Shibu has nine public baths, which any inn guest can use for free. Half an hour away (driving and then walking) is **Jigokudani**, an open-air hot spring where monkeys come down from the mountains to bathe.

Recommended buys

Chestnut sweets from the Obusedo shop in Obuse; reproduction ceramics from the Tanaka Family Mansion gift shop; and *tenugui* (rectangular cotton hand-towels) from Shibu Onsen, for collecting the stamps of the nine public baths when you visit them.

Recommended trips including Zenkoji

With so many places of diverse interest spread throughout the Zenkoji area, it is hard to plan a straightforward visit. You might need a three- to four-night trip to take in all the listed places. Here is one way of tackling the area.

● Bessho Onsen (1 night at Hana-ya, see Alternative Inns)— Zenkoji (day trip)—Togakushi (1 night)—Suzaka and Obuse (day trip)—Shibu Onsen (1 night)

IWA-NO-YU 岩の湯

LOCATION: Senni Onsen, Suzaka

Newly renovated deluxe inn with some hotel features and a bath in a cave.

RATE: From ¥19,000 w/2 meals, children from ¥9,000. **CREDIT CARDS:** Not accepted. **ROOMS:** 19 Japanese style (10 w/bath). **COMMUNAL BATHS:** 3—men's, women's, mixed w/ half-partition. **CHECK-IN:** 13:00. **CHECK-OUT:** 11:00. **LANGUAGE:** Some English.

☏ 026–245–2453 Fax: 026–248–0047
3159 Nirei, Suzaka-shi, Nagano 382–0034
〒382–0034　長野県須坂市仁礼3159

■ ACCESS

BY TRAIN: 15 min by car from Suzaka Stn (Nagano Railway).
BY CAR:　20 min (9 km) via Route 406 from Suzaka/Nagano Higashi IC (Chuo Expressway).

Room with a garden, Iwa-no-Yu

The first thing that greets you at Iwa-no-Yu is the sound of cascading water from the decorative waterfalls on the grounds; the second is the staff, cascading

Inviting Iwa-no-yu entrance

from every corner of the inn. There is almost one staff member per guest, so your comfort is guaranteed.

The Iwa-no-Yu is not a new establishment. It has been a renowned "hidden hot spring" inn for scores of years because of its unusual cave-style bath that was frequented by mountain ascetics in days gone by. In the 1980s the owner toured inns of repute throughout Japan as a prelude to a major renovation of the building. He discovered that to provide the best service an inn should have no more than ten rooms; the improved Iwa-no-Yu opened in 1990 with nineteen.

The new Iwa-no-Yu perhaps incorporates a few too many ideas from those inns he visited—a lobby fit for the Ritz is tacked onto *sukiya*-style accommodation wings and each tatami room is combined with Western-style nooks, giving the place an eclectic sort of sumptuousness. But there can be no complaints about service, comfort, food, or flowers—especially the flowers. Baskets of blooms and bouquets burst from every corner. The flower arranger must be the busiest person in the inn.

One of the great luxuries of a Japanese inn is having meals brought to your room, but like many other modern establishments the Iwa-no-Yu has stopped doing this. Instead, meals are served in separate private rooms with gardens, which is certainly better than facing a dining room full of other bleary-eyed breakfasters. The advantage of this is that you do not have to fit in with the "Good morning Mr. Tanaka, it's 7:30. Time for breakfast!" routine. Just get up and have your breakfast when you feel like it—as long as it is before check-out time. The fare is a first-class choice of Japanese-style country food or a Western-style feast of scrambled eggs, crêpes, and croissants, with fresh local apple juice and homemade jam. The inn makes a point of preparing meals using only local produce, which, in this case, means there is no seafood.

The cave bath at the Iwa-no-Yu is lukewarm, but the steamy interior makes it feel like a sauna. You emerge refreshed, not boiled alive. There are private sections for men and women on either side of a wall, but the inner section is mixed. If cave bathing does not sound appealing, there is another bathroom with a square bath and garden view.

I mentioned that the sound of water greets you at the Iwa-no-Yu. If you go in winter this may not be so; then everything is silenced under snow.

Nearby

Iwa-no-Yu is close to two towns of cultural interest:
Suzaka and Obuse, both introduced earlier.

GOHONJIN FUJIYA 御本陣藤屋

LOCATION:
Zenkoji

Funky old inn right on the doorstep of Zenkoji with twenty-three spacious rooms and one deluxe suite.

RATE: From ¥9,000 w/2 meals, ¥6,500 w/breakfast, ¥5,500 w/o meals, children 30% off. **CREDIT CARDS:** AMEX, VISA. **ROOMS:** 24 Japanese style (3 w/bath). **COMMUNAL BATHS:** 3—men's, women's, private (*kazoku-buro*). **CHECK-IN:** 14:00. **CHECK-OUT:** 10:00. **LANGUAGE:** English spoken.

☎ 026–232–1241 Fax: 026–232–1243
INTERNET: www.abisnet.or.jp/`fuziya/
E-MAIL: fuziya@avisnet.or.jp
80 Daimon-cho, Nagano-shi, Nagano 380–0841
〒380–0841　長野県長野市大門町80

Stone façade,
Gohonjin Fujiya

■ ACCESS

BY TRAIN: 10 min by car from Nagano Stn (JR Nagano *shinkansen*).
BY CAR:　Nearby Zenkoji temple, 30 min (10 km) from Nagano IC (Joshin'etsu Expressway).

In 1611, when the Tokugawa shogunate established its network of official highways so that all roads led to the capital city of Edo (now Tokyo), Zenkoji temple found itself on one of these routes. The approach to Zenkoji was designated a highway station and was soon lined with inns. In 1776 an ancestor of the Gohonjin Fujiya's present owner started a *honjin* (an inn exclusively for the accommodation of *daimyo*), thus beginning the establishment's three hundred-year-long history.

Now nothing remains of the original *honjin*. In 1923 the Gohonjin Fujiya was rebuilt in Western style and that building still stands today—a stern, three-story, stone-faced structure that looks more like a bank than an inn, in prime position on the lovely boulevard leading to the temple. It has definitely seen better days, but merits inclusion here because it is the funkiest inn in an intriguing town.

Courtyard garden,
Gohonjin Fujiya

The foyer gives a hint of its former glory, with its giant murals of wisteria and maidens (the *"fuji"* of Fujiya means "wisteria"). A handsome British club-type drawing room lies to the left, and a 1920s reception counter staffed by the elegant lady of the house, Mrs. Keiko Fujii, a sixteenth-generation Fujii, is found to the right. A grand staircase rises to the second floor, where the "poorer accommodations" can be found. These are cavernous, high-ceilinged tatami rooms of a former era, neglected, but with a certain faded elegance. I enjoyed mine very much even though the rest rooms are shared, dormitory-style, and the communal bath is downstairs.

The more comfortably equipped rooms with their own toilets are on the ground level. If you want to make your visit to Zenkoji a truly special occasion, there is one suite with its own garden view to which they have added a splendid new bathroom—complete with a private cypress bath.

The food at the Gohonjin Fujiya, served in a depressing Western-style room, is unspectacular. Feast yourself on what is left of the atmosphere instead.

Nearby

The Gohonjin Fujiya is a five-minute stroll from the gates of Zenkoji temple. Attending sutra readings in the main hall of the temple at 6:30 A.M. is a recommended experience. There are other interesting shops along this street as well. The road closer to Zenkoji is lined with souvenir stalls and *shukubo* (temple accommodations), some with rather handsome façades. I asked one of the hawkers whether it was worth staying at any of them, but got the thumbs down. "The temples that run them are dubious," she said.

NAKATANI 中谷旅館

LOCATION: Togakushi

Well-cared-for pilgrims' lodgings on the approach to Togakushi shrine.

RATE: From ¥15,000 w/2 meals, 30% off w/o meals, children 30% off. **CREDIT CARDS:** AMEX, DC, MC, VISA. **ROOMS:** 16 Japanese style (4 w/bath). **COMMUNAL BATHS:** 3—men's, women's, 1 private (*kazoku-buro*). **CHECK-IN:** 14:00. **CHECK-OUT:** 10:00. **LANGUAGE:** No English, reservations in Japanese.

☎ 026–254–2533 Fax: 026–254–2885
3503 Togakushi, Togakushi-mura, Kami-Minochi-gun, Nagano 381–4101
〒381–4101　長野県上水内郡戸隠村戸隠3503

■ ACCESS
BY TRAIN: 1 hr by bus from Nagano Stn (JR Nagano *shinkansen*).
BY CAR:　30 km via Togakushi Bird Line from Nagano IC (Joshin'etsu Expressway).

Nakatani

Once upon a time, says the legend, the Sun Goddess took off in a huff and hid herself in a cave in Kyushu. The gods were most concerned because the world was in darkness. So they all gathered outside the cave and one of the lady gods performed a naughty dance that made the others laugh so much that the Sun Goddess could not control her curiosity. When she opened the cave door to peek out, a god managed to put his toe in the doorway and then hurled the stone door far away. The world became light again—and the place where the door fell, thousands of kilometers away in Nagano Prefecture, became Mount Togakushi. This explains the origin of the strange name *togakushi*—"the door that hides."

Mount Togakushi has long been a place of pilgrimages and asceticism, where Shugendo priests practiced their curious mixture of Shinto, Buddhism, and magic. It revolved around the three shrines of Togakushi—Hokosha, Chusha, and Okusha. Rows of lodgings sprang up along the roads leading to the shrines for the accommodation of pilgrims, mostly at Chusha. The Nakatani is the grandfather of them all, with a history that goes back to the 1600s. The present building is a hundred years old.

Gate leading to Okusha shrine

Even though other lodgings may be a little less expensive and have more exotic-looking façades, I recommend the Nakatani for its old-fashioned comfort, cleanliness, and service. The rooms are spacious, and the wholesome, simple meals contain an abundance of local wild greens, plus the inevitable—and overrated—Togakushi buckwheat noodles. Meals are served in a big room downstairs that adjoins a shrine room. If you peer into its dim interior you can make out a sacred mirror, representing the gods, with offerings nearby.

Today there are few mountain ascetics and more tourists than pilgrims at Togakushi; in summer, people come for the scenery and the birdwatching (access from Nagano Station is via the "Togakushi Bird Line") and, in winter, for the ski slopes. The quiet seasons are highly recommended—just after Golden Week in early May, and between the end of the summer holidays and the start of the autumn colors. At these times you will get a cheaper rate at the Nakatani and find yourself virtually alone on your walks to the holy places.

Nearby

Do walk the fifty minutes from Chusha shrine to Okusha shrine along an awesome cryptomeria-lined forest path. Unfortunately people have been stealing the bark from the beautiful cryptomeria trees (it is used for roof tiles), but this is a lovely, relaxing place. The start of the path is a ten-minute drive from the Nakatani, but the energetic can walk there via a hiking trail that passes through fields of *mizubasho* (skunk cabbage) and brings you in contact with rare bird and plant life. A short way along the path is a sign marking the spot where a Buddhist temple was torn down during the purge of Buddhism that took place after Meiji-period (1868–1912) oligarchs proclaimed Shinto the state religion. Until then Buddhism and Shinto had coexisted peacefully.

RINSEN-KAKU 御宿 臨仙閣

LOCATION:
Shibu Onsen

Classic wooden hot spring inn.

RATE: From ¥15,000 w/2 meals. **CREDIT CARDS:** AMEX, DC, VISA. **ROOMS:** 14 Japanese style (5 w/bath). **COMMUNAL BATHS:** 2—men's, women's. **CHECK-IN:** 15:00. **CHECK-OUT:** 10:00. **LANGUAGE:** No English, reservations in Japanese.

☎ 0269–33–2521 Fax: 0269–33–2523
Shibu Onsen, Yamanouchi-cho, Shimo-Takai-gun, Nagano 381–0401
〒381–0401　長野県下高井郡山ノ内町渋温泉

■ ACCESS
BY TRAIN: 5 min by car from Yudanaka Stn (Nagano Railway).
BY CAR: 25 min (8 km) via Route 292 from Shinshu Nakano IC (Joshin'etsu Expressway).

From the highway, Shibu Onsen looks like the worst sort of concrete chaos. But once you are in the little *onsengai* (hot spring town), it is suddenly all picture-postcard charm. The main street, a narrow, stone-paved road that winds precariously up to a shrine, is full of shops, 1920s inns, and public baths that do not seem to have changed since they were built at the turn of the century. This is in large part due to the efforts of the owner of the Rinsen-kaku, Shimpei

Rinsen-kaku

Nishiyama, who has a plan to preserve and enhance the atmosphere of Shibu Onsen's little street.

Shibu Onsen is the perfect place to put on *yukata* and geta and go walking about the streets. There are nine public baths, each decoratively marked, and each with its own claims to protect you from various misfortunes—bad health, fire, and plague. Your inn will give you a key to visit them all and you can also obtain a *tenugui* (rectangular cotton cloth) to collect the stamps of each as a memento of your visit. Number Nine is the bath where most townspeople go, and where they still engage in *hadaka no tsukiai* ("naked communication"). Whatever other ills you may have had, at least all your inhibitions will have gone by the time you emerge, steaming, from Number Nine.

Draped entrance to a public bath, Shibu Onsen

The Rinsen-kaku itself does not face the steep main street, but looks out on a bigger street across from the highway. It is an unusual three-story wooden building with big rooms and high ceilings that was completed in 1928. The corridors on the third floor have been decorated to resemble the walls of a castle town.

The massive rock at the back of the inn's famed "Dragon God Bath" is said to have emerged from subterranean depths following a torrential downpour when the inn was being built—a gift from the Dragon God.

Nearby

It is a fifteen-minute taxi ride from here to Jigokudani Onsen, where monkeys come down from the mountains to bathe. From the carpark you need to hike for fifteen minutes along a gorge to reach the monkeys' pool. Try to make it there at about 8 A.M. when the monkey bathing is at its most picturesque. Those prepared to rough it a bit can stay at the Koraku-kan (℡ 0269–33–4376), the only *ryokan* in Jigokudani Onsen. There are two inside baths, two outside baths (one exclusively for women), and two *kazoku-buro* for private bathing with your partner or family. The food specialties here are duck hot-pot and *tempura* of wild mountain vegetables, plus carp sashimi and grilled river fish.

12

NOZAWA ONSEN

Ogama

ATTRACTIONS

Abundant hot spring baths in a ski town.

Long a favorite soaking spot for skiers, Nozawa's best attractions are its **thir-teen *soto-yu*** (public baths). In the 1990s, ¥80 million was spent on renovating **Oyu**, the most beautiful of all the *soto-yu*, into a classic Edo-period (1600–1868) wooden bathhouse—a wise investment in the town's future.

Local townspeople operate all the *soto-yu* and use them themselves every day, which ensures that they are well maintained. Out-of-towners are welcome to use the baths for a small fee, as long as they observe bathing etiquette: no soap, shampoo, towels, or face cloths in the tub; be friendly but not loud; clean up after yourself; and don't drip water in the changing rooms.

Nozawa is most famous, though, for its small town square with steaming hot spring pools of 90°C (194°F) that would poach a human bather alive—but are perfect for boiling the veggies. And, indeed, innkeepers and local people come to the *ogama* (literally, "hemp pot") every day with baskets of greens to cook.

From early November the whole town begins *o-sai arai*, which literally means "washing the veggies." The greens are simmered in the hot waters before being preserved in salt for the long, snowy Nozawa winter, when no fresh greens can be found—or so the tradition goes. Of these veggies, *Nozawa-na*, a slightly bitter leaf served as a pickle, is so good it has made Nozawa a household name. It is now sold nationwide, but only the *Nozawa-na* boiled in this town's hot spring is the genuine item.

Seasonal tip

One of three big fire festivals in Japan is the Dosojin Hi-matsuri, held here on February 15.

Recommended buys

Nozawa-na, the local pickle, is the natural choice if you enjoy pickles.

Recommended trips including Nozawa

From Nozawa you can go two ways. Toward Nagano are the lively Zenkoji pilgrimage temple (Destination 11) and the interesting neighboring towns of Obuse and Suzaka. But the Uonuma-gun area of Niigata Prefecture (Destination 17) comprises the most glorious rice paddy country in Japan. This is best explored by car, taking the mountain roads to such isolated spots as Matsunoyama.

- Nozawa (1 night)—Zenkoji or Togakushi (1 night)— Suzaka/Obuse (day trip, Destination 11)
- Nozawa (1 night)—Minami Uonuma-gun (1 night, Destination 17)

Note: For area map, see Destination 11.

SUMIYOSHI-YA 村のホテル住吉屋

A comfortable, well-established inn with a folk-style decor. Generous helpings of country cooking served in an old kura.

RATE: From ¥18,000 w/2 meals, 20% off w/breakfast, from ¥10,000 w/o meals, children 30–50% off. **CREDIT CARDS:** AMEX, DC, VISA. **ROOMS:** 15 Japanese style (4 w/bath). **COMMUNAL BATHS:** 3—men's, women's, outdoor bath (alternating) **CHECK-IN:** 12:00. **CHECK-OUT:** 11:00. **LANGUAGE:** Some English.

☎ 0269–85–2005 Fax: 0269–85–2501

87–3 Toyosato, Nozawa Onsen-mura, Shimo-Takai-gun, Nagano 389–2502

〒389–2502　長野県下高井郡野沢温泉村豊郷87–3

■ ACCESS

BY TRAIN: 75 min by bus from Nagano Stn or 20 min by bus from Togari Nozawa Onsen Stn (JR Iiyama Line).

BY CAR: 25 km via Route 117 from Toyoda/Iiyama IC (Joshin'etsu Expressway), or 55 km via Routes 353 & 117 from Shiozawa/Ishiuchi IC (Kan'etsu Expressway).

Across the street from the *ogama* (vegetable-washing hot spring) is the Sumiyoshi-ya, the oldest, most venerable *ryokan* in Nozawa. Instead of becoming greedy and turning the old inn into a concrete mammoth as did the owners of many of the other old, respected inns of Japan, the proprietors of the Sumiyoshi-ya have kept it small. The present building dates to 1870 and feels like someone's lovingly cared-for home, with a beautiful and unpretentious interior decor in the *mingei* tradition.

Sumiyoshi-ya as seen from the Ogama

Rooms are not large, but they are intimate and warm. Meals are served in a low-ceilinged, one-hundred-year-old former storehouse. Here guests dine on such foreigner-friendly foods as small potatoes in their jackets that have been fried and then boiled in soy sauce and a little sugar, sweetly seasoned beans, preserved fish, fresh meats, and many different wild mountain greens boiled—of course—in the hot spring waters across the road. In a departure from the usual small, individual portions of a *kaiseki*-style meal, large bowls of food are passed among the guests. The soft-boiled eggs at breakfast are also cooked in the hot waters of the town square.

EIRAKU-YA 永楽屋

LOCATION: Nozawa Onsen

An ancient, thatched building with two rooms and intimate service provided by a legendary owner-chef.

RATE: From ¥17,000 w/2 meals. **CREDIT CARDS:** Not accepted. **ROOMS:** 1 Japanese style (w/o bath). **COMMUNAL BATHS:** 2—men's, women's. **CHECK-IN:** 12:00. **CHECK-OUT:** 12:00. **LANGUAGE:** No English, reservations in Japanese.

☎ 0269–85–2023 Fax: 0269-85–4503
Shinyu, Nozawa Onsen-mura, Shimo-Takai-gun, Nagano, 389–2500
〒389–2500　長野県下高井郡野沢温泉村真湯

■ ACCESS
BY TRAIN: 1 hr by bus from Nagano Stn, or 20 min by bus from Togari Nozawa Onsen Stn (JR Iiyama Line).
BY CAR: 25 km via Route 117 from Toyoda/Iiyama IC (Joshin'etsu Expressway), or 55 km via Routes 353 & 117 from Shiozawa/Ishiuchi IC (Kan'etsu Expressway).

This old thatched house, with its crooked pillars, sloping floors, and age-stains on the earthen walls, is on its last legs. And yet, if you can pry a list of favorite inns out of the most seasoned Japanese travelers, those who really know Japan will murmur confidentially: "Eiraku-ya."

For me this inn's magic lies in the angled, stained walls, and the obvious fact that somebody has loved this old building with its gleaming wooden floors throughout its three hundred years. For many others, I suppose, the charm is in the small-inn intimacy. And for everybody, it is Mieko Kono, the beautiful, hard-working owner of Eiraku-ya, who collects mountain vegetables, prepares them in delicious ways, and serves them herself to her guests—no more than four people a night—around one big, square table.

Far more solidly preserved than the guest rooms, the inn's bathing facilities do complete justice to the waters of this famous hot spring. The separate women's and men's facilities are surrounded in stone and impeccably clean, like everything else at Eiraku-ya.

Of course, because Eiraku-ya is so small and has such a dedicated band of admirers, reservations will be difficult. But give it a try.

13

HIDA-TAKAYAMA

Hida-Takayama in spring

ATTRACTIONS

Abundant old houses, excellent crafts and antique shops in Takayama City, famous spring festivals here and at neighboring Furukawa.

An hour after getting on the Takayama Line from Nagoya, the train is weaving its way among tall mountains, crossing and recrossing the aqua Shirakawa river. Before the smile has faded from your face you are in **Hida-Takayama**, a provincial city with an elegant culture nestled in the snow-capped Japanese Alps. Put on your walking shoes, because it is a great walking town.

From the station it is just a fifteen-minute stroll to all the major attractions: **Takayama Jinya** (handsome and fascinating former provincial government offices), the **morning market** around Takayama Jinya, **Sanno-machi** (a block of Edo-period (1600–1868) houses, now craft shops and restaurants), the **Kusakabe Mingei-kan** (Folk Art Museum) in a former wealthy merchant's mansion, the **Yoshijima-ke** saké merchant's house, and the **Takayama Yatai Kaikan**, which displays floats for the spring and autumn festivals in rotation. This is almost a better way of seeing the floats than competing with the crowds at festival time.

If you do not have two hours to visit Shirakawa-go (Destination 14), a genuine village of historic A-frame thatched farmhouses called "praying hands"

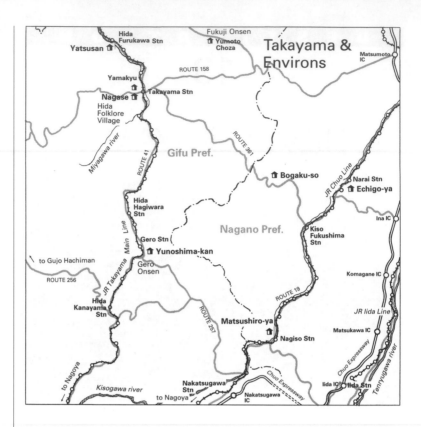

Takayama & Environs

(*gassho-zukuri*), the alternative is the fifteen-minute bus ride to the **Gassho-zukuri Minka-en** (Hida Folklore Village), an open-air museum of *gassho-zukuri* and other structures that show how local peasants lived in simpler times. The Hida area was full of praying-hands structures until dams and other developments engulfed most of the villages. A large number of farmhouses were relocated to other parts of Japan. In Hida today, craftsmen work on the premises displaying the particular Hida skills of lacquering and carving yew wood.

Takayama has dozens of mediocre inns and one very special one, the Nagase. To see Takayama, spend at least one night in the town itself and then head for a hot spring inn on the second night. The Yumoto Choza at Fukuji Onsen and the Yunoshima-kan at Gero Onsen, both about an hour away in opposite directions, are two rather distinctive types of hot spring inns—the first a rustic establishment with contemporary flair, the other a classic inn patronized by royalty. Another interesting alternative to staying in Takayama would be a night in neighboring **Furukawa-machi**, a small town noted for its raucous April festival and for harboring one of the few traditional candlemakers in Japan. The Yatsusan inn there is excellent.

Seasonal tips
Mid-April is a good time to visit this area because you can do a fantastic festival

crawl—the Takayama Spring Festival on April 14–15 (antique festival floats with performances by amazing mechanical dolls), the Furukawa Okoshi-daiko Festival at Furukawa on April 19–20 (a raucous procession at night featuring a huge drum, and processions of festival floats like the Takayama ones during the day), and the Mino Festival on the second weekend in April (floats draped in long sprigs of pink paper flowers, with competing groups fighting at intersections; see Destination 15. If you are not planning to go until the fall, you can experience the Takayama Autumn Festival (October 9–10) and the Doboroku Festival at Shirakawa-go (October 14–19; see Destination 14), which has colorful processions through the fields and opportunities to drink the milky-white, unrefined local saké after which this festival is named.

Bear in mind that this is high-mountain country, so winter brings heavy snows that may prevent passage to some places, notably Kami-Kochi and the Sea of Japan coast. Some years, the roads do not open until May.

Recommended buys

Hand-colored woodblock-print votive pictures of horses (*ema*). Hang them facing inside your home so the horse doesn't gallop out the door, taking your good luck with it. There is a fair especially for these, the Ema-ichi, on August 9–10. Lacquered items in the rich caramel-colored *shunkei-nuri* lacquerware loved by tea ceremony aficionados. Gracefully tapered red or white handmade candles from the Mishima-ya shop at Furukawa-machi, made of vegetable wax over a thick wick of *igusa* (tatami rushes). Aromatic miso grilled on a big, dry magnolia leaf over an individual brazier (standard breakfast fare at all inns). All the ingredients for this, as well as the inexpensive braziers, can be bought at the Takayama morning market.

Recommended trips including Hida-Takayama

Hida-Takayama really is a trip in itself. With a few days available, you can combine it with a rewarding visit to Matsumoto via the Kaida Kogen Plateau (see Destinations 9 and 10), remembering that the road may be closed in winter. A more common choice is to combine Hida-Takayama with Shirakawa-go, Japan's famous World Heritage village of "praying-hands" farmhouses (see Destination 14). Also nearby is Mino (Destination 15), another worthwhile detour .

● Hida-Takayama/Furukawa (1 or 2 nights)—Kaida Kogen/Narai
(1–2 nights, Destination 10)—Matsumoto (1 night)
● Takayama/Furukawa (1 or 2 nights)—Shirakawa-go (1 night, Destination 14)
Mino (1 night, Destination 15)—Gujo-Hachiman/Kokin Denju-no-Sato
(day trip)—Hida-Takayama (1–2 nights)

NAGASE 長瀬旅館

LOCATION:
Central
Takayama

Elegantly renovated 250-year-old merchant house.

RATE: From ¥15,000 w/2 meals, children 30% off. **CREDIT CARDS:** VISA. **ROOMS:** 10 Japanese style (8 w/bath). **COMMUNAL BATHS:** 2—men's, women's. **CHECK-IN:** 15:00. **CHECK-OUT:** 10:00. **LANGUAGE:** Some English.

☏ 0577–32–0068 Fax: 0577–32–1068
10 Kami Nino-machi, Takayama-shi, Gifu 506–0845
〒506–0845　岐阜県高山市上二之町10

■ ACCESS

BY TRAIN: 5 min by car from Takayama Stn (JR Takayama Main Line).
BY CAR: 2 hr via Route 158 from Matsumoto IC (Chuo Expressway).

The room where Bernard Leach stayed

Miso grilled on a magnolia leaf— a local delicacy

After doing battle with the rest of the tourists in Takayama, stepping into the quiet interior of the Nagase is like arriving at an oasis. The faceless wooden grilles of the façade glide open onto the luxury of a welcoming entrance and spacious lobby crafted in powerful Hida architecture—the very same into which stepped British potter Bernard Leach (1887–1979) in the company of Shoji Hamada (1894–1959) on one of their legendary searches for dying folkcrafts. Others who have stayed here were potter-designer Rosanjin Kitaoji (1883–1959), sculptor Isamu Noguchi (1904–88), and the explorer Sir Edmund Hillary (1919–).

But that was over fifty years ago. Since then, ninth-generation inn master Keiichi Nagase has thoughtfully renovated the establishment, parts of which date back 250 years to its merchant-house days. Far from compromising the original design, Mr. Nagase has preserved the integrity of the old accommodations while adding to their comfort with charming pocket-sized gardens adjoining each of the eleven rooms, giving them a feeling of space and luxury. These small gardens all have their own rocky waterfalls and flowing streams, which are transformed into miniature snowscapes in winter. The veranda of each room incorporates a low, black lacquered table for two designed by Mr. Nagase for viewing the garden. His attention to detail has allowed the Nagase to maintain its standing as Takayama's most trustworthy inn.

When it comes to meals, the Nagase surpasses most Takayama inns by serving formal Kyoto-style cuisine. This is not a pretension, but the honoring of a long tradition, for the rich merchants and craftspeople of Hida were no strangers to the elegance of Kyoto culture. Their wood craftsmen had gone to work on the temples, shrines, and palaces of the ancient capital for generations and, when they returned, they brought back an appreciation of the Kyoto style. Takayama is still known as "the Little Kyoto of Hida." Local flavor in the meal comes from additions such as Hida beef and Takayama's famous aromatic miso grilled on a magnolia leaf over individual braziers.

If your only trip into the Japanese countryside is to Takayama, a night at this inn is very worthwhile—despite its higher price—for the comfort, the good taste, and the traditional experience it offers.

Nearby

Nagase is a short distance from Sanno-machi, Takayama's picturesque street of shops and houses.

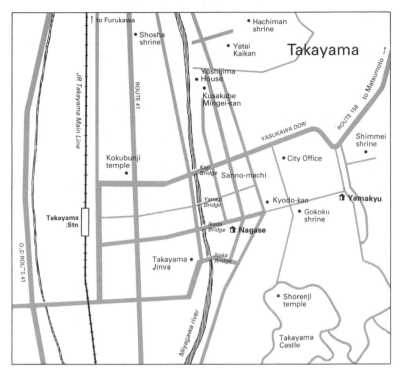

- to Furukawa
- Shosha shrine
- Hachiman shrine
- Yatai Kaikan
- Takayama
- Yoshijima House
- Kusakabe Mingei-kan
- JR Takayama Main Line
- ROUTE 41
- ROUTE 158 to Matsumoto
- YASUKAWA DORI
- Shimmei shrine
- Kokubunji temple
- Kaji Bridge
- Sanno-machi
- City Office
- Yanagi Bridge
- Kyodo-kan
- 🏠 Yamakyu
- Takayama Stn
- Ikada Bridge
- 🏠 Nagase
- Gokoku shrine
- OLD ROUTE 41
- Takayama Jinya
- Naka Bridge
- Miyagawa river
- Shorenji temple
- Takayama Castle

YATSUSAN 八ツ三旅館

LOCATION: Furukawa-machi

Splendid former merchant house with interesting history in a quiet town two stops from Takayama.

RATE: From ¥15,000 w/2 meals, children 30% off. **CREDIT CARDS:** Not accepted. **ROOMS:** 15 Japanese style (14 w/bath). **COMMUNAL BATHS:** 6–2 alternating, 2 outdoor (men's, women's), 2 private (*kazoku-buro*). **CHECK-IN:** 15:00. **CHECK-OUT:** 10:00. **CLOSED:** 12/26–1/1. **LANGUAGE:** Some English.

☎ 0577–73–2121 Fax: 0577–73–3910
1–8–27 Mukai-machi, Furukawa-machi, Yoshiki-gun, Gifu 509–4241
〒509–4241 岐阜県吉城郡古川町向町1–8–27

■ ACCESS
BY TRAIN: 7 min on foot from Hida Furukawa Stn (JR Takayama Main Line).
BY CAR: 2 hr 30 min via Routes 158 & 41 from Matsumoto IC or 3 hr via Routes 257 & 41 from Nakatsugawa IC (Chuo Expressway).

Historic warehouses near Yatsusan

Yatsusan's original quarters

The original owner of the Yatsusan first put up lodgings here 130 years ago and dealt in rice on the side. The *honkan* (main building) is built in the style typical of a two-story Hida merchant house—with towering pillars and beams and a shaft that reaches right up to the roof, allowing light to pour down to the first floor with its big sunken hearths. You can see several examples of this impressive style of architecture in neighboring Takayama, but you can't spend a night in any of them. This is what makes the Yatsusan special—and a good reason to stay in Furukawa-machi.

As you contemplate the massive pillars of the Yatsusan's old wing, spare a thought for the many young women who once stayed here, when, at the end of the 1900s, the Yatsusan served as an official wayhouse for girls who had been sent by their fathers to work at the textile factories of neighboring Nagano Prefecture. These girls, many just out of primary school, walked treacherous mountain roads, traversing the infamous Nomugi Toge Pass, to get to their destination and a life that was nothing short of slavery. The trip was dangerous at any time, but especially in the bitterly cold winter, when many of the girls died. So that they would not be tempted to run away, they were allowed to stay in only certain inns en route. Some scenes in *Ah, Nomugi Toge*, a film documenting this bleak episode in history, were filmed at Yatsusan.

Today you will be accommodated in the new *sukiya*-style section of the Yatsusan. Kazumi Ikeda, the seventh-generation owner, and her husband have earned the inn a new reputation for elegant cuisine.

Nearby

The Mishima-ya candle shop is the big attraction in the town of Furukawa-machi, and a carp-filled canal lined with old warehouses adds to the atmosphere. They are all walking distance from the Yatsusan. The time to visit is April, when the famous drum festival takes place, a few days after Takayama's spring festival. The Yatsusan fills up early for this period, so make reservations well in advance.

YUNOSHIMA-KAN 湯の島館

LOCATION: Gero Onsen

A classic rambling wooden inn, with a grand entrance and superb wooden architecture, this inn has received innumerable imperial guests.

RATE: From ¥18,000 w/2 meals, 20% off w/breakfast only, 30% off w/o meals, children 30–50% off. **CREDIT CARDS:** AMEX, DC, MC, VISA. **ROOMS:** 73 Japanese style (44 w/bath). **COMMUNAL BATHS:** 8—men's, women's, 2 outdoor (men's, women's), 4 private (*kazoku-buro*). **CHECK-IN:** 14:00. **CHECK-OUT:** 10:00. **LANGUAGE:** No English, reservations in Japanese.

✆ 0576–25–3131 Fax: 0576–24–1882
645 Yunoshima, Gero-cho, Mashita-gun, Gifu 509–2207
〒509–2207 岐阜県益田郡下呂町湯之島645

BY TRAIN: 5 min by car from Gero Stn (JR Takayama Main Line).
BY CAR: 1 hr via Route 257 from Nakatsugawa IC (Chuo Expressway).

Embraced by ancient cryptomeria and cypress groves, the Yunoshima-kan, though officially in Gero, maintains a regal detachment from that tawdry riverside town in the valley below Yunoshima Mountain, famous for its hot spring discovered in the tenth century. This inn was built in 1931, when standards of carpentry were still high, and the owner employed the best timbers and materials he could buy. Indeed, for the dignity of its classic wooden architecture and the elegance of its interiors, there aren't many inns that outrank it.

Yunoshima-kan

The low tables and other furnishings in the rooms are a little worn now, but they were created when objects were made to be beautiful forever. The wing in which I stayed was built so that each room juts out just a little further than the last, and I have an indelible picture in my mind of that zigzag row of rooms glowing with warm light through bamboo blinds. I thought such sights were gone for good.

Exploring the rambling buildings on the forested hillside is a fun thing to do at Yunoshima-kan. At one end of the Frank Lloyd Wright–influenced Western-style building that adjoins the main wing, and after the "ballroom," is a fenced-off area leading to the Shunkei-so, a grand structure in the *shoin-sukiya* style that was favored by lords. Emperor Showa (formerly known as Emperor Hirohito; 1901–89) stayed in the Shunkei-so when he visited in 1958. The pillars are lacquered in *shunkei-nuri*, the rich, toffee-colored lacquer from the Hida area. There is a small Japanese artifacts museum at this end of the building, too.

Guest room, Yunoshima-kan

The water at Gero is wonderful and the Yunoshima-kan provides a variety of ways to enjoy it. There are a couple of large indoor baths, one lined with windows looking out on the Hida Mountains. For privacy, but no view, choose one of the *kazoku-buro*. There are four of these old-fashioned, private bathrooms, each with a spacious dressing room and bath area. The water is very hot, but at least in private you can control your cooking temperature.

You are overfed at the Yunoshima-kan, but standards are so high you forgive them.

This inn has made only one concession to the modern traveler—a sparkling glass-enclosed extension that is used as a coffee shop. If you can reconcile stepping from old wood and bamboo into pastel carpet and velvet, you will enjoy a pleasant morning cup of coffee.

Nearby

The Gassho Mura museum, showing examples of praying hands–style houses, is five minutes by taxi from Gero Station.

14

SHIRAKAWA-GO and GOKAYAMA

Shirakawa-go

ATTRACTIONS

Both villages are World Heritage Sites, so designated because of the large number of centuries-old "praying-hands" farmhouses preserved in each community. Many of these farmhouses now double as guest-houses, offering a chance to experience life in an old farming village and meals around an open hearth.

People along the Shokawa river in Gifu and Toyama prefectures are said to have made buildings in the dramatic style of architecture known as *gassho-zukuri* (praying-hands houses) for eight hundred years. *Gassho-zukuri* are A-frame farmhouses with either three or four stories. Traditionally people lived crammed together on the first floor, while silkworms lived luxuriously on the upper levels.

In the sixties, whole communities of these praying-hands structures were removed for the construction of a dam. Only two of the original villages are still intact—Shirakawa-go on the Gifu side of the prefectural border, and Gokayama on the Toyama side—and both are now designated UNESCO World Heritage Sites.

Staying a night in a towering praying-hands farmhouse in one of these villages is one of those "must" experiences of Japan, like seeing the Zen garden of Ryoanji in Kyoto or cormorant fishing in Iwakuni.

There are no inns here, only *minshuku*. Comfort and privacy are not big priorities for the innkeeper: the meals served around the open hearth are smoky; the baths and toilets are shared; and your room may be partitioned off by nothing more than a flimsy sliding door through which a stranger may come stumbling through in the dark in search of the lavatory at three in the morning (as happened to me). But it is an opportunity to experience, in a touristic sort of way, a farmhouse lifestyle (minus the silkworms) and, best of all, to see the villages in silence.

Hearthside country-style cooking

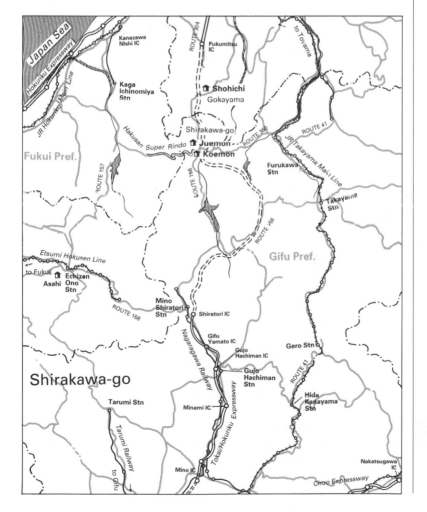

It is hard to recommend one village over the other. Shirakawa-go offers a panorama of one hundred praying-hands structures, with twenty-three offering lodgings, and it has a museum, a shrine, and a temple, which makes for a pleasant stroll. Gokayama is smaller (only twenty houses in all), but it is picturesque and, in addition to a museum, there is an intriguing papermaking display.

Minshuku in Shirakawa-go and Gokayama

Three *minshuku* are recommended here. For *minshuku* reservations in Shirakawa-go or Gokayama other than those listed here, ask for help at the Japan National Tourist Organization (JNTO) Tourist Information Center (☎ 03–3201–3331).

Seasonal tip

The Doburoku Festival celebrating the harvest is held in Shirakawa-go in mid-October, with colorful processions and dances.

Recommended trips including Shirakawa-go

Pairing Hida-Takayama with Shirakawa-go is a natural choice. From here you can visit Toyama via the high and winding Hakusan Supaa Rindo Highway and then on to Kanazawa and the Noto Peninsula (Destinations 21 and 22).

● Hida-Takayama (1–2 nights, Destination 13)—Shirakawa-go (1 night)—Hakusan Supaa Rindo (scenic drive)

KOEMON　幸エ門

RATE: From ¥8,000 w/2 meals. **CREDIT CARDS:** Not accepted. **ROOMS:** 5 Japanese style (w/o bath). **COMMUNAL BATHS:** 2—men's, women's. **CHECK-IN:** 15:00. **CHECK-OUT:** 9:00. **LANGUAGE:** Some English.

☎ 05769–6–1446　Fax: 05769–6–1748
456 Ogi-machi, Shirakawa-mura, Ono-gun, Gifu 501–5627
〒501–5627　岐阜県大野郡白川村荻町456

■ ACCESS
BY TRAIN: 2 hr 30 min by bus from Takayama Stn (JR Takayama Main Line).
BY CAR:　4 hrs via Takayama from Nakatsugawa IC (Chuo Expressway) or 1 hr half via Route 156 from Shiratori IC (Tokai/Hokuriku Expressway).

Sunken brazier, Koemon

The Koemon is located close to Myozenji temple and the Shirakawa Hachiman shrine, the home of the Doburoku Festival; it is also where members of the Japan National Trust make their base when they come to Shirakawa-go on their regular visits to help rethatch roofs in the village.

In the old days people would just spread their futons out in the big open space around the sunken brazier on the first floor, but paying guests now receive a degree of privacy with partitioned-off rooms. Nevertheless, the open hearth is still the center of all activity and where you will have your meal of homemade grilled miso, tofu, mountain greens, and *dokudami* herb tea.

JUEMON 民宿 十右エ門

LOCATION: Shirakawa-go

RATE: From ¥8,000 w/2 meals, from ¥6500 w/breakfast, from ¥5,500 w/o meals, children from ¥7,000. **CREDIT CARDS:** Not accepted. **ROOMS:** 7 Japanese style (w/o bath). **COMMUNAL BATH:** 1—alternating. **CHECK-IN:** 15:00. **CHECK-OUT:** 9:30. **CLOSED:** Year end/New Year holidays. **LANGUAGE:** Some English.

☎ 05769–6–1053 Fax: 05769–6–1016
1653 Ogi-machi, Shirakawa-mura, Ono-gun, Gifu 501–5627
〒501–5627　岐阜県大野郡白川村荻町1653

■ ACCESS
BY TRAIN: 2 hrs by bus from Takayama Stn (JR Takayama Main Line).
BY CAR:　4 hrs via Takayama from Nakatsugawa IC (Chuo Expressway), or 1 hr 30 min via Route 156 from Shiratori IC (Tokai Hokuriku Expressway).

Typical Shirakawa-go farmhouse

The Juemon is a neatly kept, modest three-story house, about 270 years old. One room—a second-floor tatami room that used to house silkworms—is especially pleasant, with a view over rice paddies. The owners are farmers as well as innkeepers.

After a simple dinner of grilled river fish, lightly flavored boiled vegetables, soba, and tofu, the lady of the household may serenade you on a lively stringed instrument, the *shamisen*.

SHOSHICHI 庄七

LOCATION: Gokayama

RATE: From ¥7500 w/2 meals, children 20% off. **CREDIT CARDS:** Not accepted. **ROOMS:** 5 Japanese style (w/o bath). **COMMUNAL BATH:** 1—alternating. **CHECK-IN:** 15:00. **CHECK-OUT:** 10:00. **LANGUAGE:** No English, reservations in Japanese.

☎ 0763–66–2206 Fax: 0763–66–2206
421 Ainokura, Taira, Higashi Tonami-gun, Toyama 939–1915
〒939–1915　富山県東砺波郡平村相倉421

■ **ACCESS**
BY TRAIN: 20 min by taxi from Johana Stn (JR Johana Line; transfer at Takaoka Stn, JR Hokuriku Main Line).
BY CAR: 30 min via Route 304 from Fukumitsu IC (Tokai/Hokuriku Expressway).

The 180-year-old Shoshichi is a thatched building right in the middle of the most picturesque part of the village, with a white *kura* at the back. It has high ceilings on the first floor, and big rooms.

The excellent home-cooked meals include carp sashimi, boiled vegetables, grilled fish, and vegetable tempura.

Pick up a guide to the local places of interest: these include a museum, a papermaking display, and even an Edo-period (1600–1868) thatched jailhouse a short drive away.

15

MINO

*Scenic Gifu along
the Kisogawa river*

ATTRACTIONS

*An atmospheric street of Edo-period (1600–1868) houses and other relics
of Mino's former wealth as Japan's premier paper-producing district.*

In the days when *washi* (handmade paper) was made entirely by hand, Mino
was one of the biggest, most active centers of commerce in the country. Echizen
papers from the Sea of Japan coast were the choice of artists and calligraphers,
but Mino paper fed the voracious appetite for books among the increasingly lit-
erate residents of Edo (Tokyo) during the Edo period. The fine, blemish-free
Mino paper, sold at bulk discounts, was so popular with Edo woodblock printers
that the size of the Mino molding frames determined the standard sizes of
books. And rather as Westerners now call crockery "china," the generic name for
the most common scroll-mounting paper is still *mino-gami*.

The only visible remains today of the hundreds and hundreds of papermakers
who once lined the banks of the Itadorigawa river are two *hon-mino-gami* (genuine Mino paper) masters who are designated "living national treasures." Their
homes still have tall boards propped out in front to dry the fruits of their considerable labor. Real sun-dried *washi*, once the norm, is now by far the exception

because of the tremendously labor-intensive processes involved. There are other papermakers who mold paper by hand but employ machinery for the rest of the process and many more who have switched entirely to mechanization.

Mino is worth a trip for reasons other than its paper. Strangely enough, Japanese tourists have yet to discover this charming township, in spite of its street full of Edo-period houses. The **Imai House**, which is open to the public, belonged, naturally, to a paper baron. One of the home's unusual features is a wooden shaft that stretches from floor to roof to let in light. In the garden there is a *suikin-kutsu*, an ingenious device that sings with a pleasant, bell-like sound as water trickles into a large pottery urn buried underground.

All the houses on this street have in common an unusual architectural device called *udatsu*. *Udatsu* started as simple firebreak walls erected between dwellings, but the wealthier residents began adding decorative tiled "roofs," and *udatsu* became a symbol of affluence. In modern Japanese, the phrase "*udatsu ga agaranai*" ("has not erected an *udatsu*") refers to a person who has not made it in the world. Few Japanese today are aware of the origin of this saying.

Down by the **Nagaragawa river** there is further evidence of Mino's former glory—the handsome, wooden, nine-meter- (twenty-nine-foot-) high **Kozuchi riverside lighthouse**. But the best reason of all to visit Mino is the

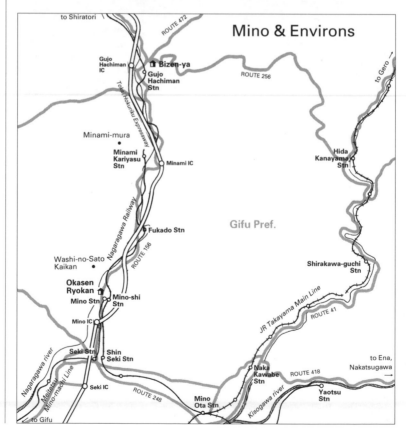

warm and elegant Okasen Ryokan. My suggestion would be to arrive in Mino around lunchtime, explore the town, spend a quiet night at the Okasen Ryokan, and rise early for a day trip on the **Nagaragawa Railway**. For the first stop, get off at Minami-kariyasu and take a taxi from there to the **Minami-mura Enku-no-Furusato** (¥300; closed Mondays and the day after public holidays), a museum that has ninety-five statues carved by Minami-mura-born woodcarver –Buddhist priest Enku (1632–95). This museum, and the nearby **Minami-mura Seikatsu Shiryo-kan**, which depicts the lives of Minami-mura loggers in the Edo period, are next to **Hoshinomiya shrine**, which is dedicated to left-handed people. It features an outside wall covered in left-handed scythes.

Genuine Mino paper set out to dry

The Nagaragawa Railway continues along to **Gujo Hachiman**, a former castle town whose main claim to fame is now a popular **summer festival** in mid-August. This usually quiet riverside town goes into a frenzy of all-night dancing for over a week, and anyone is welcome to learn the traditional steps by joining in. It is not quite Rio, but it is fun, with live drum-and-flute music and quite complex dance steps. So bring along your *yukata* and geta and learn how by joining a circle of dancers.

Gujo Hachiman is compact enough to negotiate on foot and has one main attraction, a famous well, **Sogisui Spring**, named in 1985 as the purest underground spring water in Japan. There are quite a few craft shops on either side of the river, and some interesting little museums and shops in an area called **Yanakamizu-no-Komichi**. A good meal, which features the famous local miso, can be enjoyed at a restaurant called **Daihachi** (☎ 0575–65–3709). I have been told the town's best inn is **Bizen-ya**.

Having come this far, I would suggest a car or bus trip to a rather unusual museum called **Kokin Denju-no-Sato**. (Take the road that leads to Shiratori and there's a signposted detour on the way.) This museum is dedicated to the legacy of the Toh clan, which carried on a tradition of Heian-period (794–1185) classical poetry by teaching it to initiates. The family occupied this district from the thirteenth to sixteenth centuries.

The museum's displays may be of limited interest since they consist mainly of scrolls of calligraphy, but the view of the mountain scenery from a large tatami room in the museum's partly thatched rear building makes the ¥1,000 entrance fee well worth the visit. You might also splurge on a meal at the gorgeously situated French restaurant on the grounds.

Seasonal tips

The spring festival of Mino is close to the Takayama Festival (see Destination 13) in mid-April (☎ 0575–33–1122, city office). Mino's colorful celebration has palanquins, decorated with magnificent sprigs of pink paper flowers, jostling for supremacy at crossroads. At the end of the festival people clamor to grab the pink sprigs to take home and place on their roofs as protection for the household.

The summer dancing at Gujo Hachiman takes place during the second and third weeks of August. Each section of the town has its night of dancing, and the festival culminates in one or two days when the whole town and hundreds of tourists join in. The dates change every year, so call the Gujo Hachiman tourist office to confirm (☎ 0575–67–0181).

Recommended buys

Mino's biggest miracle is that it has so far been spared "souvenir-shopitis." There was not much to buy in the tourist street of Mino where the Imai House is located—except a small selection of sweets (French almond wafers and similar items) and one paper shop, which was closed when I was there. Apart from this, there is the Washi-no-Sato Kaikan (☎ 0575–34–8111) on the city's outskirts, where you can see displays on the paper-making process, make a *washi* post-card, and buy paper products.

Your other best buys from the area will be postcards or a color catalog from the Enku museum, or *gujo tsumugi*, the expensive but beautiful hand-woven and dyed silk with a four-hundred-year history, available from such shops as Tanizawa Gofuku-ten in the *hommachi* district of Gujo Hachiman.

Recommended trips including Mino

- Mino (1 night)—Minami-mura/Gujo Hachiman/Kokin Denju-no-Sato
  (day trip taking them all in or with overnight at Gujo Hachiman)

In Praise of Japanese Paper

Washi, or handmade Japanese paper, is made from one of three types of bushes that have especially long fibers, the most common being *kozo* (paper mulberry). The long fibers are beaten and cleaned by hand and suspended in water with a mucilage. Then the papermaker moves a fine-mesh mold in a rhythmic swishing motion, causing the fibers to entwine in a complex way. This process makes *washi* the strongest handmade paper in the world. In Mino's case, the craftsmen created a very fine and very white paper. Their methods were once tenaciously guarded trade secrets. Mino's success also allowed it to trade in bulk at low prices.

Mino paper is all natural plant matter and thus alkaline, which means that even over centuries it does not develop brown acid spots or disintegrate. The only cause of disintegration is due to insects, who find it delicious. Handmade papers are still made in Japan, and are also used for the repair of precious documents around the world. Traditional artists, calligraphers, and scroll makers will not use anything else. But beware, not all products being sold as "*washi*" on the world market are the real handmade article.

OKASEN RYOKAN　岡専旅館

LOCATION: Central Mino City

*Elegant former salt magnate's home, once
a stopover accommodation for the lord of Gujo Hachiman.*

RATE: From ¥7,500 w/2 meals, ¥6,500 w/breakfast, ¥5,000 w/o meals. **CREDIT CARDS:** Not accepted. **ROOMS:** 7 Japanese style (w/o bath). **COMMUNAL BATH:** 1—alternating. **CHECK-IN:** 16:00. **CHECK-OUT:** 10:00. **CLOSED:** Jan 1–3. **LANGUAGE:** No English, reservations in Japanese.

☎ 0575–33–0140
2190–1 Uoya-cho, Mino-shi, Gifu 501–3724
〒501–3724　岐阜県美濃市魚屋町2190–1

■ **ACCESS**
BY TRAIN: 10 min on foot from Mino Stn (Meitetsu Mino-machi Line).
BY CAR: 5 min from Mino IC (Tokai/Hokuriku Expressway).

*Okasen's elegant
courtyard garden*

Have you wondered why there is so little traditional architecture visible in Japan today and why it is conspicuously absent where it should be most prevalent—in provincial towns? In postwar years provincial civil servants were sent on a campaign to purge their hometowns of "undesirable relics of the feudal past" and have them replaced with concrete, carpet, and curtains. Shop- and inn-owners who experienced this tell of the overzealous official who arrived at their door one day: "Madame, your old wooden inn is an eyesore. It doesn't fit in with our image of the city of the future. Anyway, it is a fire hazard. I'm afraid we'll have to ask you to replace it with something a little more modern."

Streets full of lovely wooden buildings in towns and cities all over Japan succumbed in this way. If only a few more people had stood up to this pressure—like the owner of the Fuji-ya in Nagano City, who refused to tear down her inn, or the owner of this inn, the Okasen, who compromised by replacing the inn's "unfashionable" wooden gable entrance with a concrete façade—Japan might be a more architecturally attractive place today.

Behind the unattractive façade of the Okasen the former home of a wealthy salt merchant is still intact, with a lovely Edo-period (1600–1868) garden and its own *inari* shrine. Several old salt warehouses still stand to the left of the garden. In Edo days the home had the distinction of accommodating the lord of Gujo Hachiman on his trips to Takayama down the Nagaragawa river.

The plain but finely crafted rooms at Okasen are beautifully cared for. The downstairs corner room is especially lovely for its ninety-degree outlook on the elegant garden with its rare, gnarled trees. This garden is tended by the elderly proprietor himself. "He weeds and picks up fallen leaves every day. That is why it stays so nice," says his wife. Together they keep the old place immaculate.

Toilets and bath are shared, but no one can complain considering the price, which also includes a delicious home-cooked meal. The night I was there, dinner consisted of grilled fish with rice, miso soup, and savory egg custard. You could not get more basic than that, but the rice was fragrant, the soup tasty and mild, and the custard big and full of tasty bits of chicken and mushrooms—a commoner's meal fit for a lord.

Nearby

The Okasen has a great location: it sits right on Mino's street of old houses with their beautiful *udatsu*. Of these old houses, the Imai House, formerly owned by a paper magnate, is open to the public. Take a little time to wander the lanes behind this main street to see some picturesque architecture.
From the inn, it's a twenty-minute walk to the riverside, where you will find the old wooden lighthouse that used to service the bustling river traffic.

16

ISE and AICHI

*Ohashi-ya depicted
by Hiroshige*

ATTRACTIONS

Millions of pilgrims have made their way over the centuries to the Grand Shrines of Ise, and the shopping streets approaching the Naiku (inner shrine) have grown to serve this trade. Ise can be combined with a visit to Mikimoto Pearl Island or with sight-seeing in Aichi Prefecture, including a night in the only original inn on the Old Tokaido Highway.

The Grand Shrines of Ise, consisting of inner and outer shrines to the Sun Goddess set in a splendid forest, were once Japan's prime tourist destination. Even if the whole family could not afford to go, one lucky member would make the pilgrimage on their behalf to bring back the shrines' blessings. This was a chance for high adventure, and the traveler might even combine the pilgrimage with a trip to Kyoto to bathe in the elegant traditions of the imperial capital.

At times during the 1700s and 1800s, thousands upon thousands of people a week made frenzied pilgrimages to the shrines, attracted by talk of miracles attributed to the gods enshrined there. In some months, up to three million people journeyed to receive the blessings of the Sun Goddess, making Ise one of the busiest places in Japan.

If you were to visit Ise now around the New Year, you might think that things have not changed very much—the river of people is six-wide on the gravel paths leading to the sanctuaries. Even ordinarily, Ise attracts more visitors than most other places in Japan. The unfailing popularity of the Ise pilgrimage is immediately obvious in **the streets that lead to Naiku**, the inner shrine. For the traveler jaded by the skin-deep Japanesque style of the many towns that have refashioned themselves into "mini-Kyotos" and "mini-Edos," it's a welcome surprise to find a town where so much of the architecture is genuinely beautiful and the shops are in good taste. Even the local delicacy, *akafuku*, a red-bean paste sweet, is excellent. I was particularly impressed to find something I haven't seen elsewhere: a thriving *shogi* **(Japanese chess) hall** in a beautifully reconstructed wooden building.

It's a pity the developers of the seaside spot of **Futamigaura**, ten minutes away by car, are not following Ise's lead. Before visiting the shrines, pilgrims used to make an obligatory trip to Futamigaura to perform ablutions in the Pacific. Today the place is a virtual ghost town, with the only reminder of its former prosperity a handful of gracious old wooden inns wedged in amongst 1960s ferroconcrete structures. I wish I could say that Futamigaura was a charming seaside resort and the old inns were worth visiting, but the town just looks sad and the inns have caught the malaise. Nevertheless, the more devout pilgrims still make the trip here to pray to the creator gods Izanami and Izanagi, represented by "male" and "female" rock-islands just off the coast.

Toba, home of the late pearl baron Kokichi Mikimoto (1858–1954), is another disappointment. However, it's worth paying ¥1,200 to visit **Mikimoto Pearl Island**, as the displays on pearl cultivation and Mr. Mikimoto's life are

Cauldrons at Aka-fuku main shop

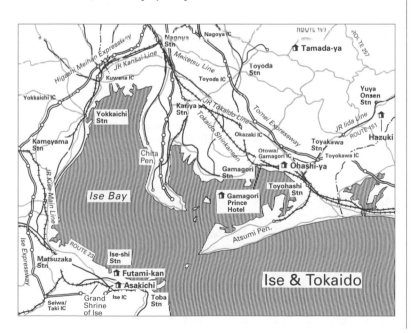

Ise & Tokaido

interesting. The tour also includes a diving demonstration by *ama*, the women pearl divers (these days wearing thermal underwear inside their white cotton diving suits), and the shop and restaurant are not too obtrusive. But Toba itself, a seaside town crowded with ugly commercialism around the pretty pine-clad island, is so grim that it spoils what could be a pleasant half-day by the sea. I didn't bother with the aquarium, which now attracts most of the crowds.

If you have a week free, I would recommend combining an Ise trip with a visit to Kumano in Wakayama (a couple of hours along the coast) and from there going on to Ryujin Onsen and holy Mount Koya before finishing back at either Osaka or Nara. With less time to spare, I saved the Kumano trip and instead combined Ise with some sight-seeing in Aichi Prefecture. This included a night in **Akasaka-juku** at the Ohashi-ya, the only original inn that remains on the **Old Tokaido Highway**, and a visit to the town of **Asuke**, an hour out of Toyota City. Asuke is a strange collection of old houses on the ancient Halfway Horse Highway, close to a very pretty river. Although it's not easy to reach, this unpretentious old town deserves a half-day or more exploring. I regret not having been able to get to **Arimatsu**, another town with many old houses. Famous for its *shibori* textile tradition, Arimatsu is just two stops down the train track from Akasaka-juku.

If you are going to be in the Nagoya-Toyohashi district, a beautiful hot spring for a night's stay (or just lunch and a bath) is **Yuya Onsen**; see Hazuki in this section. In Ise itself, the fun choice for a night's stay is Asakichi.

Recommended buys

In Ise, *akafuku* sweets (rice cakes lathered with an excellent quality red-bean paste) at a shop of the same name and crafts made from Matsuzaka indigo cotton cloth (available on the same street as Akafuku); on Mikimoto Pearl Island, pearls; and in Arimatsu, crafts made from *shibori* tie-dyed cloth.

Recommended trips including Ise

- Yuya Onsen (1 night)—Akasaka-juku (1 night)—Arimatsu (half-day trip) —Asuke (day trip or 1 night)—Ise

- Ise (1 night)—Toba (1–2 hours)—Kumano and extended trip in Wakayama (Destination 25)

ASAKICHI 麻吉

LOCATION: Ise City

Formerly a restaurant in the busy pleasure quarters of Ise, now a partly renovated inn in a quiet, elevated location.

RATE: From ¥10,000 w/2 meals. **CREDIT CARDS:** Not accepted. **ROOMS:** 16 Japanese style (3 w/bath). **COMMUNAL BATHS:** 2—men's, women's. **CHECK-IN:** 16:00. **CHECK-OUT:** 10:00. **LANGUAGE:** Some English.

☎ 0596–22–4101 Fax: 0596–22–4102
109 Nakano-machi, Ise-shi, Mie 516–0034
〒516–0034 三重県伊勢市中之町109

■ ACCESS

BY TRAIN: 10 min by car from Uji Yamada Stn (Kintetsu Shima Line).
BY CAR: 2 min (1 km) from Ise IC (Ise Expressway).

A pilgrim to Ise two or three centuries ago would first head for Futamigaura to perform ablutions in the sea, then move on to the Grand Shrines to pray, and finally descend on the pleasure quarters to undo all the good he had just done. An Ise pilgrimage might be the only trip in a lifetime for a commoner of the Edo period (1600–1868), so he made the most of it.

Ise's pleasure quarters then ranked among the nation's big five, along with Yoshiwara in Edo, Shimabara in Kyoto, Shimmachi in Osaka, and Maruyama in Nagasaki. The Asakichi was right in the middle of the brothels and inns, providing both dining and private rooms for many types of pleasure.

In *kanji*, Asakichi's name contains the character for "hempen cloth," which suggests it might once have been among the many shops in Ise dealing in hemp or silk—both common shrine offerings. Whatever its origins, it seems that the Asakichi was serving as a restaurant by the beginning of the nineteenth century, for it appears as such in *Tokaido Chu Hiza Kurige*, one of the famous comic adventures of the buffoons Yaji and Kita, written by Jippensha Ikku about 1809.

Nowadays, few relics of the old pleasure quarters remain, except perhaps the lanterns at the Asakichi's entrance and the old laneway that snakes down the steep slope to which three stories of the inn precariously cling.

Much of the building dates back to the second half of the nineteenth century, yet the Asakichi is one place where I would advise that you ask for a "new" rather than an "old" room. The big old rooms at the front (usually recommended for foreign visitors) probably had a pleasant forest outlook until the mountain was bulldozed and a highway planted outside. But the three new rooms with bath and toilet are significantly more comfortable than the old, shared facilities.

Excellent Asakichi seafood

An old part of the inn worth seeing is the *kura* (storehouse), now converted into a three-story museum of Asakichi history. Ask the friendly lady of the house to show you.

Asakichi's food is excellent, a combination of fresh fish and tender Matsu-zaka beef, plus savory egg custard, and oysters in winter.

Nearby

There are numerous shrines and temples lining the old highway that leads from the Asakichi area to the Grand Shrines, but I would head straight for the main shrines.
Ise is a difficult place to negotiate with or without a car. The problem for train travelers is the considerable distance from the station to both outer and inner shrines; if you are in a car, there is an acute lack of parking. If you are coming by train, charter a taxi for a day or half a day unless you have the energy to wait around for shuttle buses. If you have a car, visit the shrines before breakfast, while the parking lots are still empty.

Apart from the shrines, the main attraction of Ise is Oharai-cho, the shopping street that leads away from the Naiku (the inner shrine). Here most people head straight for the beautiful Akafuku sweet shop, halfway down the street. You can tell it by the big red cauldrons of boiling water in the front. For ¥230 you will get a healthy serving of *akafuku* (rice cakes smothered with a smooth, sweet bean paste) and tasty *bancha* tea made with water heated over wood-fired ovens in those generous cauldrons.

Next to the Akafuku sweet shop is the Akafuku souvenir shop, which stocks Ise *chiyo-gami* (woodcut prints in charming patterns) and lovely papier-mâché dolls. Next door is a converted storehouse featuring an excellent display on Ise shrine festivals, recreated with expressive dolls. Entry costs ¥100.

At most shops you can find a map of the town that indicates the other main attractions, such as Okageyoko-cho with its fascinating history museum. The day I was at Ise there were even lion dances in the street. I wish I had allowed myself much more time for all there was to offer—I even missed out on the famous Ise *udon* noodles.

FUTAMI-KAN 二見館

LOCATION: Futamigaura

Exquisitely crafted late-nineteenth-century building in a "ghost resort."

RATE: From ¥16,000 w/2 meals, ¥12,000 w/o meals, children 30–50% off. **CREDIT CARDS:** AMEX, DC, MC, VISA. **ROOMS:** 43 Japanese style (w/2 bath). **COMMUNAL BATHS:** 3—men's, women's, 1 private (*kazoku-buro*). **CHECK-IN:** 14:00. **CHECK-OUT:** 10:30. **LANGUAGE:** Some English.

☎ 0596–43–2003 Fax: 0596–42–1224
Ei 569–1, Futami-cho, Watarai-gun, Mie 519–0602
〒519–0602　三重県渡会郡二見町江569–1

■ ACCESS
BY TRAIN: 20 min by bus from Uji Yamada Stn (Kintetsu Shima Line).
BY CAR: 4.5 km from Ise IC (Ise Expressway).

Futami-kan

Imperial visits to Ise became a great deal more frequent after the advent of State Shinto (an institutionalized version of the indigenous religion). A group of Ise shrine promoters called the Shin'enkai (Garden of the Gods Society) therefore decided that members of the imperial family needed a suitable place to stay on their visits to the shrine. To this end the Hinjitsu-kan, which is the oldest part of this inn, was built in 1887, just twenty years into the Meiji period (1868–1912). The two-story building was located right on the seashore at Futamigaura, a short distance from the famous male and female rocks, Meoto-iwa. Emperor Taisho and a succession of other imperial family members stayed there over the next thirty years or so.

Just five years before the Hinjitsu-kan was built, Japan had designated its first public swimming beaches at Kobe and Hayama, and Futamigaura became the third. The peaceful Hinjitsu-kan thus found itself in the middle of a tourist mecca. In 1904 and 1905, the area became even busier as more and more common people flocked to Ise to pray for Japan's victory in the Russo-Japanese war.

In 1911, the Shin'enkai group was disbanded and the inn next door, the Futami-kan, purchased the Hinjitsu-kan. Times were prosperous and, in 1930, both inns underwent major renovations under the direction of Oe Shintaro, a leading architect in the Japanese style. The Hinjitsu-kan was given a banquet hall of majestic proportions, with 120 mats and massive chandeliers. The place must have been glorious.

Intricate woodwork, the Emperor's room, Futami-kan

Time has since stood still for the Futami-kan and Hinjitsu-kan. The imperial visits stopped as the demands for modern security could not be met without extensive alterations to the old wooden structures. Futamigaura has also suffered a worrisome decrease in tourists and now nobody seems to know how to jolly up the remnant of one of Japan's first beach "resorts."

The Hinjitsu-kan remains one of Japan's architectural masterpieces, but unless you pay a large enough sum of money to occupy the former imperial suites, you will be accommodated in the adjoining Futami-kan with its musty, old-fashioned rooms. Still, this does not stop you from taking a stroll through to the more beautiful Hinjitsu-kan for a look. On the way is an artifacts display with funny retro postcards from the inn's more swinging days.

Nearby

The big attraction at Futamigaura beach is Meoto-iwa, the "male" and "female" rocks representing the gods Izanami and Izanagi. They are accompanied by an unattractive shrine and shop.
The strip of beach in front of the Futami-kan is where people would take a purifying dip before proceeding to the Grand Shrines. This custom seems to have died out now, taking with it most of the reason for a visit to Futamigaura. Even the beach is almost nonexistent because of erosion. With the exception of the Futami-kan, the shops and inns along the beach front are an eyesore although the backstreets are more interesting.
The same people who built the Edo-Mura theme park in Tochigi Prefecture have built a theme park very close to Futamigaura which re-creates the adventures of the Warring States period (1482–1573). The eye-popper you see as you approach the "Pearl Road" highway toll gate is a replica of warlord Oda Nobunaga's gaudy Azuchi Castle. The Pearl Road leads to Toba, where you will find Mikimoto Pearl Island.

HAZUKI はづ木

LOCATION: Yuya Onsen

A heart-warming wooden hot spring inn in a riverside setting, serving Chinese medicinal food.

RATE: From ¥20,000 w/2 meals, from ¥10,000 w/breakfast, from ¥8,000 w/o meals, children 30% off. **CREDIT CARDS:** AMEX, DC, MC, VISA. **ROOMS:** 5 Japanese style, 2 semi-Japanese style—all rooms w/bath. **COMMUNAL BATH:** 2—*hinoki* bath (alternating), outdoor bath (alternating). **CHECK-IN:** 13:00. **CHECK-OUT:** 11:00. **LANGUAGE:** Some English.

☎ 05363–2–1211 Fax: 05363–2–2121
Yuya Onsen, Horai-cho, Minami Shidara-gun, Aichi 441–1631
〒441–1631　愛知県南設楽郡鳳来町湯谷温泉

■ **ACCESS**
BY TRAIN: 3 min from Yuya Onsen Stn (JR Iida Line).
BY CAR: 45 min via Route 151 from Toyokawa IC (Tomei Expressway).

Hazuki

When Hiroaki Kato and his wife Shinko opened the Hazuki in Yuya Onsen, they made a deal with a top Shanghai restaurant to supply chefs on a rotating basis who could prepare *yakuzen ryori* (Chinese food with medicinal properties). The Chinese chefs supervise the preparation of a fifteen-course meal designed to remove toxins, strengthen the immune system, balance pH, and improve the skin. You may not expect to warm immediately to the flavors of the seaweed and jellyfish appetizer, the frog ovary soup with Chinese ham powder for respiratory ailments, the turtle and mushroom insomnia-killer, or the lotus seed, cloud ear, abalone, and bamboo shoot soup for fatigue, but you will probably be pleasantly surprised at how good they all taste, especially the beef, the snail kebabs, and the juicy dumplings with powdered pearl. The food, tea, and Chinese wine come in a pretty palette of terra-cotta-colored vessels with some Japanese pottery mixed in.

The Hazuki is a beautifully crafted former *ryotei* from the 1950s. The Katos had it moved to this scenic spot by the river and renovated the entrance and lounge into the kind of place you'd like to call home. The five spacious guest rooms were formal tatami dining rooms and bear the mark of high-quality carpentry; two have anterooms with beds, the bedcovers stylishly hand-dyed in indigo and white. Meals are taken with other guests in a dining room with tables and chairs.

Yuya Onsen dates back a thousand years. An important highway turned it into a thriving resort in the eighteenth century, but it was left behind by the faster highways and trains of the 1950s. All the better for the Hazuki. Now, when you step onto the platform at Yuya after the one-hour chug-along trip from Toyohashi, you wonder: Is this really a Japanese station? Where are the souvenir shops, the pachinko parlors? Instead, around the corner from the station, there is just an appealing street that looks like it is in a quiet suburb. On this main street is the Hazuki.

The Hazuki is, in fact, one of four fine inns owned by the Katos in Yuya; their first and the one closest to their hearts is the Hazu Bekkan, which is two houses down the street from the Hazuki. The most luxurious is the Hazu Gassho, two magnificent farmhouses from Toyama that the Katos took apart and reassembled at the top of a scenic gorge five minutes from the Hazuki. Hazu Gassho is an upmarket, country-style establishment serving Kyoto *kaiseki* cuisine.

Its majestic farmhouse proportions, classic cuisine, and gorgeous open-air baths mean that the Hazu Gassho is the most popular inn for taking foreign guests. But for me the choice is not so simple. With its more delicate, sophisticated urban structure, the Hazuki captivates, and the added fascination of the Shanghai medicinal food is hard to beat. But the Hazu Bekkan—the least expensive of the three—has a beautiful atmosphere, too, with its splendidly crafted, high-ceiling, *mingei*-style rooms. Even the rooms facing the road instead of the river have charm, due in part to the old handmade glass window panes.

All of the inns have excellent cypress baths, and a choice of outdoor and indoor bathing. All offer the very special service of devoted innkeepers. Which one to choose? The easy answer is to visit all of them at different times.

OHASHI-YA 旅籠 大橋屋

An antique treasure on the Old Tokaido Highway,
with only the basics in food and bathing, but the maximum in atmosphere.

LOCATION: Akasaka-juku

RATE: From ¥8,000 w/2 meals. **CREDIT CARDS:** Not accepted. **ROOMS:** 7 Japanese style (w/o bath). **COMMUNAL BATH:** 1—alternating. **CHECK-IN:** 15:00. **CHECK-OUT:** 10:00. **LANGUAGE:** No English, reservations in Japanese.

☎ 0533–87–2450
127 Benizato, Akasaka, Otowa-cho, Hoi-gun, Aichi 441–0202
〒441 0202　愛知県宝飯郡音羽町赤坂紅里127

■ ACCESS
BY TRAIN: 8 min on foot from Meiden Akasaka Stn (Meitetsu Nagoya Line).
BY CAR:　5 min (2 km) from Otowa/Gamagori IC (Tomei Expressway).

Ohashi-ya entrance

I wonder how many people have been inspired to try and walk the Old Tokaido Highway out of nostalgia for Ando Hiroshige's nineteenth-century series of prints, "Fifty-three Stations on the Tokaido." A visitor's book at the Ohashi-ya in Akasaka-juku, one of the stations on the old highway, contains a number of entries that begin proudly: "Have come this far, walking the Old Tokaido…" For these people the trip must be ninety-nine percent imagining and one percent actually experiencing anything resembling the beauty of those Hiroshige prints.

The Ohashi-ya is an oasis in a historical desert—the only original inn left on the old Tokaido. It is even depicted in one of Hiroshige's prints, showing a view from a courtyard garden of a room with men and women cavorting inside. A tall cycad stands in the foreground. Sadly, the section of the inn depicted was burned down in the 1920s and the only part that remains is the front section, built in 1716, that faces the old Tokaido. This has been preserved in its original state. Though its floorboards are now blackened with use and its ceilings decaying, the rooms are spotlessly clean and are offered with quiet hospitality by the nineteenth-generation owners.

Facing the Old Tokaido

An uninteresting new section has been added at the back of the Ohashi-ya, but the innkeepers usually offer guests the three old rooms in the front "because people prefer them." These rooms are reached by a steep old staircase that rises up among impressive rafters and are separated only by sliding doors. If all three rooms were occupied it might be a bit too close for comfort, I suspect, but the rarity of old Tokaido fanatics means you are more than likely to have all three rooms to yourself.

If you are used to Tokyo and Kyoto flavors, meals at the Ohashi-ya might be a trial for the tastebuds: Aichi people like their miso very salty and their sauces very sweet. But the inn's specialty—sticky potato poured over noodles or rice—is said to be very good for you.

Nearby

The Tokaido Highway was once entirely lined with trees, and I was excited to find that there is still a pine tree–lined section at Goyu, a ten-minute walk from Akasaka-juku. These two stations have the distinction of being the closest together of all the stations (1.7 kilometers/1 mile apart). Between them were sixteen inns and, though there wasn't anything very special or scenic about the area, they apparently flourished because of their female amusements.

A walk to Goyu will give you a hint as to how pretty the whole highway probably once looked. The taller pines were planted in 1604 by the shogunate, but many of them, blighted by pine-munching bugs, have been replaced by spindly seedlings. Two stops down the track from Akasaka-juku on the Meitetsu Nagoya Honsen Line is the town of Arimatsu, which has the reputation of being the best preserved of all the Tokaido towns and also has an illustrious *shibori* (tie-dyeing) tradition.

TAMADA-YA 玉田屋

LOCATION: Asuke

Unassuming historic inn way off the beaten track.
Shared bath and toilet. Good home-cooked food.

RATE: From ¥7,000 w/2 meals, from ¥5,500 w/breakfast, from ¥5,000 w/o meals. **CREDIT CARDS:** Not accepted. **ROOMS:** 6 Japanese style (w/o bath). **COMMUNAL BATH:** 1—alternating. **CHECK-IN:** 15:30. **CHECK-OUT:** 9:30. **CLOSED:** Jan 1. **LANGUAGE:** No English, reservations in Japanese.

☏ 0565–62–0170 Fax: 0565–61–2010
36 Asuke Nishi-machi, Asuke-cho, Higashi Kamo-gun, Aichi 444–2424
〒444–2424　愛知県東加茂郡足助町足助西町36

■ ACCESS

BY TRAIN: 50 min by bus from Toyoda-shi Stn (Meitetsu Mikawa Line).
BY CAR: 40 min (25 km) via Route 153 from Toyoda IC (Tomei Expressway).

Old Asuka alleyway

A pamphlet put out by the Asuke municipality states that the town aims to become the Shangri-La of Japan. My traveling companion unkindly said it had already reached its goal, if the pamphlet was referring to some underdeveloped Tibetan village.

Asuke is on what was known in the Edo period (1600–1868) as the Chuma, or Halfway Horse Highway. The highway was so named because it was the road used to transport salt by horse from the coast to inland areas of Shinshu (present-day Nagano). At the foot of the mountains, the salt had to be repackaged into smaller bundles so that sturdier mountain steeds could transport it over the steep terrain into Shinshu. Asuke was where the salt was off-loaded and repacked by local wholesalers for the onward journey, so the salt arrived in Shinshu under the "Asuke" brand.

Entrance hall,
Tamada-ya

As there is no railway station in Asuke, the only way to get there is by car or bus (fifty minutes by bus from Toyota). A similar blessing has left the town of Fukiya in Okayama Prefecture exquisitely pristine. Unfortunately, Asuke is not as beautifully preserved as Fukiya since it is less remote, but it nevertheless retains its old-town appeal. If the buildings along the shallow but picturesque Asuke river could only be restored to their former beauty, Asuke might indeed become a Shangri-La.

While the attractions are few, there is one rather spectacular lane called Manrin-koji, which begins on the corner of the handsome Manrin bookstore. And local picnickers love Korankei Gorge for its splendid autumn colors. The *momiji* maples at the edge of the gorge were planted here 360 years ago. At the Sanshu Asuke Yashiki along the gorge, craftsmen and -women make cloth and paper and do smithing (open 9:00–17:00, closed Thursdays, small entry fee). There is also a pleasing view of the valley from the local castle replica.

Tamada-ya is the only inn left on the Halfway Horse Highway, and the inn building dates to the Edo period. It is an unassuming place with simple home-cooked food and clean shared facilities. A good base for a day exploring a future Shangri-La.

DESTINATION
17

NIIGATA PREFECTURE

Thatched cottage in the Northern Culture Museum complex

ATTRACTIONS

The Northern Culture Museum set around the former homestead of one of Japan's richest families; stunning rice-paddy country at Minami Uonuma-gun; an old hot spring town where the geisha culture is still alive; and, on the northern coast, a seaside town with an important legacy from a legendary poet-priest.

The *shinkansen* journey from Tokyo to Niigata lasts only two hours. If you were so inclined, you could get to Niigata, do some sight-seeing, and be back in Tokyo in as long as it would take to visit Hakone. It's that easy.

But I suggest staying the night at the Dairo-an, the charming inn in the grounds of the **Northern Culture Museum**, and then heading the next day to either Sado Island, Aizu Wakamatsu (in Fukushima Prefecture), or Niigata's beautiful rice country in Minami Uonuma-gun.

Niigata is a place I am drawn to again and again, as there is so much interesting country to see and so many fascinating detours. It helps to have a car; it is almost impossible to explore the rice country without one, and the roads, at least in the countryside, are empty and easy to negotiate.

The place to go for rice country is **Minami Uonuma-gun**. Some of the best scenery is on the way to **Matsunoyama Onsen**, where terraced paddies cling to steep mountains. No machines can get there, so all cultivation is done by hand. The flavor of this rice is said to be outstanding.

As you get closer to the coast, the rice paddies take on a different appearance. Farmers in these parts used to grow rows of trees in between the paddies for putting up trellises to dry the rice straw. Most of these trees have now been uprooted and the only spot that preserves this unique scenery is **Natsui**, not far from **Iwamuro Onsen**. Photographers and artists come from far and wide to record the scene.

The proprietor of the Memmen-tei Wata-ya inn in Iwamuro tells of a close call: "I thought that the local farmers were preserving the trees intentionally until one day an artist happened to mention that there were fewer trees 'again' this year. I made some enquiries and learned that the farmers were on the verge of selling all the trees to a maker of golf-club heads. So I asked them to preserve them for the sake of Niigata and they said they had never realized their value."

Iwamuro Onsen—not a terribly remarkable place these days—was an important post station on an official highway from the seventeenth to nineteenth

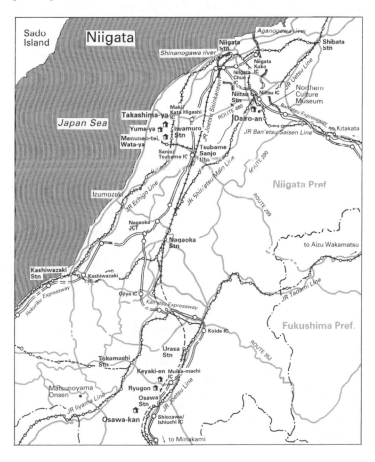

centuries, and because of its thermal springs and proximity to the pilgrims' shrine of **Yahiko**, it grew into quite a good-time town. A healthy geisha tradition in fact lives on in Iwamuro and is undergoing a quiet revival. I found it astounding that there are still some eighty geisha learning to become proficient traditional entertainers. About half of them are in their twenties and thirties. Stroll the streets of this quiet town, you are likely to hear them practicing on their *shamisen*.

The two main inns are the imposing Takashima-ya and the Yume-ya. Also noteworthy is the friendly Memmen-tei Wata-ya, where you can stay in the truly charming Baisho, an old, rustic-style tearoom with a garden view. The rest of the inn is rundown, but plans for renovation are underway and the owner is genuinely interested in preserving local culture. The food is excellent *kaiseki*-style cuisine.

One Niigata spot that must be mentioned is **Izumozaki**, on the coast south of Iwamuro Onsen, with a view of Sado Island in the distance. Izumozaki has two main streets of old houses, beautiful in their weather-beaten way, which date back to the middle of the Edo period (1600–1868), when the town was a bustling jump-off point to Sado and had a healthy population of 20,000 (including temporary laborers). Things went downhill quickly with the coming of the modern era. Izumozaki's main claim to fame now is as the birthplace of Ryokan (1758–1831), a wandering Zen priest who lived from hand to mouth and was loved for his childlike antics and profound verse. All along the Niigata coast as far as Iwamuro Onsen, you will find **statues of Ryokan** and pieces of his calligraphy displayed with great reverence. One of the best-loved images of Ryokan shows him sitting in his one-room hut, Gogyo-an, looking pleased with himself for having cut away part of his stairs to let a bamboo shoot come up. This hut still exists and is open to the public; a museum dedicated to him, the **Ryokan Kinen-kan**, is situated on a hill overlooking Izumozaki.

In the town, the culinary specialty is ***hamayaki***, whole fish grilled over hot coals in sand. Traditionally this was done right on the beach, but now local women are restricted to grilling the fish in sandpits along the town's main street—a curious sight. Izumozaki is also the home of waxed paper toy balloons and has a sweet shop, Daikoku-ya, with a 120-year history.

There are two decent-looking inns in Izumozaki. The Kuruma-ya (☎ 0258–78–2148) dates back to the seventeenth century, but appears to have undergone a stylish renovation, while the Horizen (☎ 0258–78–2051) is close to the swimming beach and so is popular in summer. It might be fun to spend a night in this remote seaside town, but I cannot vouch for either of these inns.

I have not included a listing for **Sado Island** in this book, since there is ample information in other guidebooks and plenty of cheap accommodation. I have investigated only two inns on the island. The Yawata-kan (☎ 0259–57–2141) on Mano Bay, where royalty has stayed, has its own forest of elegant red pines in spacious grounds, but it seemed gloomy. I preferred the faded, two-story wooden Seishin-tei (☎ 0259–74–2019), which is the century-old former home of a Mitsubishi trading company man who was in charge of running the **Sado gold mine**. Unfortunately, the inn is not in a convenient location for much more than swimming or exploring the mine, which is a twenty-minute walk away. **Shukunegi** in Ogi is home to Sado's most interesting streets of old buildings.

Seasonal tips

The best time for exploring Niigata by car is May–June, when all is green. Mid-winter, when the area is deep under snow, is also beautiful. Summer on Sado Island is the time of the Kodo drummer performances and each August an annual music festival is held in Ogi; the beaches and ferries become very crowded.

The Iwamuro Onsen Festival is held each July 24–25, while the Funamatsuri of Izumozaki is August 14–15. The latter is a colorful parade of fishing boats commemorating the days when gold from the Sado mines was loaded onto the wooden *kitamae-bune* boats for their trip to Osaka.

Recommended buys

Famous among tea-ceremony aficionados, Wasambon sweets can be bought from the Daikoku-ya Kashiten (0258–78–2101) on the main street in Izumozaki. They are feather-light and not too sweet. Waxed paper balloons can be bought from the Isono Kamifusen shop (0258–78–2045) or in local souvenir stalls.

Recommended trips including the Northern Culture Museum

If your preference is mountain scenery, explore Uonuma-gun by car; if you prefer the sea, choose Izumozaki and/or Sado Island. Surprisingly convenient to Niigata is Aizu Wakamatsu (Destination 18). Not so convenient but very worthwhile is a trip combining Tsuruoka, Asahi-mura, and the holy mountains of Dewa Sanzan (Destination 19). One of the most spectacular drives in Japan is from Tsuruoka to Yamagata via Asahi-mura. Take time to get off the main highway and explore the mountain farmlands.

- Northern Culture Museum (1 night)—Uonuma-gun (day trip)
—Nozawa Onsen (1 night, Destination 12)
- Northern Culture Museum (1 night)—Aizu Wakamatsu
(1–2 nights, Destination 18)
- Northern Culture Museum (1 night)—Tsuruoka/Asahi-mura
(day trip)—Dewa Sanzan (1–2 nights, Destination 19)
- Northern Culture Museum (1 night)
—Iwamuro Onsen (1 night)
- Northern Culture Museum (1 night)—Izumozaki (day trip)
—Niigata/Sado Island (2 nights)

DAIRO-AN 大呂庵

LOCATION: Niitsu

Meticulously kept and appointed 1930s Japanese house with four rooms and a stylish new sun-room, in the grounds of the magnificent Northern Culture Museum.

RATE: From ¥15,000 w/2 meals, children 50% off. **CREDIT CARDS:** Not accepted. **ROOMS:** 6 Japanese style (w/o bath). **COMMUNAL BATHS:** 2—men's, women's. **CHECK-IN:** 15:00. **CHECK-OUT:** 10:00. **LANGUAGE:** No English, reservations in Japanese.

☏ 025–385–2100 Fax: 025–385–2006
Soumi, Yokogoshi-machi, Naka Kambara-gun, Niigata 950–0205
〒950–0205　新潟県中蒲原郡横越町沢海

■ ACCESS
BY TRAIN: 10 min by car from Niitsu Stn (JR Shin'etsu Line).
BY CAR: 8 min (4 km) from Niitsu IC (Ban'etsu Expressway).

The owner of the Northern Culture Museum (Hoppo Bunka Hakubutsu-kan) in Niigata believes that if you have to pay for advertising, the product you are offering is not worth it. That is why you may never have heard of one of the finest cultural attractions in Japan, nor the gem of an inn on its grounds, the Dairo-an.

The Northern Culture Museum is a misleading name: the museum is not about the culture of Japan's north, although this is one of the country's more northerly areas. Rather, it is a gathering of traditional Niigata structures, from homes and storehouses to carpenters' quarters and teahouses, centered around the mansion of the Ito family. Among the wealthiest landowners in Japan, the Ito family had its own temple and even its own crematorium; its telephone number was 0001, one ahead of the city office.

The grounds of the Northern Culture Museum are so full of interesting buildings and gardens that it is easy to get lost. The most impressive is the Ito family's own sixty-room homestead, which has been in the family since 1750. Its massive kitchen has a wood-fire hearth that was used each day to cook an amount of rice that would feed one modern family for a year. In the compound there are no fewer than five teahouses. They include a fascinating triangular building called Sanraku-tei, where every corner is a forty-five-degree angle, even on the tatami and in the cupboard drawers.

This impressive museum has a remarkable story attached to its survival. After World War II, the whole Ito family property was to have been demolished and turned into apartment complexes by the Occupation Forces under the Land Reform Act. It was saved thanks to an encounter two months after the war between the seventh-generation Bunkichi Ito, a graduate of Pennsylvania University, and a certain Lt. Ralph Wright, who was the officer in charge of educational affairs for the Occupation Forces. After a plea from the English-speaking Ito not to tear down the house, Wright advised headquarters that the Ito home should be saved by classifying it as a museum.

When the eighth-generation Bunkichi "Bunny" Ito became head of the Ito family, he went to the United States to look for the man who had saved the family home. He found Wright through a series of serendipitous events and brought him to Japan for an emotional celebration of appreciation.

The wonderful 1920s house that is now the Dairo-an inn was built for one of the members of the Ito family. It is *haikara* ("high collar"), meaning that it incorporated fashionable Western-style features, such as imported English timbers. The workmanship of this old building is superb, with highly polished wooden floors and banisters and large tatami rooms with handmade glass window panes. The striking indigo-and-white floor cushions and all the *futon* covers have been beautifully fashioned out of the family's old ikat-weave quilts.

When the house was turned into an inn in the 1980s, some modern comforts—such as a big sun-room and a modern jacuzzi bath—were added. The guest rooms don't have their own bath or toilet, but two state-of-the-art toilets are shared by the four rooms.

Most meals are served in one of two dining rooms downstairs—the main dining room at night and the recently added sun-room for breakfast. The meals are home-style feasts of local produce.

The great thing about the Dairo-an is its location. In the midst of all the beautiful old architecture and gardens, no industry can be seen, no cars can be heard. You wake to the sound of cocks crowing, cows mooing, and the elegant rattle of those handmade window panes, and can look out over a sea of old tiled roofs. There is no television or karaoke, and the only telephone is a pay phone downstairs.

Entry to the museum is free for the Dairo-an's guests.

TAKASHIMA-YA （高志の宿）高島屋

LOCATION: Iwamuro Onsen

The former home of a rich merchant, with massive beams and a gorgeous garden, in a quiet, one-time geisha hot spring

---

RATE: From ¥20,000 w/2 meals, 20% off w/breakfast, ¥30% off w/o meals, children 50% off. **CREDIT CARDS:** AMEX, DC, MC, VISA. **ROOMS:** 24 Japanese style (15 w/bath). **COMMUNAL BATHS:** 3—men's, women's, outdoor (alternating). **CHECK-IN:** 14:00. **CHECK-OUT:** 11:00. **LANGUAGE:** No English, reservations in Japanese.

☎ 0256–82–2001 Fax: 0256–82–4124
678–Ko Iwamuro, Iwamuro-mura, Nishi Kambara-gun, Niigata 935–0104
〒935–0104 新潟県西蒲原郡岩室村大字岩室678甲

■ ACCESS
BY TRAIN: 8 min by car from Iwamuro Stn (JR Echigo Line).
BY CAR: 20 min (11 km) via Route 460 from Maki/Kata Higashi IC (Hokuriku Expressway).

This inn has nothing to do with the department store of the same name; it is an historic headman's home that was turned into an inn by a family called Takashima after the post-feudal land reforms made it impossible for this wealthy family to survive on rice-tax income. The seventh-generation head of

Tea is served at the big hearth, Takashima-ya

Individual iron-pot baths, Takashima-ya

the family is said to have been the one who first discovered the hot spring in Iwamuro in 1713. Takashima-ya is the grandest inn in Iwamuro Onsen, and the massive proportions of the 240-year-old main building give a vivid sense of the wealth invested here.

Upon arrival you will be seated at the edge of the ample hearth on the ground floor and invited to take whisked green tea to the ticking of an antique pendulum wall clock while enjoying the grand outlook onto the inn's splendid garden, with its four-hundred-year-old pine tree. Whereas a lot of old buildings of this sort and size suffer from dreary, dark interiors, the garden outlook helps to make the Takashima-ya open, light, and uplifting. If all the rooms were in this part of the building, then it would be perfect. Most of the guest rooms have been built on as new wings and though they are in perfectly good taste, I found myself longing for the grandeur of the old main house.

There is one old guest room in an adjoining building and it has a most interesting feature—a "raining roof." The proprietress borrowed this idea from an eighty-year-old house she once saw. A sprinkler system has been installed around the edge of the roof and, on a hot day, the water can be turned on to create a cooling, rainlike shower all around the house. "If eight people share this big room, the cost per person goes down to ¥25,000. Not bad at that price, eh?" she said.

The food at Takashima-ya is so good that the inn warrants a visit for a meal even if you don't stay the night (call ahead for reservations). The specialty is *noppo-jiru*, a mainly vegetable concoction that is stewed for four days and imparts a satisfying depth of flavor.

The baths at the Takashima-ya are also a treat. In addition to a big main bath with a garden view, you can have the unique experience of immersing yourself in an iron pot of hot water heated from underneath.

OSAWA-KAN 大沢館

LOCATION:
Osawa Onsen

Superb hot spring baths in a well-appointed,
isolated mountain inn located in exhilarating Niigata snow country.

RATE: From ¥12,000 w/2 meals, children 30% off. **CREDIT CARDS:** Not accepted. **ROOMS:** 16 Japanese style (w/o bath). **COMMUNAL BATHS:** 4—men's, women's, 2 outdoor (men's, women's). **CHECK-IN:** 15:00. **CHECK-OUT:** 10:00. **LANGUAGE:** No English, reservations in Japanese.

☏ 0257–83–3773 Fax: 0257–83–4777
Osawa, Shiozawa-cho, Minami Uonuma-gun, Niigata 949–6361
〒949–6361　新潟県南魚沼郡塩沢町大沢

■ ACCESS
BY TRAIN: 5 min by car from Osawa Stn (JR Joetsu Line).
BY CAR: 2 km from Shiozawa/Ishiuchi IC (Kan'etsu Expressway).

An imposing samurai-mansion gate stands at the entrance to the Osawa-kan. I half expected the military motif to be continued in the rest of the inn, but on entering the lobby the theme turned to rural life in the snow country. In the room adjoining the lobby we found an open fireplace with a big kettle simmering, a dish of rice-cake wafers to grill, a bear rug with claws still attached (this is Niigata bear country), and straw sandals strewn over a wooden frame above the fire, just as they would have been after a day in the fields.

Samurai mansion-style gate

The unassuming proprietress greeted us herself and allowed us to choose between the old wing and the new. The new wing (*bekkan*) was about ¥5,000 more per person, but we settled on the best and biggest new room, Iwai. It features a coffered ceiling and intricately carpentered, *shoin*-style *shoji* (screens) and *chigai-dana* (shelves). Iwai was a considerable leap in luxury from the basic, rather small old-wing rooms without their own toilets. In fact, it was pure indulgence.

A bracing walk along a pleasant corridor, then over wooden planks like those you find in an iris garden, took us to the outdoor pool. The bath had a view of the brilliant green mountains of early spring; in winter this would all be covered in snow. The wooden baths were pristine and overflowed with pure hot spring water.

The indoor bath, with a large lantern and Buddhist statue and expansive mountain views through big windows, is exotic. The inn provides a complimentary drawstring bag containing a loofah, pumice stone, small towel, toothbrush, and a pair of *tabi* socks, as well as large yellow bath towels.

Men's open-air bath, Osawa-kan

Dinner featured excellent wild vegetables, which were especially good when we visited in early spring. Eel was a speciality, served in individual hot pots with sliced burdock root and wild mushrooms. The other delicacy was the rice: this region claims it grows the best in Japan. For a large party of guests, the master of the inn starts up his wood-fired rice cooking stove outside.

At check-out time the owner will drop you at the unmanned Osawa Station for the twelve-minute ride on the Joetsu Line to Echigo Yuzawa, where you can connect with the *shinkansen*. Pay for your ticket at the end of the ride.

18

AIZU WAKAMATSU

Mukaitaki

ATTRACTIONS

The town of Aizu Wakamatsu is renowned for its handsome food and craft shops and unusual eateries. Here you can visit a lord's mansion with a herb garden and a samurai museum in a town with a legacy of warrior bravery. There is a classic inn at Higashiyama Onsen, and the nearby town of Kitakata is full of houses built in the traditional kura (storehouses) style.

"Are you sure you got our order?"

Twenty minutes had passed since we sat down at the counter of **Mitsuta-ya** restaurant for a taste of old Aizu, and nothing had happened. A red-faced man sitting at the counter took note of our impatience: "It was an hour before we received our order," he said. "So relax, friends, and enjoy the saké. This is Aizu, not Tokyo."

The forty-minute wait turned out to be worth it—the skewered slabs of tofu, *konnyaku*, yam, fish, and rice cakes, covered with wholesome miso pastes of different hues and aromas, were simply exquisite. All were grilled over a charcoal fire tended by two ladies with the broadest of Tohoku accents. (In Aizu, *ginko* [bank] becomes *jinko* and "parking" becomes "parjing." I remember this because we were instructed that the "parjing" was next to the *jinko* and were none the wiser.)

The Mitsuta-ya originally produced only miso, but now it also sells a variety of natural foods including hand-pressed oils, pickles, *umeboshi* plums, and plum wine. Eating here is still one of the great Aizu things to do, as are exploring the smattering of old shops in the town center, enjoying the variety of dramatic *noren*, and buying souvenirs from such institutions as the **Suzuki-ya Rihei Shoten** lacquerware shop or the **Taketo** bamboo-goods shop. Aizu is also famous for its saké production and it is worthwhile paying a visit to a restored saké distillery, such as **Kaishu-ichi Zohin-kan**.

But to get into the right mood for Aizu Wakamatsu, it is only proper to start with **Tsuruga Castle**. Just inside the entrance to the castle is large, old wooden *dojo*, a martial arts practice hall which was shaking under hundreds of small thumping feet on the day I was there. It was *kendo* (fencing) practice for the local kids and handsome little warriors in cloth helmets were charging each other with blood-curdling shouts.

Aizu has a reputation to uphold in the warrior stakes: it was here that the antirevolutionary forces held out against the pro-imperialists in the face of the *fait accompli* of the Meiji Restoration. It was also here in 1868, the year of the Restoration, that a tragic band of nineteen teenage samurai called the "White Tigers" (Byakkotai) slaughtered themselves because they mistakenly thought their lord's castle had fallen. The site of their suicide, **Iimori-yama**, is a famous Aizu sight. I was told that local people continue to respect the martial arts more than other places in Japan, and those little kendoists were certainly a stirring sight as, knowingly or not, they took up the banner of their gutsy forebears.

After the castle, it was time for lunch, so my next stop was the Mitsuta-ya. But an equally impressive place to eat is the atmospheric **Takino Wappameshi** restaurant, where the specialty is rice with delicious toppings like wild mountain vegetables, mushrooms, or salmon, served in the bentwood boxes characteristic of Aizu.

It is hard to get around Aizu Wakamatsu on foot; apart from the downtown area, the sights are scattered far and wide. You will have to take a car or bus to the next suggested stop, the **Buke Yashiki**, a spic-and-span reproduction of a high-ranking samurai's residence that even has a working rice mill.

Onyakuen

A short drive away is **Onyakuen** (literally, "garden of medicinal plants"), the former villa of an Aizu lord that has a stroll garden, tea arbors, and a big plot of herbs. The property has an endearing disheveled look about it and a pond with the fattest, hungriest carp I have ever fed.

It is hard to choose between staying at Shibukawa Donya inn or at the classic Mukaitaki in Higashiyama, a hot spring town on the edge of Aizu Wakamatsu. Perhaps the easiest way is to spend a night at each. Another possibility is going to **Kitakata** to stay in a *kura*, a renovated fireproof storehouse, such as the Sasa-ya Ryokan (✆ 0241–22–0008) or the Osaragi-no-Yado (see Alternative Inns).

Kitakata City has become known as "the City of *Kura*," since there are said to be 2,400 *kura*-style structures in the town. The proliferation of these sturdy,

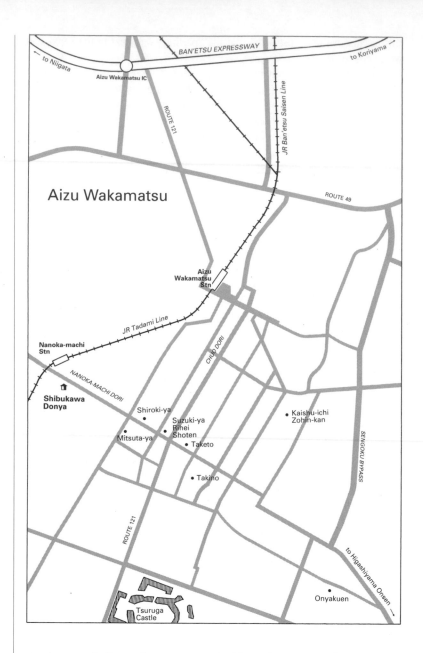

storehouse-style fireproof structures resulted from the townspeople's experience with a devastating fire in 1880. When the flames died down and residents returned to sift through the ashes, they were astonished to see all their storehouses still standing, while everything else was reduced to cinders. From that time, people with means built every possible structure they could in *kura*-style—a wood frame with layers of plaster or even brick or stone on the outside.

I wish I could say that Kitakata is a picturesque *kura*-filled townscape. One beautiful old home, **Kai Honke**, and even a temple built in *kura* style, **Anshoji**, are open to the public, along with scattered clusters of *kura* that have been turned into souvenir shops. There is also an excellent saké brewery open to the public on a street with other *kura*. But most of the *kura* remain hidden behind unattractive canopies and concrete façades, so a casual stroll reveals little.

For some mysterious reason, the town of Kitakata has also come to be known as "the Town of *Ramen*." Each *ramen* shop competes with the next for the tastiest soups and toppings. Some are very good, but there's no secret recipe.

Horse-drawn wagons operate from the station to ferry people around the Kitakata sights. This would have been a good idea if the sights on the way had been more appealing and the wagons less shabby. Only do this if you are not in a hurry. Otherwise hire bikes or a taxi.

Recommended trips including Aizu Wakamatsu

- Aizu Wakamatsu (1–2 nights)—Northern Culture Museum (Niigata) (1 night, Destination 17)
- Aizu Wakamatsu (1–2 nights)—Kitakata (day trip)—Yonezawa/Shirabu Onsen (1 night, Destination 19)

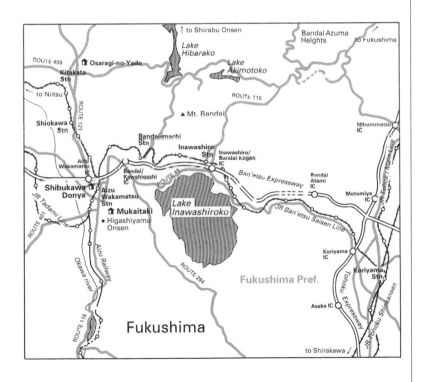

SHIBUKAWA DONYA 渋川問屋

Once the mansion and storehouses of a wealthy cod and herring dealer, this is now a good-value inn with interesting food.

RATE: From ¥10,000 w/2 meals, no children. **CREDIT CARDS:** Not accepted. **ROOMS:** 16 Japanese style (w/o bath). **COMMUNAL BATHS:** 2—men's, women's. **CHECK-IN:** 16:00. **CHECK-OUT:** 10:00. **LANGUAGE:** No English, reservations in Japanese.

☽ 0242–28–4000 Fax: 0242–26–6464

3–28 Nanoka-machi, Aizu Wakamatsu-shi, Fukushima 965–0044

〒965–0044　福島県会津若松市七日町3–28

■ ACCESS
BY TRAIN: 5 min by car from Aizu Wakamatsu Stn (JR Ban'etsu Saisen Line).
BY CAR:　10 min from Aizu Wakamatsu IC (Ban'etsu Expressway).

Shibukawa Donya with New Year's decorations

It may not seem strange that the traditional diet of Aizu Wakamatsu includes cod and herring until you realize that Aizu is landlocked snow country. Marine products traveled on the *kitamae-bune* ships that used to sail from Hokkaido to Osaka via points along the Sea of Japan coast, and were then transported overland to Aizu. The fish products were brought in their dried and salted form, then reconstituted and turned into delectable foods by either simmering in soy sauce and *mirin* (rice vinegar), or pickling. This was not an easy process; reconstituting dried cod, which has the consistency of rock-hard beef jerky, can take over a week.

Shibukawa Donya was one of the handful of seafood wholesalers in Aizu Wakamatsu that imported and sold not only cod and herring but a whole range of sea products, including giant kelp, an important base for soup stocks. Shibukawa Donya's business started in 1868, the dawn of Japan's modern era, and the company grew so wealthy that at one stage there were more than fifty people living in the establishment, including six families and their servants.

One hundred and thirty years on, Shibukawa Donya has been transformed into an inn that serves some of those same traditional marine products of Aizu to guests. The cod is succulent and tasty, while the pickled herring is along the lines of good blue cheese; both are served in a course with more familiar items, such as red salmon sushi, and complemented with wholesome buckwheat gruel.

Refurbished thirteen years ago, the inn is an eclectic gathering of living quarters and converted storerooms, with some of the buildings dating from the 1890s. Regrettably, there is limited accommodation available in the quiet wooden, 1920s section of the complex, but young Japanese tourists tend to prefer the inn's "ladies' hotel." This "designer dormitory" adjoins an old herring warehouse, which acts as its lobby. It has space-age interiors in steel, chrome, and stained glass; compact tatami rooms with silver wallpaper and high-sloping ceilings; dramatic orange and black striped doors; and trendy louvered windows.

Though a "ladies' hotel," men can stay if they are accompanied by a woman. In spite of the assault on my senses from all that chrome and silver, I spent a cozy night here and, for the same price, it was much better value than a business hotel.

The "ladies' hotel," Shibukawa Donya

The shared bath was pleasant. Dinner was served in the old *kura* adjoining the hundred-year-old reception area and was excellent. I learned later that, for an additional sum, I could have ordered the acclaimed Aizu Shiokawa beef to go with my traditional Aizu meal. A wholesome Japanese breakfast with complimentary coffee is served in a cozy morning room with tables and chairs. The food is, in fact, one of the reasons that many Japanese choose to stay at Shibukawa Donya. The night I was there, for example, a mother and daughter on a nostalgic journey back to their old hometown had chosen to stay at the inn because of the quality of the food and the low rates, both of which compensate for its relative isolation.

Literature buffs will be interested to know that the writer Yukio Mishima (1925–70) visited this inn to learn more about a black sheep of the Shibukawa family, who was jailed for his part in the February 26 Incident, a failed coup d'état in 1936. Mishima dubbed his room "the patriot's room"; unfortunately it is not open to the public.

MUKAITAKI 向瀧

LOCATION: Higashiyama Onsen

*Classic old wooden inn close to Aizu Wakamatsu,
once chosen as accommodation for the imperial household.*

RATE: From ¥19,000 w/2 meals, 20% off w/breakfast only, 30% off w/o meals, children 30% off. **CREDIT CARDS:** AMEX, DC, VISA. **ROOMS:** 28 Japanese style (3 w/bath). **COMMUNAL BATHS:** 8 2 men's, 2 women's, 4 private (*kazoku-buro*). **CHECK-IN:** 15:00. **CHECK-OUT:** 10:00. **LANGUAGE:** Some English.

☎ 0242–27–7501 Fax: 0242–28–0939
INTERNET: www.mukaitaki.com/
E-MAIL: ryokan@mukaitaki.com
200 Kawamuko, Yumoto, Higasiyama-cho, Aizu Wakamatsu-shi, Fukushima 965–0814
〒965–0814　福島県会津若松市東山町湯本川向200

■ ACCESS
BY TRAIN: 10 min by car from Aizu Wakamatsu Stn (JR Ban'etsu Saisen Line).
BY CAR: 10 min from Aizu Wakamatsu IC (Ban'etsu Expressway).

The Mukaitaki is one of those heady old Japanese places that has not sold its soul, although asphalt is creeping to its doorstep and towers of concrete are encroaching. More like a historic building than an inn, it has just eleven rooms in elegant *sukiya* style that sit ornately around an intimate classic garden with

Mukaitaki hillside garden

mountains for a backdrop. In the garden are many trees of venerable gnarl—cherry and expertly clipped azaleas.

I could find little about the Mukaitaki in any of my Japanese guidebooks, but was excited to find a small item written by the daughter of Kakuei Tanaka (1918–93), the former Japanese prime minister, noting that this was one of the great man's favorite inns—interesting for someone who once sought to "pave Japan in asphalt."

Historic Mukaitaki structures

The Mukaitaki was build in 1873, the sixth year of the Meiji period (1868–1912). The spot where it stands had long been a hot spring called the "Fox Bath" (Kitsune-yu), where the warriors of the Aizu clan used to soothe their battle wounds. The present buildings date mainly from the 1930s and all reflect wonderful use of wood. The Paulownia Room, Pine Room, Maple Room, and Bamboo Room each feature the given type of wood. All of the wooden surfaces on the outside of the inn are sanded and repolished every five years to preserve the beauty of the building's exterior.

The Mukaitaki baths here lack the decadent size and brimming luxury characteristic of many late-twentieth-century Japanese inns, but have a classic elegance that suits their vintage, especially the men's Saru-no-Yu ("Monkey Bath") with its marble relief of a naked nymph. Mukaitaki also has *kazoku-buro*, smaller baths for more intimate bathing.

The food, while standard fare, comes in copious quantities, one dish after another. It is a pleasure to eat with a view of the garden illuminated at night. Higashiyama is a geisha town, so if you are feeling game, why not request a geisha to help pour your drinks? A geisha's presence costs about ¥10,000 for a couple of hours; ask at the reception.

19

YAMAGATA PREFECTURE

Yamabushi at Dewa Sanzan

ATTRACTIONS

A fascinating farm and fishing museum; neglected thatch farmhouses in spectacular countryside; and three holy mountains.

I have never failed to enjoy a trip into the countryside of Tohoku, and Yamagata has a great deal to see. Like all trips in Tohoku, I recommend having a car—you miss out on so much of the scenery traveling by train.

One of the most famous places in Yamagata is the city of **Sakata**, on the Sea of Japan coast. Sakata was once a thriving commercial port with flourishing arts and crafts, but little of the traditional culture is to be seen now. Nevertheless, I enjoyed visiting the **old rice warehouses** that house displays on the rice trade in the Edo period (1600–1868). Try lifting the bales of rice that they man-handled in those days! A museum on the outskirts of the city dedicated to the work of photographer **Ken Domon** (1909–80), with its modern garden and sculpture by the late Isamu Noguchi (1904–88), is also a must.

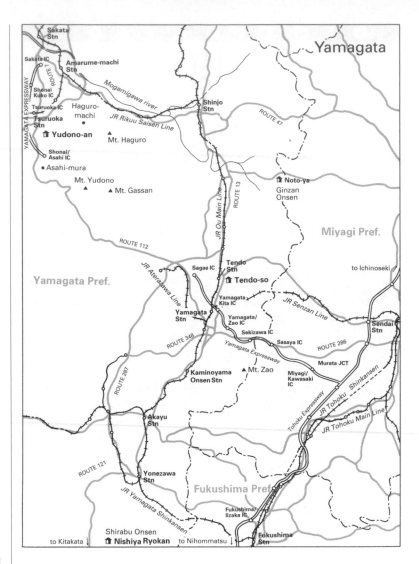

Yamagata

Rice storehouses,
Sakata

Tsuruoka on the Sea of Japan coast is somewhat more worthwhile than Sakata, mainly for the chance to see the **Chido Hakubutsu-kan**, which has one of Japan's most fascinating and well-presented collections of fishing and farming tools and folk crafts, along with a perfectly preserved example of the rarely seen *kabuto* (helmet)-style thatch farmhouse. The house was brought from the village of Tamugimata, where two other examples still exist.

I recommend driving from Tsuruoka to Tendo or Yamagata City along Highway 112. The scenery is spectacular in May, when snow-capped mountains, cherry blossoms, and new shoots all vie for attention.

On the way, take a detour at **Asahi-mura** to the marvelous old Churenji temple, which has a mummified holy man as one of its objects of worship. The nearby village of **Tamugimata** may also be of interest for its two *kabuto*-style thatch farmhouses. One, the *minshuku* Kayabuki-ya (☎0235–54–6103), provides cheap lodgings. But for exquisite, tumbledown thatch farmhouses, I found it more rewarding to drive from Asahi-mura to an eerie lake called **Otori-ike**, which is said to be inhabited by a Japanese Nessie called Taki Taro.

From Asahi-mura you are close to the three holy mountains—Gassan, Yudono-san, and Haguro-san—known collectively as **Dewa Sanzan**, where the *yamabushi* (mountain ascetics) practice. Lodgings for pilgrims line the approaches to the main shrines on all of these mountains; many of them are highly picturesque and some serve vegetarian food. Ministrations to comfort are minimal, however, and I would recommend a night at the Yudono-an on the outskirts of Tsuruoka for greater luxury.

From Asahi-mura return to the highway and continue on to Tendo, outside Yamagata City, and stay at the excellent Tendo-so inn. Alternatively, travel to the historically important **Yonezawa**, which has picturesque **Shirabu Onsen** on its outskirts. In Yamagata City itself is **Ginzan Onsen**, a cluster of atmospheric wooden inns straddling a small river. Their style is right out of the 1920s. The funkiest-looking is the Noto-ya Ryokan. The very first inn that the Emperor Showa (previously known as Emperor Hirohito; 1901–89) stayed at after Japan's defeat in World War II was the Murao (☎ 0236–72–2111) in Kaminoyama City, just south of Yamagata City near the Mount Zao ski slopes. Shinshun-no-Ma, the lavishly decorated, pond-side detached suite where the emperor stayed, is available for plebeian guests at a royal rate.

Recommended trips including Yamagata Prefecture

● Sakata (half day)—Tsuruoka (1 night at Yudono-an)—Asahi-mura,
Churenji temple and Yudono-san (day trip)—Tendo (1 night)
Yonezawa (1 night at Shirabu Onsen)

TENDO-SO 天童壮

LOCATION:
Tendo

Classic sukiya inn offering maximum value for money.

RATE: From ¥25,000 w/2 meals, 30% off w/breakfast only, 40% off w/o meals, children 30% off. **CREDIT CARDS:** DC, VISA. **ROOMS:** 18 Japanese style (13 w/bath). **COMMUNAL BATHS:** 2—men's, women's—each connects to outdoor bath. **CHECK-IN:** 14:00. **CHECK-OUT:** 11:00. **LANGUAGE:** No English, reservations in Japanese.

☎ 023–653–2033 Fax: 023–654–8875
2–2–18 Kamata, Tendo-shi, Yamagata 994–0024
〒994–0024　山形県天童市鎌田2–2–18

■ ACCESS
BY TRAIN: 5 min by car from Tendo Stn (JR Ou Main Line).
BY CAR:　12 min via Route 13 from Yamagata Kita IC (Yamagata Expressway).

Tendo-so

It is tragic that this *sukiya*-style *ryokan* is not closer to Tokyo—I would recommend it above almost anyplace in Izu. The *mingei* façade and foyer are quietly dignified, and the interior décor and service can compete with the best in the world at this price.

The owner of the Tendo-so was a man with a mission. A former designer, he made a point of displaying the beauty of wood in every part of this single-story inn. His wife, a lover of the tea ceremony, then set about making it feel like home—the kind of home most people would dream of. The black-and-white, *mingei*-style reception area leads to eighteen spacious *sukiya* guest rooms, and there are seven somewhat more expensive *hanare*. A classic teahut has been made in the garden. The big communal bathroom is all in black marble, with wooden tubs and a small open-air jacuzzi.

The proprietors go to great pains to decide on the menu and are so insistent that the food vessels show off the food to its best advantage that they handpick these when they travel. The meal—creative *kaiseki*—could not be faulted. I was only sorry I had not ordered *unagi* (grilled eel): in its former incarnation, this inn was a restaurant specializing in eel and, if I had placed an order in advance, I could have had a taste of their hundred-year-old recipe.

The Tendo-so is located in a modest hot spring town that caters to Yamagata City dwellers, and the most interesting tourist spots are quite a distance away. But if you are traveling near Yamagata City, this inn is well worth the detour.

NISHI-YA RYOKAN 西屋旅館

LOCATION:
Shirabu Onsen

Thatched hot spring inn on the mountainous outskirts of Yonezawa.

RATE: From ¥8,000 w/2 meals, 10% off w/breakfast only, 40% off w/o meals, children 40% off. **CREDIT CARDS:** VISA. **ROOMS:** 20 Japanese style (w/o bath). **COMMUNAL BATHS:** 3—men's, women's, 1 private (*kazoku-buro*). **CHECK-IN:** 15:00. **CHECK-OUT:** 10:00. **LANGUAGE:** Some English.

☏ 0239–55–2480 Fax: 0238–55–2212
E-MAIL: nishiya@mail.dewa.or.jp
(Shirabu Onsen) 1527 Seki, Yonezawa-shi, Yamagata 992–1472
〒992–1472　山形県米沢市関1527（白布温泉）

■ ACCESS
BY TRAIN: 40 min by car from Yonezawa Stn (JR Ou Main Line).
BY CAR:　1 hr 45 min via Yonezawa from Fukushima/Iizaka IC (Tohoku Expressway).

Nishi-ya Ryokan

Shirabu Onsen is a seven-hundred-year-old hot spring situated in particularly lovely mountain country thirty minutes from Yonezawa. Nishi-ya Ryokan is one of three impressive thatch-roofed inns—Higashi-ya, Naka-ya, and Nishi-ya (the East House, the Middle House, and the West House, respectively)—that dominate Shirabu. Nishi-ya Ryokan has the most atmospheric accommodations, with parts that date from the mid-Edo period (1700s) and the rest being from after the war. Old and new harmonize well, and the bathhouse, with its high rafters that let in natural light, is spectacular in its simplicity.

YUDONO-AN 湯どの庵

Comfortingly refined but unprepossessing ryokan *in an unlikely town.*

LOCATION: Yutagawa Onsen, Tsuruoka

RATE: From ¥20,000 w/2 meals, children 50–70% off. **CREDIT CARDS:** VISA. **ROOMS:** 14 Japanese style (2 w/bath). **COMMUNAL BATHS:** 2—*hinoki*-wood bath, stone bath—both alternate. **CHECK-IN:** 15:00. **CHECK-OUT:** 10:00. **LANGUAGE:** No English, reservations in Japanese.

☎ 0235–35–2200 Fax: 0235–35–2201
Otsu–38 Yutagawa, Tsuruoka-shi, Yamagata 997–0752
〒997–0752　山形県鶴岡市湯田川乙38

■ ACCESS
BY TRAIN: 20 min by car from Tsuruoka Stn (JR Uetsu Main Line).
BY CAR:　1 hr half from Sagae IC (Yamagata Expressway).

I have found some of the most elegant establishments in the most unlikely places. One is Yudono-an, in a hot spring enclave on the outskirts of Tsuruoka, which is so isolated and quiet you wonder if you got off at the wrong bus stop. About halfway down the Yutagawa Onsen "hot spring street," with its three dusty shops and a handful of inns, are the high walls of one grand establishment, above which peek a well-crafted wooden building with a heavy, tiled roof. This is Yudono-an.

Tatami-matted lobby, Yudono-an

From the hushed, dimly lit foyer, your eyes are drawn to the light filtering through delicate maple leaves in the pretty courtyard garden. A tatami-covered sitting room adjacent to the foyer, with small, low tables and plump cushions, ideal for viewing the garden, is where guests first alight for cherry-blossom tea before being shown to their room.

No slippers are provided. Everyone pads around in bare or stockinged feet, for the inn is spotless. The only other inn brave enough to attempt this is the Kayo-tei in Yamanaka Onsen. Hallways and stairs leading to rooms in the concrete annex of the original wooden building are carpeted. The rooms are unexceptional, but wait for the bath and the meal—this is where the Yudono-an shines.

Yudono-an has two superb bathhouses, each smallish and cozy. One bath is of stone and one is of old cypress. The men's and women's designations are reversed at 8 P.M. so that guests can sample both. The cypress bath has a lower water temperature than the stone, but it was perfect for me; the warmth seeped slowly in.

The dining room is worthy of a *daimyo*, with a high coffered ceiling and handsomely crafted staggered shelves. Partitioned off, it provides absolute privacy in a grand setting, making one willing, even eager, to forgive Yudono-an for its ordinary guest rooms.

The inn was originally built as a place for the local Tsuruoka lord to relax, which explains its exalted atmosphere. While the oldest parts of the building have been rebuilt and originate in the Meiji period (1868–1912), the craftsmanship is well beyond most modern equivalents.

If a Japanese travel writer were assigned to cover this inn, I have no doubt he or she would first praise the food. Like the Kayo-tei in Yamanaka Onsen, the inn's pride simply glows through the food, so superbly is it presented, in elegant Kyoto style, and so delicate and well chosen are its flavors.

Like all the best encounters, this is not an inn that overwhelms you at first meeting, but like its hot spring water it works its magic slowly.

Nearby

Tsuruoka has one of the most interesting museums in Japan, the Chido Hakubutsu-kan. In addition to accommodating a collection of local historic buildings of both Japanese and Western style, it has some fascinating displays pertaining to local Shonai (Yamagata area) fishing and rice culture. Most unusual are the *iwai-bandori* (padded backpacks) made in festive designs for celebratory occasions (such as carrying a bride's dowry) and the collection of sleek bamboo fishing rods belonging to the samurai of the local lord, who were encouraged to learn martial skills and endurance through fishing.

20

IWATE, AKITA, and AOMORI PREFECTURES

Indoor women's bath, Kuro-yu Onsen

ATTRACTIONS

This spectacular countryside, dotted with hot springs, is worthy of a prolonged driving holiday.

Tohoku, the great northern frontier, has room to breathe. It is a great place to explore by car precisely because it is without the irksome challenge of negotiating the narrow, congested streets that prevail in overdeveloped Kanto and Kansai. It is surprising how much of Tohoku is still untouched, but you will not see this if you stay on trains.

Maybe I am doing Tohoku an injustice by breaking it into just three sections (Aizu Wakamatsu, Yamagata Prefecture, and these three prefectures together), but with the exception of a handful of ¥40,000 to ¥60,000 places, the kind of inns I relish are few in Tohoku. Were this a book about hot springs, I could have filled a whole volume on rustic Tohoku *onsen* inns alone. I have confined myself here to very special hot spring *ryokan*, in or near interesting places.

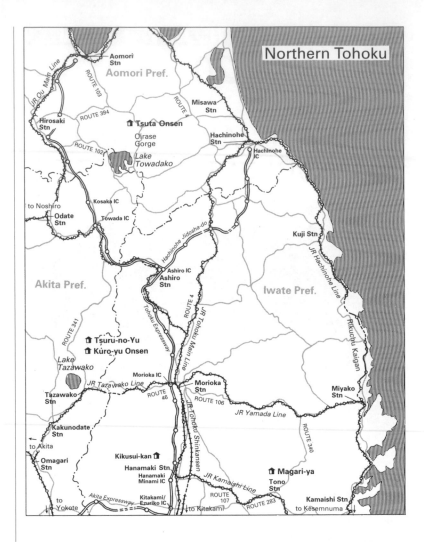

IWATE PREFECTURE

Tono and **Morioka** are the places to go in Iwate.

In Tono, don't limit yourself to the attractions listed in the tourist pamphlets (**Kappabuchi Pond** or the pristine **Chiba House**). Try and get out on the quiet country roads that link the seven villages of Tono to see some working farms, exquisitely decrepit *torii* (shrine gates), and the last of the living *magari-ya* (L-shaped farmhouses). Also don't miss the **Five Hundred Rakan Statues** carved on rocks in a stunning ravine. The **Denshoen complex**, which seeks to re-create traditional culture has a beautifully renovated *magari-ya* with one display room dedicated to an eerie collection of *o-shira-sama* dolls—the local deity of sericulture.

In Morioka City, Iwate's capital, head for the **Kogensha folk craft complex** (① 019–622–2894). There are several other good crafts and antiques shops close by.

Osawa Onsen at Hanamaki is the most pleasant of the hot springs in Iwate. The Kikusui-kan inn there is a classic.

AKITA PREFECTURE

The **Nyuto Onsen** group (two hours' drive from Morioka) has beautiful inns for staying at hot springs such as Kuro-yu and Tsuru-no-Yu. From here it is an hour to **Kakunodate**, an interesting place to visit for its relics of samurai culture (two mansions, Japanese and Western-style, to explore) and fine **cherry-bark crafts**.

AOMORI PREFECTURE

Aomori's cultural center is **Hirosaki**, a city well worth visiting. But I recommend approaching Aomori Prefecture from its southern end, driving up from the Nyuto Onsen group in Akita through spectacular beech-covered mountains to the stunning **Lake Towada** and the **Oirase Gorge**. Drive when there are few cars on the road—after Golden Week in May is one good time. The **Tsuta Onsen** *ryokan* is the classic old inn of Aomori, reached via Oirase Gorge. The much advertised Aoni Onsen is disappointingly commercialized.

Cherry-bark craft

Recommended trips in North Tohoku

The easiest way to travel in Tohoku is to get the *shinkansen* to a major city and rent a car from there. Here is just one trip I would recommend.

- Tohoku *shinkansen* to Morioka (day excursion)—Hanamaki Onsen (1 night)—Kakunodate (stopover)—Kuro-yu or Tsuru-no-Yu Onsen (1 night)—Tsuta Onsen via Lake Towada and Oirase Gorge (1 night)—Hirosaki.

If you are short of time, I recommend returning the car in Aomori and taking a plane back to Tokyo.
Another route back from Tsuta Onsen is along the scenic eastern coastline, especially via the Rikuchu Kaigan National Park, before making a detour to Tono, then getting back onto the main route to visit the historically important city of Hiraizumi

---

KURO-YU ONSEN 黒湯温泉

LOCATION: Nyuto Onsen group

*Milky baths and thatch buildings
in a primeval setting.*

RATE: From ¥10,000 w/2 meals. **CREDIT CARDS:** Not accepted. **ROOMS:** 20 Japanese style (w/o bath). **COMMUNAL BATHS:** 6—2 men's, 2 women's, 1 mixed, 1 outdoor mixed bath. **CHECK-IN:** 14:00. **CHECK-OUT:** 9:00. **CLOSED:** Nov–Apr. **LANGUAGE:** No English, reservations in Japanese.

☎ 0187–46–2214 Fax: 0187–46–2280
2–1 Kuroyusawa, Obonai, Tazawako-machi, Semboku-gun, Akita 014–1201
〒014–1201   秋田県仙北郡田沢湖町生保内黒湯沢2–1

■ **ACCESS**
BY TRAIN: 55 min by bus from Tazawako Stn (JR Tazawako Line).
BY CAR: 1 hr 40 min via Routes 46 & 341 from Morioka IC (Tohoku Expressway).

Kuro-yu

The road that links the hot springs in the Nyuto Onsen group—part of what is called the "New" Narrow Road to the Deep North—ends in a confusion of signs. So I ended up leaving the car at a dead end where the sign pointed to Magoroku Onsen. The Kuro-yu Onsen was supposed to be just round the bend from there.

The fifteen-minute walk, along a slushy mountain trail in rugged terrain, next to a snow-swelled stream, turned out to be a spectacular way to approach the Kuro-yu Onsen. From this rear approach, the *ryokan* seemed a craggy, steamy, infernal sort of place dotted with old wooden buildings, some charmingly thatched, some for sleeping, some for bathing. Though the buildings look like they have been there since Edo times, the oldest one is only about seventy years old. The loveliest of them was built especially for a visit by a member of the imperial family and has been locked up ever since.

Thermal waters bubbling up at Kuro-yu

When I tried to make a reservation at the Kuro-yu Onsen, there were rooms left only in the *jisuibu*, the self-cooking section. This was a chance for a new experience. In the *jisuibu*, a thin *futon* in a sparse but clean room with torn *shoji* was provided for ¥2,500 a person per night, along with everything needed to cook your own meals. All sorts of people were hard at work in the communal kitchen, washing *daikon* radishes and spinach leaves in the sink, steaming rice, and choosing eating utensils, bowls, and plates from the cupboards. It looked like so much fun I began wishing we had a party of friends along with us, not to mention something better to eat than *oden* stew purchased at a highway rest stop.

Baths are scattered throughout the complex. We first went to the ladies' indoor bath, a big wooden tub brimming with very hot milky water, and with the cold tap at hand. The outdoor pool was a little too small for mixed company, but picturesque with its pillars made of beech-tree trunks. Some people were stood under a stream of water pouring from overhead bamboo pipes to massage their necks and backs. In another indoor *utase-yu* bathhouse, a dachshund was having his third bath of the day in his own private styrene tub (therapy for a hernia). This was one of few inns I had come across where pets were allowed.

Nearby

If you are a hiker, the Nyuto Onsen group is a great place to spend a few days hopping in and out of the different baths in the area while exploring the mountains. After the Kuro-yu Onsen, perhaps try the Magoroku inn (☎ 0187–46–2224) just down the track. Don't miss a trip to Tsuru-no-Yu, about fifteen minutes away by car. The end of winter, when the snow is still on the ground in the beech forests, is an excellent time to see this countryside.

TSURU-NO-YU 鶴ノ湯温泉

LOCATION: Nyuto Onsen group

Euphoric "hidden hot spring" experience.

RATE: From ¥8,000 w/2 meals, ¥3,500 w/o meals, children 20% off. **CREDIT CARDS:** VISA. **ROOMS:** 40 Japanese style (w/o bath). **COMMUNAL BATHS:** 6—men's, women's, mixed, 3 outdoor (2 women's, 1 mixed). **CHECK-IN:** 15:30. **CHECK-OUT:** 10:00. **CLOSED:** 11/16–18. **LANGUAGE:** No English, reservations in Japanese.

☎ 0187–46–2214/2139 Fax: 0187–46–2761

50 Kokuyurin, Aza Sendatsuzawa, Obonai, Tazawako-machi, Semboku-gun, Akita 014–1201

〒014–1201　秋田県仙北郡田沢湖町生保内字先達沢国有林50

■ ACCESS

BY TRAIN: 40 min by bus from Tazawako Stn (JR Tazawako Line).
BY CAR:　90 min via Routes 46 & 341 from Morioka IC (Tohoku Expressway).

Gate to Tsuru-no-Yu

The steep road spirals down into a valley full of beeches to the hot spring gully of Tsuru-no-Yu with its excellent hot spring inn. Lit by oil lamps at night, the thatched-roof lodge provides meals served around your own private *irori* sunken hearth, and the baths are the kind that epitomize the *onsen*.

On weekends and holidays, loads of day tripper dippers and curious tourists come to spy on Tsuru-no-Yu's hidden hot spring charms. But instead of erecting barbed wire fences, the owners apparently decided "if you can't beat 'em, join 'em." They adjusted the facilities for day visitors by increasing the number of baths and adding a rustic café (serving splendid pound cake and excellent coffee, plus some basic meals like curry). It's all done very tastefully. By 5 P.M. all the tourists are gone, leaving guests to their private haven.

Hearth-side meal, Tsuru-no-Yu

When I went in May, there was still some snow on the ground and the beech trees were beginning to bud. Going there in the grip of winter to soak in the outdoor pools with the silence and snow up around your ears must be magical. The Tsuru-no-Yu keeps its roads free of snow all year round, unlike some of the others in the Nyuto group, which become snowbound. Many people combine a visit with daytime skiing.

A word of warning: Tsuru-no-Yu is so popular that it is hard to get a room in the *honkan* (original wing). Don't be tempted, though, into trying the "new wing" fifteen minutes down the road.

TSUTA ONSEN 蔦温泉旅館

LOCATION: Tsuta Onsen

A classic north-country inn, with good old-fashioned food and service, close to the natural wonders of Oirase Gorge and Lake Towada.

RATE: From ¥10,000 w/2 meals, from ¥8,000 w/breakfast, from ¥7,000 w/o meals, children 30–50% off. **CREDIT CARDS:** Not accepted. **ROOMS:** 47 Japanese style, 3 semi-Japanese style—4 rooms w/ bath. **COMMUNAL BATHS:** 2—men's, women's. **CHECK-IN:** 14:00. **CHECK-OUT:** 10:00. **LANGUAGE:** Some English.

☎ 0176–74–2311 Fax: 0176–74–2244
Okuse, Towadako-machi, Kamikita-gun, Aomori 034–0301
〒034–0301　青森県上北郡十和田湖町奥瀬

■ ACCESS
BY TRAIN: 110 min by bus from Aomori Stn (JR Tohoku Main Line).
BY CAR:　90 min via Lake Towada from Kosaka IC (Tohoku Expressway).

Tsuta Onsen

The word *tsuta* means vine, and the owner of the Tsuta Onsen inn says that the name reflects the abundance and variety of vine plants found in the forests around the inn. And vines in all their sinewy forms abound here, thick stocks used in the banisters on staircases, decorating the transoms in some of the rooms, and climbing to the ceiling as pillars. Some of the most impressive examples are found in the barriers between urinals in the shared toilets.

In the wild, most of the vines climb up beech trees, largely because these are the most abundant trees in the area. The beech forests are so vast that the area is known as Lake Towada Jukai—"The Lake Towada Ocean of Trees."

For years Tsuta loomed in my mind as *the* inn to see in Tohoku, but it took me fifteen years to get there. Anticipation of the much-awaited experience at Tsuta Onsen had not prepared me for what was even more impressive than the inn itself—the beauty of Lake Towada and Oirase Gorge, and the beech-covered banks of the high mountains that can be experienced on roads to and from the hot spring.

Tsuta Onsen *ryokan*, the patriarch of Tohoku inns, continues to deserve its reputation as a true old-fashioned *ryokan*. Like the generations of owners before him, the present owner of the Tsuta Onsen insists that your evening meal be served in your room in grand old *ryokan* style, regardless of the strain this places on kimono-clad maids who must negotiate several flights of aged wooden stairs to bring you this fourteen-course feast.

Our wing was added to the existing 1920s structure in 1960. If I had realized this, I would have chosen to stay in the distinctive older wing with its lumpy tatami and doors without locks. At least we were spared the carpet and steel of the 1995 hotel-style addition. However, all guests are served breakfast in the new dining room of this wing, a pleasant area with big picture windows that look out onto the garden.

In 1996 the inn rebuilt its ancient bathhouse—a blackened old place that was made entirely of beechwood—and created separate facilities with cathedral-high ceilings. Now only the floors are made of beech planks, while the walls are made of cypress-smelling *asunaro* wood, also from the nearby forests.

MAGARI-YA 民宿 曲がり家

LOCATION: Tono

*Rare L-shaped wooden farmhouse that serves
excellent grilled foods around an open hearth.*

RATE: From ¥9,800 w/2 meals, no children. **CREDIT CARDS:** Not accepted. **ROOMS:** 15 Japanese style (w/o bath). **COMMUNAL BATHS:** 2—men's, women's. **CHECK-IN:** 16:00. **CHECK-OUT:** 9:00. **LANGUAGE:** No English, reservations in Japanese.

☎ 0198–62–4564
30–58–3 Niisato, Ayaori-cho, Tono-shi, Iwate 028–0531
〒028–0531　岩手県遠野市綾織町新里30–58–3

■ ACCESS
BY TRAIN: 10 min by car from Tono Stn (JR Kamaishi Line).
BY CAR:　1 hr via Routes 107 & 283 from Kitakami/Ezuriko IC (Tohoku Expressway).

"Magari-ya" is the generic name for the L-shaped farmhouses that were once common in Tono. People and animals lived under the same roof in the *magari-ya*—humans in the long part of the L, horses and cows in the short leg. (Tono was traditionally a horse-breeding district, originally of draft horses and later of horses for war.)

When I first visited in 1994 I expected to see sterile renovated *magari-ya,* but I did not anticipate finding *magari-ya* "in the wild." So it was thrilling to drive around the seven villages that make up Tono and find quite a number of these impressive structures still standing. On closer inspection, however, more than a few of them revealed gaping holes in their thatch—the result of heavy rains in 1993—and they were simply crumbling away at the backs of properties since nobody had the money to repair them.

Magari-ya

Magari-ya is a well-preserved *magari-ya*, and its constantly burning open hearth helps preserve the thatch by killing insects that may breed there. The perpetual fire in the hearth also fills the inn with smoke, which is forever getting in your eyes. But you forgive any discomfort after sampling the excellent food at the Magari-ya, which consists of wild vegetables, free-range chicken, and river fish grilled over the coals.

There are no televisions and no newspapers at Magari-ya. Instead you can ask for a storyteller to come to the inn and recite the ghostly Tono folk tales around the hearth for a fee—or just chat with the other guests and the owner of the inn until he shoos you off to bed after a bath at 10 P.M.

21

KANAZAWA

Kutani ware

ATTRACTIONS

Relics of a sumptuous culture, including a rich legacy of decorative arts and one of Japan's most famous gardens.

During the Edo period (1600–1868), Kaga, which is what Kanazawa was then called, was the richest domain in the land. Kaga was so wealthy that when its lord went to Edo for *sankin kotai* (compulsory castle attendance), he took a retinue of two to three thousand retainers, servants, cooks, stable hands, keepers of the tea utensils, and so on. Sometimes the tail end of the procession had not left the last post station before the front end reached the next one. The Kaga lords became rich and stayed affluent by sponsoring pottery kilns that copied the polychrome export ceramics of the Kyushu kilns, lacquer workshops that produced the highest quality gold-relief lacquerware, and dye shops that shipped elaborately decorated silks around Japan and competed for prestige with Kyoto textiles.

The modern-day Kaga is a mini-Tokyo with all the attendant urban clutter and a cultural heritage harder to ferret out than Kyoto's. But a glimpse of the former glory of the richest domain can be found at such places as the **Kenrokuen garden** (one of Japan's top three); the palatial **Seisonkaku villa**,

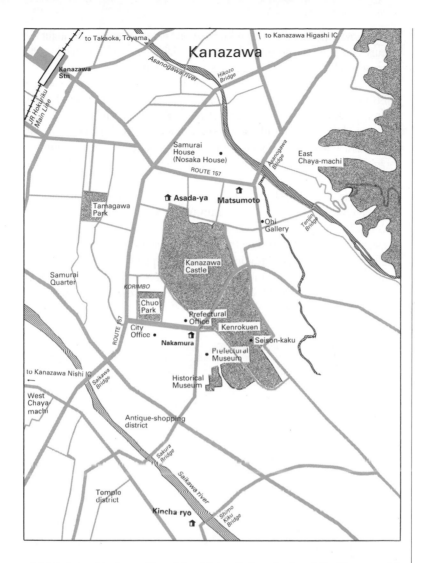

Kanazawa

to Takaoka, Toyama

to Kanazawa Higashi IC

Kanazawa Stn

Asanogawa river

Hikozo Bridge

JR Hokuriku Main Line

Samurai House (Nosaka House)

ROUTE 157

Asanogawa Bridge

East Chaya-machi

Tamagawa Park

Asada-ya   Matsumoto

Ohi Gallery

Tenjin Bridge

Samurai Quarter

KORIMBO

Kanazawa Castle

Chuo Park

Prefectural Office

Kenrokuen

City Office

Nakamura

Seison-kaku

ROUTE 157

to Kanazawa Nishi IC

Saikawa Bridge

Prefectural Museum

West Chaya-machi

Historical Museum

Antique-shopping district

Sakura Bridge

Saikawa river

Temple district

Kincha ryo

Shimo Kiku Bridge

which belonged to the mother of the thirteenth Kaga lord; and the **Nagamachi old samurai quarter**, now in a neighborhood with a Dunkin' Donuts.

One feature of Kanazawa culture very much alive is the use of the startling "traditional Kanazawa colors"—shocking blue and red—on the interior walls of traditional Japanese houses. Some of these blue and red interiors are visible today at the Seisonkaku villa in Kanazawa. The tour guide was adamant that, yes, the walls originally were those colors.

But what of mauve, pink, and lime green? These are some of the other "traditional Kanazawa colors" that the finer inns and eating establishments of Kanazawa are reviving. They certainly are a change from the more earthy, subdued tones of Kyoto. Two very colorful inns, Matsumoto and Kincha-ryo, are listed in this section.

Kanazawa, incidentally, is regarded as second only to Kyoto for the quality of its cuisine, and for the prices at which it is available. The higher-priced inns do offer undeniably superb food experiences, so consider indulging yourself.

Ceramics and lacquerware industries still thrive in Kanazawa, with younger artists moving energetically in new directions. Kutani ware, Kanazawa's famous ceramic, is found in shops that line the streets to Kenrokuen garden.

Lovers of tea ceramics will also enjoy a visit to the **Ohi Gallery**, for a look at the masterpieces of successive generations of Kanazawa's most famous tea ceramics family. However, modern production from this kiln is discouragingly pricey.

Several inns are listed here for Kanazawa itself, but also consider hot spring resorts outside of Kanazawa. One is **Yamanaka Onsen**, site of the unusual Cat's Cradle Bridge, where the Kayo-tei inn signals relief from the big-city frenzy of Kanazawa. If you fly into Komatsu Airport, a good first stop before going into Kanazawa is Yamanaka (thirty minutes from the airport).

More comprehensive information on Kanazawa is available in *Gateway to Japan* by June Kinoshita and Nicholas Palevsky, or *Kanazawa* by Ruth Stevens (Kanazawa Tourist Association).

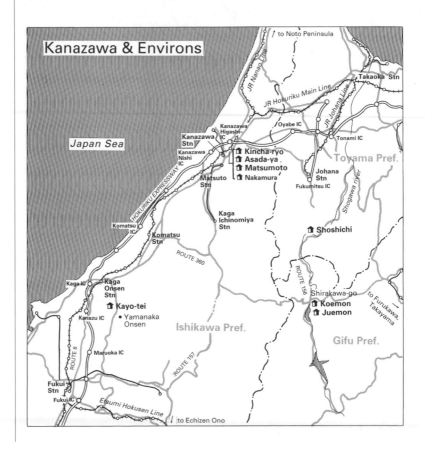

Kutani ware ceramics: even mass-production pieces can be very attractive and are at least reasonably priced. Also watch for examples of the somberly elegant **Echizen ware**, a natural ash glaze pottery from neighboring Fukui Prefecture. **Yamanaka lacquerware** is a less expensive alternative to Wajima lacquerware. I was told by the chagrined lacquerers of Yamanaka that in the Edo period (1600–1868) their wood-turning and lacquering skills used to be far superior to Wajima's, but Wajima eventually beat them at the marketing game.

Recommended trips including Kanazawa

- Kanazawa and/or Yamanaka Onsen (1–2 nights)
  —Noto Peninsula (2–3 nights, Destination 22)
- Kanazawa and/or Yamanaka Onsen (1–2 nights)—Eiheiji (day trip)—
  Echizen Ono (1 night at Asahi Ryokan, see Alternative Inns)

KINCHA-RYO 金茶寮

LOCATION: Kanazawa City

Kanazawa's picturesque, secluded, and sumptuous VIP retreat, home of formal Kanazawa cuisine.

RATE: From ¥30,000 w/2 meals. **CREDIT CARDS:** AMEX, DC, VISA. **ROOMS:** 5 Japanese style (w/bath). **COMMUNAL BATHS:** None. **CHECK-IN:** 16:00. **CHECK-OUT:** 10:00. **CLOSED:** 12/26–1/4. **LANGUAGE:** English spoken. Some German.

076–243–2121 Fax: 076–244–1411
1–8–50 Tera-machi, Kanazawa-shi, Ishikawa 921–8033
〒921-8033　石川県金沢市寺町1-8-50

■ ACCESS
BY TRAIN: 20 min by car from Kanazawa Stn (JR Hokuriku Main Line).
BY CAR: 20 min (7 km) from Kanazawa Nishi IC (Hokuriku Expressway).

The Kincha-ryo is head and shoulders above other Kanazawa inns when it comes to location. This former villa of a principal Kaga clan retainer looks out over the Sai River, and has six rooms in separate *sukiya*-style buildings that cascade down the steep hill among azaleas, maples, and cherries.

The maids here make sure that guests don't ever have to meet one another on the paths or in the lobby, by ushering them discreetly in and out of back and front entrances using a system of signals. This attention to privacy is essential for the Japanese politicians and VIPs who choose the Kincha-ryo as a retreat for themselves or their overseas guests. The stunning lady of the house has a manner as fresh and natural as a spring breeze, and even the stern-faced Henry Kissinger is said to have melted into smiles under her gentle care.

Among Kanazawa locals, the Kincha-ryo is recognized for high-class private

Voluptuous Kincha-ryo room

dining. Less well known is that this expensive *ryotei* on the hill also serves as an inn. The second-generation master of the Kincha-ryo is a top chef himself, following in the footsteps of his father, the very man who is said to have created the original *Kaga kaiseki*—Kanazawa's famed formal cuisine—after a long apprenticeship in Kyoto kitchens.

Essential to every Kaga meal is *gori-jiru* (a white miso soup containing an ugly but delectable little fish called *gori*), *jibu-ni* (a stew with generous amounts of meat and vegetables), and *ama-ebi* (small, sweet prawns served raw). At the Kincha-ryo, fish are not taken from their tanks until a guest has placed an order.

Kanazawa natives are proud of the sumptuousness of their culture, and rooms of amazing hues can be found in many city inns and restaurants. The Kincha-ryo is no exception: Henry Kissinger's suite was mauve. Colored rooms are novel, but my favorite at the Kincha-ryo is the somber-walled O-chin, an ancient suite with an equally ancient (150-year-old) tearoom attached. O-chin is reserved exclusively for private dining.

Nearby

Kincha-ryo is in Tera-machi, the temple quarter that houses seventy temples. Among them is Myoryuji, better known as the Ninja temple, where a guided tour reveals the concealed rooms, secret passages, and emergency escape hatches used by the ninja, the sixteenth-century spies employed by the shogunate and local lords. Tours by appointment (☏ 0762–41–2877).

ASADA-YA 浅田屋

LOCATION:
Kanazawa City

Hushed, exclusive Kyoto-style inn, priding itself on its elegant cuisine.

RATE: From ¥50,000 w/2 meals. **CREDIT CARDS:** AMEX, DC, VISA. **ROOMS:** 5 Japanese style (w/bath). **COMMUNAL BATHS:** 1—private (*kazoku-buro*). **CHECK-IN:** 14:00. **CHECK-OUT:** 11:00. **LANGUAGE:** Some English.

☏ 076–231–2228 Fax: 076–231–2229
23 Jukken-machi, Kanazawa-shi, Ishikawa 920–0906
〒920–0906　石川県金沢市十間町23

■ ACCESS
BY TRAIN: 5 min by car from Kanazawa Stn (JR Hokuriku Main Line).
BY CAR:　20 min (7 km) from Kanazawa Nishi IC (Hokuriku Expressway).

Right across the street from the Omi-cho Market, with its mountains of crabs and other seafood that end up daily in the best kitchens of Kanazawa, is the Asada-ya, one of the city's most expensive inns.

To overcome the inner-city malady of limited space for rooms and gardens, the owners pulled down the former thirty-three-room Asada-ya at the start of the 1980s and built a luxury establishment of just five rooms. Four of these rooms have their own tiny gardens, while another has an indoor rock garden.

Only the best will do at the Asada-ya. Upon your arrival the staff welcomes you in the inn's hushed reception room with its exquisitely crafted Hida-style *hibachi*, and serve you a salty-plum-flavored beverage followed by whisked green tea and a sweet from the city's most exclusive confectioner. You are then guided to your room, past corridors lined with glass cases displaying the inn's fine collection of sword hilts.

The flower arrangement in the alcove of your sparse but impeccably appointed room deserves special attention. It will be the creation of the owner's daughter-in-law, who takes care of the day-to-day running of the inn, and who has a passion for wild flowers. "I keep a collection of wild plants in pots at home to be able to gauge when each of them will be coming into bloom in the mountains. They usually bloom in the mountains about a week later, and that's when I get in the car and go off on flower hunts," she said.

Understated Asada-ya elegance

The great joy for a guest staying at the Asada-ya is the evening's gourmandizing. Asada-ya's *kaiseki* meal is partly Kaga style and partly international in origin. The chef enjoys using non-Japanese ingredients, so your meal might begin with the freshest raw sweet prawns served with caviar, followed by shark-fin soup and foie gras.

Each dish is brought to your room and you are pampered in the very best of Japanese traditions. The Asada-ya sometimes has foreign VIPs staying for several days in a row; different menus, with the main dish alternating between fish and beef, are then prepared each day. Breakfast is either *asagayu*, a delicate rice gruel with deluxe accompaniments, or Western style with toast and jam. Like all the best inns, the Asada-ya keeps a record of guests' preferences to ensure perfect service next time.

The Asada-ya was not always so sumptuous. The proprietress remembers nothing but hard work from the inn's former incarnation as a thirty-three-room travelers' lodge. "We couldn't afford to have laundry done for us so we had to do it all ourselves, and that included washing and starching all the linen. We even made the starch ourselves from rice. And we sewed all the *yukata*. I much prefer it these days."

MATSUMOTO 料理旅館 まつ本

LOCATION: Kanazawa City

Startling Kanazawa colors are on parade in the newly renovated interiors of this former restaurant. The food is upmarket hot-pot cooking.

RATE: From ¥25,000 w/2 meals, children 30% off. **CREDIT CARDS:** VISA. **ROOMS:** 10 Japanese style (3 w/bath). **COMMUNAL BATH:** 1—alternating. **CHECK-IN:** 16:00. **CHECK-OUT:** 10:00. **CLOSED:** 12/31–1/3. **LANGUAGE:** No English, reservations in Japanese.

☏ 0762–21–0302 Fax: 0762–21–0303
1–7–2 Owari-cho Kanazawa-shi, Ishikawa 920–0902
〒920–0902　石川県金沢市尾張町1–7–2

■ ACCESS
BY TRAIN: 10 min by car from Kanazawa Stn (JR Hokuriku Main Line).
BY CAR: 20 min from Kanazawa Higashi IC (Hokuriku Expressway).

Matsumoto

When this inn undertook expensive renovations in the 1980s (¥200 million was spent on two rooms alone), it created rooms in all three of the so-called "Kaga-colors": military blue, red, and lime green. With the exception of the red room, whose atmosphere is rich and warm, the result is an intense assault to the senses. This is not to say you should not try them—for a change.

For a more restful atmosphere there's the *hanare*, a handsome converted plaster storehouse. Thick white and black doors lead into a dining room downstairs with its own garden; upstairs are sleeping quarters with "non-Kaga-colored" walls.

The storehouse was attached to a home that was the residence of a timber merchant during the Edo period (1600–1868). In 1930 it was turned into an inn specializing in *yosenabe*, a hot-pot of seafood, meat, and vegetables. This was a novelty in Kanazawa, where hot-pot cooking was regarded strictly as home fare.

Yosenabe meal, Matsumoto

The inn's present proprietor not only refurbished the inn but built a reputation for quality food. The hot-pot (available September to April) includes winter delicacies from the Sea of Japan—sea bream, crab, sweet prawns, and angler fish—in a tasty broth simmered slowly over hot coals. In other seasons the inn serves formal Kaga cuisine, which includes duck with *shiitake* mushrooms and *jibu-ni*, a soup containing copious servings of *sudare-fu*, an interesting wheat-gluten product.

Nearby

Matsumoto is a block or so away from Terajima Kurando-tei, a two-hundred-year-old house that once belonged to a middle-ranking samurai. Although not lavish, it has exquisite details in the furnishings and a special tranquility. Note the lovely tearoom with its unusual door.

KAYO-TEI　かよう亭

LOCATION: Yamanaka Onsen

Exclusive establishment in a serene hot spring town offering unforgettable food.

RATE∕ATE: From ¥30,000 w/2 meals, from ¥20,000 w/breakfast, from ¥15,000 w/o meals, children 50% off. **CREDIT CARDS:** VISA. **ROOMS:** 10 Japanese style (6 w/bath). **COMMUNAL BATHS:** 2—men's, women's. **CHECK-IN:** 12:00. **CHECK-OUT:** 12:00. **LANGUAGE:** English spoken.

☎ 07617–8–1410 Fax: 07617–8–1121
1–Ho–20 Higashi-cho, Yamanaka-machi, Enuma-gun, Ishikawa 922–0114
〒922–0114　石川県江沼郡山中町東町1–ホ–20

■ ACCESS
BY TRAIN: 15 min by car from Kaga Onsen Stn (JR Hokuriku Main Line).
BY CAR:　20 min via Route 364 from Kaga IC (Hokuriku Expressway).

In 1978, when every other inn in Japan seemed to be adding new wings as fast as they could pour cement, the owner of the Kayo-tei tore down his family's forty-room establishment to build in its place an inn of intimate proportions with food for gourmets.

Kayo-tei's success is due to a chef who does not think it too much trouble to drive the hour to the Shiramine Mountains just to pick butterbur and wild fern fronds for tempura. Dinner is an exquisitely aesthetic affair of the best mouthwatering seafood and mountain vegetables from the Sea of Japan region. I especially loved breakfast at the Kayo-tei, where brittle sheets of rare *iwanori* (dried river algae) were served with their own small brazier to keep them crisp until we were precisely ready to eat them. A maid prepared a delicate soup with freshly made *yuba* (soy milk curds) at the table and grilled delicious *hata-hata* fish over another miniature brazier while we savored succulent bite-size Japanese omelettes.

Path to Kayo-tei

The Kayo-tei will not wake its guests in the morning until they are ready to be woken, unlike many inns, which rouse you from sleep for breakfast more to suit their own timetable than the guest's. Another welcome detail is the provision of complimentary *tabi* (split-toed socks) for guests, along with *yukata* cotton robes. You can wear the *tabi* or walk barefoot throughout the inn on the lovely rush matting. All of the rooms are on the same floor; there are no elevators or stairs, except for the stairs up from the reception.

The only disappointment at the Kayo-tei might be the bath. Though it uses hot spring water, it lacks the sophistication given to the rest of the inn.

Nearby

Yamanaka Onsen is a sleepy hot spring town beside a picturesque gorge, half an hour from Kanazawa. The Kayo-tei is at the start of a scenic riverside walking course along the gorge, which is distinguished by a small thatched arbor dedicated to the poet Matsuo Basho (1644–94). Basho wrote several poems in praise of the area. The walk continues for 1.3 kilometers (0.8 miles) along a winding river where egrets alight on rocks, and where little shrines and Buddhist guardians are cared for and given daily offerings of food and flowers by the locals.

Do walk this path at least as far as the Cat's Cradle Bridge (*Ayatori-bashi*), which was built in the 1980s by the famous flower artist Hiroshi Teshigahara (1927–). This outrageous purple-colored bridge with its sinuous, twisting form somehow looks perfect where it is. If you have the energy to continue farther, you will find the second of Yamanaka Onsen's three famous bridges, an all-cypress span called the Cricket Bridge (*Korogi-bashi*), which is torn down and rebuilt every twenty years—just like the Grand Shrines of Ise. The third well-known bridge is made of stone.

The Kiku-no-Yu men's public bath in its classic bathhouse is the other main attraction in Yamanaka. Across from it is an even more astonishing public lavatory complex. To enter this facility, you will need to walk under a sheet of water. There is a covered path, but you will still get splashed. A whole book could be written about the imaginative public facilities that were built around Japan in the cash-crazed "bubble" years of the 1980s.

22

NOTO PENINSULA

Coastline, Suzu

ATTRACTIONS

Some of the most untouched coastal and mountain scenery in Japan; pristine villages. In Noto is Wajima, home of refined lacquerware; also two of the best-value inns in the land.

Sosogi coast

The logical extension of a trip to Kanazawa is to travel up the Noto Peninsula. I recommend driving—driving is easy on Noto, and once you get out onto the country roads, highly rewarding. I especially enjoyed the sunset drive up the rugged top end of the peninsula's **west coast** (Oku-Noto) to Wajima. Along this coast I found one unsullied seaside village after another—like the Japan of old and not some pachinko parlor–infested wasteland.

Before reaching Wajima make a detour to **Monzen**, where you can take in the soaring **Sojiji**, an important Soto Zen temple. It is an impressive sight, and it is possible to stay in the *shukubo* (temple lodgings) there. Staying in this real training temple must be a wonderful experience, but they advise all but the hardiest travelers to avoid the winter months since no heating is provided. You are woken at 3:30 A.M.—you have no choice in the matter—to attend the early-morning Buddhist service. Softies may forgo the accommodation and book here for a lunch of Buddhist vegetarian cuisine. To make a reservation (for either food or accommodation), submit an application in writing a week in advance (☎ 0768–42–0005; in Japanese).

In Wajima itself, the big attraction is supposed to be the morning market (from 8 A.M. on the main strip), but fame has gone to its head and the market is now littered with too many cheap souvenirs and too little local produce. Still the weather-beaten farming and fishing women who bring in their wares to sell make a short visit worthwhile.

The quality of genuine **Wajima lacquerware** is legendary and you will see dozens of lacquerware shops in Wajima. Beware the plastic imitations and those with bases made of compressed sawdust instead of quality wood.

The Noto Peninsula has two superb contemporary inns: the Urushi-no-Yado Yashiki in Wajima, and the Sakamoto inn at Suzu on the opposite coast. Do try to experience both of them. On the way from Wajima to Suzu, I suggest stopping to explore the grand **Tokikuni-ke** houses at Sosogi. They belonged to a powerful local family descended from a noble of the Taira clan, which was defeated in a war with the Minamoto and banished here in 1185. The butterfly crest is that of the Taira.

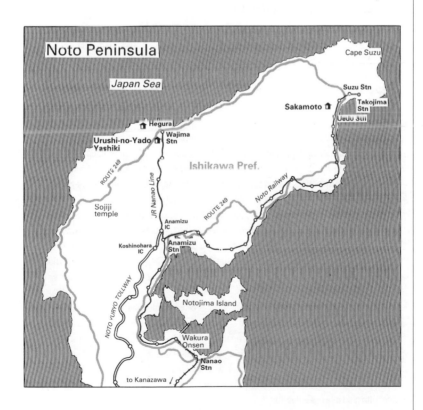

Good lacquerware is the obvious choice. You can observe two streams of lacquer craft in Wajima today: the traditional black or red with gold relief decoration; and the contemporary stream led by such artists as Isaburo Kado, who first brought the linen layer to the surface of bowls for the pure enjoyment of its texture (see side-bar for more information on Wajima lacquer). Examples of contemporary lacquer work can be seen at two excellent shops in Wajima: Tefu-tefu (☏ 0768–22–6304) and Quai, both under the same ownership. At these shops you may also find the rare black Suzu pottery, and handmade products by paper artist Kyomi Tomi, who lives just outside Wajima City.

Another of Wajima's famous products is *yubeshi*, a confection made in a complicated process by stuffing a hollowed *yuzu* citrus fruit with the fruit's flesh mixed with miso paste, and then drying it. The preserve is eaten in paper-thin slices.

Recommended trip including the Noto Peninsula

● Kanazawa (1–2 nights, Destination 21)—Wajima/Sojiji (1–2 nights)—Suzu (1 night at Sakamoto)

In Praise of Wajima Lacquerware

Lacquerware has been produced in Wajima for over a thousand years, evolving into a product that is durable, spotlessly finished, and laboriously decorated. While the craftsmanship is impeccable, the real reason for the success of Wajima lacquerware in the marketplace has been aggressive marketing. As early as the Edo period (1600–1868), Wajima salesmen strapped samples to their backs and trudged across the country, selling the product door-to-door. They were particularly attentive to after-sales services, such as repairs that may become necessary after long use.

Making lacquerware is a highly labor-intensive process. It begins by applying a layer of dichotomous clay to fill the grainy surface of the wooden base, attaching linen cloth to the base and rim to prevent breakages when dropped, and then applying layer after layer of lacquer, each of which requires humid conditions and up to a week to dry before the next layer is added. After this comes decoration with gold relief or engraving work.

This is the stuff of heirlooms. In the past, nearly every household in Japan owned at least one set of Wajima bowls and stacked lacquer boxes for special occasions, and these were passed down from generation to generation. They would be polished with veneration and stored away after each use, the patina becoming more beautiful with age. When, after several generations, they were chipped or cracked, the owners would send them back to the original maker in Wajima for sanding and relacquering.

Such establishments still exist, but the number of people who make use of them has greatly declined. Genuine handmade lacquerware is beyond the means of the average modern household, so people tend to buy the cheaper imitations (with bases of compressed sawdust or plastic), and lacquerware gets a bad name. It is a tragedy, one which is being alleviated only by the energy of some modern lacquer artists who have been boosting the popularity of lacquerware by taking it in new directions, exploring its textural potential rather than decorating elaborately with gold relief (see Recommended buys).

URUSHI-NO-YADO YASHIKI
うるしの宿やしき

*Tastefully renovated inn, serving an
inspired sampling of traditional Wajima food.*

RATE: From ¥15,000 w/2 meals, children 30% off. **CREDIT CARDS:** Not accepted. **ROOMS:** 8 Japanese style (1 w/bath) **COMMUNAL BATHS:** 3—men's, women's, 1 private (*kazoku-buro*). **CHECK-IN:** 15:00. **CHECK-OUT:** 10:00. **LANGUAGE:** No English, reservations in Japanese.

☎ 0768–22–0138 Fax: 0768–22–5729

15 Kawai-cho, Wajima-shi, Ishikawa 928–0001

〒928–0001　石川県輪島市河井町15

■ ACCESS
BY TRAIN: 3 min by car from Wajima Stn (Noto Railway).
BY CAR:　22 km from Anamizu IC (Noto Yuryo Tollway).

"Urushi-no-Yado" means "inn of *urushi*" (lacquer craft)—an appropriate name for an inn in Wajima, the home of premium lacquerware *par excellence*. This claim to being the "inn of lacquer craft" would have been reason enough for some inns to install black-lacquered toilet seats with gold-relief cherry blossoms. But the lacquer at Urushi-no-Yado Yashiki appears in only the most modest of forms, evoking quiet respect in the glowing black edges on the sliding doors, as a light coating on the exposed wooden surfaces, and in the excellent Meiji-Taisho dinner bowls and plates. Some exquisite examples of superb lacquer craft—in the form of exquisitely decorated bowls and trays—are displayed in the reception room inside an original *urushi* mixing tub.

Urushi-tree pillar, contrasted with pink and gray walls, Urushi-no-Yado Yashiki.

Two other features of this inn are worth noting. The quiet pink and gray of the interior walls, a subtle change from brown, is highly attractive, and in most rooms an actual *urushi* tree trunk is used as a pillar in the alcoves, the wood still showing the cuttings in the bark from which the *urushi* was extracted. All in all, the inn is an inspiring example of what can be done to renovate a Japanese interior tastefully—and thank goodness for the interior, because Yashiki wouldn't attract a second look if one passed it on the street.

Urushi-no-Yado has been an inn since 1935, but the third-generation owner began renovating at the end of the 1980s, first by knocking out walls to make the sixteen small rooms into eight large ones. These range in size from six- to fifteen-mat. All rooms bear names that are connected with lacquer crafting.

Wajima is not only a town of lacquer. It has a major culinary legacy as well, and for those jaded by *kaiseki* cuisine, dinner at the Yashiki will deliver plenty of surprises. Why not vegetable broth in two-inch thick wooden bowls warmed with a sizzling-hot rock inside, or crab claws grilled on hot rocks at the table? These special heat-retaining rocks come from a place called Kameyo on the Noto Peninsula.

Incidentally, soup in Wajima is quite often not the familiar broth of giant kelp or fish but what is known as *ishiru*, which is made with squid and is reminiscent of Thailand's *nam pla*.

At night there are also handmade soba noodles, and in the morning handmade tofu. You haven't tasted tofu until you've eaten it like this.

SAKAMOTO さか本

LOCATION: Suzu City

Unusual modern epicurean's inn serving the finest natural produce and handmade soba and tofu; guests dine together around a beautiful open hearth.

Mr. Sakamoto tends the hearth

RATE: From ¥13,000 w/2 meals. **CREDIT CARDS:** Not accepted. **ROOMS:** 4 Japanese style (w/o bath). **COMMUNAL BATHS:** 2—stone bath, lacquer bath—each alternating. **CHECK-IN:** 15:00. **CHECK-OUT:** 10:00. **CLOSED:** Jan, Feb. **LANGUAGE:** No English, reservations in Japanese.

☏ 0768–82–0584
Uedo-machi Jisha, Suzu-shi, Ishikawa 927–1216
〒927–1216　石川県珠洲市上戸町寺社

Tefu-tefu

■ ACCESS
BY TRAIN: 15 min on foot from Uedo Stn (Noto Railway Line).
BY CAR:　50 km via Route 249 from Anamizu IC (Noto Yuryo Doro).

Shinichiro Sakamoto, owner-chef of the Sakamoto, is up at daybreak making breakfast. He makes the soup and steams the rice, and also prepares the tofu that goes with it—from scratch. Making tofu is a process that alone requires a couple of hours of work, and Mr. Sakamoto never does things by half measures—he gets salt water from the Sea of Japan to use as a natural coagulant.

When I stayed at the Sakamoto, it was his day to buy a fresh supply of *himono* (sun-dried fish), so he piled everyone from the inn into his minivan (fortunately there is room for only six guests at the inn) for a ride to the beachside hut of his favorite supplier, a sun-dried gent himself who lovingly dries his fish so they are pink and impeccably clean.

Back at the inn, the little fish went straight onto the charcoal grill in the open hearth while we dug into his delicious tofu, miso soup, and mix of brown and white rice.

The night before we also had a culturally eclectic dinner with some very good Okinawan white liquor and hilarious conversation. Mr. Sakamoto made his own soba and also served up delicious rare mushrooms.

In spite of a physical disability that makes it difficult for him to walk, let alone cook and run an inn, Mr. Sakamoto is a world traveler and a man of the finest taste in all things—a true epicure. Dishes, trays, cups, glasses, and bowls used at the inn are hand-picked from the work of the best contemporary crafts-men in Noto.

His sensibilities show in the *ryokan* itself. Before rebuilding the old inn that he had inherited from his father, he spent months poring over plans with top Wajima architect Shinji Takagi to design a place that would retain the best of Noto architecture and reflect the Noto way of life. The result is a simple wooden structure made from local *asunaro* timber, which is coated with *urushi* lacquer for durability. As is typical of traditional Japanese architecture, the cooking hearth is the center of all things. Two guest rooms on the upper level are reached by a narrow balcony overlooking the hearth. They are beautiful and sparse, with lovely, slightly curved wooden ceilings.

The three guest rooms do not have toilets or baths, but this gives you a chance to experience one of the many unique characteristics of the Sakamoto—the toilets are reached via a wide corridor open to the elements. It makes for a bracing walk in winter. The washbasins are also open, permitting the refreshing experience of brushing your teeth with a full breeze on your face while meditating on a garden.

Don't quote me on this, but as far as I know the Sakamoto has the only lac-querware bathtub in the world. It sits by a window because Mr. Sakamoto's dream was to have a bath into which the moonlight flooded. "There's nothing lovelier than a woman in a moonlit bath," he said. (This does not mean that Mr. Sakamoto has a peephole to spy on moonlit ladies.) The moon wasn't out the night I was there, but sitting in this lacquered bathtub was like being enveloped in satin.

Incidentally, Mr. Sakamoto does not provide complimentary toothbrushes nor the small washing towels that you receive at other inns, believing that this is a waste of expense that can better be spent on other more important things—like the food and their vessels. Nor does he pamper guests with overly attentive service. Even so, everything about the Sakamoto sets it apart from every other *ryokan* I have ever experienced. The Sakamoto breaks all the molds and does it with great success.

Nearby

The Sakamoto is located in the town of Suzu, home to a very unusual form of pottery called *Suzu-yaki*. This ceramic ware is easily distinguished by its black color and a sparkling surface, due to the carbon in the clay. This pottery, which died out from the end of the fifteenth century to the early sixteenth century, has seen a revival in the last twenty years. If you cannot find any in Suzu itself, try the Quai or Tefu-tefu (☎ 0768–22–6304) shops in Wajima City. These are both owned by innovative lacquer artist Kunikatsu Seto.

23

KYOTO

Shin'nyo-do temple

ATTRACTIONS

The great center of aristocratic culture for 1,200 years. Kyoto was not bombed in World War II, so much more of the old city remains than in Tokyo. Just outside Kyoto is the former castle town of Hikone and an hour away is the idyllic farm village of Miyama-cho.

David Kidd, a late Kyoto personality who lived there for over twenty years, said that Kyoto "gets uglier and uglier" as you drive through the ancient capital. "Get off the main streets and walk," was his advice. Diane Durston, who explores the traditional shops and inns of the city in her excellent guide, *Old Kyoto*, makes a similar recommendation.

The first-time visitor to Kyoto should also guard against temple burnout by taking the best ones in small doses. These include **Kinkakuji** (Golden Pavilion) and **Ginkakuji** (Silver Pavilion), which were the villas of aristocrats and are now temples; **Ryoanji**, the temple that houses the most famous Zen garden; and **Sanjusangendo**, with its one thousand statues covered in gold leaf. **Kiyomizu temple** is also popular, in good part due to the shopping on the steep lanes—**Ninenzaka, Sannenzaka, and Gojozaka**—leading up to its hill-

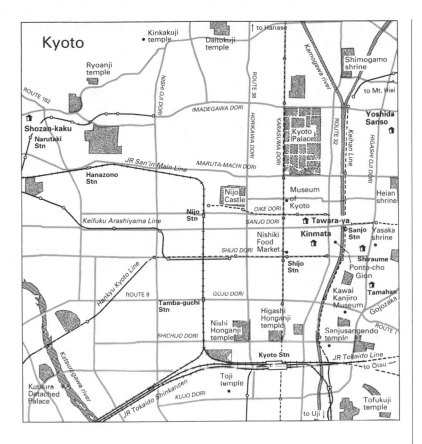

Kyoto

Kinkakuji temple
Daitokuji temple
↑ to Hanase
Ryoanji temple
Shimogamo shrine
ROUTE 162
to Mt. Hiei
NISHI OJI DORI
ROUTE 38
HORIKAWA DORI
KARASUMA DORI
Kamogawa river
ROUTE 32
Keihan Line
HIGASHI OJI DORI
IMADEGAWA DORI
Yoshida Sanso
↑ Shozan-kaku
Kyoto Palace
Narutaki Stn
JR San'in Main Line
MARUTA-MACHI DORI
Hanazono Stn
Keifuku Arashiyama Line
Nijo Castle
Museum of Kyoto
Heian shrine
Nijo Stn
OIKE DORI
Hankyu Kyoto Line
SANJO DORI
↑ Tawara-ya
Nishiki Food Market
Kinmata ↑
Sanjo Stn
Yasaka shrine
SHIJO DORI
Shiraume
Ponto-cho Gion
Shijo Stn
ROUTE 9
GOJO DORI
Kawai Kanjiro Museum
Tamahan
Tamba-guchi Stn
Gojozaka
ROUTE 1
Higashi Honganji temple
Nishi Honganji temple
SHICHIJO DORI
Sanjusangendo temple
Kyoto Stn
JR Tokaido Line
to Otsu
Katsuragawa river
JR Tokaido Shinkansen
KUJO DORI
Toji temple
Kutsura Detached Palace
Tofukuji temple
to Uji ↓

side perch. On **Gojozaka**, which is packed with ceramics shops, you are just a ten-minute walk from the home of the late potter and mystic **Kawai Kanjiro** (1890–1966), whose inspiring house and workshop are open to the public. Longtime residents of Kyoto almost without exception recommend walking on the **Philosopher's Path** by an old canal lined with cherry trees, linking Ginkakuji and **Nanzenji** temples. I also recommend **Hakusa Sonso Garden** on the Philosopher's Path, built by the artist Kansetsu Hashimoto (1883–1957) in 1916, and another stunningly composed garden in northeast Kyoto at the **Shisendo temple**, formerly the villa of writer and calligrapher Ishikawa Jozan (1583–1672).

Nijo Palace is magnificent, with its squeaky "nightingale floorboards" designed to warn against approaching intruders. For a complete change of pace, stroll the **Nishiki food market**. It is a short walk from there to the **Museum of Kyoto** on Sanjo Street.

At night head to **Pontocho** or **Gion**. The big **antique/flea markets** of Kyoto are at Toji temple—rain or shrine—on the twenty-first of every month, and at Kitano Shrine on the twenty-fifth. **Shimmonzen** and **Furumonzen streets** are also for antique hunters.

You might want to leave some time at the end of your Kyoto visit to explore **Kyoto Station**, which has the feeling of a set for *2001: A Space Odyssey*. The top is reached by ascending its *Stairway to Heaven* escalators.

It is impossible to list all of the great classic inns in Kyoto. I chose to give the space over to some slightly less expensive, more interesting alternatives that retain the Kyoto feel. Of the classics, Tawara-ya remains the quintessential Kyoto inn, but other superb inns deserving mention include Sumi-ya (☎ 075–221–2188), the tea aficionados' favorite, and Hiiragi-ya (☎ 075–221–1136), which also has a more affordable branch called Hiiragi-ya Bekkan (☎ 075–231–0151). For inns under ¥8,000, see page 276.

HIKONE (ONE HOUR BY TRAIN FROM KYOTO)

One of Japan's great statesmen, Ii Naosuke (1815–60), had his **castle** in Hikone. After undergoing a major renovation in the 1990s, it now houses a **museum** with a small but thoughtfully displayed collection of superb armor, and Noh masks and costumes. There is also a **Noh stage**. The Ii family were great patrons of Noh and the other arts.

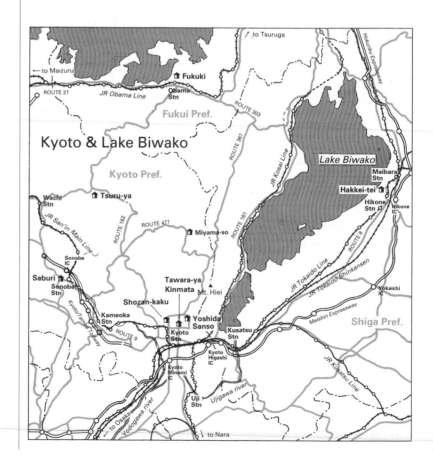

Not far away is the family's former pleasure villa, **Hakkei-tei**, which is now an inn (see listing in this section), with a **stroll garden**, **Genkyu-en**, open to the public.

Hikone City has been working hard to tidy up the town and has built a replica row of old shops called the **Yume Kyobashi Castle Road.** Ask for information in English at the tourist information office next to Hikone Station.

There are also two interesting temples in the Hikone vicinity: **Ryotanji**, which has a raked stone garden, and **Tenneiji**, home to five hundred statues of Rakan (Buddha's saints)—there's a face in there that you know. Also recommended is the Koto-Sanzan bus tour to see, among other things, **Hyakusaiji**. This is the oldest temple in Shiga Prefecture, with a superb garden that borrows scenery from the Suzuka Mountains.

Recommended buys

In Kyoto, paper, incense, fans, and pottery. For other recommendations, see Diane Durston's *Old Kyoto*.

Recommended trips including Kyoto

The list is endless. Kyoto was the center of culture for so long that all the places of the greatest cultural and historical interest seem to be packed around it. I mentioned Hikone, but there is also Nara (Destination 24) and Miyama-cho (Destination 28), both of which have their own sections in this book. Other recommendations are Tamba Sasayama, Uji, Ohara, Shigaraki, and Kurodani (see *Old Kyoto*).

- Nara (1–2 nights, Destination 24)—Kyoto (2–3 nights)
- Kyoto (2–3 nights)—Miyama-cho (1 night)—Obama/Ama-no-Hashidate (1 night, Destination 28)
- Kyoto (2 nights)—Hikone (1 night)

TAWARA-YA 俵屋旅館

LOCATION:
Central Kyoto

Kyoto's most famous inn, deserving of its reputation.

RATE: From ¥35,000 w/2 meals, children 30% off. **CREDIT CARDS:** AMEX, VISA. **ROOMS:** 18 Japanese style (w/bath). **COMMUNAL BATHS:** None. **CHECK-IN:** 13:00. **CHECK-OUT:** 11:00. **LANGUAGE:** English spoken.

☎ 075–211–5566 Fax: 075–211–2204
Oike-sagaru, Fuyamachi-dori, Nakagyo-ku, Kyoto-shi, Kyoto 604–8094
〒604–8094　京都市中京区麩屋町通り御池ドル

■ **ACCESS**
BY TRAIN: 15 min by car from Kyoto Stn (JR Tokaido *shinkansen*).
BY CAR:　25 min from Kyoto Higashi IC (Meishin Expressway).

For those times you feel like indulging on a night to remember, a Kyoto inn is

Tawara-ya's signature courtyard garden

the thing on which to splurge. And if you are going to do it, you may as well do it properly on Kyoto's oldest, most famous, and most exorbitant inn, the three-hundred-year-old Tawara-ya. You will be in great company—the Rothschilds, the Rockefellers, European royalty, Leonard Bernstein, and Marlon Brando have all tested the tatami at the Tawara-ya.

Walking into the Tawara-ya is—for the romantic—like finding the Japan you have always read about, but which now exists only in coffee-table books. There are wooden corridors here, soft lights from paper-covered lamps there, a basket of wild flowers, and those shadowy rooms where a whole wall opens to reveal a mossy garden, like in some magical forest.

Garden as an extension of the room, Tawara-ya

Owner Toshi Satow is responsible for keeping the Tawara-ya in this state of dreamlike suspension between Genji Japan and the modern world. "I like things that are just on the point of disintegration—a sad kind of ending beauty," says Ms. Satow. If you tune into Satow's "beauty of the full-blown," you will experience what is called *mono no aware* (the "ah"-ness of things) in the aesthetic glossary of Japan.

Satow has been able to maintain this stirring tension by two simple commandments—that no one element in any room shall stand out above any other, and a refusal to revere the old for old's sake. If it is new and it fits, use it.

Nearby

The Tawara-ya is within walking distance of one of my favorite parts of Kyoto, Sanjo. In the area near the Heian Museum are many trendy shops, as well as workshops where craftspeople make old fans, incense, and *tabi* (split-toed socks). It is also walking distance from the Nishiki food market.

KINMATA 懐石宿 近又

First-class, foreigner-friendly gourmet establishment redolent of old Kyoto.

RATE: From ¥25,000 w/2 meals, from ¥15,000 w/breakfast, children 20% off. **CREDIT CARDS:** AMEX, DC, MC, VISA. **ROOMS:** 7 Japanese style (w/o bath). **COMMUNAL BATH:** 1 private (*kazoku-buro*). **CHECK-IN:** 15:00. **CHECK-OUT:** 10:00. **CLOSED:** Wed. **LANGUAGE:** Some English.

☎ 075–221–1039 Fax: 075–231–7632
407 Shijo-agaru, Gokomachi-dori, Nakagyo-ku, Kyoto-shi, Kyoto 604–8044
〒604–8044　京都市中京区御幸町通四条上ル407

■ ACCESS
BY TRAIN: 10 min by car from Kyoto Stn (JR Tokaido *shinkansen*).
BY CAR: 30 min from Kyoto Minami IC (Meishin Expressway).

We did not reach the Kinmata until ten at night. We had spent the previous half hour driving around in circles in the narrow one-way streets of the city, made narrower by drunkenly weaving bodies. Lesson number one about central Kyoto: do not come here by car.

Happily, the inn was a true traveler's haven. The Kinmata is exactly what a good inn should be—a world apart, where you leave your worries at the doorstep.

Kinmata

Haruji Ukai, the proprietor, was immediately at our side, pouring the best, strongest green tea we had had in four days of traveling. Mr. Ukai's hospitality was warm yet professional. Even late at night, his starched white chef's jacket did not have a stain or a wrinkle in it, which epitomizes the level of service you can expect. Everything in the Kinmata is just so. But it is not overdone: this is like the well-loved home of a proud housewife.

Mr. Ukai is also the inn's chef, and his creations help to make the Kinmata special. He trained as a fishmonger before becoming a chef, and his food is superb. The porcelains and lacquerware he uses are more often than not ones cherished by his parents before him and their parents before them. The Kinmata opened its doors in 1801.

Six of the seven rooms in this former townhouse have neither bath or toilet, which is partly why the inn is so reasonable relative to its high quality. Guests must use the shared toilet and bathing facilities, which are spotless. "It's the Japanese people who comment about not having a bath and toilet in the rooms these days," says Mr. Ukai. "I've never had a foreign guest complain."

Kinmata landing

Personally, I love the lack of facilities in the rooms, as well as the fact that you are separated from the neighboring room and corridor by nothing but a membrane of wood and paper. Where else can you experience what it might have been like to live in a Kyoto house two hundred years ago? Mr. Ukai loves the inn as it is and cares for it as if it were a living thing. His effort shows in the gleam of its polished surfaces.

In one of the corridors is a framed photograph showing Mr. Ukai's great-grandfather as a little boy on the upstairs balcony. The building today is the same as it was then, except for renovations—a new kitchen, refurbished bath and toilets, and a compact *kaiseki* restaurant with modern Japanese sensibilities, where the old kitchen once was. Of course the rooms are air-conditioned and the paper lamps are electric, but nothing modern is obtrusive. In all other ways a stay here is like stepping back into 1801. The mini-garden (*tsubo-niwa*) and a bigger garden at the back are both good examples of how beauty is created in small spaces—something Kyotoites do so well.

Nearby

This is the center of Kyoto proper, so you are near to department stores, Pontocho, and the Nishiki market.

SHOZAN-KAKU 松山閣

A little-known, luxury gourmet inn set among pine-forested mountains.

RATE: From ¥30,000 w/2 meals, from ¥15,000 w/breakfast, no children.   **CREDIT CARDS:** VISA.
ROOMS: 4 Japanese style (w/o bath).   **COMMUNAL BATH:** 1—alternating.   **CHECK-IN:** 16:00.
CHECK-OUT: 10:00.   **LANGUAGE:** No English, reservations in Japanese.

☎ 075–461–4970 Fax: 075–461–4997

20 Utanodani, Narutaki, Ukyo-ku, Kyoto 606–8251

〒606–8251　京都市右京区鳴滝宇多野谷20

■ ACCESS

BY TRAIN: 30 min by car from Kyoto Stn (JR Tokaido *shinkansen*).
BY CAR:　40 min via Route 162 from Kyoto Minami IC (Meishin Expressway).

Food cooked in
a paper "pot,"
Shozan-kaku

A 30-minute taxi ride from Kyoto Station is an inn where the air is so fresh it comes as a shock to pollution-adulterated senses, and where *tanuki* (badgers) come out to play at night. Not many people know about the Shozan-kaku, and those who do would probably like to keep things that way.

Pine-covered mountains and intimate gardens surround the Shozan-kaku. The inn makes luxurious use of space. While downtown Kyoto inns are inspiring examples of the Japanese genius for squeezing so much elegance out of such small spaces, the Shozan-kaku is the kind of place where you can take a big breath and fling your arms out wide—without punching a hole in the *shoji*.

Known more among locals as a retreat for gourmandizing than as an inn, the Shozan-kaku's specialty is *yuba*, a nutritious and highly digestible soybean food that is one of the jewels in the crown of Kyoto cuisine. Made from the skin that is skimmed off simmering soymilk, *yuba* is such a superior food that it is a shame more Kyoto establishments do not give it more prominence on their menus. Then again, *yuba* is an expensive delicacy.

That's why the Shozan-kaku's Yuba Oke-Zen, a set-course meal sampled as lunch or dinner, is such a treat. Its centerpiece is a wooden tub full of delicious *yuba*. The bucket is made of Kitayama-*sugi* cedar, a precious timber usually reserved for feature pillars in the best teahouses. The meal that accompanies this tub is a lyrical experience full of allusions to classical Japanese literature and the seasons. On a summer day, I had chopped fresh bamboo shoots served in a miniature porcelain flute along with some delectable warm-weather fish in a miniature lacquerware drum, reminders of the music of summer festivals.

Now forty years old, the Shozan-kaku's twelve *sukiya*-style guest rooms are becoming more beautiful as the well-polished wood takes on the graceful patina of age. As is common in inns of this vintage, the guest rooms do not have their own bathrooms and toilets. But the shared bath is total modern indulgence, with a garden view from full-length windows.

The proprietress of the Shozan-kaku, all smiles and polite phrases, is one of Kyoto's gracious ladies. She and her inn embody the very best of Kyoto.

The Shozan-kaku now has a branch restaurant, of the same name, in the Kyoto Station building, where you can sample the marvelous *yuba* dishes.

Nearby

The paths of the garden behind the inn are lined with weeping cherries and other varieties of cherry tree; they bloom in April. Red maples are characteristic of November; different flowers keep this area a picture through spring and summer.

YOSHIDA SANSO 吉田山荘

LOCATION: Kyoto

Former home of royalty, now a bustling business.

RATE: From ¥30,000 w/2 meals, from ¥20,000 w/breakfast, from ¥15,000 w/o meals. **CREDIT CARDS:** AMEX, DC, VISA. **ROOMS:** 10 Japanese style (1 cottage w/bath). **COMMUNAL BATHS:** 2—men's, women's. **CHECK-IN:** 15:30. **CHECK-OUT:** 10:00. **LANGUAGE:** Some English.

☎ 075–771–6125 Fax: 075–771–5667
59–1 Shimo-Oji-machi, Yoshida, Sakyo-ku, Kyoto 606–8314
〒606–8314　京都市左京区吉田下大路町59–1

■ ACCESS
BY TRAIN: 20 min by car from Kyoto Stn (JR Tokaido *shinkansen*).
BY CAR:　20 min from Kyoto Higashi IC (Meishin Expressway).

Formerly the second house of Prince Higashi Fushimi, this 1930s structure is made entirely of precious Japanese cypress. Western features include a round stained-glass window in the entry and stained-glass panels in place of the breezy wooden transoms. Roof tiles and door pulls are adorned with imperial chrysanthemum crests.

Aristocratic Yoshida Sanso

Once a serene estate in a quiet part of Kyoto, the house has now lost some of its dignity to tourism. Crowds throng here for lunch in the busy Kyoto seasons, especially in mid- to late November, when the Japanese maples in nearby Shin'nyo-do temple are at their most stunning.

Considering the crowds and the fact that baths and toilets are shared, Yoshida Sanso may seem overpriced. But consider also that there are twenty people serving just ten rooms.

Yoshida Sanso is a wonderfully quiet place to stay in Kyoto's uncrowded winter months. But you may like to save your money and simply partake of the imperial atmosphere over lunch.

SABURI さぶり

LOCATION:
Sonobe
(one hour from
Kyoto by train)

Country farmhouse turned gourmet inn.

RATE: From ¥18,500 (tax and service fee included) w/2 meals. **CREDIT CARDS:** Not accepted. **ROOMS:** 2 Japanese style (w/o bath). **COMMUNAL BATH:** 1—alternating. **CHECK-IN:** 16:00. **CHECK-OUT:** 10:00. **LANGUAGE:** Some English.

☎ 0771–62–1007 Fax: 0771–62–1007
Senzuma, Sonobe-cho, Funai-gun, Kyoto 622–0024
〒622–0024　京都府船井郡園部町千妻

■ ACCESS
BY TRAIN: 7 min by car from Sonobe Stn (JR San'in Main Line).
BY CAR: 2 min from Sonobe IC (Kyoto/Tamba Doro).

Mr. Yasushi Saburi, proprietor of this unique country inn, accepts one party of four to seven guests at a time, either for lunch or as guests for the night. He is the sole proprietor, chef, bed-maker, bartender, and bottle-washer at this three-hundred-year-old thatch-roofed farmhouse, now an inn with wonderful food.

I arrived at the Saburi expecting to find a sophisticated country inn in well-tended surroundings, but found the place rather unkempt and needing, perhaps, a woman's touch. But the atmosphere is very much in keeping with the rest of the unprepossessing farmhouses in this enclave, where life does not seem to have become any better or worse for the past hundred years.

Mr. Saburi invites newly arrived guests to lounge in the two-room living-cum-sleeping quarters with a cup of *bancha* (roasted tea) and a handful of crunchy sugar-coated sweets. Meanwhile, he conceals himself in the kitchen doing what he knows and loves best—making food. He was the chef at his own restaurant specializing in home cooking in Gion, Kyoto, for twenty years before retiring here to his country retreat in the latter half of the eighties.

At mealtime, Mr. Saburi slides open the doors of the "dining room" with a theatrical flourish and steps back proudly as a sparkling scene is revealed to his guests. The open fire in the sunken hearth is the main star, burning brightly, with a supporting cast of antique trays studded with dishes of colorful appetizers. We take to our cushions on the floor and wait for the first act.

I have been to several country inns where the food is served around an open fire, but none do it with quite this flair. Such places are usually catered by a team of women slaving in the kitchen. Here, Mr. Saburi sits with you at the fire and cooks the feast before your eyes.

We had an intriguing array of food that was not all Japanese, even though the meal started with sashimi. Mr. Saburi does his own smoking, so we had portions of smoked free-range chicken, and smoked scallops.

Over the coals went a square of *mochi* rice cake for everyone. Mr. Saburi placed a big iron pot of delicate broth on the fire and, with a practiced hand, transformed it into a refreshing soup of mushroom, tofu, and chicken, with citron zest. The gently browned *mochi* arrived, couched in sheets of *nori* seaweed.

An enormous wooden tray filled with a feast of vegetables appeared as the final act, its centerpiece a square lacquerware bowl of fat *udon* noodles.

Mr. Saburi has a thing about pots over open fires. Even the bath at the Saburi is a giant version of the soup pot—an iron pot over a wood fire, called a *goemon-buro*. You will not experience one of these farmhouse baths in many other places, so make the most of it. Stand on the wooden board and ease yourself down into its warmth and enjoy.

Nearby

One of the pleasant things about the Saburi is that it is in the middle of nowhere. Mr. Saburi has antiques for sale in an adjoining storehouse, so spend a while sifting through them. Also go for a little walk to the tiny Asakura shrine, where the protected giant cedar tree dwarfs the modest sanctuary. The Saburi is sixteen kilometers (ten miles) from the rapids of Hozu on the Sea of Japan coast. To make reservations for a ride down the rapids, call ② 0771 22 5846 in Japanese.

HAKKEI-TEI 八景亭

LOCATION: Hikone

Spectacularly dilapidated former pleasure villa in a famous stroll garden.

RATE: From ¥17,000 w/2 meals. **CREDIT CARDS:** Not accepted. **ROOMS:** 5 Japanese style (w/o bath). **COMMUNAL BATH:** 1—private (*kazoku-buro*). **CHECK-IN:** 16:00. **CHECK-OUT:** 10:00. **LANGUAGE:** English spoken.

② 0749–22–3117 Fax: 0749–22–3120
E-MAIL: kitake@ops.dti.ne.jp (Kiyotaka Takenaka)
3–41 Konki-machi, Hikone-shi, Shiga 522–0061
〒522–0061 滋賀県彦根市金亀町3–41

■ ACCESS
BY TRAIN: 3 min by car from Hikone Stn (JR Tokaido Line).
BY CAR: 2.5 km from Hikone IC (Meishin Expressway).

With so much to see in Kyoto, many people don't make the excursion to the castle town of Hikone. But there is a unique *ryokan* in Hikone which alone makes the trip worthwhile.

The Hakkei-tei has been standing for 320 years, which makes it possibly the oldest structure in Japan being used as an inn. It is part of a complex of structures set in a luxurious garden built originally as the pleasure villa for the Ii clan, one of the most illustrious families in Japan. The family's most famous

Hakkei-tei with Hikone Castle

member was Ii Naosuke (1815–60), who was the first lord of Hikone Castle and chief minister to the second-to-last shogun, Tokugawa Iemochi (1846–66). Hakkei-tei and its twin Raku-Raku-tei (no longer in use) are where successive generations of the Ii family entertained state guests.

The Hakkei-tei was built in 1677, and no expense was spared on its superb stroll garden, landscaped round a massive pond. The Hakkei-tei's rooms stand with their pillars in the water, looking out over this pond—and the view is pure magic.

At the end of the feudal age, ownership of the estate passed from the national government to Shiga Prefecture and finally to Hikone City itself, which now leases out the buildings. City Hall pays for the upkeep of the grounds and buildings, while leasees operate the inn.

There are only two rooms for overnight guests. Apart from the expansive view, the rooms are unremarkable, even with their considerable size and a secret closet inside a *tokonoma* where the lord's bodyguards used to hide. Three other small rooms are available for private dining at lunch or dinner. These, too, have marvelous views of the pond.

There is another small price to pay for enjoying the Hakkei-tei's lordly view—a certain lack of privacy. The public pays a nominal fee to stroll around the inn's pond-garden, which is known as Genkyuen, and you, inside the Hakkei-tei, become part of their view. You may feel a bit exposed, but the hours that you require privacy are mostly the hours when the gates are closed.

The Hakkei-tei does not advertise itself as an inn because there are only the two rickety old rooms, the facilities are not quite up to scratch (there are no baths or toilets in the rooms), and the place is creaky and falling to bits. But at the Hakkei-tei that is really half the fun.

Nearby

The castle museum and tourist shops are walking distance from the inn.

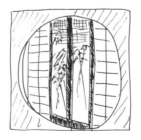

24

NARA

Yakushiji

ATTRACTIONS

A history older than Kyoto's, the ruins of Japan's first capital, and both the oldest and largest wooden buildings in the world—each a World Heritage Site. An interesting side trip can be made to Imai-cho. Nara is also the gateway to Yoshino, with its sacred mountains and cherry blossoms.

Nara always gets lost in the shadows of its more famous neighbor, Kyoto. It may not have as many gilded pavilions or Zen gardens as Kyoto, but it has a fascinating—and older—history. A serious student of Japan would do well to start here before moving on to Kyoto. Nara is really where Japan's written history began, in the fifth to sixth centuries, when Buddhism was brought in via Korea. Prince Shotoku (574–622), who some believe was a Korean himself, propagated it among his peers at the same time he is said to have introduced the country's first constitution.

The two most famous places in Nara, **Horyuji temple** (with the oldest wooden structure in the world) and **Todaiji temple** (the largest wooden building in the world) are linked to Buddhism's earliest days in Japan. Horyuji

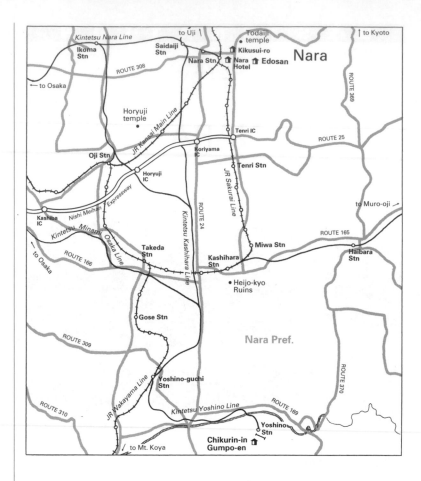

was built by Prince Shotoku, while Todaiji (completed in 752) was used to propagate Buddhism as the state religion, a politically motivated decision designed to unify the nation. Todaiji was built as the head temple that would oversee branches all over the country.

You see the result today—Buddhism's presence is everywhere. Ten thousand people attended the "opening of the eyes" of the Daibutsu (Great Buddha) in Todaiji when it was completed in A.D. 752, and includes overseas guests. Its construction almost bankrupted the nation. Todaiji has been rebuilt several times since, the latest being in the early 1700s.

Once a year the treasures of the **Imperial Treasure House** (Shoso-in) at Todaiji are shown to the public. It is a remarkable collection of 1,300-year-old objects that belonged to the Emperor Shomu (701–56), and includes foreign gifts made of such rare materials as European lapis lazuli and African rhinoceros horn. Japan was not—as some in Nara claim—the last stop on the Silk Road; what is true is that Japanese envoys brought back many precious items from China that had arrived via the Road. More significantly, Japan sent regular missions to China, each with up to six hundred people, to learn from Chinese civilization, at a time when such long journeys were treacherous. Both Horyuji and Todaiji are UNESCO World Heritage Sites, along with **Toshodaiji** and **Yakushiji**.

It is a sign of Japan's great reverence of T'ang China that the T'ang capital, Chang'an, was chosen as the model for the new capital city at present-day Nara. In a town where there had formerly been thatched huts, the walled capital of **Heijo-kyo** must have held people in awe with its vermilion pillars and black-tiled roofs. The excavated ruins of the old capital city can be viewed today.

The other big attraction in Nara is **Kasuga shrine**, a short walk from Todaiji. This shrine, which is famous for the deer in its parkland, enshrines the tutelary gods of the Fujiwara, a clan that manipulated Japanese politics from the 700s to the Meiji Restoration of 1868. In the deer park is the charming Edosan inn.

Some travelers prefer to avoid all the above major sights and head for the more remote and rustic temples of old Nara, such as **Muro-oji**, **Gansenji**, **Joruriji**, and **Enjoji**.

Nara's shopping center, on the approach to the deer park, turned trendy in the 1980s to keep abreast of the younger generation. Young visitors come in bus loads on school excursions every day and are more interested in T-shirts of pop idols than boxes of *nara-zuke*, the saké-imbued pickles for which Nara is most famous. The offerings therefore are eclectic. Old and new merge in a funky blend in phone booths on the main street with stained-glass ceilings depicting the Great Buddha.

One of Japan's classic old hotels, the Nara Hotel, is probably where I would choose to stay at a future time, but it was delightful staying at the Edosan for its location in the park. Nara's top inn, the Kikusui-ro, where the Emperor stayed, has been listed as an alternative choice because of its equally exalted price.

On the way to Nara from Kyoto you could visit **Uji.** The Japanese culture professor at my university always claimed that the most beautiful temple in Japan was Uji's **Byodoin**, with its Phoenix Hall (Hoodo). Seen from overhead, the temple is shaped like a bird in flight, and two of the imaginary birds are perched on the building's roof. It was built to house a stunning statue of Amida, the Buddha who was to save people from a Buddhist doomsday (*mappo*) predicted for the eleventh century. Angels playing musical instruments frolic on the walls around Amida's head, and his face is framed from the opposite bank of the temple's pond, where aristocrats spent idle hours boating.

Uji itself is a pleasant spot with its wide river and old teahouses—the district is said to grow Japan's best tea.

I would also like to add a word in praise of **Imai-cho**, a remarkable little haven from urban progress on the outskirts of Nara City. Imai-cho has several blocks of late Edo- and early Meiji-period (mid-nineteenth century) houses on streets too narrow for cars to enter, and is virtually untouched by tourism. Like Mino in Gifu Prefecture, Imai-cho has been buffered by the more famous places on either side of it. When I was there, it did not even have a shop selling film.

Hardly had I asked a group of ladies where I might buy some when a young fellow, who had overheard the conversation, rode up on a bicycle, pressed a roll of film into my hand, then cycled off without a word. There are seven houses open to the public, the most impressive being the Imanishi-ke.

Special times

The Nigatsudo Hall of Todaiji is the scene of one of the most spectacular festivals in Japan. Held every March 12, Omizutori is a ceremony of accepting water from a well said to be linked by an underground tunnel to Obama on the Sea of Japan coast. The festival takes place at night with the brandishing of huge fire torches. The "water" is ritually "sent" from a waterway in Obama by priests of the syncretic Jinguji temple in Obama (see Destination 28), in a ceremony called "the sending of the water."

Recommended buys

Nara is famous for its ink sticks and calligraphy brushes. *Nara-zuke* pickles, the traditional souvenir of the city, are an acquired taste. Uji is famous for its tea.

For some of the finest *mitarashi dango* and freshly made, old-fashioned sweets, look for the Okuta shop (☎ 0742–23–0058) in the Alte-kan, down the street between Sumitomo Bank and the Zeitaku Mame store in downtown Nara.

Recommended trips including Nara

It seems only natural to combine Kyoto with Nara because of their proximity, but Kyoto alone is worth a week of exploring, and most people think they have had enough of traditional culture after that. To preclude cultural burnout in Nara, I would suggest separate trips to each city. Limit yourself to Nara with a side trip to Uji and Imai-cho, or make Nara part of a longer tour to Yoshino and then Wakayama.

- Nara (2 nights)—Yoshino (lunch at Gumpo-en or overnight stay)—Ryujin Onsen (1 night, Destination 25)—Taiji (day excursion) —Kii Katsuura (1 night, Destination 25)
- Kyoto (2 nights, Destination 23)—Uji (day excursion)—Nara (2 nights)

EDOSAN 江戸三

LOCATION: Nara Park, Nara City

Unusual inn consisting of eleven huts in different architectural styles set in the Nara deer park.

RATE: From ¥18,000 w/2 meals, children 30% off. **CREDIT CARDS:** AMEX, DC, MC, VISA. **ROOMS:** 10 Japanese style (1 w/bath). **COMMUNAL BATHS:** 2—private (*kazoku-buro*). **CHECK-IN:** 15:00. **CHECK-OUT:** 10:00. **CLOSED:** Year end/New Year holidays. **LANGUAGE:** Some English.

☎ 0742–26–2662 Fax: 0742–26–2663
1167 Takabatake-cho, Nara-shi, Nara 630–8301
〒630–8301 奈良県奈良市高畑町1167

BY TRAIN: 5 min by car from Nara Stn (Kintetsu Line).
BY CAR: 30 min via Route 169 from Tenri IC (Nishi Meihan Expressway).

*One of eleven
Edosan cottages*

A wealthy cad in the good old days of the Meiji era (1868–1912) would have spent his money on partaking in tea ceremonies, *geisha asobi*, or both. The second, meaning "entertainment by geisha," did not necessarily refer to a Tom Jones–type of philandering. A man entertained by geisha not only got his fill of food, wine, song, dance, and party games, but he had to be worthy of his female entertainer's company by matching her in wit and repartee.

The original owner of the buildings that now comprise the Edosan, a certain Mr. Yamato, was one such man. Not content to do his *geisha asobi* in any old downtown joint, he built his own *ryotei* in 1907—and not just one building, but eleven, spread amongst the tall trees in the sacred precincts of Nara Park.

Each of the huts is in a different architectural style, and since they were built in the days before telephones, each one had its own distinctive bells and clappers to call the main house with requests such as: "More beer, and send me a different woman." This is why the buildings have such names as Shoko ("Bell and Drum"), in the case of a shrinelike building with a high, thatched roof; Suzu ("Jingling Bell"), for a farmhouse-style one; and Dora ("Gong"), a *machi-ya* –style house. As Dora is quite a distance from the main house, it needed a resounding gong. There is also a tiny thatch hut called Taiko ("Drum") with a round window, and Gyoku ("Fish-shape Buddhist Drum"). Other names such as Happo-tei ("The Octagonal House") reflect the design.

Those were the days.

As pretty as these little Meiji-period huts are to see, however, the fourth-generation Mr. Yamato might have tried harder to protect them from the intrusion of air conditioners, telephones, and TVs, which make their small interiors somewhat cramped. But can you really complain about being in a corner of Nara Park with deer nosing around outside your bedroom?

It is said that no funny business went on in these elegant little huts because they lacked bathing facilities in the rooms. There are still no baths in all but one of the huts; everyone else shares the communal baths in a separate hut posed beside a pond.

Wakakusa-nabe, a hot pot, is one of the famed dishes served at the Edosan.

Nearby

You are a five-minute walk (amongst the deer) to Todaiji, the hall of the Daibutsu (Great Buddha), and a ten-minute walk the other way to the Nara shopping street—hangout of the high-school set.

CHIKURIN-IN GUMPO-EN
竹林院群芳園

LOCATION:
Yoshino

*Ryokan-like temple lodgings with a renowned garden,
in the famed cherry blossom mecca of Yoshino.*

RATE: From ¥15,000 w/2 meals, from ¥10,000 w/breakfast, children 50% off. CREDIT CARDS: AMEX, DC, MC, VISA. ROOMS: 55 Japanese style (34 w/bath). COMMUNAL BATHS: 2—men's, women's. CHECK-IN: 15:00. CHECK-OUT: 10:00. LANGUAGE: Some English.

☎ 07463–2–8081 Fax: 07463–2–8088
Yoshinoyama, Yoshino-cho, Yoshino-gun, Nara 639–3115
〒639–3115 奈良県吉野郡吉野町吉野山

■ ACCESS
BY TRAIN: 5 min by bus from ropeway terminal which connects to Yoshino Stn (Kintetsu Yoshino Line).
BY CAR: 35 km via Routes 24 & 169 from Koriyama IC (Nishi Meihan Expressway).

Grand entrance to the old section, Chikurin-in Gumpo-en

It was a weekday and Yoshino's famous cherry blossoms had finished, but the Chikurin-in Gumpo-en was doing a roaring trade. From each of its large and small Japanese rooms came jolly noises from gaggles of ladies out for an elegant lunch overlooking the garden, designed by a great sixteenth-century tea master.

If the ladies were from Nara it would have taken them a good hour to get here; from Kyoto, maybe three. But an excursion to lunch high up on holy Mount Yoshino, on a sunny spring day in a temple garden, was worth the trip.

Yoshino is the cherry blossom capital of the world, mainly due to the sheer abundance of trees that splash its surrounding mountains with pink every April. And if the town was this busy on an ordinary weekday in spring, I imagine it must be pure sight-seeing hell when the cherries are out. A woman working in one of the huddle of shops along the road from the Yoshino cable car station commented on how she could not even get from one side of the road to the other at the height of the blossoms, for all the people. Choose cherry time (about April 10–25) at your own risk, keeping in mind that the mountain scenery is spectacular right through the fall.

"Chikurin-in" refers to an old temple said to have been established by the sixth-century patron saint of Buddhism, Prince Shotoku, and Gumpo-en is the name of the lodgings that the temple runs. But this is not the sparse-room-and-spartan-service type of temple lodging—it is more like a real *ryokan*. Regular comforts are on tap and business is the name of the game. Unfortunately, the atmospheric rooms in the original section of the Gumpo-en, built in 1832, are for dining only. Overnight guests are accommodated in the newer concrete wing.

Nearby

Even if you do not stay at Gumpo-en, it is worth the ¥300 entrance fee to look at the temple's garden. It was first built in the Muromachi period (1392–1573) but redesigned by the renowned tea master Sen no Rikyu (1522–91) for the ruler Toyotomi Hideyoshi's (1537–98) cherry-viewing pleasures. Yoshino is home to *yamabushi* (mountain ascetics), and Chikurin-in's head priest, eighty-year-old Ryoei Fukui, has made the rounds of the *yamabushi*'s seventy-five holy places deep in the Yoshino-Omine mountains thirty-three times. Controversially, this is still an area forbidden to women.

25

WAKAYAMA
PREFECTURE

Nachi Falls

ATTRACTIONS

Temple-filled Mount Koya; Nanki Katsuura, a hot spring resort on a coastline with bizarre rock formations; Taiji, an old whaling port; Nachi Falls and a shrine with a million-dollar view; and the splendid Kumano Hongu, one of the most handsome shrines in Japan.

Wakayama is a trip to tackle if you have a week to spare. On my last visit I mistakenly tried to crowd it into four days of sight-seeing with Uji, Nara, and Yoshino. It took six hours to drive to the seaside hot spring resort of Nanki Katsuura from Yoshino. The mountain scenery was rugged and untouched, but after a while it simply became too much of a good thing—about five hours too much. I now wish I had made a detour to **Ryujin Onsen** en route, to stay at the restful Kami-goten rather than plow on through to Nanki Katsuura.

Holy **Mount Koya**, the center of esoteric Shingon Buddhism in Japan, is also in Wakayama and worthy of its own trip. This town, founded by the venerated holy man Kukai (also Kobo-daishi; 774–835), is packed with temple lodgings. Staying at such a lodging is highly recommended, and it is easy to make reservations through any travel agent. While tourists converge on Mount Koya in summer to cool off in its tall forests, my family found it especially attractive in the snow, when the temple scenery seemed otherworldly, and there was hardly another soul present. The temple where we stayed had no heating other than a *kotatsu*. Our room was so cold and there was so little to do that we turned out the light at 8 P.M. and slept—like the spokes of a wheel—with all our feet tucked under the *kotatsu*. Regardless of the spartan service, we thoroughly enjoyed the experience and the Buddhist vegetarian food, served by silent priests-in-training, was excellent.

If you stay at a temple lodging, rising at 5 A.M. for the morning chanting of sutras in the main hall is usually obligatory—and worth the effort.

The Kushimoto section of the **Nanki Katsuura** coastline has rocks and islands in bizarre shapes. If they are not sufficiently fascinating to make a special trip, do not miss the whale museum at the old whaling port of **Taiji** in the same area. It has grown a little shabby these days, but the displays related to the whaling practices of seventeenth-to-eighteenth-century Taiji are compelling. Daring men in beautifully decorated wooden boats would harpoon a whale, then haul it back to shore to festive flute and drum music. Every part of the

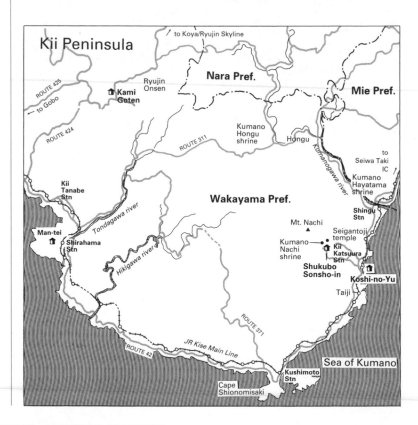

whale was processed and used (the gut was even refined for working *bunraku* puppets), and it was said that seven villages could survive for a year on a single catch. If we are to believe the official version, whaling was practiced in these parts only because of a shortage of other food, and did not become commercial until mechanized whaling practices were learned from the West.

From Taiji it is an easy drive to the two other best attractions in Wakayama: **Kumano Hongu shrine**, with its simple black shrines in the style of the Grand Shrines of Ise, and **Seigantoji temple**, overlooking **Nachi Falls**. For a million-dollar view of the falls, stay at the Sonshoin temple lodgings at Seigantoji temple itself.

Seasonal tip ▪▬▬▬▬

You'll have to brave the crowds to enjoy the famous Nachi Fire Festival (July 14), but if you can time your trip to coincide with this festival it will be worth it.

Recommended trips including Wakayama

If you come from Osaka, proceed via Mount Koya, and if you are traveling from Nara, arrive via Yoshino. Do not try to cover too much territory at once in Wakayama: with all those mountain barriers, it is bigger than you think.

- Nara (1 night, Destination 24)—Imai-cho (half-day trip, Destination 24)—Yoshino (1 night, Destination 24)—Ryujin Onsen (1 night)— Taiji (half-day excursion)—Nachi (1 night)
- Osaka—Koya-san (1 night)—Ryujin Onsen (1 night)—Shirahama/Tanabe (1 night at Man-tei, see Alternative Inns)—Taiji and Nachi (1 night)

SHUKUBO SONSHOIN 宿坊尊勝院

LOCATION: Nachi

A modern temple lodging with an unforgettable view.

RATE: From ¥8,000 w/2 meals. **CREDIT CARDS:** Not accepted. **ROOMS:** 14 Japanese style, 1 large communal room. **COMMUNAL BATHS:** 3—men's, women's, private (*kazoku-buro*). **CHECK-IN:** 17:00. **LANGUAGE:** No English, reservations in Japanese.

☽ 07355–5–0331
36 Nachisan, Nachi Katsuura-cho, Higashi-Muro-gun, Wakayama 649–5301
〒649–5301 和歌山県東牟婁郡那智勝浦町那智山36、那智山青岸渡寺 宿坊尊勝院

▪ ACCESS

BY TRAIN: 15 min by car from Kii Katsuura Stn (JR Kise Main Line).
BY CAR: 4 hr via Route 42 from Seiwa/Taki IC (Ise Expressway).

The Nachi Falls in Wakayama Prefecture are such a stunning sight as you stand in the grounds of Seigantoji temple. It is not just the drop of the 33-meter (108-

Seigantoji Pagoda and Nachi Falls

foot) falls way in the distance that makes the view so special, but the two expansive temple gardens in the foreground. The gardens are a sea of impeccably pruned azalea bushes. On my visit in April the dazzling green of new leaves sparkled with dashes of magenta, hinting that this scene might become almost too voluptuous to bear at the peak of the flowering season in May. The building that claims this incomparable mountain vista is a *shukubo* (temple lodgings) belonging to Seigantoji temple. Guests can stay there at a cost considerably lower than any *ryokan*.

Unlike the gloomy, spartan lodgings you find at temples on Wakayama's other holy mountain, Mount Koya, the *shukubo* here is a sunny little haven. At Mount Koya young priests silently serve meals of tofu, rice, and miso soup in black lacquer bowls, their solemnity reflecting the long, dark path they probably see ahead of them. At this *shukubo*, the Sonshoin, on the other hand, the attitude seems to be: "Here is heaven, come and get it, and there might even be fish for dinner." Attendance at the early morning chanting of the sutras in the main temple hall is not compulsory—but definitely desirable.

Nearby

The Seigantoji temple, Nachi, and Nachi Falls are what most people come to see here. This temple, though a Zen site, is the first station on a pilgrimage of thirty-three temples dedicated to the bodhisattva Kannon, "the compassionate one." The famous fire festival is in July. You might also consider the walk to the shrine at the base of Nachi Falls.

KOSHI-NO-YU 越之湯

LOCATION: Nanki Katsuura Onsen

A big modern inn that offers a boat trip to a very special hot spring bath.

RATE: From ¥18,000 w/2 meals, children 30% off. **CREDIT CARDS:** AMEX, DC, MC, VISA. **ROOMS:** 78 Japanese style, 1 Western style—37 w/bath. **COMMUNAL BATHS:** 5—men's, women's, 3 outdoor (men's, women's, mixed). **CHECK-IN:** 15:00. **CHECK-OUT:** 10:00. **LANGUAGE:** No English, reservations in Japanese.

☎ 0735–52–1414 Fax: 0735–52–0605
1108 Yukawa, Nachi Katsuura-cho, Higashi-Muro-gun, Wakayama 649–5336
〒649–5336　和歌山県東牟婁郡那智勝浦町湯川1108

■ ACCESS
BY TRAIN: 3 min by car from Kii Katsuura Stn (JR Kise Main Line).
BY CAR: 3 hr half via Route 42 from Seiwa/Taki IC (Ise Expressway).

View of Camel Rock from Koshi-no-Yu bath

The coastline at Nanki Katsuura in Wakayama is dotted with little islands, natural arches, and rocks in animal shapes. A particularly incredible one is called "Camel Rock." Its camel shape can only be seen from the shore, and since the shore is a sheer rock face the average tourist never gets to see it at all. But if you stay at the Koshi-no-Yu, you will have the chance to see Camel Rock from a hot spring bath.

The owners of the Koshi-no-Yu knew there was a hot spring in the rock face when they bought this land, but it took them until the early 1990s to get permission to build a bath. This is a national park: they first had to prove that their bath (and changing sheds) would not be a blight on the scenery.

The two baths they subsequently built are for the enjoyment of hotel guests only. The hotel ferries guests to the bath, just a five-minute ride round a promontory, in the morning and evening for a ¥500 fee.

Male and female guests all bathe together, so the hotel provides moo-moos with elastic tops for the ladies and bathing pants for the men. You are asked to change into these in a makeshift hut. "Canadian guests last year stripped their clothes right off and even dived into the sea for a swim!" said the man who looks after the baths. He begged us not to do this because naked bathers constitute a blight on the scenery.

The Camel Rock spa is a must, for its scenery and because the hot spring water is so primally pure that you know this is the real thing. The water comes out of the mountainside at 60°C (115°F), but instead of diluting it with cold water from another source, it has been piped on a roundabout course to cool it down. The result is just right.

Back at the Koshi-no-Yu there are three other baths as well, the best ones being the *rotemburo* in the old wing. Incidentally, the old wing is marginally less ordinary than the new. This is the only "hotel-style" *ryokan* I have included in this book, and I have only done so because of their Camel Rock bath.

Meals were a mixed bag. The dinner was disappointingly short on fresh seafood, and included imported lobster in French sauce gone cold. This was somewhat compensated for by a nourishing *chawan mushi* (savory custard) and a small hot-pot of leeks and pork cooked at the table. The most interesting item was the *kakinoha* sushi, a ball of rice wrapped in a persimmon leaf. Breakfast was a forgettable *bento* with a poached egg. The service was exceptionally friendly, however, and it was surprising that, at an inn of this size, the *okami* came round personally at dinner time to greet each room of guests. What a job!

KAMI-GOTEN　上御殿

LOCATION:
Ryujin Onsen

Splendid, wholesome, old-fashioned inn
with river views, a hot spring, and healthy food.

RATE: From ¥15,000 w/2 meals, children 30–50% off. **CREDIT CARDS:** Not accepted. **ROOMS:** 11 Japanese style (w/o bath). **COMMUNAL BATHS:** 3—men's, women's, outdoor private (*kazoku-buro*). **CHECK-IN:** 15:00. **CHECK-OUT:** 10:00. **LANGUAGE:** No English, reservations in Japanese.

Intricately restored Onari-no-Ma, Kami-Goten

☎ 0739–79–0005 Fax: 0739–79–0526
Ryujin, Ryujin-mura, Hidaka-gun, Wakayama 645–0525
〒645–0525　和歌山県日高郡龍神村龍神

■ **ACCESS**
BY TRAIN: 1 hr by bus from Kii Tanabe Stn (JR Kise Main Line).
BY CAR: 2 hr via Route 425 from Gobo IC (Yuasa/Gobo Doro) via Hanwa Expressway.

River view, Kami-Goten

This is the grandmother of old, no-nonsense inn buildings. Most recently renovated in 1886, it is a fine example of how good timbers just get better with age.

The Kami-goten is the oldest inn at Ryujin Onsen, so named after the Ryujin family that settled in this pleasant riverside spot eight hundred years ago. The present-day *okami* is cheerful seventy-seven-year-old Aya Ryujin, who traces her ancestry back twenty-eight generations to the Minamoto clan. It was not until the early Edo period (1600–1868), almost four hundred years ago, that the lord of the Kishu domain ordered her family to build an inn here so that he and his samurai retainers could enjoy the hot spring (the lower ranks were provided with a separate building).

The waters of Ryujin Onsen have long been acclaimed for their professed ability to whiten the skin (female beauty in Japan is traditionally synonymous with white skin), and this hot spring is ranked among the three best for "beautifying women," along with Kawanaka Onsen in Gumma Prefecture and Yunokawa Onsen in Shimane Prefecture. In addition to making the skin white and blemish-free, the waters are also said to be effective against "nervous ailments, skin disorders, and hysteria." Both indoor and outdoor baths are segregated and have mountain and river views.

"When I first took over the inn from my parents," the modest Mrs. Ryujin is quoted as saying in *Kateigaho* magazine, "I made a firm decision to become the best inn maid in Japan. I just do things the old way as my parents taught me." This includes serving wholesome country food to guests in the good old-fashioned way, by carrying each course to your room.

A terrible fire destroyed the first lodge in the Meiji period (1868–1912) but at least one of the rooms was rebuilt in its original finery: the Onari-no-Ma in the old section (*kyukan*). This room features many timbers not commonly used in Japanese carpentry, such as mulberry, black persimmon, azalea, and even loquat.

As if in tribute to the inn's roots, Mrs. Ryujin stubbornly preserves the traditional integrity of the Japanese inn and its culture by refusing to install karaoke sets or even a vending machine.

26

ARIMA ONSEN

*Noh at Kasuga shrine,
Tamba-Sasayama*

ATTRACTIONS

A quiet leafy retreat in the hinterland of the international port of Kobe.

The local people still talk about January 17, 1995, the day that the earth rocked **Kobe** like a giant shaking a cocktail. The Great Hanshin Earthquake killed 5,000, and many more have died since of broken hearts or lack of care. A visit to Kobe shows how the city has recovered on the surface, but not the deeper scars.

Kobe is totally new now, apart from the **Ijin-kan**—European-style residences of early foreign traders and businessmen. An international port since the 1800s, Kobe has always had a cosmopolitan population, which brought exotic styles of living. The Ijin-kan houses, as the focus of nineteenth-century foreign activity, have long been one of the main tourist attractions in Kobe. I find the Western-style architecture there stifling compared to the lightness and openness of Japanese houses —the Ijin-kan reminded me of my childhood in a stuffy English house. Still, despite being the premier tourist spot of Kobe, it is nevertheless an animated part of town.

Instead of staying in Kobe, I recommend taking a forty-minute train ride through the countryside to **Arima Onsen**, home of **Tosen Goshobo**, one of the best inns in this book. Several of the large inns at Arima suffered serious damage in the Kobe earthquake, but Tosen Goshobo did not move an inch.

For possible day trips to combine with a night in Arima Onsen, I recommend Himeji or Tamba-Sasayama.

Himeji has Japan's finest original castle and is altogether a very pleasant, foreigner-friendly town.

Tamba-Sasayama is a former merchants' quarter with a well-preserved street full of historic buildings. There are crafts and antiques shops; an excellent museum of Tamba ware (the local stoneware favored by tea masters), called the **Tamba Koto-kan**; and a **Noh drama museum** (Nohgaku Shiryo-kan). Tamba-Sasayama has a long history as a center of Noh, and the local **Kasuga shrine** holds special performances in mid-April and mid-September. *Okina*, the a sacred dance for the gods, is presented at midnight on New Year's Eve, and anyone is welcome to stand in the snow and watch the performance. The audience wraps money in paper and throws it on the stage. Afterward cups of warm *amazake* (sweet saké) are passed around.

In the winter months, Tamba-Sasayama restaurants and inns feature **wild-boar hot pot**. One newly refurbished and reasonably pleasant inn serving this special local dish is Jinyo-ro (☎ 0795–52–0021).

Seasonal tips ▌

Mid-April, mid-September, and New Year's Eve (a free performance) are the

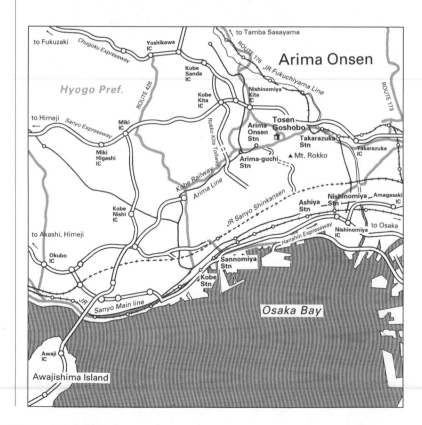

times for Noh drama at Kasuga Shrine. There is a Tamba pottery fair at Tachikui on October 19–20.

Recommended buys

Tamba ware can be purchased at the Tamba Koto-kan or souvenir shops in the old merchant quarter, but the main center of Tamba ware production is the village of **Tachikui**, thirty minutes away by car. The works of famed artists in this folkware are often as pricey as Bizen ware.

Japanese people know Tamba-Sasayama best for its *kuromame* (black beans). Good breads and steamed buns filled with sweetened black beans are available from shops in the thriving market street where the Jinyo-ro inn is located.

Recommended buys in Arima Onsen

Arima Kago, bamboo wicker baskets at Kutsuwa (☎ 078–904–0364).

Recommended trips including Kobe/Arima Onsen

In addition to the suggestions below, a visit to Kobe and Arima Onsen could be combined with a trip to Kinosaki Onsen (Destination 27) and its surroundings. Also, it's just a short hop from Kobe on the *shinkansen* to areas further west like Kurashiki and Hiroshima.

- Arima Onsen (1 night)—Himeji (day excursion)
- Arima Onsen (1 night)—Tamba-Sasayama
  (day excursion or overnight at Jinyo-ro)

TOSEN GOSHOBO 陶湶 御所坊

LOCATION: Arima Onsen

Chic lodgings in a long-venerated hot spring town.

RATE: From ¥20,000 w/2 meals, children from ¥15,000. **CREDIT CARDS:** AMEX, DC, VISA. **ROOMS:** 20 Japanese style (13 w/bath). **COMMUNAL BATHS:** 3   men's, women's, mixed w/half-partition. **CHECK-IN:** 15:00. **CHECK-OUT:** 10:00. **CLOSED:** Mon. **LANGUAGE:** Some English.

☎ 078–904–0551 Fax: 078–904–3601
858 Arima-cho, Kita-ku, Kobe-shi, Hyogo 651–1401
〒651–1401　兵庫県神戸市北区有馬町858

■ ACCESS

BY TRAIN: 5 min on foot from Arima Onsen Stn (Kobe Railway, Arima Line).
BY CAR:　5 km from Nishinomiya Kita IC (Chugoku Expressway).

The Tosen Goshobo quietly upstages all the other inns in Arima Onsen. Its three-story, sand-colored buildings stand in a leafy glade by a stream. Yet the gleaming black London taxi outside does not seem out of context, and as you step into the foyer you know that this is definitely an extraordinary place.

Tosen Goshobo

Shoin-style window,
Tosen Goshobo

The proprietors of Tosen Goshobo are among the precious few in Japan who stand for an artistic integrity that allows new ideas to mix gracefully with old.

Arima Onsen has an eight-hundred-year history. In the twelfth century, a priest set up twelve temple lodgings here, each dedicated to one of the *juni shinsho* (twelve guardian gods of Buddha). Ever since, Arima has been renowned as the place where one could worship and simultaneously be healed by hot spring waters. Many of the inns in Arima, including this one, still carry the suffix *"bo"* ("temple lodge"), and Tosen Goshobo was the most distinguished of them all, being the choice of aristocrats and men of letters from long ago. National unifier Toyotomi Hideyoshi (1537–98) was fond of Arima, and he ordered the bathing facilities at Arima Onsen to be repaired for his pleasure at the end of the sixteenth century. In more recent times, such greats as Hirobumi Ito (1841–1909), Japan's first prime minister, and novelists Jun'ichiro Tanizaki (1886–1965) and Eiji Yoshikawa (1892–1962), have been guests.

The present owner, Hironobu Kanai, was responsible for the thorough and thoughtful renovation that brought the inn into the twentieth century. Completed in 1991, this renovation left a portion of 1920s architecture intact but added a contemporary flair to the twenty guest rooms. The style is eclectic Japanese-Western—a marriage of poetic elegance and modern convenience.

Happily, nothing is lost by choosing a room at the lower end of the rate scale, as the same menu is served to all guests. And food is another area in which this inn truly shines. The proprietors are diligent in choosing only the best local produce from Hyogo and surrounding areas. Highlights include tofu with plump black beans from Tamba, soy milk skin (*yuba*—a Kansai specialty), the best Kobe beef, free-range chickens, fresh local *wasabi* to go with Inland Sea sashimi, and organically grown rice.

This inn is a part of its local community, too. It has a chic saké bar with its own saké sommelier and a restaurant-cum-party room with a sun terrace, plus coffee shops, tennis courts, and a swimming pool, all of which have become elegant local hangouts. Its upbeat presence is having an effect on the owners of neighboring buildings, who one by one are raising their own game. Under Kanai's influence, this is a town with a future.

Arima hot spring waters are terra-cotta-colored because of a high iron content, and this accounts for the first part of the inn's unusual name, *"tosen,"* which means "clay spring." The ladies' bath has a unique water-filled passageway leading to the bath proper. The wall between the ladies' and the men's bath gets lower and lower until it peters out altogether, thus offering the unique choice of private or mixed bathing. When warmer days arrive, the shutters are opened to let in the breeze and open the view to the green leaves outside.

The famous tea master Sen no Rikyu (1522–91) accompanied Toyotomi Hideyoshi to Arima Onsen and paid a visit to Zuihoji temple. Ever since, Arima has been revered for its associations with tea. The forebears of Tosen Goshobo's present owner were also tea aficionados, and displays of some of their precious utensils may be found in glass cases in the room that Tanizaki Jun'ichiro once used.

DESTINATION

27

KINOSAKI ONSEN

Willow-lined river, Kinosaki Onsen

ATTRACTIONS

Just before the Sea of Japan coast of Hyogo Prefecture (capital, Kobe) is the idyllic hot spring town of Kinosaki, a retreat for writers and artists since the early nineteenth century. The area has spectacular coastal scenery at Kasumi and the little-known former station town of Izushi.

People have all but forgotten that **Kinosaki** town was wiped out by a massive earthquake seventy years ago. Now, it is one of the prettiest hot spring towns in Japan, with a willow-lined stream and neat rows of inns where people go out strolling in *yukata* and *geta*. If you want to join in, your *ryokan* will be able to provide the necessary accouterments. While your promenade may reveal nothing more than a handful of mediocre sweet and souvenir shops, and a snooty antique store with a sign saying "Don't bother if you don't know what you're looking at," the atmosphere more than compensates for the minor disappointments.

Most people out in their *yukata* are doing the rounds of the *soto-yu*, the **six public baths**. Ichino-yu (propitious for passing exams and traffic safety) is the most picturesque; then there is Yamagi-yu for fertility, Gosho-yu for

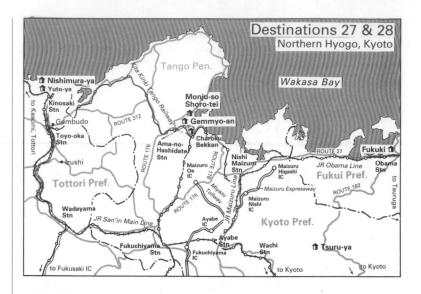

fortuitous relationships and protection against disasters, Mandara-yu for prosperous business and good harvests of the five grains, Jizo-yu for family safety
and lost children, and Kono-yu for good conjugal relations and long life. All these
luck-enhancing bathing opportunities are complimentary to guests of any Kinosaki inn, so just ask for your free pass. Day-trippers may also bathe, for a fee.

Kinosaki is near some of Japan's most scenic countryside. Close by is
Kasumi, which has spectacular pine-covered cliffs and a temple, **Daijoji**, with
marvelous sliding screen murals painted in the mid-1700s by one of Japan's
most noted artists, Maruyama Okyo (1733–95) and his students. Seven minutes
away by car from Kinosaki are the **Gembudo Caves**. These spectacular rock
formations were created ten thousand years ago when this part of the coast was
still under the sea and Mount Kuruhi erupted, sending lava into the waves where
it cooled in fantastic ripples.

Izushi, a former castle town and station on the highway from Tottori, is
another half an hour on. One of its highlights is the Sukyoji temple; it is also
known as **Takuandera** after Takuan Soho (1573–1645), the mid-seventeenth-
century Zen priest and legendary mentor of swordsman Miyamoto Musashi
(1584–1645). He also gave his name to the ubiquitous *takuan* (giant-radish
pickles). Born in Izu-shi, Takuan stayed at this temple for thirty-three years.
Izushi also features old samurai quarters, an impressive wooden clock tower,
and forty-odd soba shops.

A regular tourist bus (Zentan Busu Teiki Kanko) from Kinosaki does the
rounds of the Gembudo Caves, the Nakashima shrine (dedicated to the god of
sweets), and Izushi. But I would recommend hiring a car to enjoy the pastoral
scenery. Particularly lovely is the road from Kasumi to sleepy **Iwai Onsen**,
where there is a pleasantly faded country inn, the Hana-ya (☎ 0857–
72–1431). If you bathe at Iwai, ask them to demonstrate the unique custom of

smacking the water rhythmically with a ladle then pouring water over your towel-bedecked head.

If you are exploring the entire San'in region, also visit the city of **Tottori** for its sand dunes and the **Folk Art Museum** (Tottori Mingei Bijutsu-kan; ☎ 0857–26–2367). Not far from Tottori is the quaint old town of **Kurayoshi**, which has made a feature of its public lavatories. The inn of note in Kurayoshi is Shofu-so (☎ 0858–22–6363). Nearby Misasa Onsen has the well-established Saiki Bekkan Inn, which is "perfectly" appointed in an overdone and overpriced sort of way (☎ 0858–43–0331).

Recommended trips including Kinosaki

Kinosaki is only two hours and thirty minutes by train from Himeji and its
magnificent castle. You could also come from Kyoto and include a
day trip to Ama-no-Hashidate around the other side
of the Tango Peninsula (see Destination 28).

- Kobe and Arima Onsen (1 night, Destination 26)
  —Himeji (day trip)—Kinosaki (1 night)
- Kasumi (half-day)—Kinosaki (1 night)
  —Izushi (day excursion)
- Kyoto (Destination 23)—Kinosaki (1 night)—Ama-no-Hashidate
  (1 night, Destination 28)

NISHIMURA-YA　西村屋

LOCATION: Kinosaki Onsen

A classic Japanese inn, in a picturesque hot spring town near the Sea of Japan coast.

RATE: From ¥28,000 w/2 meals, children 30–70% off. **CREDIT CARDS:** DC, MC, VISA. **ROOMS:** 35 Japanese style (w/bath). **COMMUNAL BATHS:** 6–2 men's, 2 women's, 2 outdoor bath (men's, women's). **CHECK-IN:** 15:00. **CHECK-OUT:** 11:00. **LANGUAGE:** No English, reservations in Japanese.

☎ 0796–32–2211 Fax: 0796–32–4456
469 Yushima, Kinosaki-cho, Konosaki-gun, Hyogo 669–6101
〒669–6101　兵庫県城崎郡城崎町湯島469

■ ACCESS
BY TRAIN: 3 min from Kinosaki Stn (JR San'in Main Line).
BY CAR:　2 hr (80 km) via Route 312 from Fukusaki IC (Chugoku Expressway).

Balcony,
Nishimura-ya

Nishimura-ya is an inn among inns: one of those impeccable and deeply comfortable havens where you can escape and relax completely. I can't pinpoint just what it is that makes an inn feel this good. Perhaps it has something to do with the textures of the burnished wood, paper, silk, lacquer, and tatami; or perhaps it is the security you feel from the size of the rooms, the height of the ceilings, and the thickness of the walls. Whatever it is, this inn has it.

Nishimura-ya has been operating for one hundred and forty years, though the present buildings date from after the big Kinosaki earthquake seventy years ago. A newcomer to the business would find it hard to compete with the solid tradition of quality that epitomizes this inn. Mrs. Nishimura, the present *okami*, says her only goal in life is to carry on the same high standards of service as the generations of *okami* before her.

The orthodox Kyoto-style *kaiseki* meal is served in your room. The eight courses are presented one by one, starting with an aperitif, clear soup, and sashimi, then followed by an assortment of dishes accompanied by pickles, rice, and miso soup. Nishimura-ya also provides high-quality beef from the Tajima area in a delicious *shabu-shabu* that comes with a *miso*-flavored dipping sauce. Sea of Japan crab is a specialty year-round, but is particularly good in the winter months.

Leave enough time to inspect the inn's "display room," which has treasures from its century-and-a-half existence. These reveal a noted clientele: potters such as Rosanjin Kitaoji (1883–1959), Shoji Hamada (1894–1978), and Kanjiro Kawai (1890–1966); the woodblock artist Shiko Munakata (1903–75); and some of the country's most acclaimed novelists, who left behind pieces of their calligraphy.

The inn has bright, modern bathrooms, which look out on a stately garden.

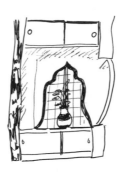

28

MIYAMA-CHO and AMA-NO-HASHIDATE

ATTRACTIONS

The idyllic hamlet of thatched farmhouses in Miyama-cho. A two-hour drive through lovely countryside takes you to the formerly bustling port of Obama. A further two hours along the Sea of Japan coast gets you to Ama-no-Hashidate, the "Bridge of Heaven."

That Kyoto is only about a three-hour drive from the Sea of Japan coast is something worth remembering when making travel plans. A visit to Kyoto always combines well with a trip along the Sea of Japan—whether you go to Kinosaki Onsen and the scenic Kasumi coast (see Destination 27) or, in this case, through Miyama-cho to Obama and Ama-no-Hashidate.

The road linking Kyoto and **Obama** has a fascinating history as the "mackerel route," the road along which running couriers transported freshly caught mackerel to the tables of Kyoto.

Obama, a natural harbor, was one of the main points of contact with Korea and China and was also a stopping-off point for the *kitamae-bune*—the wooden ships that transported goods such as giant kelp (an essential ingredient in Japanese cuisine) from Japan's far north to Osaka. When the ships would stop at Obama, goods for Kyoto would be unloaded and carried overland. All this trade made Obama rich—and wherever there is wealth, there are expensive souls to save. This is one reason why Obama has more than its fair share of temples, even earning the moniker "Nara by the sea."

If you have just come from Kyoto, you may be templed-out, but save enough energy to visit some of the temples and shrines of Obama. The **Hachimangu shrine**, with its god "lodges" set aside for gods who may be visiting from other parts of the country, and **Jinguji**, an imposing thatch-roofed temple that preserves relics from the time when temples and shrines were one, are especially worth seeing. Not far from Jinguji is the water course from which water is ritually "sent" to Nara for the famous Omizutori Festival at Todaiji temple (see Destination 24).

As the country opened and railways spread in the early twentieth century, and as Japan's main gateway shifted to Edo (modern-day Tokyo), there was no more need for the *kitamae-bune*. An era ended for Obama, and it was forgotten until years later, when the coast became famous for nuclear power plants instead.

The atmospheric old center of Obama was brutally demolished in the late 1980s to make way for a supermarket and an eight-story hotel, and the famous **Obama fish market** is now in a tourist arcade. But the damage stopped when the economic "bubble" burst, and if you go to Obama now you can still find many old buildings in the backstreets—especially in the former geisha quarter, **Sanno-machi**.

When the center of Obama was torn down, one of its gracious old wooden inns, the Sekumi-ya, went with it. The Sekumi-ya has since become a faceless hotel. The only inn of distinction that I know of in Obama is the Fukuki.

A good alternative to staying in Obama is to go the extra two hours to **Ama-no-Hashidate** ("Bridge of Heaven"), a three-kilometer-long (two-mile) pine-covered sandbar. It is traditionally best seen by standing with your back to it, bending over, and looking between your legs; in this way, it becomes a bridge across the sky.

I first saw the **Bridge of Heaven** blanketed under a late December snowfall. Viewing it upside down, it did look like a white bridge in the sky and the seaside town below seemed quaint and underpopulated—just like the idyllic fishing village I had envisaged—and I was thoroughly taken in. People said I was lucky to come in winter because the snow covered up the sins of development. So I did not really expect to be impressed when I went back again in the warmer months. I must have been lucky, however. On a sparkling blue Sunday in early May, Ama-no-Hashidate's seaside was pretty, and animated with lots of young people crowding into the bayside temple, **Chionji**, and cruising the bay.

For all its beauty and fame, though, the Bridge of Heaven suffered from overdevelopment in the sixties and seventies, and some shabby shops and hotels from that time remain. Fortunately, a belated face-lift does appear to be underway.

A recommended route to Obama and Ama-no-Hashidate is by driving from Kyoto through the Kitayama cypress forests—stopping at the **Kitayama Cypress Museum** (Kitayama Sugi Shiryo-kan) on the way—via Miyama-cho.

At **Miyama-cho** you will find a small community called **Kitamura** that has 250 buildings with thatched roofs, beautifully preserved in a somewhat gentler style than those of Shirakawa-go (Destination 14). It is possible to stay at a *minshuku* in the preserved village. For accommodations in a farmhouse *minshuku*, call the Miyama-cho Tourist Association (☎ 0771–75–0310) or the Tourist Information Center at (☎ 0771–75–0815), both in Japanese. If you just want to take a day trip from Kyoto to Miyama-cho, it will take about two and a half hours by bus. Ask at the Kyoto Tourist Information Center (☎ 075–371–5649). An interesting alternative to a *minshuku* in Kitamura hamlet is the eccentric Tsuru-ya in Miyama-cho town proper.

Recommended trips including Miyama-cho / Obama /Ama-no-Hashidate

Miyama-cho is in a part of Japan called Tamba, the capital of which is the interesting town of Tamba-Sasayama. This does not mean that it is practical to combine Tamba-Sasayama and Miyama-cho in one trip—better to visit Tamba-Sasayama with Arima Onsen (Destination 26) and combine Miyama-cho with the Sea of Japan coast. It is also easy to carry on to the Kinosaki Onsen area (Destination 27) from Ama-no-Hashidate.

● Kyoto (Destination 23)—via Kitayama to Miyama-cho (1 night)—Obama (1 night)—Ama-no-Hashidate (1 day sight-seeing or overnight)

Note: For area map, see Destination 27.

MONJU-SO SHORO-TEI 文珠荘 松露亭

LOCATION: Ama-no-Hashidate

Superb one-story, sukiya-*style inn in a liberating seaside location.*

RATE: From ¥30,000 w/2 meals, no children. **CREDIT CARDS:** AMEX, DC, MC, VISA. **ROOMS:** 12 Japanese style (11 w/bath). **COMMUNAL BATHS:** 2—men's, women's. **CHECK-IN:** 14:00. **CHECK-OUT:** 10:00. **LANGUAGE:** No English, reservations in Japanese.

☎ 0772–22–2151 Fax: 0772–22–2153
Monjudo Misaki, Amano Hashidate, Miyazu-shi, Kyoto 626–0001
〒626–0001　京都府宮津市天橋立文殊堂岬

■ **ACCESS**
BY TRAIN: 5 min on foot from Amano Hashidate Stn (Kita-Kinki Tango Railway).
BY CAR: 30 km via Routes 175 & 176 from Maizuru/Ooe IC (Miyazu Doro) via Maizuru
Expressway.

Monju-so Shoro-tei

From Ama-no-Hashidate Station it is a five-minute saunter to the busy little sea-side temple of **Chionji**, known for its Chie no Monju ("Bodhisattva of Wisdom") and its Chie no Mochi ("Rice Cakes of Wisdom"). Right behind the temple, on prime bayside real estate and jutting out into the lovely Miyazu Bay, is the exquisitely renovated Monju-so Shoro-tei, formerly the Monju-so Bekkan.

The only thing separating the Monju-so Shoro-tei from the shore and sky is an elegant garden, with windswept pines and one absolutely ancient gnarled plum.

As early as 1690, a pleasure villa occupied this location. Nine years after World War II, the property was turned into a *ryokan*. Some exquisite new rooms were added in 1995, when forty years of wear were also sandpapered off the existing wooden floors and pillars in a painstaking renovation. Monju-so Shoro-tei is now undoubtedly the best inn Ama-no-Hashidate has to offer and among the finest in Japan. It does not have the view of the Bridge of Heaven, but it has the sea at its doorstep.

I was astounded by the beauty of its biggest corner suite, called "Kumoi," which has its own stunning three-mat tearoom attached. If I had the extra money to spend, I would be tempted to reserve this room—even over one at the Tawara-ya in Kyoto—for a premier *ryokan* experience.

GEMMYO-AN 玄妙庵

LOCATION:
Ama-no-
Hashidate

*Respectable concrete inn frequented by royalty
for its spectacular views of the Bridge of Heaven.*

RATE: From ¥25,000 w/2 meals, from ¥20,000 w/breakfast, from ¥18,000 w/o meals, children 30–50% off. **CREDIT CARDS:** AMEX, DC, MC, VISA. **ROOMS:** 28 Japanese style (w/bath). **COMMUNAL BATHS:** 2—men's, women's. **CHECK-IN:** 15:00. **CHECK-OUT:** 10:00. **LANGUAGE:** English spoken.

☎ 0772–22–2171 Fax: 0772–25–1641
Ama-no-Hashidate, Miyazu-shi, Kyoto 626–0001
〒626–0001　京都府宮津市天橋立

■ **ACCESS**
BY TRAIN: 5 min by car from Ama-no-hashidate Stn (Kita-Kinki Tango Railway).
BY CAR: 30 km via Routes 175 & 176 from Maizuru/Ooe IC (Miyazu Doro) via Maizuru
Expressway.

The first book on Japanese inns I ever bought had a stunning cover photo of the view from the room in this inn where Emperor Showa (previously known as Emperor Hirohito; 1901–89) stayed in 1951. The scene was the Bridge of Heaven, the pine-covered sandbar that is one of Japan's official "three most beautiful scenes."

For twelve years I cherished the photograph and wondered whether the inn would live up to this image. Would each room have "The View"? Would the rooms themselves be able to compete with the glory of The View?

The Gemmyo-an monopolizes one of the few high places in Ama-no-Hashidate from which you can see the lovely sandbar. Guests are normally ferried to the inn from the station by private bus, but I mistakenly decided to climb the knoll myself and was covered in perspiration by the time I reached the top. The trip must certainly have been a challenge for the palanquin bearers lugging the shogun Ashikaga Yoshimitsu (1358–1408) and his fellow ascetics up to the pleasure pavilion.

When Yoshimitsu stepped unexerted from his palanquin and saw this view, he is said to have described it as "*gemmyo*" (mysteriously beautiful), and as a result his pleasure pavilion came to be named the "arbor of mysterious beauty" (Gemmyo-tei). In later times a Zen temple occupied the site, but it was later replaced by an inn—the forerunner of the present Gemmyo-an, the oldest part of which dates back only about ninety years.

As it turns out, each of the twenty-six rooms at the Gemmyo-an has The View, but only the larger, expensive rooms really do it justice. The biggest disappointment is that the inn is made of concrete; I always imagined it to be wooden.

A welcome feature of the Gemmyo-an is the *mingei*-style reception area with its high, exposed beam ceiling and a floor-to-ceiling view of the bay. One by one, the rooms have been undergoing a costly face-lift that promises to bring twenty-first-century luxury. Nevertheless, to be on the safe side, choose the bigger, more expensive ones.

The food at Gemmyo-an, which mimics Kyoto *kaiseki* cuisine, features fresh seafood from Miyazu Bay. The real feast, however, is the Bridge of Heaven.

Private bath view, Gemmyo-an

TSURU-YA つるや

LOCATION: Miyama-cho

Quaint establishment run by a lady with a passion for "flower spirits," just fifteen minutes from the picturesque farming hamlet of Kitamura.

RATE: From ¥9,500 w/2 meals. CREDIT CARDS: Not accepted. ROOMS: 5 Japanese style (w/o bath). COMMUNAL BATH: 1—alternating. CHECK-IN: 15:00. CHECK-OUT: 10:00. LANGUAGE: No English, reservations in Japanese.

☎ 0771–75–0004
Shizuhara, Miyama-cho, Kita-Kuwada-gun, Kyoto 601–0755
〒601–0755　京都府北桑田郡美山町静原

■ **ACCESS**

BY TRAIN: 30 min by car from Wachi Stn (JR San'in Main Line).
BY CAR: 50 km via Route 162 from Kyoto.

Tsuru-ya

We arrived two hours late, having become lost twice on the moonlit country roads of Tamba. As we pulled up in front of the Tsuru-ya, our headlights caught a figure standing outside, wearing *mompe* farmer's pants. She was scanning each passing car with concern. Was this finally us?

Though it was 9 P.M. already, the lady guided us with hospitable banter to our dinner. Handing us each a tall, cool glass she said, "Here, this will clear away the cobwebs. You will feel much better tomorrow." It was the colorful owner of the Tsuru-ya herself, Chizuru Okamoto, and we were drinking her famous pine-needle cider.

The cider turned out to be an aperitif preceding other brews that followed— her "flower spirits," as she calls them. These are potent little drafts of flower-soaked *shochu* (Japanese moonshine). Lined up in front of us were three liqueur glasses each containing a different flower spirit—pink rosebud, red berry, and native orchid. The flavors that the flowers and berries imparted were so subtle as to be insignificant, but they did look pretty. The *shochu* was good and strong and the food was country fare at its best.

Ms. Okamoto's "flower spirits"

An eerie spectacle is offered at the entrance to the Tsuru-ya: the room adjoining the entrance area is stacked with bottles of Ms. Okamoto's flower spirits— more than five hundred varieties of them. You need to look twice to see that this is not some gruesome laboratory. But each of those bottles—tall, small, fat, square, blue, green, and brown—contains pure beauty. Have Ms. Okamoto show you her favorites: pick them up and then hold them to the light. One that looks clear might have a bed of tiny yellow petals which cascade like a snow dome when turned upside down. Friends bring Ms. Okamoto rare flowers and berries from far and wide, so the collection grows.

The passion started with a childhood desire to preserve pretty wildflowers. She experimented with sealing them in liquor and it worked, with the colors staying the same as the day they were picked. "I gave my first bottle of flower spirits to my daughter's firstborn. The plum blossoms were in full bloom and I just sealed some in a bottle and took them to her. My daughter was so excited. She said to the baby, 'Look, this was made by grandma. We will drink it when you're twenty.' " (from Okamoto Chizuru, *Zoku: Nonohana 365 Nichi*). Ms. Okamoto has been giving away flower spirit presents ever since. "The only trouble is the colors fade as soon as the air gets into the bottle," she said. "So once you open a bottle, there is only one chance to enjoy it." Very Zen.

The inn has old and new sections. The new part is unexceptional but comfortable, and the old is in a pleasing, geriatric state.

Nearby

We chose this inn because it is a fifteen-minute drive from the Kitamura farmhouse village of Miyama-cho. Along with Shirakawa-go and Gokayama, Kitamura at Miyama-cho is one of the most preciously preserved hamlets in Japan—the kind of place where a photographer crouches at every corner snapping grannies weeding their rice patches. Kitamura was designated a village for preservation in 1994, and since then the houses with thatched roofs have received subsidies to maintain the thatch. A local resident complained about waking up to find amateur photographers in his garden, peering into his bedroom, and said he was thinking of moving out. I don't know what Miyama-cho is like on weekends, but on an early spring Monday morning there were no cheap souvenirs being sold from makeshift stalls —only farmers going about their business in a paradise lost.

FUKUKI 福喜

LOCATION: Obama

The most interesting ryokan in a great old port town.

RATE: From ¥12,000 w/2 meals, children 30% off. **CREDIT CARDS:** Not accepted. **ROOMS:** 20 Japanese style (2 w/bath). **COMMUNAL BATHS:** 2—men's, women's. **CHECK-IN:** 15:30. **CHECK-OUT:** 10:00. **LANGUAGE:** No English, reservations in Japanese.

📞 0770–52–3077 Fax: 0770–53–1178
6–17 Minato, Obama-shi, Fukui 917–0004
〒917–0004　福井県小浜市湊6 17

■ ACCESS
BY TRAIN: 10 min by car from Obama Stn (JR Obama Line).
BY CAR: 1 hr via Route 27 from Tsuruga IC (Hokuriku Expressway).

The garden of the Fukuki's dining room is spellbinding and its baths are interesting. But by far the best reason to stay here is the access it gives to one of Obama's most historic buildings—an old shipping agent's house called the Sengoku-so. The owner of the Fukuki saved the Sengoku-so from demolishers and this cultural asset is shown only to guests of the inn, and only on request. The objects displayed in the Sengoku-so, including rare tea utensils with Christian motifs, were collected by the Fukuki's owner (they did not come with the house).

Compared with this lovely building and in spite of a promising entrance, the Fukuki itself has disappointing accommodations. Food is taken communally in a big tatami dining room, which has a grand outlook on a lovely garden. The courtly Heian look is a bit overdone, though.

Elaborate Fukuki bath

29

KURASHIKI

ATTRACTIONS

Historic merchants' quarter in Kurashiki City—picturesque buildings along willow-lined canals, excellent folk museums, abundant shops selling crafts. From here, head toward the Inland Sea, to see an amazing former salt magnate's house and the gateway to one of the wonders of the modern world, the Seto Ohashi bridge to Shikoku.

Insulated from the surrounding urban clutter of the industrial **Kurashiki**, the preserved former rice merchants' quarter is a timeless world of white plaster buildings checker-boarded with black tiles along willow-lined canals. Those of us who are used to the chaos of Japanese megalopolises might call it a charming relic of old Japan. Japanese writer Shiina Makoto (1944–) calls it "silly." Regardless, Kurashiki is a gateway to so many interesting places, that I recommend a stay.

Kurashiki is at its best when it's not flustered with too many tourists; before breakfast is a good time for a contemplative stroll through the old quarter. For this reason alone I would choose an inn—like Ryokan Kurashiki—in the heart of the old area.

You'll want to stay in Kurashiki to see the **Ohara Bijutsu-kan** (Ohara Museum of Art), a museum adorned with Grecian columns. In addition to Western art, it carries a first-rate collection of folk art by potters such as Shoji

Hamada (1894–1959), Bernard Leach (1887–1979), Kanjiro Kawai (1890–1966), and Kenkichi Tomimoto (1886–1963); dynamic woodblock prints by Munakata Shiko (1903–75); and stencil-dyed masterpieces by Keisuke Serizawa (1895–1984). Two other collections of folk art in Kurashiki are worth seeing: the **Kurashiki Mingei-kan** (Museum of Folk Art), housed partly in eighteenth-century rice granaries, and the **Nihon Kyodo Gangu-kan** (Japan Folk Toy Museum). There is also a whole day's worth of browsing in craft shops and boutiques. **Bizen pottery**, from the very good to the very bad, is everywhere, precluding a visit to the town of Bizen itself.

From Kurashiki, you have easy access to Kojima, the departure point for the **Seto Ohashi bridge**—the longest bridge in the world carrying both rail and road. The ¥9,000-toll for the round trip ride is so high that the bridge is deserted most of the time, but what a trip! I never knew the Inland Sea could be so

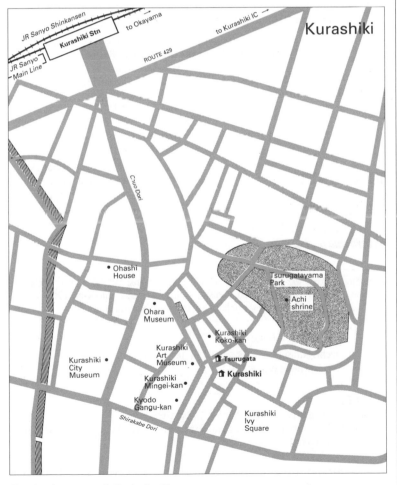

Note: See also area map in Destination 30.

spectacular. The round trip train ride is significantly cheaper, so a journey by rail is worth considering.

In Kojima itself, a must-see is the **Nozaki House**, the former home of salt baron Nozaki Buzaemon (1790–1865). Five magnificent black-and-white storehouses on the property used to house materials for salt farming. Under the pine and plum trees in the courtyard by the warehouses are clusters of rough wheel-shaped stones. They were used for weighing the coals that heated the salt water. The workers would put one stone weighing 60 kilograms (132 pounds) on a boat and measure how far the boat sank. Then they would load coal up to the same level. Do also notice the enormous flat stone in front of the reception room of the main house: important guests alighted from their palanquins on this impressive slab—a sort of rocky red carpet.

From Kojima it is a short drive to the port of Shimotsui, from where you get the boat or small ferry to **Mukuchi-jima island** with its remote inn, Mukuchi-jima Kadan. It is also just a couple of hours from Kurashiki to marvelous **Fukiya** (Destination 30).

Recommended trips including Kurashiki

- Kurashiki (1 night)—Fukiya (1 night, Destination 30)—Matsue (1 night at Shinji-cho. See Yagumo Honjin, Alternative Inns) —Izumo (day excursion, Destination 32)
- Kurashiki (1 night)—Kojima (day excursion)—Shikoku via Seto Ohashi Bridge (Destination 33)

KURASHIKI 旅館くらしき

LOCATION:
Kurashiki
(canal area)

Tastefully renovated home of a former sugar merchant in the most picturesque part of town.

Façade, Kurashiki

RATE: From ¥20,000 w/2 meals, children 30% off. **CREDIT CARDS:** AMEX, DC, VISA. **ROOMS:** 21 Japanese style (9 w/bath). **COMMUNAL BATHS:** 2—men's, women's. **CHECK-IN:** 15:00. **CHECK-OUT:** 10:00. **CLOSED:** Year end/New Year holidays. **LANGUAGE:** Some English.

☎ 086–422–0730 Fax: 086–422–0990
4–1 Hon-machi, Kurashiki-shi, Okayama 710–0054
〒710–0054　岡山県倉敷市本町4–1

■ ACCESS
BY TRAIN: 10 min by car from Kurashiki Stn (JR Sanyo *shinkansen*).
BY CAR:　15 min from Kurashiki IC (Sanyo Expressway), or 10 min from Hayashima IC (Seto Expressway).

In my experience, Okayama people really know about service. When I called the Ryokan Kurashiki to make a reservation, the greeting was genuinely welcoming, even though I was a woman traveling alone. This could be enough for many inns to turn you away—a lone female traveler traditionally spells suicide.

When I arrived, I was seated in a picturesque terrace room cozily cluttered with old English tables, and served whisked green tea to classical music.

The first-generation owner, Shigeko Hatayama, feels the inn belongs to Kurashiki, not to her. Now over eighty, she has passed the inn on to her son Riho, who is as passionate about Western traditions as he is about Eastern.

The lovely inn building, in the middle of the preserved old town, was once a sugar wholesaler's mansion. The house and its former sugar storehouse, tool shed, and rice store have all been renovated to make guest rooms. The result is that no two rooms are alike, their unique configurations being dictated by the original structures. Some are no more than four-and-a-half-mat attics, with beams so low that you must be careful not to bang your head. But from the low little windows you can peer out on the whole fascinating nest of buildings that makes up Ryokan Kurashiki. Some rooms are spacious enough to have their own bathrooms and toilets. Even if they don't, the shared rest rooms here are aesthetically pleasing.

Entrance hall,
Kurashiki

The renovators have included quite a number of antique-looking Western fittings. At times, you don't quite know where Japan ends and Europe begins, but somehow it all works very well.

The food is excellent. In the old days, fresh fish was brought to Kurashiki from the Inland Sea via the transport canals, so there was always plenty of good seafood. While the fish no longer arrive on boats running up the canals, the seafood tradition remains. In autumn, a feast from "sea and mountains" (*sankai kaiseki*) is served, consisting of fish, shellfish, mushrooms, ginkgo nuts, and chestnuts. The winter specialty is delicate steamed rice with oysters. Breakfast is a simple meal of rice, soup, and greens, or Western style. This inn is the best reason to spend a night in Kurashiki—and stroll the canal area before breakfast to see Kurashiki at its loveliest, before the crowds roll in.

MUKUCHI-JIMA KADAN 六口島花壇

LOCATION:
Mukuchi-jima
Island

Secluded, unpretentious inn on an all-but deserted island with an unimpeded outlook on the Inland Sea.

RATE: From ¥15,000 w/2 meals, children 50% off. **CREDIT CARDS:** VISA. **ROOMS:** 14 Japanese style (2 w/bath). **COMMUNAL BATHS:** 2—men's, women's. **CHECK-IN:** 15:00. **CHECK-OUT:** 10:00. **LANGUAGE:** No English, reservations in Japanese.

☏ 086–479–9093 Fax: 086–479–9093
Mukuchi-jima, Shimotsui, Kurashiki-shi, Okayama 711–0927
〒711–0927　岡山県倉敷市下津井六口島

■ **ACCESS**

BY TRAIN: 10 min by boat from Shimotsui Port (15 min by taxi from Kojima Stn; JR Seto Ohashi Line).

BY CAR: Leave your car at Shimotsui Port; 3 km from Kojima IC (Seto Expressway).

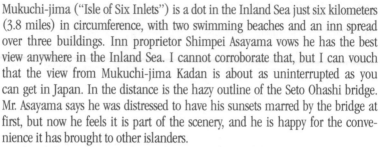

Mukuchi-jima ("Isle of Six Inlets") is a dot in the Inland Sea just six kilometers (3.8 miles) in circumference, with two swimming beaches and an inn spread over three buildings. Inn proprietor Shimpei Asayama vows he has the best view anywhere in the Inland Sea. I cannot corroborate that, but I can vouch that the view from Mukuchi-jima Kadan is about as uninterrupted as you can get in Japan. In the distance is the hazy outline of the Seto Ohashi bridge. Mr. Asayama says he was distressed to have his sunsets marred by the bridge at first, but now he feels it is part of the scenery, and he is happy for the convenience it has brought to other islanders.

Entrance, Mukuchi-jima Kadan

This convenience, however, makes little difference to Mr. Asayama. The only way to get to Mukuchi-jima is by boat—either a small commuter ferry or Mr. Asayama's dinghy. After the ten-minute ride, you alight on a beach where all that seems to exist is the lapping of water and bird song.

The Ikeda Clan, who ruled Okayama in the Edo period (1600–1868), used this island to graze horses. After World War II, Mr. Asayama's father, Katsuichi, bought the island after repatriation from China, where he had been running a factory. He settled on Mukuchi-jima in 1949, and all the landscaping work there is the result of his labors. He was an idealist who built the inn as a seaside salon for something called the "Inland Sea Culture Club" (Setonaikai Bunka Kurabu). This was to be a meeting place of minds on how to build a world where science and technology did not assume unbalanced proportions. The name *kadan* means "garden beds," and at one time this salon was indeed a garden paradise.

Private beach, Mukuchi-jima Kadan

Since Katsuichi's death in 1985, his wife and son have taken over. The flower beds are gone and the property is generally run down, but the structures are still in good shape and are kept clean and uncluttered. The most pleasant of the three lodges is the Cho-on-ro ("Sound of the Tides") on the highest point.

Mukuchi-jima Kadan must be one of the few places in Japan where guests have their own private beach. There's nothing to do but laze in the day, enjoy fresh seafood at night, and then watch seacraft bobbing like fireflies in the distant sea until falling asleep to the sound of waves. A fun way to enjoy Mukuchi-jima Kadan might be with a whole party of friends, so you can claim the entire hilltop lodge.

Nearby

Shimotsui, the port from where you get the boat to Mukuchi-jima,
is just ten minutes by car from Kojima (home of the
marvelous Nozaki House).

FUKIYA

Historic Fukiya street

ATTRACTIONS

This isolated area—home to the copper and bengara barons of old— still has amazing mansions and displays on bengara pigment production.

An excellent side trip from Kurashiki (Destination 29) is to head inland on the road to **Fukiya** on the Sea of Japan coast. This remote enclave was once Japan's center for copper and *bengara*, a red pigment used for textile dyes, pottery glazes, and tinting walls in rich people's homes. The breathtaking beauty of these walls is eloquently demonstrated by houses in Fukiya (especially in an area called Shimotani), which look their most striking when contrasted against the bright green foliage of spring and early summer.

The red pigment was a precious commodity: the wealth amassed by the local *bengara* barons is evident in two stupendous mansions that are open to the public, the **Hirokane-ke** (built in 1810) and the **Nishie-ke**.

It would be most convenient to have a car in Fukiya, first of all because the only alternative access from Bitchu-Takahashi is by infrequent bus service (forty minutes; six times a day), and secondly to let you tour the different attractions at your own pace. In addition to the Hirokane-ke and Nishie-ke mansions, these include the old ***bengara* mine** and the **Bengara-kan** (Bengara Factory

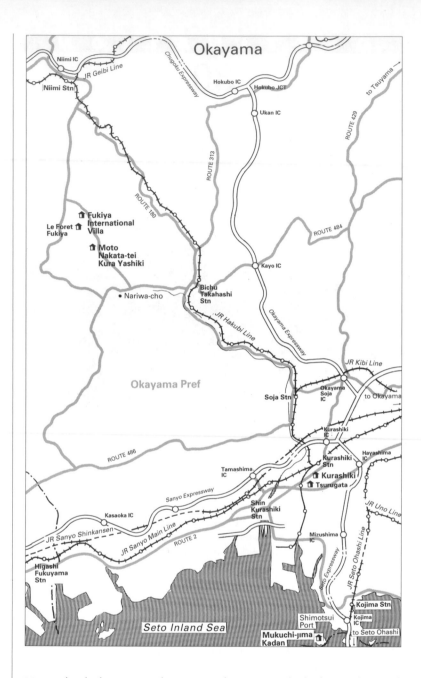

Museum), which re-creates the seventeenth-century Yoshioka factory that stood on this site until the late 1960s.

In Fukiya township itself, there is the **Fukiya Historical Museum** in the former home of the Katayama banking family. It was built in 1819 by shrine carpenters without using a nail. Note the *shoji* door that slides around a corner;

the funny little courtyard garden that is merely a lantern, a rock, and a spot of moss; and the time-worn packed-earth entrance. For something different, check out the Okinawan and other souvenirs at the **Fukiya Sanso**, which was once an inn. The owner was stationed in Okinawa during the war and developed a great fondness for the area.

Entertainment in Fukiya is nonexistent. This must be the only town in Japan without a pachinko place or a karaoke bar. That it has been left so unspoiled obviously has much to do with the isolation of the town, connected to the outside world solely by the rural road from Bitchu-Takahashi.

In **Bitchu-Takahashi**, you can visit old samurai houses, an historic miso maker's home, and **Raikyuji temple**, which has the first garden ever built by noted tea master Kobori Enshu (1579–1647). The garden is inspiring.

Recommended trips including Fukiya

Kurashiki is the natural departure point for Fukiya, but keep in mind that the train (JR Hakubi Line) from Bitchu-Takahashi heads up to Yonago, a gateway to the Sea of Japan area. From here you can explore Izumo and Matsue and then head either for Hagi (Destination 32) or in the other direction toward Kinosaki (Destination 27), or Ama-no-Hashidate (Destination 28) and from there back to Kyoto.

● Kurashiki (1 night)—Fukiya (1 night, Destination 30)—Matsue (day excursion)—Izumo (1 night, Destination 32)

FUKIYA INTERNATIONAL VILLA
吹屋 国際交流ヴィラ

Stylish, affordable lodge catering to foreign travelers, on the main street of Fukiya.

RATE: From ¥3,000 w/o meals. **CREDIT CARDS:** Not accepted. **ROOMS:** 1 Japanese style, 4 Western style—all w/o bath. **COMMUNAL BATH:** 1—alternating. **CHECK-IN:** 16:00. **CHECK-OUT:** 11:00. **LANGUAGE:** No English, reservations in Japanese.

☎ 086–256–2535 Fax: 086–256–2576
836 Fukiya, Nariwa-cho, Kawakami-gun, Okayama 719–2341
〒719–2341　岡山県川上郡成羽町吹屋836

Fukuiya International Villa

■ **ACCESS**
BY TRAIN: 50 min by bus or taxi from Bitchu Takahashi Stn (JR Hakubi Line).
BY CAR: 80 min via Route 313 from Hokubo IC (Chugoku Expressway), or 1 hr from Kayo IC (Okayama Expressway).

Okayama Prefecture gets the prize for the most tasteful "internationalization" project in Japan. Six "international villas" have been built in the prefecture where non-Japanese nationals can stay for very reasonable rates. The villa in Fukiya is a replica of the handsome soy-sauce storehouse that once stood on the site. Inside, it is more like a Western-style lodge, with four private bedrooms and one tatami room for Japanese-style sleeping. The well-equipped modern kitchen, lounge, and bathroom are all shared. When I went I had the whole place to myself, but the visitors' book indicates the villa is well used and many an "international" friendship has been formed around the wood fire. Strangers from different lands write about the great time they spent exchanging travel anecdotes and engaging in sing-alongs. You certainly do have to make your own fun; there is not even a TV.

You can do your own cooking (with supplies from an all-purpose store in the town) or eat at one of three restaurants serving noodles and other basic country food.

LOCATION: Bitchu-Uji

MOTO NAKATA-TEI KURA YASHIKI
元仲田邸くらやしき

Modern accommodations in a stunning old estate.

RATE: From ¥6,500 w/2 meals, from ¥3,000 w/o meals, children from ¥2,000. **CREDIT CARDS:** Not accepted. **ROOMS:** 5 Japanese style, 3 semi-Japanese style—all w/o bath. **COMMUNAL BATHS:** 2—men's, women's. **CHECK-IN:** 16:00. **CHECK-OUT:** 10:00. **LANGUAGE:** No English, reservations in Japanese.

☾ 0866–29–2118 Fax: 0866–29–87–2130
1757 Uji, Uji-cho, Takahashi-shi, Okayama 719–2232
〒719–2232　岡山県高梁市宇治町宇治1757

■ ACCESS
BY TRAIN: 30 min by car from Bitchu Takahashi Stn (JR Hakubi Line).
BY CAR:　1 hr via Route 313 from Hokubo IC (Chugoku Expressway), or 40 min from Kayo IC (Okayama Expressway).

The handsome original building, Moto Nakata-tei

This unusual inn is in the grounds of one of the most spectacular private homes in Japan—the former estate of the Nakata family, who were rich commodities merchants in the Edo period (1600–1868). The present buildings, decorated dramatically in black, white, and grey tiles, date from the 1930s. A former saké warehouse has been renovated to provide modern Japanese-style accommodation, and though it lacks the character of the main house, you feel privileged just to be within the estate walls. The splendid old main house can be rented for study meetings and special occasions. The food is country-style *kaiseki*, made and served by local women.

This is a tea-growing area that has come to be known as Bitchu-Uji, after Uji, the most famous of the Kyoto tea-producing areas, and driving the country roads of Bitchu-Uji is wonderfully picturesque.

31

HIROSHIMA and IWAKUNI

Miyajima Shrine

ATTRACTIONS

The nuclear bombing memorials of Hiroshima, the big red shrine in the sea at Miyajima and the serene former castle town of Iwakuni.

Hiroshima suffered the first of the two atomic bombs dropped on Japan, on August 6, 1945. The **Peace Memorial Museum in Hiroshima** preserves the sobering history of the bombing. Now fully rebuilt, Hiroshima is also the closest big city to Miyajima, site of that very Japanese icon, the lavish **Miyajima shrine**. Built on an island, the shrine is usually known as Miyajima ("shrine island"), although its real name is Itsukushima.

A-bomb dome, Hiroshima

The powerful Taira family took over the island in the late twelfth century and constructed the present red pavilions over the sea. Worshippers (but no commoners) entered through the big red *torii* gate in boats. Today, people arrive by ferry and not, unfortunately, through the *torii*. The shrine's pavilions appear to float on the water when the tide is high. The scene is made even more mysterious on those nights when the lanterns are lit around the pavilions and halls, which now also include *bugaku* (court music) and Noh stages.

There are a number of other minor attractions on the island, not least the ravenous bands of deer which will follow you into shops to get the food in your hands. Notice the stacks of maple leaf–shaped cakes filled with sweet bean paste jam on sale: the *momiji* (maple leaf) is the island's symbol. In **Momiji-dani**, a delightful glen near the Iwaso inn, over thirty varieties of *momiji* have been planted by successive generations of inn proprietors.

After Miyajima, I highly recommend making the forty-minute trip to visit **Iwakuni**—not the naval base, but the castle town district with its old streets and samurai mansions. If you can time this for the summer **cormorant fishing** season, all the better. Cormorant fishing on the placid Nishiki River, with the stunningly beautiful **Kintaikyo ("Brocade-Sash Bridge")** illuminated for your pleasure, is something out of a dream. I hear that the cherry blossoms here are magnificent, too. Inn accommodation is limited; the Hangetsu-an, though new, is a comfortable choice.

Another spot worth a detour is **Takehara,** on the other side of Hiroshima. Its name means "bamboo plains," but "salt plains" would be more appropriate because Takehara was a major salt-producing area. It started producing salt from 1650 and the wealth that accumulated here lead to a vigorous urban

culture. The Takehara historic quarter has several handsome structures that belonged to other merchants and tradesmen and a beautiful former home of a salt magnate located on a picturesque promenade. But the house that first caught my eye was Isobe Takehara, the town's tastefully refurbished old *minshuku*.

Recommended buys

The shops lining the approaches to Miyajima shrine specialize mainly in the sweet maple leaf–shaped cakes. But there is an interesting shop on the main street from the ferry, selling soy sauces, miso pastes, condiments, and pickles in handsome packaging. The *daidai shoyu* (a soy sauce flavored with tart *daidai* citrus fruit) is excellent.

Recommended trips including Hiroshima

Hiroshima and Miyajima are a natural pair. I would suggest a day in Hiroshima, ending in Miyajima for an overnight stay at the Iwaso, followed by a half-day to see the Miyajima sights.
Ferry services to Miyajima from Hiroshima are frequent and easy. It is also a quick trip to Iwakuni, although you will need to take a bus or taxi from the Sanyo Line station (Iwakuni) or *shinkansen* station (Shin Iwakuni) to get to the Kintaikyo bridge area. From Iwakuni you can extend your trip by heading to Hagi or even Kyushu, going over to Matsuyama on Shikoku, or staying on the mainland and going back to Kurashiki via Himeji.
Takehara is not far from Hiroshima, so it might make an alternative place to stay before visiting Hiroshima or on the way back from a trip to this area.

- Takehara (day excursion or overnight at Isobe Takehara. See Alternative Inns)—Hiroshima (day excursion)—Miyajima (1 night)—Iwakuni (1 night)
  - Hiroshima (day excursion)—Miyajima (1 night)—Iwakuni (1 night)—Matsuyama (by ferry; 2 nights in Matsuyama area alone, or a round trip of Shikoku requiring at least 4–5 days, Destination 33)

IWASO 岩惣

LOCATION: Miyajima

The most venerable ryokan in the Hiroshima area;
in a prime location with service and comfort worthy of royalty.

RATE: From ¥21,000 w/2 meals. **CREDIT CARDS:** AMEX, VISA. **ROOMS:** 42 Japanese style (31 w/bath). **COMMUNAL BATHS:** 2—men's, women's. **CHECK-IN:** 15:30. **CHECK-OUT:** 10:00. **CLOSED:** 12/24–12/27. **LANGUAGE:** No English, reservations in Japanese.

☏ 0829–44–2233 Fax: 0829–44–2230
Momijidani, Miyajima-cho, Saiki-gun, Hiroshima 739–0522
〒739–0522　広島県佐伯郡宮島町もみじ谷

*Iwaso's expansive
lobby*

Staying overnight on Miyajima island provides the chance for viewing the famous vermilion shrine in ways that you can't during the day—by moonlight or better still by candlelight, as well as during its quiet morning and dusk hours. To make the experience truly special, stay at the granddaddy of gracious old inns in the Hiroshima area, the Iwaso.

As the earliest inn to be built on Miyajima, the Iwaso has the monopoly on the loveliest part of Miyajima's famous Momiji-dani (Maple Leaf Glen), where a sparkling clear stream trips over rocks shaded by maples. After opening the inn in 1893, the original owner of the Iwaso developed the area by building a tea shop and filling the glen with *momiji*. The inn itself was meticulously constructed in the finest woodworking traditions of the *miya-daiku* (shrine carpenters), and has been host to royalty ever since.

Though it now has a ferroconcrete wing built in 1981, the interior is so tastefully blended with the hundred-year-old building that you scarcely know where the old part ends and the new part begins. Its lobby is a stunning gateway: expansive, stone-paved, deep, and silent.

Japan's first prime minister, Hirobumi Ito (1841–1909), novelists Soseki Natsume (1867–1916) and Ogai Mori (1862–1922), and *mingei* potter Shoji Hamada (1894–1959) all stayed at the Iwaso. Helen Keller was here in 1958. Author Eiji Yoshikawa (1892–1962) wrote his *Shin Heike Monogatari* in his favorite room, the Senshintei. Members of the imperial family have one set of *hanare* (detached rooms), the Shifuku-kan, reserved for their use.

Since this inn serves royalty, you can expect impeccable accouterments, comfort, and service in all rooms, even those in the new wing. Nevertheless, if you have the means, do try and stay in one of the original *hanare*, which are very special indeed.

Dinners are Kyoto-style *kaiseki*, starting with appetizers and clear soup and going all the way through the grilled, fried, boiled, and vinegared dishes plus *anago* (conger eel) sushi, a specialty of the area. Expect lots of oyster dishes in winter, since this is Hiroshima's main delicacy. For breakfast there is freshly brewed coffee on tap.

The area's most spectacular season is autumn, but this is also a nightmare of crowds, so you may prefer the green-leaf months or even winter, when the maple-leaf glen is sometimes covered in snow.

Nearby

From the Iwaso, Miyajima shrine is a couple of minutes on foot. The best
time to see it is before and after the daytime crowds, so take a stroll
after dinner or before breakfast. The shrine's halls are open
from 6 A.M. The deer that roam the grounds are hungry,
so if you buy a snack be prepared for the
insistent nudging of many wet noses.

SEKI-TEI 石亭

*Hot spring inn with a lovely garden
and special conger eel bento.*

RATE: From ¥21,000 w/2 meals. **CREDIT CARDS:** AMEX, DC, VISA. **ROOMS:** 10 Japanese style (7 w/bath). **COMMUNAL BATHS:** 4—men's, women's, 2 outdoor (men's, women's). **CHECK-IN:** 16:00. **CHECK-OUT:** 10:00. **LANGUAGE:** Some English.

☎ 0829–55–0601 Fax: 0829–55–0603
3–5–27 Miyahama Onsen, Ono-machi, Saiki-gun, Hiroshima 739–0454
〒739–0454　広島県佐伯郡大野町宮浜温泉3–5–27

■ ACCESS
BY TRAIN: 5 min by car from Onoura Stn (JR Sanyo Main Line).
BY CAR:　10 min from Ono IC (Sanyo Expressway).

Set in a sleepy residential area with a distant view of Miyajima, this hillside inn has a magnificently manicured garden and just ten rooms in individual structures. Though the architecture is on the cheap side and the fittings have seen better days, Seki-tei has a fine atmosphere and an excellent reputation among Hiroshima locals. Most seem to go there to enjoy an elegant lunch and hot spring bath, and it seems to prosper more as a dining venue than as an inn. The specialty here is *anago bento*—rice topped with subtly flavored grilled conger eel from Miyahama Bay, right on the inn's doorstep. This tasty morsel is presented very precisely, like a chrysanthemum flower, in a round *bento* box.

Seki-tei's immaculate garden

The original owner of Seki-tei created *anago bento* and it has since become Hiroshima's main food souvenir. The Seki-tei still makes the best in town, using only the prime specimens of the local haul, rather than Southeast Asian imports.

The inn has both a *rotemburo* and an indoor cypress bath. Lunch with a bath might be a good alternative if you have other accommodation plans.

Conger eel bento, Seki-tei

HANGETSU-AN 半月庵

*Recently refurbished, inexpensive and convenient
lodgings in a charming castle town.*

RATE: From ¥9,000 w/2 meals, from ¥12,000 w/bath, from ¥6,500 w/breakfast, from ¥5,500 w/o meals, children from ¥4,500. **CREDIT CARDS:** Not accepted. **ROOMS:** 20 Japanese style (2 w/bath). **COMMUNAL BATHS:** 2—men's, women's. **CHECK-IN:** 15:00. **CHECK-OUT:** 10:00. **CLOSED:** 12/29–1/5. **LANGUAGE:** No English, reservations in Japanese.

☎ 0827–41–0021 Fax: 0827–43–0121
1–17–27 Iwakuni, Iwakuni-shi, Yamaguchi 741–0062
〒741–0062　山口県岩国市岩国1–17–27

■ ACCESS

BY TRAIN: 10 min by car from Shin Iwakuni Stn (JR Sanyo *shinkansen*).
BY CAR:　6 km from Iwakuni IC (Sanyo Expressway).

Kintaikyo, Iwakuni

One of the best things I've done in Japan was to see cormorant fishing in Iwakuni. Compared with the commercialized spectacle at the Nagara River in Gifu Prefecture, the intimacy and beauty of cormorant fishing at Iwakuni took me by surprise. The fishermen in their grass skirts on sleek wooden skiffs, the flaming torches, and the glassy surface of the Nishiki River reflecting the lovely arches of the Kintaikyo bridge made me wonder if this was what it was like 350 years ago, when the young lord of Iwakuni first held cormorant fishing for his pleasure.

The Hangetsu-an is an old inn-turned-*kokumin shukusha* (public lodgings), which was rebuilt in concrete in the 1990s. It has been overrun by white wallpaper and fluorescent lights, but is nevertheless a welcome oasis for a weary traveler. The best thing about the Hangetsu-an is its location, right on the street where the lower-ranked samurai of Iwakuni used to live (some old residences are still present). Across the river, over Kintaikyo bridge is the road that leads to the castle high on the hill. The samurai would have made this trip on foot; now tourists can go by cable car.

The cormorant fishing takes place from June 1 (which is the start of the *ayu* sweetfish season) to August 31. The Hangetsu-an can book you onto one of the cormorant fishing viewing boats. The proprietor recommends that you have a bath, eat (a filling *bento*), and get to the riverside by about 7 P.M. in time to board the boat. You pay the inn and they pay the fishermen.

Weekends in cormorant fishing season are crowded. Try to visit on a weekday, or at least avoid Saturdays (especially the first Saturday of August, when there is also a big fireworks bash).

At Hangetsu-an, dinner is served in your room, and breakfast is eaten in the downstairs cafeteria with a garden view. Toilets and baths are shared.

Nearby

Iwakuni is worth visiting just to see Kintaikyo bridge, which is an easy walk from the Hangetsu-an. "Kintaikyo" means "bridge of the brocade sash," presumably so named because it looks like a long undulating *obi* thrown over the river. The present bridge is a replica of one built in 1673, which was swept away by a flood in 1950. The replica is all wood on stone pylons, and so well crafted that it is hard to notice the steel pin reinforcements underneath. The town's castle is also a replica (built in 1962) of one destroyed in 1615. The other place of note is Kikko Park, where the high-ranked samurai used to live, and now a pleasant leafy spot for a stroll.

32

HAGI

*Hagi ware at the
Hokumon Yashiki inn
gift shop*

ATTRACTIONS

Seaside town and home to many fathers of the Meiji Restoration (1868) and to one of the most famous tea-ceremony ceramics.

My first purpose in visiting Hagi was to do the rounds of the **Hagi ware kilns** and buy one of the tea bowls that are said to become more beautiful with age. However, the choice seemed to be mainly between production-line pieces and unaffordable one-offs. On the other hand, it was unexpectedly enjoyable to trace some of Hagi's history in this agreeable seaside town. I could imagine how this refreshingly open place with its fragrant citrus orchards became the breeding ground for the young men of progressive thought who led the revolutions that brought Japan into the modern era.

One of the best things to do in Hagi is to take a stroll or bicycle ride through the streets of **old samurai mansions** in the **Horiuchi** ("Inside the Moat") area and savor the crumbling earthen walls, samurai gates, and citrus trees. The district remembers its sons who led the Meiji Restoration and formed Japan's first modern government. Try to visit the family home of the first prime minister, Hirobumi Ito (1841–1909), and that of Takayoshi Kido (1833–77), who was influential in the first government. There is also the **Shoka Sonjuku**, the school set up by scholar Shoin Yoshida (1830–59), where many Meiji leaders gained their early education.

The most impressive Hagi sight is the Obaku Zen temple **Tokoji**, where the tombs of five of the lords of the Mori clan who ruled this domain are heralded by dramatic rows of old stone lanterns. The tombs of the even-numbered lords, side by side with their wives, are at Tokoji, while the odd-numbered lords and their wives are entombed at a somewhat quieter temple, **Daishoin**, close to Hagi Station. The stone lanterns were offered by vassals of the entombed lords in lieu of killing themselves out of loyalty.

From Hagi it is about a ninety-minute detour to **Tsuwano**, a former castle town nestled in a quiet valley whose preserved historic zone—**Tono-machi**—is famous for its picturesque narrow roadside canals full of huge red and gold carp and planted with irises.

The impressive walls in this area no longer hide the samurai mansions they once did; but museums instead. Though there is little of great substance to see, it is certainly a pleasant place to stroll. And don't limit yourself to the Tono-machi area, but continue on a bit further into *hon-machi*. You never know what you will find. I came across a handsome old pharmacy and a charming shop selling seeds, seedlings, and dried flowers.

From either Hagi or Tsuwano, I would be tempted to spend a couple of more days wending my way up the Sea of Japan coast to Izumo and then onto Matsue.

The main attraction in **Izumo** is the **Grand Shrine of Izumo** (Izumo Taisha), the second most important shrine in Japan after the Grand Shrines of Ise (Destination 16).

Though both are described as "grand shrines" in English it would not be fair to compare Ise Jingu with Izumo Taisha. Ise has received much greater patronage over the years, and this is immediately apparent in its scale and the very healthy commercialism that lines the roads to its portals. Izumo, meanwhile, is smaller and has a rather shabby road leading to its big stone *torii*, not to mention one decidedly ugly new Shinto structure in its grounds. In spite of this, though, the Grand Shrine has its own dignified charm and a marvelous patina evident in its moss-encrusted thatched roofs, which sets it apart from the ever-fresh, cypress-scented Ise. It also seems more approachable. At Ise we were held well back from the god's domain by barriers and stern guards whose lips only moved to say "No photos!" Meanwhile, the god's sanctum at Izumo, though of course sealed from view, was watched over by a rather jocular priest, and in a corner of the inner compound younger priests handed out mouthfuls of saké palm-size earthen dishes, which we were told to keep "for the memory."

On the old lunar calendar, the tenth month of the year is referred to as "Kannazuki," the "month of no gods." All of the gods, of which there are precisely eight million, are believed to congregate at Izumo Taisha at this time of year for a convocation with the resident deity, Okuninushi no Mikoto. What takes place there is not known and what the rest of Japan does without the gods, I don't know either. But notice that on either side of the Honden (the inner sanctum) are two long structures. These are called *jukusha* and they contain nineteen mini-shrines, which house all the visiting *kami* (gods). Being home to the Okuninushi no Mikoto, who among other things, is known as the god who

blesses the "joining of people" (*emmusubi*), Izumo Taisha is a favorite for weddings, which are particularly prevalent in the tenth month when all the gods are present.

Izumo is close to the city of Matsue, which was home to one of Japan's earliest and most ardent Japanofiles, Lafcadio Hearn (1850–1904), for seven months in 1890. He wrote of his experiences in such books as *Glimpses of Unfamiliar Japan*. You can see **Koizumi Yakumo Kyukyo**, the house that Hearn lived in, and the famous thatched teahouse called **Meimei-an** built in 1779 by

Matsudaira Fumai (1751–1818), a major arbiter of tea taste in the Edo period (1600–1868). His legacy dots the entire area, and is even found at the Yagumo Honjin inn (see Alternative Inns), in the form of a handsome stone waterbasin for the tea garden, which is said to have belonged to him. One of my great regrets is not having had the time to travel further out of Matsue to see an even more renowned Fumai teahouse called **Kanden-an**.

The **Adachi Museum** in picturesque farmland between Yonago and Matsue is famed for its spectacular "borrowed scenery" garden built by one of Japan's leading contemporary garden architect Kinsaku Nakane (1917–1995). The distant mountains act as a backdrop for a carefully composed foreground garden, and I must say I have never seen it done quite as dramatically. Entrepreneur Zenko Adachi built the museum in 1970 and is said to have bought much of the mountain land to the west of the garden to keep the borrowed view pristine. The garden can only be described as perfect. The museum's art, while including collections of the works of such *nihonga* greats as Taikan Yokoyama (1868–1958) and Kansetsu Hashimoto (1883–1945), and the potters Kanjiro Kawai (1890–1966) and Rosanjin Kitaoji (1883–1959), did not leave me especially inspired. The commercialism spoke a little too loudly.

Apart from the *ryokan* Yagumo Honjin, the best attraction in Shimane is **Iwami Ginzan**, the town that grew up around one of Japan's richest Edo-period silver mines, and is also synonymous in the minds of the older generation with "poison." Arsenic, a by-product of silver ore, was in great demand in the intrigue-ridden Warring States (1482–1573) and Edo periods from the fifteenth to eighteenth centuries. The township consists of one long street of Edo and Meiji/Taisho-period (1868–1926) houses meandering into the hills along a picturesque stream, a scene that has not changed since silver mining was discontinued in 1923. A lack of a railway line to this area has protected it from progress (like the *"bengara"* town of Fukiya in Okayama), and there is still a lack of tourist clutter.

An artifacts museum inside the gatehouse of the former governor's mansion at the foot of the main street explores the history of the silver mine, but soon after the town dissolves into a living community with obvious pride in its heritage. The long, narrow street of tiled-roof wooden buildings comes complete with a rickety nineteenth-century doctor's dispensary, a barber shop with one chair, an old wooden school, and a smattering of other shops making and selling daily commodities such as vinegar, miso, and sweets. On the main cross street heading out of town towards the old silver mines is a rare collection of **Gohyaku Rakan** (five hundred disciples of Buddha) inside roadside caves, definitely worth the short hike for a visit.

Apparently Iwami Ginzan is only a shadow of its former self. At one time, after it came under the direct control of the Edo shogunate, it supported a population of 200,000 and had 1,000 temples to hold funerals for the short-lived miners. But over the years it has succumbed to many fires, and finally isolation. However, that is all to its advantage today. As you enter Iwami Ginzan a banner proclaims the town's bid to become a UNESCO World Heritage Site, a designation which would assure its preservation.

I spotted two *minshuku* accommodations in Iwami Ginzan, the more homely of the two being Omori-kan (☎ 08548–9–0716). It would be fun to spend a night in this quiet town.

Iwami Ginzan is ten kilometers (six miles) from the seaside town of Oda, just out of Izumo. If you have a few extra hours, spend them exploring the privileged beach-side communities of **Oda**, with their tiny narrow streets of traditional homes, and even more so those of **Gotsu**, which is a bit further down the track. Gotsu has been home to a thriving roof-tile-making industry since the 1800s and the whole town is bedecked with gleaming red-brown and black tiles. This uniform expanse of tiled roofs is such a splendid sight, I could have spent a whole afternoon just wandering among those houses.

More information on Iwami Ginzan and indeed the whole of Shimane is contained in *Along the San'in*, by J. M. Daggett (*Imai-shoten*, Matsue).

Recommended trips including Hagi

Hagi is quite isolated at the southern end of Japan, but with enough time it can be satisfyingly combined in a round trip that could either include Kyushu (Destinations 34 and 35), or Yamaguchi City, Izumo, and Matsue, or even Hiroshima and Iwakuni (Destination 31).

● Hagi (1–2 nights)—Tsuwano (day trip)
● Kurashiki (1 night, Destination 24)—Matsue (1 night, at Yagumo Honjin, see Alternative Inns)—Izumo (day trip)—Iwami Ginzan (half-day excursion)—Tsuwano (half-day excursion)—Hagi (1–2 nights)
● Hiroshima (1 night in Miyajima)—Iwakuni (1 night, Destination 31)   Hagi (1 night)
● Hagi (1–2 nights)—Kyushu (Destinations 34 and 35)

TOMOE 萩の宿 常茂恵

LOCATION: Hagi

Deluxe contemporary ryokan *in an historic location.*

RATE: From ¥25,000 w/2 meals.   **CREDIT CARDS:** AMEX, DC, VISA.   **ROOMS:** 25 Japanese style (w/bath).   **COMMUNAL BATHS:** 2—men's, women's.   **CHECK-IN:** 15:00.   **CHECK-OUT:** 10:30.   **LANGUAGE:** English spoken.

☎ 0838–22–0150 Fax: 0838–22–0152
608–53 Kobo-ji, Hijiwara, Hagi-shi, Yamaguchi 758–0025
〒758–0025　山口県萩市土原弘法寺608–53

■ ACCESS
BY TRAIN: 3 min by car from Higashi Hagi Stn (JR San'in Main Line) or 70 min by bus from Ogori Stn (JR Sanyo *shinkansen*).
BY CAR:　50 min (45 km) via Routes 435 & 490 from Mine IC (Chugoku Expressway).

Until 1989 the Tomoe was a much-loved, two-story wooden inn dating from the 1920s. It was built to welcome home distinguished Meiji Restoration (1868)

Spacious public spaces, Tomoe

Tomoe

personalities who had moved to the new capital to build the modern Japanese state. As the most distinguished inn at Hagi, the Tomoe accommodated some of the most illustrious figures of the new era, including prime ministers Eisaku Sato (1901–75) and Nobusuke Kishi (1896–1987), and even the Emperor Showa (previously known as Emperor Hirohito; 1901–89).

In 1989, the year of the Emperor Showa's death, the old Tomoe closed and a new one opened by the Matsumoto River, not far from the waterfront where the domain boathouses once stood, the passing of the old inn coinciding with that of its most illustrious guest. The new Tomoe has the white and gray plaster walls of a castle, with the gate and façade of a high-ranking samurai mansion. Inside, it is a haven of wide open spaces and uncompromising luxury. No suite has less than one 10-mat room plus one 4 1/2-mat room; if you are in the VIP league, there are bigger rooms available. You could even book into a replica of the Kao, the room where the Emperor Showa stayed. The rooms are well spread out, so there is a feeling of total privacy.

Appointments, food, and tableware are the choice of the third-generation *okami*. She is a woman of taste who is obsessed with the finer details of service. The tableware, for example, comprises the best Hagi ware, and also handpicked ceramics from all over Japan. The windows in your room will be kept wide open to let in fresh air until just before your arrival; the *yukata* waiting for you will be a miraculously perfect fit. And if you return to the inn several years later, you will not be served the same things as during your previous visit, because records are kept of every meal that each guest eats.

Unfortunately, when the Tomoe raised its act, it also increased its prices; this is not an inn for the budget traveler. Nevertheless, the crumbling walls of Hagi's samurai mansions are very well complemented by such contemporary comfort.

Nearby

I suggest renting bicycles from the inn to explore the town.

MATSUDA-YA

LOCATION: Yuda Onsen, Yamaguchi City

The local delicacy, blowfish sashimi

A beautifully managed-hotel/inn where you can soak in the same bathtub as the plotters of the Meiji Restoration (1868).

RATE: From ¥22,000 w/2 meals, old rooms from ¥30,000, 20% off w/breakfast only, 25% of w/o meals, children 30% off. **CREDIT CARDS:** AMEX, DC, VISA. **ROOMS:** 34 Japanese style (30 w/bath). **COMMUNAL BATHS:** 4—men's, women's. 2 private (*kazoku-buro*). **CHECK-IN:** 16:00. **CHECK-OUT:** 10:00. **LANGUAGE:** No English, reservation in Japanese.

☎ 0839–22–0125 Fax: 0839–25–6111

3–6–7 Yuda Onsen, Yamaguchi-shi, Yamaguchi 753–0056

〒753–0056　山口県山口市湯田温泉3–6–7

BY TRAIN: 20 min by taxi from Ogori Stn (JR Sanyo *shinkansen*), or 10 min on foot from Yuda Onsen Stn (JR Yamaguchi Line).

BY CAR: 10 min (via Yamaguchi Bypass) from Ogori IC (Chugoku Expressway).

You will see very little of the best Japan has to offer by clinging to the main roads. Often, the choice finds are hidden on backstreets behind faceless façades. This is nowhere truer than in Yamaguchi City. The hot spring end of the city known as Yuda Onsen looks like the worst example of urban misplanning and the accommodations are all architectural abominations. So, if it had not been for an enthusiastic recommendation of an acquaintance, I would never have entertained the thought of staying at Yuda Onsen, let alone patronizing the uninviting-looking inn on the main street called Matsuda-ya. "Mind you, I haven't been there for twenty years, so I can't tell you what it's like now," said my friend putting me even more on my guard.

Historic section, Matsuda-ya

Well, the Matsuda-ya had certainly changed since my friend had been there, its modern five-story concrete wing having just emerged from a major renovation. But just as I was surveying the carpeted lobby and mentally damning the price of progress, one maid swooped gently upon us, while another took our bags. The first guided us to the display rooms ("Here are pieces of calligraphy from the key figures in the Meiji Restoration. They used to come to the Matsuda-ya for secret meetings…"), then to the baths ("Here is the bath that the plotters of the Meiji Restoration bathed in…"); and then to the garden door ("Don't miss the carp in the garden pond with long, flowing fins—bred from varieties that the emperor brought back from Southeast Asia. The garden is especially pretty at night, so do step out for a stroll in your *yukata*…"). From there we were guided to our rooms, which were of standard size but expensively fitted with high-quality timber and graceful ornamentation.

The Matsuda-ya turned out to be not only an inn with a fascinating history linked to Yamaguchi's role in nurturing the leaders of the Meiji Restoration, but an establishment where pride is evident in the poise and service of the entire management.

Unlike many similarly modernized inns, the Matsuda-ya more than makes up for its more modern leanings. Surprisingly, I did not feel particularly deprived in my fifth-story room in the new wing, and such was the comfort of the new rooms and the excellence of the meals that longings for the original wooden *honkan* never surfaced. The superb sashimi, the crushed crab soup, the *fugu* (blowfish) hot-pot, the soba noodles fried on a hot roof tile (a poetic legacy of harsher times), and the red rice with sweet *mukage* potatoes shall remain in my memory as one of the greatest inn meals I've ever had, the flavors delicate, the ingredients often unusual.

The baths were also a treat. The historic bathtub of the restoration plotters, called the "Ishin-no-Yu" can be locked for private bathing, as can another sweet-smelling cypress clad bathroom. And there are two large communal baths. More than anything, the professionalism of service was of a level that has started to disappear from even the best hotels in Tokyo.

33

MATSUYAMA

Matsuyama Castle

ATTRACTIONS

The famous Dogo Onsen area and the elaborate three-story bathhouse of the same name; a beautiful original castle; and an old candle wax-making town nearby.

My visit to the legendary **Dogo Onsen Honkan bathhouse** began at 6:30 A.M. Bodies, mainly tourists decked out in anything from hotel *yukata* to motorbike leathers, milled about on the footpath outside the Honkan. All were awaiting the beating of the drum on the phoenix-topped roof to announce the opening of the doors for the day. At the head of the line was a determined huddle of elderly ladies, who I learned were members of the local "morning bathers' club."

Five minutes after the bell, the ladies' bathroom was two- to three-deep in women soaping up and scrubbing each other's backs. After washing at the taps I squeezed my way through the barrier of bodies around the tub and slipped in. "Get that towel out of the water!" screeched an old lady, and the room of bathers turned their heads my way. "Sorry," I said self-consciously, sliding my towel to the tub edge while continuing to ease myself into the very hot water. Satisfied that I wasn't defiling the tub anymore, the old lady went back to her sit-ups at the pool's edge.

Dogo Onsen Honkan

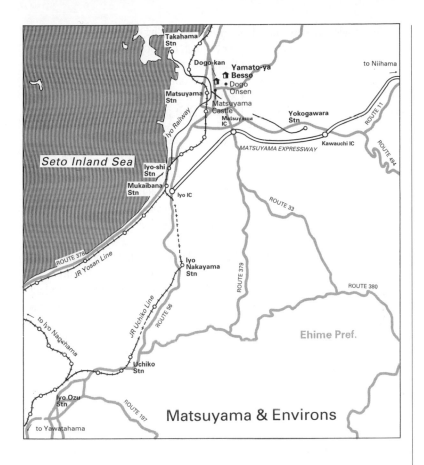

Matsuyama & Environs

Just like these ladies, the people who built the elaborate Momoyama-style bathhouse in 1894 obviously took their bathing very seriously. Perhaps they felt it necessary to do justice to Dogo's claim as the oldest hot spring in Japan (in use for about three thousand years). When an actual bathhouse was first built here in the Edo period (1600–1868), the baths were segregated into tubs for samurai and priests, for women and common people—there was even one for animals. Now it is the only public bathhouse in Japan that has a bath and changing rooms especially for the imperial family—the Yushinden, which was built in 1899. Various members of the family have taken advantage of the facilities, including Emperor Showa (previously known as Emperor Hirohito; 1901–89), who visited in 1950. The style is elaborate, with coffered ceilings and gold leaf on the walls.

The Dogo Onsen Honkan is even more famous as the bathhouse loved by Botchan in Soseki Natsume's novel of the same name. Botchan always paid a premium for a favored room on the private third floor, a room that is now predictably called "Botchan's Room." You may not be able to appreciate the joys of the bathhouse as Botchan knew it due to the endless cacophony of cars and trucks outside, but you can still enjoy its elegance by paying the few extra yen that allow you to lounge around after the bath in a Dogo Onsen *yukata* and sip tea with crackers in the second- or third-floor rooms.

If you like *sento* (public baths), I also recommend Dogo's other, newer public bath, the **Tsubaki-no-Yu** ("**Camelia Waters**"), which is at the other end of the shopping mall from the Honkan. Most of the locals go here to avoid tourists.

Matsuyama was designated by the Transport Ministry as a "model" of international tourism in the 1980s, so it is well prepared for foreign tourists with plentiful brochures and signs in different languages. The helpful staff at the Ehime Prefectural International Center (EPIC; ☎ 089–943–6688) can provide the information needed to get the most out of a visit to Matsuyama, such as details on the handsome **Matsuyama Castle**, local shrines, and nearby attractions such as **Uchiko**.

Uchiko's showpiece is the Yokaichi-Gokoku area, a stretch of restored merchants' houses dating from the late-Edo to early Meiji period (the nineteenth century). Most are modest two-story buildings, but on a road containing a half-dozen of these houses, you suddenly come to one twice as big as the others and with elaborate tile work. This house belonged to Yazaemon Haga (1801–72), a vegetable-wax baron of Uchiko, for the town's main business at that time was wax. In 1894, when Mr. Haga's daughter was to be married, he built her a new house—**the Kami Haga-tei**—just down the road. This house now contains a fascinating display of Edo-period wax making.

The wax was made from *haze* (wax tree) berries, of which there was an abundance in Ehime Prefecture. Mr. Haga developed a method of turning the naturally green wax white, and his wax, which was prized as a base for face creams, pomade, and shoe polish, won awards at international expositions in Chicago (1895) and Paris (1900). In the house are the ceramic dishes in which the Ehime wax was exported in the early 1900s.

Little folkcraft shops dot the Uchiko road, among them the **candle shop of Omori Yataro** (☎ 0893–43–0385), a family business of more than two hundred years' standing. You can watch the candlemaker working, forming the candles with his bare hands until they are thick and scaly with molten wax.

Also visit **Uchiko-za**, one of only two old Kabuki theaters left in Japan (the other famous one is in Tokushima). Built in 1916, Uchiko-za has a revolving stage, cranked by hand, and the old *masu-seki* seating in wooden squares on the floor.

In Uchiko an especially stylish place to eat is **Kawasemi** ("Kingfisher"; ☎ 0893–44–5128), with its wooden-plank counter and lute in the window. It has a comfortable farmhouse-style attic and serves sophisticated country fare.

About half an hour's drive from Matsuyama is **Baizan Commercial Pottery**, the place to see the blue-and-white **Tobe pottery** being made. *Tobe-yaki* is sturdy and excellent value. Arrange through EPIC for the people at Baizan to give you a guided tour of the workshop, the climbing kiln, and the *Tobe-yaki* museum.

Another thirty minutes from Uchiko is **Ozu**. I recommend a visit here just to see **Garyu Sanso**, the villa of a wealthy turn-of-the-century trader. The main room in the house was designed so that it could be converted into a Noh stage, and it has the requisite giant ceramic pots under the floorboards to reverberate in the foot-stamping parts of the plays. Overlooking Hijikawa river, it must have been a truly elegant country villa before the view became cluttered.

Recommended buys

Handmade candles from Uchiko; *Tobe-yaki* pottery from Tobe.

Recommended trips including Dogo Onsen

With five to seven days, you could start in Hiroshima, take the ferry to Matsuyama, see Uchiko, Ozu, and Uwajima (its castle display of samurai armor has few rivals), then backtrack to Takamatsu. In Takamatsu visit the incredible Ritsurin Koen park; an hour's drive away is the old indigo-dyeing town of Wakimachi, which has several wooden inns, for example the Zeni-ya Ryokan (℡ 0883–52–1366). Or you may prefer to see the great shrine, Kompira-san. The final leg would be back across the Seto Ohashi bridge to Kurashiki. If you have only two or three days, confine yourself to Matsuyama with a day trip to Uchiko and Ozu.

● Matsuyama (2–3 nights including day trip to Uchiko and Ozu)
● Hiroshima—Matsuyama (2–3 nights including day trip to Uchiko and Ozu)
—Wakimachi (1 night—there are several old inns in the town)
—Kompira-san—Takamatsu (day excursion)

YAMATO-YA BESSO 大和屋別荘

LOCATION: Dogu Onsen

Pure indulgence in this traditional inn modernized for absolute comfort, with superb hot spring baths.

RATE: From ¥39,100 (service charge included) w/2 meals. **CREDIT CARDS:** VISA. **ROOMS:** 19 Japanese style (w/bath). **COMMUNAL BATHS:** 2—men's, women's (each connect to outdoor bath). **CHECK-IN:** 15:00. **CHECK-OUT:** 11:00. **LANGUAGE:** No English, reservations in Japanese.

℡ 089–931–7771 Fax: 089–931–7775
2–27 Dogo Sagidani-cho, Matsuyama-shi, Ehime 790–0836
〒790–0836　愛媛県松山市道後鷺谷町2–27

■ ACCESS

BY TRAIN: 15 min by car from Matsuyama Stn (JR Yosan Line).
BY CAR:　20 min (5 km) via Route 33 from Matsuyama IC (Matsuyama Expressway).

This inn has existed since 1868, but in the 1980s the owners decided to rebuild. They traveled to top inns all over Japan, studying and refining ideas, before clos-

Yamato-ya Besso

Exquisite seafood, Yamato-ya Besso

ing for a renovation that lasted three intense years. In 1988 the Yamato-ya Besso reopened as a luxuriously appointed inn with all-cypress interiors, a generous two to three rooms per apartment, magnificent baths with garden views, well-concealed modern conveniences, subtle lighting, and alcoves decorated with calligraphy by some of Matsuyama's *haiku* greats.

Little extras such as a rejuvenating post-bathing drink of ionized water, unlimited beer for bathers, a little pre-bed snack of sushi, and truly beautiful *yukata* (with a choice of designs for women) place Yamato-ya Besso among the stars of Japanese inn-keeping. The food is classic *kaiseki* with an emphasis on Inland Sea seafood; the chef does not decide what will be on the day's menu until he has seen what is best at the markets.

34

YUFUIN and BEPPU

Antique shop, Yufuin

ATTRACTIONS

Yufuin, a world-class spa resort, and nearby Beppu, a kitsch resort renowned for its "hells," can be combined with a trip to Takachiho, where the gods first alighted in Japan.

Yufuin in the summer attracts trainloads of monied ladies. They alight from the **Yufuin-no-Mori Express**, with its wood and brass interior, wearing their Pleats Please and Jurgen Lehls, then disperse into one of the three fine inns of Yufuin—the better endowed to the **Sanso Murata**, the others to the equally elegant Kame-no-I Besso or the Tama-no-Yu. In summer, the ladies stroll around the lake to watch the fireflies, by day they pour over crafts and home-made jams in Yufuin's classy shops. They may even venture out for a bath in the pretty public bathhouse, the **Shitan-yu**.

Apart from the many craft shops in town (one of the best is **Yasugata**, specializing in indigo-dyed textiles), both the Kame-no-I Besso and the **Tama-no-Yu** have excellent coffee and gift shops open to the public.

If you are short on time, skip the **Mingei Mura folk crafts village** (pottery, glass-blowing, and so on), and go to the **Kuuso-no-Mori Bijutsu-kan**

Bubbling mud, Beppu

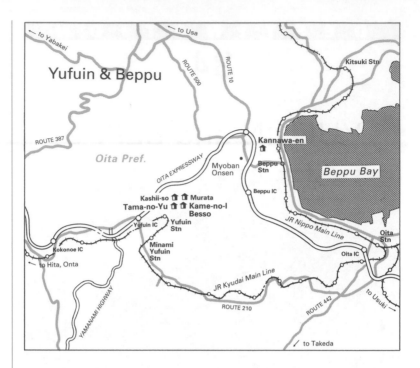

("Forest of the Imagination" museum). This inspiring collection of galleries shows old textiles, characteristic wooden and clay masks scavenged from Kyushu mountains, and other Japanese folk objects. Unless you are a hiker, you will need a taxi to get here from the city center.

The **Yufuin Bijutsu-kan** (Yufuin Art Museum), a complex designed in a circle of breezy wooden structures, is worth considering if contemporary art is your thing.

A thirty-minute bus ride up the mountain from Yufuin is **Beppu**. With its plastic souvenir dens, its bright lights, and nighttime strip joints, Beppu is the antithesis of Yufuin. A tourist dive from way back, what it lacks in class it makes up for in steam. See it coming out of pipes everywhere and feel like you're standing on the edge of creation—or destruction.

The main reason for visiting Beppu is to see the so-called **hells**—thermal pits and ponds in an amazing range of textures and colors, from spluttering mud pools to mysterious blood-red lakes. There is even a geyser that blows every 25–30 minutes—if it had not been capped with a 20-meter high (22-yard) concrete hood, it would blow 50 meters (55 yards) into the sky. Good old kitschy Beppu: I love it.

A bus does shuttles around the hells, but the most time-effective way of seeing the choicest spots is by chartered taxi, especially if a few of you can split the bill. The local taxi association has a fixed price for a couple of hours visiting the five most interesting hells (note that there is a small entrance fee to each of them as well). Our driver also took us to see **Myoban Onsen**, where hot spring mineral deposits (*yu-no-hana*) are "cultivated" in straw-roofed huts, then "harvested" and sold in porous bags for throwing into your own bath at home. You can bathe at Myoban Onsen in the hot spring baths in little thatched structures, or you can patronize the mud and sand baths on the way there.

Also in the general Beppu area, though an hour's drive away on confusing country roads, is **Onta**, the *mingei* pottery town par excellence. Onta's potters still pound rocks to produce clay with waterwheel-driven pounders. The British potter Bernard Leach (1887–1979) spent time here learning the Onta technique of skip decoration, and it seems his visit encouraged the local potters to uphold their traditions.

If you go to Onta, you may as well go the little extra distance to **Hita**. This is one of the so-called Little Kyotos because of the way it developed a refined culture mimicking the sophisticated capital. Some relics of this bygone elegance are preserved in the old part of town, and interesting finds are waiting in the area's antique shops. Get a map from the helpful people at the tourist information center near the station.

Near Beppu are the **Usuki** *sekibutsu* (stone statues). The statues date from the Kamakura period (1185–1333), but their origins and reason for existence are still a total mystery. They have been cleaned up for the tourists recently, which may have also cleaned up some of their charm.

Takachiho—best reached from the town of Nobeoka on a marvelous scenic railway, the Takachiho-go (two round trips a day)—is where the mythical Sun Goddess (the deity from whom the imperial line is said to have descended) hid herself in a cave until she was lured out by the gods laughing at a lewd dance. Takachiho is a truly picturesque gorge with fascinating folded rock faces that conjure up a suitably primeval ambience. Despite the lack of

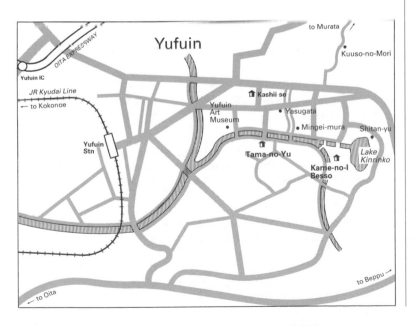

really recommendable facilities at Takachiho, an overnight stay there is recommended in order to see the **Yokagura**, a set of ancient dances, performed in a moldy hall at Takachiho shrine every night from 8 P.M. About four hundred farmers are part of a cooperative set up to keep the full repertoire of thirty-three ancient dances alive. Five members take turns performing four dances each night, including the dance of Ameno-Uzume, the female deity who lured the Sun Goddess from her cave. Some of the scenes are quite ribald.

The green, rolling countryside around the volcano **Mount Aso** is quite unlike any other in Japan. As for Mount Aso itself, tourists have been known to be struck by flying volcanic matter as they peered into the crater, so perhaps, like Mount Fuji, it is best seen from afar.

Recommended buys

Bamboo craft from Beppu; *mingei* pottery from Onta

Recommended trips including Yufuin

If you have a week to tour Kyushu, my choice would be to arrive in Hakata and then go to Karatsu, Arita, and Hirado (Destination 35). Then carry on to Kumamoto (which has a castle, famous garden, and excellent museums), Takachiho, Nobeoka (just to change trains), Yufuin, and Beppu, with side trips to Usuki and Onta/Hita.
If you only have a few days and your prime goal is a leisurely time in Yufuin, then try to arrive first in Beppu, go on to Yufuin to stay, and if you like, take side trips to Usuki, Onta/Hita, Mount Aso, and Takachiho.

- Beppu (day trip)—Yufuin (1–2 nights)
- Beppu (day trip)—Yufuin (1–2 nights)—Mount Aso—Takachiho
(from here to either Kagoshima or on to Nagasaki, Hirado, Arita, and Karatsu, Destination 35)

KAME-NO-I BESSO　亀の井別荘

LOCATION: Yufuin

A success story in contemporary Japanese inn-keeping, with splendid hot spring baths and wholesome foreigner-friendly cuisine.

RATE: From ¥30,000 w/2 meals. **CREDIT CARDS:** AMEX, DC, VISA. **ROOMS:** 15 Japanese style, 6 Western style—all w/ bath. **COMMUNAL BATHS:** 2—men's, women's (each connects to outdoor bath). **CHECK-IN:** 15:00. **CHECK-OUT:** 11:00. **LANGUAGE:** English spoken.

☎ 0977–84–3166 Fax: 0977–84–2356
2633–1 Kawakami, Yufuin-cho, Oita-gun, Oita 879–5102
〒879–5102　大分県大分郡湯布院町川上2633–1

■ ACCESS

BY TRAIN: 5 min by car from Yufuin Stn (JR Kyudai Main Line).
BY CAR:　10 min (2 km) from Yufuin IC (Oita Expressway).

Kame-no-I Besso

The Kame-no-I Besso started out eighty years ago as a thatched cottage in a forest. Its visionary owner, Kentaro Nakaya, later transformed it into a collection of twelve *minka*-style *hanare*, with outdoor cypress baths for guests and other lovely structures in the large grounds. There is a twenty-four-hour public hot spring bath called Kusa-no-Yu.

In the 1980s, the Kame-no-I Besso became a legend in its own time for a revolutionary new approach to innkeeping. Innkeepers from all over Japan still make the pilgrimage to Yufuin to take lessons from its success.

The Kame-no-I Besso's great innovation was to open its doors to the tourist on the street by adding public spaces to the inn, such as coffee shops, restaurants, and a gift shop. This concept was alien to the more traditional innkeepers of Japan, for whom *ryokan* were behind-closed-doors havens for overnight guests only.

The Kame-no-I Besso seized an opportunity to attract more customers in a resort town that certainly lends itself to this kind of enterprise. Yufuin is a perfect strolling town, with lovely public baths and interesting craft and antique shops in one compact area. The inn next door to the Kame-no-I Besso, the Tama-no-Yu, followed its neighbor's lead by opening its own restaurant and coffee shop for outside customers. And so a trend was set.

Quite apart from the effect that it has had on its surroundings, the Kame-no-I Besso is simply a very special inn. The finer details of its appointments and service make it a joy to visit. In autumn, I was most impressed to find that our room had its own *hibachi* with live coals and an iron kettle of hot water simmering on it, from which the maid served tea.

The Kame-no-I uses only fresh water from its own spring, and the preparation of food certainly benefits. In addition, extreme care is taken to acquire only the best and safest ingredients for meals, including organically grown vegetables and handmade tofu. Dinner during my visit included a delicious local beef steam-seared on the outside, turtle soup containing rice cakes, and eggplant stuffed with beef, mushrooms, and pine nuts. You can choose between Western-style or Japanese breakfasts.

After dinner, you simply must take coffee here. The Kame-no-I has converted a two-hundred-year-old former saké brewery into a large shop displaying beautiful local crafts and boutique foodstuffs, with a coffee shop and bar upstairs. This structure's amazing beams will tempt you to think that the place was built as some sort of architectural parody—but this formidable structure is for real.

Nearby

Next door is the other great inn of Yufuin, Tama-no-Yu.
All other tourist sites are also accessible on
foot except for Kuusoo-no-Mori.

TAMA-NO-YU 玉の湯

LOCATION:
Yufuin

*Detached cottages in leafy surroundings with
a choice of menu and equally elegant Western-
or Japanese-style accommodations.*

RATE: From ¥30,000 w/breakfast, children 30–50% off. **CREDIT CARDS:** AMEX, DC, VISA. **ROOMS:** 3 Japanese style, 15 semi-Japanese style—all w/bath. **COMMUNAL BATHS:** 4—men's, women's, 2 outdoor baths (men's, women's). **CHECK-IN:** 13:00. **CHECK-OUT:** 12:00. **LANGUAGE:** English spoken.

☎ 0977–84–2158 Fax: 0977–85–4179
Yunotsubo, Yufuin-cho, Oita-gun, Oita 879–5197
〒879–5197　大分県大分郡湯院町湯の坪

■ ACCESS
BY TRAIN: 5 min by car from Yufuin Stn (JR Kyudai Main Line).
BY CAR:　10 min (2 km) from Yufuin IC (Oita Expressway).

Tama-no-Yu

Tama-no-Yu is a complex of cottages in a grove that runs wild with uncut grass and shady trees. The first thing I wondered when I saw it was why they did not cut the grass. Silly me: the unkempt grassiness is part of the calculated charm. There is the aesthetic of decay, so why not the aesthetic of weeds?

Lolling in this wild grove are the inn's fourteen *hanare*, joined by walkways. Three of the fourteen are pure Japanese (two tatami rooms plus bathroom); a further ten are a mix of Japanese and Western, with a Western-style bedroom adjoining a tatami room. The beds, made of Swedish white wood and covered with hand-woven Japanese *ikat*, are a delight.

When in Yufuin, it is always hard deciding whether to stay at the Kame-no-I Besso or the Tama-no-Yu because they are both such excellent inns. Tama-no-Yu was, in fact, built along the same lines as its neighbor, the Kame-no-I Besso.

Perhaps the Tama-no-Yu is the place to choose when you are ready for a bit of Western-style comfort. This is not just because there are beds. Unlike almost any other inn in Japan, here you are not force-fed a set menu but have a choice of meals—say, between a main dish of locally raised beef with wild mountain vegetables or a free-range chicken hot-pot with all the healthy trimmings. The food is served in simple folk-style crockery from the ancient pottery village of Onta. All the maids are dressed in *mompe* farmers' pants, adding another dimension to the rustic atmosphere.

The rooms at the Tama-no-Yu have their own sweet-smelling cypress baths and the *yukata* are supplied in pretty bamboo baskets. There are also outdoor baths for men and women, of a type known as *utase-yu*, meaning that there are overhead bamboo pipes releasing a firm stream of water (ideal for aching shoulders). This idea is borrowed from the nearby Suji-yu hot spring. All the rooms have been built to allow ample space for people in wheelchairs. There is also a reading room for guests.

Departures are not rushed at the Tama-no Yu — checkout is at noon and you will not be woken if you want to sleep in. Breakfast is either Japanese, or Western-style with scrambled eggs.

The inn has its own restaurant and coffee shop (with great homemade ice cream). So if you do not stay at the Tama-no-Yu, at least come and enjoy its aesthetic of weeds over coffee or lunch. There is also a shop selling select local crafts.

Summer and spring are wonderful in Yufuin, and autumn is famous for the morning mists that rise from Lake Kinrinko and the Oita River. But if you are lucky to catch the Tama-no-Yu in the snow, they say it is the time that will really stay in your heart.

Nearby

Next door is the other great inn of Yufuin, Kame-no-I Besso.
The other tourist sites are also accessible on foot except
for Kuuso-no-Mori.

KANNAWA-EN 神和苑

LOCATION: Beppu

Exotic old-style inn with its own steaming hot spring pools.

RATE: From ¥20,000 w/2 meals, from ¥13,000 w/breakfast, children 40% off. **CREDIT CARDS:** Not accepted. **ROOMS:** 17 Japanese style (8 w/bath). **COMMUNAL BATHS:** 4–3 private (*kazoku-buro*), 1 outdoor (mixed). **CHECK-IN:** 15:00. **CHECK-OUT:** 10:00. **LANGUAGE:** Some English.

☎ 0977–66–2111 Fax: 0977–66–2113
Miyuki 6–kumi, Beppu-shi, Oita 874–0045
〒874–0045　大分県別府市御幸6組

■ ACCESS
BY TRAIN: 15 min by car from Beppu Stn (JR Nippo Main Line).
BY CAR:　2.5 km from Beppu IC (Oita Expressway).

The Kannawa-en is one of the best places to get into the Beppu mood. Driving into the inn was like entering an exotic dream world. The Kannawa-en consists of one majestic old wooden building and a number of separate huts set in a lush garden, enshrouded by the billows of steam rising from its very own "hell" of hot spring water. This hell is smaller than Beppu's other infernal sites, but just as impressive.

By a stroke of luck, the hut we were given had an adjoining tearoom with a beautifully crafted wooden ceiling. This tearoom was our bedroom for the night. The food—in usual voluminous *kaiseki* style—could have been more exciting for the ¥20,000 per head we paid, but the setting and service were faultless. To be on the safe side, pay the extra fee to get the better *hanare* rooms.

Kannawa-en

SAGA PREFECTURE

Arita ware in Arita

ATTRACTIONS

In Karatsu, the Karatsu Kunchi festival (November 2–3 every year), the warm and hospitable Yoyo-kaku inn, and the simple yet profound Karatsu ware pottery. A visit to Karatsu can be easily combined with a trip to the porcelain kilns of Arita, the public baths of Takeo, and the first Dutch traders' port at Hirado.

On November 2, the day the **Karatsu Kunchi** begins, boys start gathering in the streets dressed in *happi* coats, short white cotton leg-huggers and split-toed socks with straw sandals, their heads tied with a twisted cotton cloth. Each neighborhood group wears its own distinctively designed style of *happi*.

The highlight of the first day is the nighttime procession of floats, which is more like a race to see how fast each group can pull its float around corners without having a hideous accident. A float once toppled into the river and its town group has watched the festival from the sidelines ever since, as the historical float made of lacquered papier-mâché was too costly to rebuild. The oldest Karatsu Kunchi float dates back to 1819, the most recent to 1876; all have been crafted with the most extraordinary skill and sense of design. One distinctive

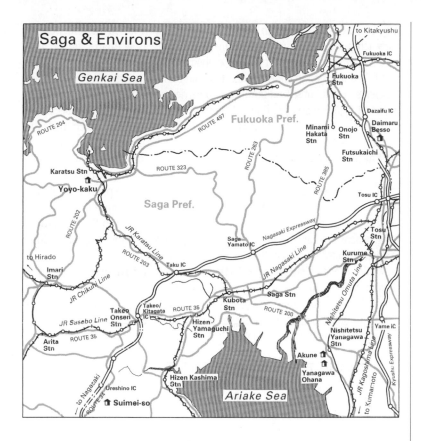

Saga & Environs

Genkai Sea

Fukuoka Pref.

Saga Pref.

Ariake Sea

entry consists of a wide-eyed, bright red sea bream—a fish often served on auspicious occasions—that bobs up and down as it is pulled along.

Karatsu residents lay on feasts and declare open house for the duration of the festival. On the second day, the floats are paraded around the neighborhoods to bestow blessings on the residents before converging at the beach for a grand finale. The media helicopters overhead now mar this stage of the festival, but the exuberant cries of the float carriers—*Enya! Enya!*—still ring in the ears long after the carnival is over. (If you miss the festival, you can see the floats at the **Hikiyama Tenjijo**, the festival exhibition hall.)

I recommend visiting some of the galleries and shops specializing in **Karatsu ware**, the local pottery especially prized by tea-ceremony people for its simple designs in iron underglaze on a beige-gray background. The most famous Karatsu ware kiln is that of **Nakazato Taroemon**, now presided over by the thirteenth-generation Taroemon (1923–). The beautiful gallery is open to the public and sells some affordable wares produced by apprentices, in addition to the high-priced pieces of the master.

This part of Japan is a real ceramics paradise. **Arita**, the home of the famous blue-and-white and polychrome porcelains, is an easy stopping-off point on the way to Nagasaki. Though the actual kilns were at Arita and nearby Okawachiyama, the porcelains became known overseas as Imari ware, because it was exported from this port to Europe aboard Dutch ships.

I found it easiest to charter a taxi to explore the Arita area. Worth a visit are the elegant estates of several families who carried on the secret Imari ware techniques of applying designs in red pigment to ware that had been first decorated with blue underglaze. One is the **Imaizumi Imaemon kiln**, which made the precious Iro-Nabeshima ware exclusively for the Nabeshima *daimyo*. Another is the **Sakaida Kakiemon kiln**, whose persimmon-colored glaze was applied to a non-underglazed surface. Kakiemon is an impeccably groomed establishment, more of interest for its buildings and gardens than the pretty white porcelains with their over-the-top prices. You need to apply in advance if you want to see the workshop. To see work in progress it is easier to go to the **Genemon kiln,** where you can spend an absorbing time looking through glass windows at steady-handed artists painting intricate designs on pots.

While in Arita visit the historic **Okawachiyama kiln area**, where the Kyushu clans first brought Korean potters to impart their knowledge. It is still crowded with kilns. There is a graveyard with the tombs of more than eight hundred Korean potters, including a monument to Ri Sampei (1579–1655), who started the whole Kyushu porcelain industry after discovering kaolin clay in the area.

The big **Arita Pottery Fair** (Arita Toki Ichi) is held every year from April 29 to May 5—probably a good time to avoid the place.

If you are unable to get accommodation in Karatsu, **Ureshino Onsen** or **Takeo Onsen** are alternatives. Suimei-so Wata-ya Besso is a high-class inn located in Ureshino, while the old public baths in Takeo (modern on the outside, wood-paneled inside) are the best reason to go there. This whole area is also a famous **tea-producing district**.

Considered an alluring destination by Japanese travelers for its early Western-style mansions, Nagasaki is indeed special. But if your time is limited, I suggest skipping this city and heading for the even more exotic **Hirado**. This is the port where the first Dutch merchants traded in the early 1600s. The Jesuit missionary Francis Xavier (1506–52) lived in Hirado for a time, and the British navigator William Adams (1564–1620) died here.

The highlight here is the absorbing **Matsu'ura Shiryo Hakubutsu-kan** (Matsu'ura Historical Museum). Situated on the estate of the Matsu'ura clan, which ruled Hirado for seven hundred years, the museum has fascinating relics of samurai culture as well as assorted objects from Japan's first contact with the West, including cannons, guns, and clothing. Even if you think you have seen enough Japanese museums to last a lifetime, give this one a try. You can also take tea in the marvelous thatched teahouse on the grounds.

Hirado Castle, a replica, has a great view over the port. But my favorite place in Hirado is **Kairakuen**. It is not on the Hirado tourist map and requires a fifteen-minute taxi drive, but you should not miss it. The house was frequented by the Hirado lord Matsu'ura Hiromu (1791–1867) at the end of the

Edo period (1600–1868) and it was here that he employed a tea master to have tea with him and talk of life and art. A delightful lady who is descended from the tea master himself presides over the house. Visitors pay a small fee at the end of her tour.

At the beginning or end of your trip to this part of Kyushu you will almost certainly find yourself in Fukuoka—either at Fukuoka Airport, or Hakata Station on the *shinkansen* line. Just fifteen minutes from Fukuoka, in the small hot spring enclave of **Futsukaichi Onsen**, is the Daimaru Besso, a superbly appointed inn (actually more like a first-class hotel with tatami rooms and inn-style service) that has been patronized by the imperial family. If you are planning just a quick trip to Kyushu with a day trip to the Arita and Karatsu kilns out of Fukuoka, for example, this would be an excellent inn to choose. It is also close to the ancient provincial capital of **Dazaifu**, which has Temman-gu, dedicated to the deified scholar Sugawara no Michizane (845–903), the shrine most visited by students praying for good results in their exams.

Seasonal tip

Karatsu Kunchi (November 2–3) is one festival for which I would risk the crowds. The Arita Pottery Fair from April 29 to May 5 is a good time to pick up bargains.

Recommended trips including Karatsu

From Fukuoka get the local train to Karatsu, spend the night there, move on to Hirado the next day, visiting Arita on the way. Most travelers take the Red Express from Hakata straight to Nagasaki, but this leaves quite a haul to get to Hirado. I made the mistake of doing the Hirado trip by bus from Nagasaki—a grueling three hours. Because of the distance involved, you might consider staying overnight in Hirado rather than Nagasaki.

● Hakata (Fukuoka) (1 night at Daimaru Besso, see Alternative Inns)—Karatsu (1–2 nights)—Arita (day excursion)—Hirado (1 night) —Kumamoto—rest of Kyushu (Destination 34)

YOYO-KAKU　洋々閣

One of the must-stay inns of Japan—a few rooms around an elegant seaside garden, country food served with affection and flair, and a gallery of work by world-renowned potter Takashi Nakazato.

RATE: From ¥17,000 w/2 meals, 30% off w/breakfast only, 50% off w/o meals, children 50% off.
CREDIT CARDS: AMEX, DC, VISA. **ROOMS:** 20 Japanese style (18 rooms w/bath). **COMMUNAL BATHS:** 2—men's, women's. **CHECK-IN:** 15:00. **CHECK-OUT:** 10:00. **LANGUAGE:** Some English.

☎ 0955–72–7181 Fax: 0955–73–0604
2–4–40 Higashi Karatsu, Karatsu-shi, Saga 847–0017
〒847–0017　佐賀県唐津市東唐津2–4–40

■ ACCESS

BY TRAIN: 5 min by car from Karatsu Stn (JR Chikuhi Line).
BY CAR:　40 min (35 km) via Route 203 from Taku IC (Nagasaki Expressway).

Yoyo-kaku

When I asked Japanese travel writer Kozaburo Arashiyama to recommend inns for foreign travelers, he suggested the Yoyo-kaku in Karatsu and the Fujiya Hotel in Hakone. I can see why he chose the Yoyo-kaku. The elegance of the inn itself and the affable personalities of the inn's owners, Mr. and Mrs. Okochi, make the Yoyo-kaku one of *the* special inns in Japan.

The Yoyo-kaku was built as an exclusive restaurant in the early 1900s. Although additions have since been made, even the concrete sections of the new buildings are designed with such sensitivity you would never guess they were not part of the original wooden structure.

That the Yoyo-kaku has a gallery dedicated to the work of Takashi Nakazato is not surprising, considering that his pottery and the inn are so alike in their quiet beauty. Takashi, who is the black sheep of the famous Nakazato family of potters, makes pots in a way that is as frank and natural as clay itself. Since he is also a cook, he knows how to make pots for food.

Karatsu-ites living all over the country will do anything to come home for the Karatsu Kunchi, the city's annual festival. It is a time when every household prepares a feast and opens its doors to everyone else in a spirit that is not unlike Christmas in the West. The Yoyo-kaku prepares a feast, too, and gathers all the inn's guests and friends into a candle-lit tatami room featuring a spectacular spread of festive dishes. The centerpiece is a huge fish called *ara*, a great delicacy which can run to several thousand dollars for a large specimen. The inn also has musicians come by and play flutes and drums, after they have finished participating in the festival processions.

The two-story inn is right on the seashore, and though it is not a particularly attractive beach this location gives the inn a refreshing openness. Some of the pines in the inn's garden are over two hundred years old; all twenty rooms have a garden view. Enjoy the patina of beautiful timbers, such as zelkova and cedar, in the old building.

SUIMEI-SO WATA-YA BESSO
水明荘 和多屋別荘

*A huge hotel in a featureless hot spring town—
but its ten detached suites are a world apart.*

RATE: From ¥30,000 w/2 meals for Suimei-so (lower rates for rooms in Tower block), children 30% off. **CREDIT CARDS:** AMEX, DC, MC, VISA. **ROOMS:** 10 Japanese style (w/bath). **COMMUNAL BATHS:** 5—men's, women's, 3 outdoor bath (men's, women's, mixed). **CHECK-IN:** 15:00. **CHECK-OUT:** 10:00. **LANGUAGE:** No English, reservations in Japanese.

☎ 09544–2–0210 Fax: 0954–42–0222
INTERNET: www.saganet.ne.jp/wataya
E-MAIL: wataya@po.saganet.
Otsu–738 Shimojuku, Ureshino-cho, Fujitsu-gun, Saga 843–0301
〒843-0301　佐賀県藤津郡嬉野町下宿乙738

■ ACCESS
BY TRAIN: 25 min by car from Takeo Onsen Stn (JR Sasebo Line).
BY CAR:　3 min (1 km) from Ureshino IC (Nagasaki Expressway).

Two hundred years ago Ureshino was still a post town on the old Nagasaki Kaido highway; now it is a tacky hot spring resort, with the nightly entertainment strictly for men. But since Ureshino (along with neighboring Takeo) is also the closest hot spring town to the ceramic meccas of Karatsu and Arita, it does make a good base from which to nose around the kilns.

Suimei-so

Set in luscious gardens and on both sides of the Ureshino river, this inn is the best in town and does have a distinguished history. Its forerunner was frequented by the Shimazu clan lords in the Edo period (1600–1868) and once accommodated the Nagasaki-based German physician Philipp Franz von Siebold (1796–1866) in the early 1880s.

In spite of the fact that the Wata-ya Besso has since spawned a dreadful twelve-story "Tower Block," there is a lot to be said for the beauty of its *sukiya*-type rooms in the Kachoen, Aosan-so, and Suimei-so detached rooms.

It seemed like miles from the reception desk, past gaudy shopping stalls and across the river, to this row of low-slung wooden structures strung out along the bank. Our room was in the Suimei-so block of suites. In contrast to the faceless rooms likely to be experienced in the Tower Block, the room in the Suimei-so was spacious, with a view through floor-to-ceiling sliding windows onto grass, shrubs, and water. There was a private bathroom in the suite, but there were also a number of inviting outdoor and indoor baths.

The food was above-average *kaiseki* style, with excellent seafood, served in the very best of local ceramic ware, as one would expect from a first-class *ryotei*.

When the Emperor Showa (formally Emperor Hirohito; 1901–89) visited Kyushu in 1961 he stayed in the beautiful Senshin no Ma ("Spirit Cleansing Room"). You can stay there too.

ALTERNATIVE INNS

When I made my rounds, I found a number of other inns of merit that did not make the final cut for one reason or another, but could serve as alternative selections should your first choice be fully booked, too pricy, or not quite what you are seeking at the moment. Each inn here is worthy of mention for one or more aspects of its situation, service, or presentation.

Still other perfectly respectable inns, such as the Daimaru Besso outside of Fukuoka and the Wasure-no-Sato Gajoen in Kagoshima, fell outside the boundaries of a target Destination, but offer ideal lodging for those touring the area or traveling from one Destination to the next. These inns appear in the listing here near the Destinations they are geographically closest to. The access information will allow you to pinpoint them on a map.

I have also included inns for Saitama, Hokkaido, the Tama area of Tokyo, and several other areas outside the scope of the thirty-five Destinations, which are also listed in approximate geographical order.

DESTINATION

TAMA, ON THE OUTSKIRTS OF TOKYO

KABUTO-YA 兜家
Location: Hinohara-mura, Tokyo.
Handsome, well-looked-after thatch-roofed minshuku *with good country food.*

RATE: From ¥8,500 w/2 meals. **LANGUAGE:** No English, reservations in Japanese.

☎ 042–598–6136 Fax: 042–598–6741
INTERNET: www2n.biglobe.ne.jp/˜kabutoya/
E-MAIL: kabutoya@mxm.mesh.ne.jp
2612 Kazuma, Hinohara-mura, Nishi Tama-gun, Tokyo 190–0221
〒190–0221　東京都西多摩郡桧原村数馬2612
■ **ACCESS**
BY TRAIN: 70 min by bus from Musashi Itsukaichi Stn (JR Itsukaichi Line).
BY CAR: 40 min from Uenohara IC (Chuo Expressway).

MITAKE SANSO 御岳山荘
Location: Mount Mitake, Tokyo.
One of the original lodgings for pilgrims to Mount Mitake. With eighteen hiking courses, the mountain is now a favorite among hikers.

RATE: ¥8,000–10,000 w/2 meals. **LANGUAGE:** No English, reservations in Japanese.

☎ 0428–78–8474 Fax: 0428–78–8727
123 Mitake-san, Ome-shi, Tokyo 198–0175
〒198–0175　東京都青梅市御岳山123
■ **ACCESS**
BY TRAIN: 10 min on foot from the top of Mt. Mitake; via cable car & bus from Mitake Stn (JR Ome Line).
BY CAR: 60 km from Tokyo via Route 411 (Ome Kaido).

DESTINATION

SAITAMA PREFECTURE

KYO-TEI 京亭
Location: Yorii, Saitama Prefecture

Former riverside pleasure retreat belonging to Tokyo composer and stage producer Sassa Koka in the 1930s and now a rare example of superb old wooden architecture close to Tokyo. Scrumptious ayu-meshi (sweetfish mixed with delicately flavored steamed rice) is the specialty of the inn year-round. A wooden bath is available for restaurant or inn guests twenty-four hours a day. Though not a hot spring ryokan, Kyo-tei is worth a visit to contemplate the architecture.

RATE: From ¥15,000 w/2 meals. **LANGUAGE:** Some English.

☎ 0485–81–0128 Fax: 0485–81–5898
547 Yorii, Yorii-machi, Osato-gun, Saitama 369–1203
〒369–1203　埼玉県大里郡寄居町寄居547
■ **ACCESS**
BY TRAIN: 10 min on foot from Yorii Stn (Tobu Tojo Line).
BY CAR: 60 km from Hanazono IC (Kan'etsu Expressway).

DESTINATION
3

KITA ONSEN 北温泉
Location: Nasu, Tochigi Prefecture.
A rambling, rustic wooden hot spring inn set down in the wilds of Nasu. The location, reached by a 10-minute mountain trek, is very attractive, but the rooms are basic—good for a family holiday. There are three baths to choose from and a hot spring swimming pool. Wear your swimsuit. Food is average and served in a big barn of a room.

RATE: From ¥7,500 w/2 meals. **LANGUAGE:** No English, reservations in Japanese.

☎ 0287–76–2008 Fax: 0287–76–4171
151 Yumoto, Nasu-machi, Nasu-gun, Tochigi 325–0301
〒325–0101　栃木県那須郡那須町湯本151
■ **ACCESS**
BY TRAIN: 1 hr by bus from Kuroiso Stn (JR Tohoku Main Line).
BY CAR: 30 min from Nasu IC (Tohoku Expressway).

NIKI CLUB 二期倶楽部
Location: Nasu, Tochigi Prefecture.
Contemporary hotel-inn featuring the beautiful brown-speckled Oya stone from a local quarry. Only six rooms (two of them Japanese).

Secluded location. Top-class accommodations with every comfort. Contemporary kaiseki meal with Western and Japanese elements is shared in a posh, hushed dining room.

RATE: Twin w/o meals from ¥28,000 for 2. **LANGUAGE:** English spoken.

☎ 0287–78–2215 Fax: 0287–78–2218
2301 Michishita, Takaku-Otsu, Nasu-machi, Nasu-gun, Tochigi 325–0303
〒325–0303　栃木県那須郡那須町高久乙道下2301
■ **ACCESS**
BY TRAIN: 30 min by car from Nasu Shiobara Stn (JR Tohoku shinkansen).
BY CAR: 15 min (10 km) from Nasu IC (Tohoku Expressway).

DESTINATION
5

GORA KANSUI-RO 強羅環翠楼
Location: Gora, Kanagawa Prefecture.
One of three former summer houses belonging to the Iwasaki family, founders of the Mitsubishi group. Splendid old wooden building in quiet woody garden, looked after by an older caretaker.

RATE: From ¥25,000 w/2 meals. **LANGUAGE:** Some English.

☎ 0460–2–3141 Fax: 0460–2–3143
1300 Gora, Hakone-machi, Ashigara Shimo-gun, Kanagawa 250–0408
〒250–0408　神奈川県足柄下郡箱根町強羅1300
■ **ACCESS**
BY TRAIN: 3 min on foot from Gora Stn (Hakone Tozan Railway).
BY CAR: 30 min from Gotemba IC (Tomei Expressway).

DESTINATION
6

ASABA あさば
Location: Shuzenji, Izu Peninsula.
First-class hot spring inn with its own Noh stage —brought from Tokyo in the early 1900s.

RATE: From ¥30,000 w/2 meals. **LANGUAGE:** Some English.

☎ 0558–72–7000 Fax: 0558–72–7077
3450–1 Shuzenji, Shuzenji-machi, Tagata-gun, Shizuoka 410–2416

〒410–2416　静岡県田方郡修善寺町修善寺3450–1
- **ACCESS**
BY TRAIN: 7 min by car from Shuzenji Stn (Izu Hakone Railway).
BY CAR: 45 min from Numazu IC (Tomei Expressway).

GYOKUHO-KAN 玉峰館
Location: Izu-Kawazu, Izu Peninsula.
Owner Inaba Takashi, an interior designer with a passion for Indonesia, has spruced up his family inn with ethnic furniture from other parts of Asia. The food is innovative, with some Southeast Asian flavors. Their cypress semi-outdoor hot spring bath has a view of one of the inn's hot spring geysers. The other baths are old-fashioned, from its former incarnation.

RATE: From ¥25,000 w/2 meals. **LANGUAGE:** No English, reservations in Japanese.

☎ 0558–32–1031 Fax: 0558–32–2786
440 Mine, Kawazu-machi, Kamo-gun, Shizuoka 413–0511
〒413–0511　静岡県賀茂郡河津町峰440
- **ACCESS**
BY TRAIN: 3 min by car from Kawazu Stn (Izu Kyuko Line).
BY CAR: 90 km via Odawara/Atsugi Doro & Route 135 from Atsugi IC (Tomei Expressway).

KIUN-KAKU 起雲閣
Location: Atami, Izu Peninsula.
Former luxurious holiday home of the founder of the Tobu railway set in an expansive classical Japanese garden. The main building was built in the 1920s.

RATE: From ¥25,000 w/2 meals. **LANGUAGE:** No English, reservations in Japanese.

☎ 0557–81–3623 Fax: 0557–81–9795
4–2 Showa-machi, Atami-shi, Shizuoka 413–0022
〒413–0022　静岡県熱海市昭和町4–2
- **ACCESS**
BY TRAIN: 10 min by car from Atami Stn (JR Tokaido Main Line).
BY CAR: 80 min via Odawara/Atsugi Doro from Atsugi IC (Tomei Expressway).

TEPPO 民宿 鉄砲
Location: Izu-Kawazu, Izu Peninsula.
A minshuku utilizing a 200-year-old former village headman's house with namako-kabe (black-and-white tiled walls). Handsome mingei-style rooms. Excellent bath, food, and

site for such a reasonably priced minshuku. Winter meals may include wild boar or pheasant hot-pot.

RATE: From ¥8,500 w/2 meals. **LANGUAGE:** No English, reservations in Japanese.

☎ 0558–35–7501 Fax: 0558–36–8276
175 Nashimoto, Kawazu-machi, Kamo-gun, Shizuoka 413–0501
〒413–0501　静岡県賀茂郡河津町梨本175
- **ACCESS**
BY TRAIN: 15 min by bus from Kawazu Stn (Izu Kyuko Line).
BY CAR: 90 km via Odawara/Atsugi Doro & Route 135 from Atsugi IC (Tomei Expressway).

NANZAN-SO 南山荘
Location: Izu Nagaoka, Izu Peninsula.
Twenty-two detached structures in a large undulating garden with serene, carp-filled ponds.

RATE: From ¥18,000 w/2 meals. **LANGUAGE:** No English, reservations in Japanese.

☎ 0559–48–0601 Fax: 0559–47–0601
1056 Nagaoka, Izu Nagaoka-cho, Tagata-gun, Shizuoka 410–2211
〒410–2211　静岡県田方郡伊豆長岡町長岡1056
- **ACCESS**
BY TRAIN: 5 min by car from Izu Nagaoka Stn (Izu Hakone Railway).
BY CAR: 30 min from Numazu IC (Tomei Expressway).

SANYO-SO 三養荘
Location: Izu Nagaoka, Izu Peninsula.
Former holiday home belonging to the Iwasaki family, founders of the Mitsubishi group, set in a large, splendid garden with ponds, streams, small waterfalls, and precious stone lanterns and Buddhist statues. Classic elegance accompanied by perfect accouterments and service.

RATE: From ¥35,000 w/2 meals. **LANGUAGE:** Some English.

☎ 0559–47–1111 Fax: 0559–47–0610
INTERNET: www.princehotels.co.jp/sanyo-so
270 Mamanoue, Izu Nagaoka-cho, Tagata-gun, Shizuoka 410–2204
〒410–2204　静岡県田方郡伊豆長岡町墹之上270
- **ACCESS**
BY TRAIN: 5 min by car from Izu Nagaoka Stn (Izu Hakone Railway).
BY CAR: 30 min from Numazu IC (Tomei Expressway).

SEIRYU-SO 清流荘
Location: Shimoda, Izu Peninsula.

The best inn in historic Shimoda, renovated to the heights of slick luxury in the 1990s.

RATE: From ¥35,000 w/2 meals. **LANGUAGE:** Some English.

℡ 0558–22–1361 Fax: 0558–23–2066
2–2 Kouchi, Shimoda-shi, Shizuoka 415–0011
〒415–0011　静岡県下田市河内2–2
■ **ACCESS**
BY TRAIN: 5 min by car from Shimoda Stn (Izu Kyuko Line).
BY CAR:　100 km via Odawara/Atsugi Doro & Route 135 from Atsugi IC (Tomei Expressway).

TSUBAKI 海石榴
Location: Oku-Yugawara, Izu Peninsula.

One of the famed luxury inns of Japan. Total perfection. The garden's 700 camellia trees cover 150 varieties of the species.

RATE: From ¥37,000 w/2 meals. **LANGUAGE:** Some English.

℡ 0465–63–3333 Fax: 0465–63–6640
776 Miyakami, Yugawara-cho, Ashigara Shimo-gun, Shizuoka 259–0304
〒259–0304　神奈川県足柄下郡湯河原町宮上776
■ **ACCESS**
BY TRAIN: 7 min by car from Yugawara Stn (JR Tokaido Main Line).
BY CAR:　1 hr via Odawara/Atsugi Doro from Atsugi IC (Tomei Expressway).

MARU-YA まるや
Location: Shimo-Suwa, Nagano Prefecture.

Spacious accommodations and friendly service that seem more inviting than those of the better-known Minato-ya, but are also more expensive, and come without a sampling of the region's famous side dish of baby bees.

RATE: From ¥22,000 w/2 meals. **LANGUAGE:** No English, reservations in Japanese.

℡ 0266–27–5151 Fax: 0266–27–0615
3304 Tatsu-machi, Suwa-gun, Nagano 393–0015
〒393–0015　長野県諏訪郡下諏訪町立町3304
■ **ACCESS**
BY TRAIN: 5 min by car from Shimo Suwa Stn (JR Chuo Main Line).
BY CAR:　10 min from Okaya IC (Chuo Expressway).

KIKU-NO-YU 菊の湯
Location: Asama Onsen, Matsumoto, Nagano Prefecture.

Comfortable inn constructed in the elegant traditional Nagano farmhouse style with a long sweeping roof.

RATE: From ¥15,000 w/2 meals. **LANGUAGE:** No English, reservations in Japanese.

℡ 0263–46–2300 Fax: 0263–46–0015
1–29–7 Asama Onsen, Matsumoto-shi, Nagano 390–0303
〒390–0303　長野県松本市浅間温泉1–29–7
■ **ACCESS**
BY TRAIN: 15 min by car from Matsumoto Stn (JR Chuo Main Line).
BY CAR:　15 min from Matsumoto IC (Chuo Expressway).

NUNO-YA 旅館 ぬのや
Location: Matsumoto, Nagano Prefecture.

This cheap inn is right in the middle of Naka-machi, the main tourist street. Old building, warm atmosphere. Mediterranean food is available if you book three days in advance and specify this preference.

RATE: From ¥8,000 w/2 meals. **LANGUAGE:** Some English.

℡ 0263–32–0545 Fax: 0263 32 0545
3–5–7 Chuo, Matsumoto-shi, Nagano 390–0811
〒390–0811　長野県松本市中央3-5-7
■ **ACCESS**
BY TRAIN: 10 min on foot from Matsumoto Stn (JR Chuo Main Line).
BY CAR:　10 min from Matsumoto IC (Chuo Expressway).

TATESHINA AI たてしな 藍
Location: Tateshina, Nagano Prefecture.

Luxurious country inn that makes a feature of indigo-dyed fabrics. Indulgent indoor and outdoor baths.

RATE: From ¥24,000 w/2 meals. **LANGUAGE:** No English, reservations in Japanese.

℡ 0266–67–5030 Fax: 0266–67–4647
Yokoyakyo-guchi, Chuo Kogen, Chino-shi, Nagano 391–0000
〒391–0000　長野県茅野市中央高原横谷峡口

■ **ACCESS**

BY TRAIN: 20 min by car from Chino Stn (JR Chuo Main Line).

BY CAR: 30 min from Suwa IC (Chuo Expressway).

DESTINATION

11

HANA-YA 花屋

Location: Bessho Onsen, Nagano Prefecture.

Splendid collection of old mazelike wooden buildings with handsome white plaster façade. Highly professional service puts you at ease. All of the meals are served in your room by a tireless staff. Baths, both indoor and outdoor, are beautiful. Highly recommended as a weekend hot spring trip from Tokyo, but book early—Hana-ya fills up quickly on the weekends.

RATE: From ¥15,000 w/2 meals. **LANGUAGE:** Some English.

✆ 0268–38–3131 Fax: 0268–38–7923

169 Bessho Onsen, Ueda-shi, Nagano 386–1431

〒386–1431 長野県上田市別所温泉169

■ **ACCESS**

BY TRAIN: 3 min on foot from Bessho Onsen Stn (Uedakotsu Bessho Line).

BY CAR: 30 min from Ueda/Sugadaira IC (Joshin'etsu Expressway).

KANAGU-YA 金具屋

Location: Shibu Onsen, Nagano Prefecture.

Original four-story wooden section of the inn built in the 1920s has interesting interior details, including inserts of superannuated waterwheel parts. Elegant gourd-shaped indoor bath called the "Kamakura-buro."

RATE: From ¥8,000 w/2 meals. **LANGUAGE:** No English, reservations in Japanese.

✆ 0269–33–3131 Fax: 0269–33–3135

INTERNET: www.avisnet.or.jp/~kanaguya/

Shibu Onsen, Yamanouchi-machi, Shimo Takai-gun, Nagano 381–0401

〒381–0401 長野県下高井郡山ノ内町渋温泉

■ **ACCESS**

BY TRAIN: 5 min by car from Yudanaka Stn (Nagano Railway).

BY CAR: 25 min from Shinshu Nakano IC (Joshin'etsu Expressway).

DESTINATION

13

YAMAKYU 山久

Location: Takayama City, Gifu Prefecture.

The best things the Yamakyu has going for it are its quiet location (opposite Hokkeji Temple) and its reasonable price. The rooms are small and the garden needs care, but the lobby overflows with the owner's collection of 1920s glass, lamps, clocks, you-name-it, and the inn has a friendly, homey atmosphere. The food is home-style Hida cooking.

RATE: From ¥7,000 w/2 meals. **LANGUAGE:** No English, reservations in Japanese.

✆ 0577–32–3756 Fax: 0577–35–2350

58 Tenshoji-machi, Takayama-shi, Gifu 506–0832

〒506–0832 岐阜県高山市天性寺町58

■ **ACCESS**

BY TRAIN: 5 min by car from Takayama Stn (JR Takayama Main Line).

BY CAR: 2 hrs from Matsumoto IC (Chuo Expressway).

YUMOTO CHOZA 湯元長座

Location: Fukuji Onsen, Gifu Prefecture.

Farmhouse-style inn constructed from the timber of a hundred-year-old Niigata mansion, tastefully decorated in mingei*-style. Meals are taken around large open fireplaces, the centerpiece being delicious rice patties on sticks flavored with* miso*. In winter, enjoy the Hida beef hot-pot. Indoor and outdoor hot spring baths.*

RATE: ¥16,000–28,000 w/2 meals. **LANGUAGE:** No English, reservations in Japanese.

✆ 0578–9–2146 Fax: 0578–9–2010

Fukuji Onsen, Kami Takara-mura, Yoshiki-gun, Gifu 506–1434

〒506–1434 岐阜県吉城郡上宝村福地温泉

■ **ACCESS**

BY TRAIN: 1 hr by bus from Takayama Stn (JR Takayama Main Line).

BY CAR: 75 min from Matsumoto IC (Chuo Expressway).

ASAHI 阿さひ
Location: Echizen Ono, Fukui Prefecture.
Uncompromisingly old-fashioned, two-story wooden inn with ten rooms and good solid meals in the quiet Teramachi part of the old castle town Echizen Ono. Close to the morning market area.

RATE: From ¥9,000 w/2 meals. **LANGUAGE:** No English, reservations in Japanese.

☎ 0779–66–2075 Fax: 0779–66–1793
5–12 Nishiki-cho, Ono-shi, Fukui 912–0024
〒912–0024　福井県大野市錦町5–12
■ **ACCESS**
BY TRAIN: 7 min on foot from Echizen Ono Stn (JR Etsubi Hokusen Line).
BY CAR: 32 km via Route 158 from Fukui IC (Hokuriku Expressway).

BIZEN-YA びぜんや
Location: Gujo Hachiman, Gifu Prefecture.
Old wooden inn with a reputation for good food. You need to book early if you want to stay here at the time of the Gujo Odori, a famous summer dance festival.

RATE: From ¥10,000 w/2 meals. **LANGUAGE:** No English, reservations in Japanese.

☎ 0575–65–2068 Fax: 0575–67–0007
264 Yanagi-cho, Hachiman-machi, Gujo-gun, Gifu 501–4214
〒501–4214　岐阜県郡上郡八幡町柳町264
■ **ACCESS**
BY TRAIN: 5 min by car from Gujo Hachiman Stn (Nagaragawa Railway).
BY CAR: 10 min from Hachiman IC.

SENZAI-RO 千歳楼
Location: Yoro-machi, Gifu Prefecture.
Picturesque and delicately constructed traditional ryokan built in 1872 in a mountain setting, with dramatic interior features. The inn is close to the famous Yoro Falls, where it is said a devoted son's desire to give his father
a drink of saké resulted in the falls turning from water to saké.

RATE: From ¥16,000 w/2 meals. **LANGUAGE:** No English, reservations in Japanese.

☎ 0584–32–1118 Fax: 0584–32–1117
Yoro Koen, Yoro-machi, Yoro-gun, Gifu 503–1254
〒503–1254　岐阜県養老郡養老町養老公園
■ **ACCESS**
BY TRAIN: 5 min by car from Yoro Stn (Kintetsu Yoro Line).
BY CAR: 30 min from Ogaki IC (Meishin Expressway).

KEYAKI-EN 欅苑
Location: Muika-machi, Niigata Prefecture.
Former village chief's house in a forest setting with a towering 1,500-year-old zelkova tree. Stay in a simple newly built lodge in the grounds, but dine in the rambling old house. Magnificent country food, almost entirely vegetarian, served on antique wares from the village head's household.

RATE: From ¥12,000 w/2 meals. **LANGUAGE:** No English, reservations in Japanese.

☎ 0257–75–2419 Fax: 0257–75–2419
24 Nagamori, Muika-machi, Minami Uonuma gun, Niigata 949–7112
〒949–7112　新潟県南魚沼郡六日町長森24
■ **ACCESS**
BY TRAIN: 15 min by car from Urasa Stn (JR Joetsu *shinkansen*).
BY CAR: 12 min (9 km) from Muika-machi IC (Kan'etsu Expressway).

MEMMEN-TEI WATA-YA
めんめん亭 綿屋
Location: Iwamuro Onsen, Niigata Prefecture.
Modest inn run by an owner genuinely interested in preserving local culture. Ask for the room called Baisho, a former rustic tearoom with a garden view. An excellent kaiseki meal is served.

RATE: From ¥16,000 w/2 meals. **LANGUAGE:** No English, reservations in Japanese.

☎ 0256–82–2030 Fax: 0256–82–4637
Iwamuro, Iwamuro-mura, Nishi Kambara-gun, Niigata 953–0104
〒953–0104　新潟県西蒲原郡岩室村岩室

■ **ACCESS**

BY TRAIN: 8 min by car from Iwamuro Stn (JR Echigo Line).

BY CAR: 30 min from Maki/Katahigashi IC (Hokuriku Expressway).

RYUGON 龍言

Location: Muika-machi, Minami-Uonuma-gun, Niigata Prefecture.

Splendid structure belonging to an upper-class advisor to the warrior Uesugi Kenshin (1530–78), relocated here in 1964.

RATE: From ¥22,000 w/2 meals. **LANGUAGE:** No English, reservations in Japanese.

☏ 0257–72–3470 Fax: 0257–72–2124

Sakado, Muika-machi, Minami Uonuma-gun, Niigata 949–6611

〒949–6611　新潟県南魚沼郡六日町坂戸

■ **ACCESS**

BY TRAIN: 15 min by car from Urasa Stn (JR Joetsu *shinkansen*).

BY CAR: 10 min from Muikamachi IC (Kan'etsu Expressway).

YUME-YA ゆめや

Location: Iwamuro Onsen, Niigata Prefecture.

Deluxe contemporary inn with only ten rooms, intimate service, and luxurious indoor and outdoor hot spring baths.

RATE: From ¥30,000 w/2 meals. **LANGUAGE:** No English, reservations in Japanese.

☏ 0256–82–5151 Fax: 0256–82–5153

905–1 Iwamuro, Iwamuro-mura, Nishi Kambara-gun, Niigata 953–0104

〒953–0104　新潟県西蒲原郡岩室村岩室905–1

■ **ACCESS**

BY TRAIN: 8 min by car from Iwamuro Stn (JR Echigo Line).

BY CAR: 15 min from Maki/Katahigashi IC (Hokuriku Expressway).

DESTINATION

18

OSARAGI-NO-YADO おさらぎの宿

Location: Kitakata Onsen, Kitakata, Fukushima Prefecture.

Casual, contemporary country inn set down in rice paddy country on the outskirts of

Kitakata, "the town of kura (storehouses) and ramen (noodles)." All of the rooms are set around a garden. Free drinks are available for guests in the high-ceilinged lobby after dinner. The inn takes pride in its food, especially its "zaku-zaku-ni," an old Aizu home-style country dish that includes burdock, daikon (giant white radishes), carrots, and yams in a nourishing broth. Guests may have as many helpings as they wish.

RATE: From ¥22,000 w/2 meals, from ¥15,000 w/breakfast, children 30% off. **LANGUAGE:** No English, reservations in Japanese.

☏ 0241–23–1126 Fax: 0241–23–2318

4113–1 Aza Sojabara, Miyazu, Iwatsuki-cho, Kitakata-shi, Fukushima 966–0002

〒966–0002　福島県喜多方市岩月町宮津字荘社原4113–1

■ **ACCESS**

BY TRAIN: 10 min by car from Kitakata Stn (JR Ban'etsu Saisen Line).

BY CAR: 30 min via Route 121 from Aizu Wakamatsu IC (Ban'etsu Expressway).

DESTINATION

19

NOTO-YA RYOKAN 能登屋旅館

Location: Ginzan Onsen, Yamagata Prefecture.

The most splendid of the several three-story wooden inns in this small 1920s hot spring town. The area had a population of 220,000 in the mid-seventeenth century when a silver mine was operating nearby. This inn was one of the places where the wildly popular television drama Oshin, about the heartbreaking misfortunes of a girl from a poor Tohoku family, was filmed.

RATE: From ¥12,000 w/2 meals. **LANGUAGE:** No English, reservations in Japanese.

☏ 0237–28–2327 Fax: 0237–28–2177

Ginzan Onsen, Obanazawa-shi, Yamagata 999–4333

〒999–4333　山形県尾花沢市銀山温泉

■ **ACCESS**

BY TRAIN: 40 min by car from Oishida Stn (JR Ou Main Line).

BY CAR: 90 min from Yamagata Kita IC (Tohoku Expressway).

KIKUSUI-KAN 菊水館（大沢温泉）
Location: Osawa Onsen, Iwate Prefecture.

Atmospheric old wooden buildings adjoining a tasteful but expensive new wing and a cheap, fend-for-yourself section, all sharing excellent baths. The rotemburo *is mixed.*

RATE: From ¥6,700 w/2 meals. **LANGUAGE:** No English, reservations in Japanese.

☎ 0198–25–2233 Fax: 0198–25–2551
181 Osawa, Yuguchi, Hanamaki-shi, Iwate 025–0244
〒025–0244　岩手県花巻市湯口字大沢181

■ **ACCESS**
BY TRAIN: 30 min by bus from Hanamaki Stn (JR Tohoku Main Line).
BY CAR: 20 min from Hanamaki IC (Tohoku Expressway).

GINRIN-SO 銀鱗荘
Location: Otaru, Hokkaido.

Palatial former home of a herring-fishing baron that was relocated to this site in 1939 and renovated in 1986. Splendid building, beautifully cared for.

RATE: From ¥36,000 w/2 meals. **LANGUAGE:** No English, reservations in Japanese. **CLOSED:** Nov–Apr.

☎ 0134–54–7010 Fax: 0134–52–2011
1–1 Sakura, Otaru shi, Hokkaido 047–0156
〒047–0156　北海道小樽市桜1–1

■ **ACCESS**
BY TRAIN: 8 min by taxi from Otaru Stn (JR Hakodate Main Line).
BY CAR: 8 min from Asari IC (Sapporo Expressway).

NISHIN-GOTEN 鰊御殿
Location: Suttsu, Hokkaido.

Built by a businessman who made a fortune by buying herring and herring roe from cash-strapped fishermen and selling them for a profit. The house was built at great expense using glass imported from Holland and cloth from Spain for the sliding door coverings. It was converted to an inn after the herring

suddenly stopped migrating to the seas near here in the 1920s to 1940s.

RATE: From ¥10,000 w/2 meals. **LANGUAGE:** No English, reservations in Japanese.

☎ 0136–64–5321 Fax: 0136–64–5322
Utasutsu, Suttsu-machi, Suttsu-gun, Hokkaido
〒048–0415　北海道寿都郡寿都町歌棄

■ **ACCESS**
BY TRAIN: 2 hrs by bus from Otaru Stn (JR Hakodate Main Line).
BY CAR: 1 hr 50 min from Otaru IC (Sapporo Expressway).

NAKAMURA なかむら
Location: Central Kanazawa, Ishikawa Prefecture.

Cheap, conveniently located lodgings in an old Kanazawa house, where the fake mud-colored wallpaper is peeling off the walls. Within easy walking of the busiest eating and entertainment area of Kanazawa, so meals are not served here. Recommended if you are on a budget or don't want inn food. Ninety percent of the customers are foreigners. A portion of the old building has been given over to a small "international café" called Chabo Nakamura, where locals and visitors can rendezvous over a cup of amerikan *(weak coffee).*

RATE: From ¥5,000 w/2 meals. **LANGUAGE:** No English, reservations in Japanese.

☎ 076–231–1806 Fax: 076–231–7806
1–6–6 Hirosaka, Kanazawa-shi, Ishikawa 920–0962
〒920–0962　石川県金沢市広坂1–6–6

■ **ACCESS**
BY TRAIN: 10 min by car from Kanazawa Stn (JR Hokuriku Main Line).
BY CAR: 30 min from Kanazawa Higashi IC (Hokuriku Expressway).

HEGURA へぐら
Location: Wajima, Ishikawa Prefecture.

A cheap minshuku *with the most rudimentary accommodations and food, but interesting since the old building is an original lacquer workshop.*

RATE: From ¥7,000 w/2 meals. **LANGUAGE:** No English, reservations in Japanese.

☏ 0768–22–1018 Fax: 0768–22–1018

91 Kami-machi, Fugeshi-machi, Wajima-shi, Ishikawa 928–0077

〒928–0077　石川県輪島市鳳至町上町91

■ **ACCESS**

BY TRAIN: 5 min by car from Wajima Stn (Noto Tetsudo Line).

BY CAR:　30 min (20 km) from Anamizu IC (Noto Doro).

D E S T I N A T I O N
23

MIYAMA-SO　美山荘
Location: Kyoto.

The original building was an old temple lodging (shukubo). Magnificent in every detail of accouterments and service. The meals feature fresh country produce worked into Kyoto's refined cooking style. Though within Kyoto city limits, Miyama-so is an hour by car from Kyoto Station.

RATE: From ¥35,000 w/2 meals. **LANGUAGE:** No English, reservations in Japanese.

☏ 075–746–0231 Fax: 075–746–0233

Daihizan, Harachi-cho, Hanase, Sakyo-ku, Kyoto 601–1102

〒601–1102　京都市左京区花背原地町大悲山

■ **ACCESS**

BY TRAIN: 50 min by taxi from Kitaoji Stn (subway).

BY CAR:　1 hr by car from Kyoto Minami IC (Meishin Expressway).

SHIRAUME　白梅
Location: Gion, Kyoto.

A two-story wooden inn with only eight rooms, facing the picturesque cherry-tree dotted Shirakawa river in Gion, which was once used by yuzen dyers to wash the wax resist from their gorgeous textiles. Shiraume used to be a Japanese-style restaurant with private rooms, where guests would have been entertained by geisha. Though renovated in 1997, it retains most of its elegant interior features. The name Shiraume, "White Plum," is a nod

to one-hundred-year-old plum trees flanking the small bridge that leads to the inn's entrance.

RATE: From ¥18,000 w/2 meals. **LANGUAGE:** Some English.

☏ 075–561–1459 Fax: 075–531–5290

Shijo Nawate-Agaru, Higashi-Iru, Gion Shimbashi, Higashiyama-ku, Kyoto 605–0085

〒605–0085　京都市東山区祇園新橋四条縄手上ル東入る

■ **ACCESS**

BY TRAIN: 15 min by taxi from Kyoto Stn (JR Tokaido *shinkansen*).

BY CAR:　15 min from Kyoto Higashi IC (Meishin Expressway).

TAMAHAN　玉半
Location: Gion, Kyoto.

Originally built as the second home of an Osaka stock trader. Opened in 1929 as an elegant inn specializing in Kyoto cuisine. The lovely embracing garden is designed for the enjoyment of different flowers all year round. The bekkan, a section attached later, adjoins the cobblestone street of atmospheric Ishibe koji, close to Gion.

RATE: From ¥25,000 w/2 meals. **LANGUAGE:** Some English.

☏ 075–561–3188 Fax: 075–531–5128

477 Shimogawara-cho, Gion, Higashiyama-ku, Kyoto 605–0825

〒605–0825　京都市東山区祇園下河原町477

■ **ACCESS**

BY TRAIN: 15 min by car from Kyoto Stn.

BY CAR:　15 min from Kyoto Higashi IC (Meishin Expressway; call ahead to reserve parking space).

D E S T I N A T I O N
24

KIKUSUI-RO　菊水楼
Location: Nara.

Opened in 1868 at a corner of Nara Park. A classic, top-quality inn with a hundred-year-plus history of entertaining VIPs.

RATE: From ¥39,000 w/2 meals. **LANGUAGE:** No English, reservations in Japanese.

☏ 0742–23–2001 Fax: 0742–26–0025

1130 Takabatake-cho, Nara-shi Nara 630–8301

〒630–8301　奈良県奈良市高畑町1130

■ ACCESS
BY TRAIN: 5 min by car from Nara Stn (Kintetsu Line).
BY CAR: 40 min from Tenri IC (Nishi Meihan Express-
           way).

■ ACCESS
BY TRAIN: 5 min on foot from Kinosaki Stn (JR Sanin
           Main Line).
BY CAR: 2 hrs from Fukusaki IC (Chugoku Expressway).

D E S T I N A T I O N
25

MAN-TEI 万亭
Location: Shirahama, Wakayama Prefecture.

A classic half-Western, half-Japanese structure situated on a high point in Nanki Shirahama, a popular old hot spring resort by the beach. Renovated in 1943. One of the detached guest rooms is also a teahouse.

RATE: From ¥25,000 w/2 meals. LANGUAGE: No English, reservations in Japanese.

☎ 0739–43–5005 Fax: 0739–42–5353
920–16 Shirahama-cho, Nishi Muro-gun, Wakayama 649–2211
〒649–2211 和歌山県西牟婁郡白浜町920–16
■ ACCESS
BY TRAIN: 10 min by car from Shirahama Stn (JR Kise
           Main Line).
BY CAR: 90 min from Gobo IC (Yuasa/Gobo Doro) via
           Hanwa Expressway.

D E S T I N A T I O N
27

YUTO-YA ゆとうや
Location: Kinosaki Onsen, Hyogo Prefecture.

The Yuto-ya was built in 1688 solely for offi-cers of the Tokugawa shogunate. In 1868, it became a regular inn, and was rebuilt in the 1930s. The owners are foreigner-friendly, and the buildings offer some marvelous details redolent of a former era when carpentry was a high art.

RATE: From ¥18,000 w/2 meals. LANGUAGE: No English, reservations in Japanese.

☎ 0796–32–2121 Fax: 0796–32–2255
INTERNET: www.globe.or.jp/kinosaki/
373 Yushima, Kinosaki-cho, Kinosaki-gun, Hyogo 669–6101
〒669–6101 兵庫県城崎郡城崎町湯島373

D E S T I N A T I O N
28

CHAROKU BEKKAN 茶六別館
Location: Miyazu, Kyoto Prefecture.

One of the famous inns on the Sea of Japan coast. Eclectic sukiya *and* shoin *architectural styles and a classic garden.*

RATE: From ¥20,000 w/2 meals. LANGUAGE: Some English.

☎ 0772–22–2177 Fax: 0772–22–2178
Shimazaki Kaigan, Miyazu-shi, Kyoto 626–0017
〒626–0017 京都府宮津市島崎海岸
■ ACCESS
BY TRAIN: 10 min on foot from Miyazu Stn (JR Kita Kinki
           Tango Tetsudo Line).
BY CAR: 35 min (30 km) from Maizuru/Oe IC (Kyoto
           Jukando Miyazu Doro), via Maizuru Expressway.

D E S T I N A T I O N
TOTTORI PREFECTURE

HANA-YA 花屋
Location: Iwai Onsen, Tottori Prefecture.

A modest hot spring ryokan in the quiet hot spring town of Iwai set in peaceful farm country.

RATE: From ¥13,000 w/2 meals. LANGUAGE: No English, reservations in Japanese.

☎ 0857–72–1431 Fax: 0857–73–0745
Iwai, Iwami-cho, Iwami-gun, Tottori 681–0024
〒681–0024 鳥取県岩美郡岩井町岩井
■ ACCESS
BY TRAIN: 5 min by car from Iwami Stn (JR Sanin Main
           Line).
BY CAR: 1 hr 50 min from Fukusaki IC (Chugoku
           Expressway).

SHOFU-SO 松風荘旅館
Location: Kurayoshi, Tottori Prefecture.

A modestly attractive, down-to-earth ryokan in a town with rows of old houses and inventive public lavatories.

RATE: From ¥10,000 w/2 meals. LANGUAGE: No English, reservations in Japanese.

☎ 0858–22–6363 Fax: 0858–23–0520
Sezaki-cho, Kurayoshi-shi, Tottori 682–0863
〒682–0863　鳥取県倉吉市瀬崎町

■ ACCESS
BY TRAIN: 10 min by car from Kurayoshi Stn (JR Sanin Main Line).
BY CAR: 40 min from In-nosho IC (Chugoku Expressway).

DESTINATION

29

TSURUGATA　鶴形
Location: Kurashiki canal district, Okayama Prefecture.

A more conservative and expensive alternative to Ryokan Kurashiki, but Tsurugata sits in the same beautiful canal area, built in 1744 as a merchant's quarters.

RATE: ¥15,000–32,000 w/2 meals. LANGUAGE: No English, reservations in Japanese.

☎ 086–424–1635 Fax: 086–424–1650
1–3–15 Chuo, Kurashiki-shi, Okayama 710–0046
〒710–0046　岡山県倉敷市中央1-3-15

■ ACCESS
BY TRAIN: 7 min by car from Kurashiki Stn (JR Sanyo Main Line).
BY CAR: 12 min from Kurashiki IC (Sanyo Expressway).

DESTINATION

30

LA FORET FUKIYA　ラフォーレ吹屋
Location: Fukiya, Okayama Prefecture.

Tastefully built to match the beautiful old wooden Fukiya primary school next door, this hotel was especially designed to accommodate study groups and nature lovers who come to hike, bird-watch, and mountain climb in the untouched surrounding countryside. Both Western and Japanese-style accommodations.

RATE: Twin w/o meals from ¥5,000. LANGUAGE: No English, reservations in Japanese.

☎ 0866–29–2000 Fax: 0866–29–2005
611 Fukiya, Nariwa-cho, Kawakami-gun, Okayama 719–2341

〒719–2341　岡山県川上郡成羽町吹屋611

■ ACCESS
BY TRAIN: 50 min by car from Takahashi Stn (JR Hakubi Line).
BY CAR: 40 min from Niimi IC (Chugoku Expressway).

DESTINATION

31

JUSEN-SO　寿仙荘
Location: Yuno Onsen, Tokuyama, Yamaguchi Prefecture.

A modest entrance belies the extent of the huge garden at the back of the inn, which used to be the property of a high-ranking samurai of the powerful Choshu clan. Some trees are several hundred years old. Six separate buildings in the garden, each with its own charming characteristics, make up the inn. The most luxurious and most expensive building has two expansive rooms overlooking a pond, plus one for the maid—should you bring one along.

RATE: From ¥16,000 w/2 meals. LANGUAGE: No English, reservations in Japanese.

☎ 0834–83–2280 Fax: 0834–83–2088
Yuno, Tokuyama-shi, Yamaguchi, 745–1132
〒745–1132　山口県徳山市湯野

■ ACCESS
BY TRAIN: 25 min by car from Tokuyama Stn (JR Sanyo Main Line).
BY CAR: 5 min from Tokuyama Nishi IC (Sanyo Expressway).

DESTINATION

32

HOKUMON YASHIKI　北門屋敷
Location: Hagi, Yamaguchi Prefecture.

A classic sukiya inn with glitzy contemporary flair, Hokumon was frequented by Japanese royalty. The inn is situated within the moat area of the former Hagi Castle, where the higher-ranking samurai under the Mori Clan built their mansions.

RATE: From ¥25,000 w/2 meals. LANGUAGE: No English, reservations in Japanese.

☎ 0838–22–7521 Fax: 0838–25–8144

210 Horiuchi, Hagi-shi, Yamaguchi 758–0057

〒758–0057　山口県萩市堀内210

■ **ACCESS**

BY TRAIN: 15 min by car from Higashi Hagi Stn (JR San'in Main Line).

BY CAR: 40 min (45 km) from Mine IC, or 47 km from Yamaguchi IC (Chutoku Expressway).

SANSUIEN　山水園

Location: Yuda Onsen, Yamaguchi Prefecture.

Originally the summer house of a 1920s shipping magnate, Sansuien later became a hot spring inn and was tastefully modified under the eye of its tea-ceremony-loving new owner. The rooms are now in the process of being splendidly refurbished. Ornamental features of each room are playfully different and the tokonoma *are especially beautiful. You'll find no televisions in the alcoves here. Emperor Showa (formerly Emperor Hirohito; 1901–89) and several members of the imperial family have stayed here. Enjoy the garden with its mountain backdrop. This is one of the few superb old wooden inns in the country that has not added on a ferroconcrete extension. A treat for the architecturally alert.*

RATE: From ¥20,000 w/2 meals.　**LANGUAGE:** No English, reservations in Japanese.

☎ 0839–22–0560 Fax: 0839–21–0600

4–60 Midori-cho, Yamaguchi-shi, Yamaguchi 753–0078

〒753–0078　山口県山口市緑町4–60

■ **ACCESS**

BY TRAIN: 10 min by car from Yamaguchi Stn (JR Yamaguchi Line).

BY CAR: 15 min from Ogori IC (Chugoku Expressway).

YUI-NO-IE　YUIの家

Location: Nagato, Yamaguchi Prefecture.

A contemporary hotel-inn with a splendid view of the sea. Both Western- and Japanese-style rooms available. Two meals are included in the tariff, centering on local seafood. Yui-no-Ie offers both hot spring bathing and a hot spring swimming pool.

RATE: From ¥12,000 w/2 meals.　**LANGUAGE:** No English, reservations in Japanese.

☎ 0837–37–2578 Fax: 0837–37–2577

1707–2 Kami Isoda, Heki, Heki-machi, Otsu-gun,

Yamaguchi 759–4401

〒759–4401　山口県大津郡日置町日置上磯田 1707–2

■ **ACCESS**

BY TRAIN: 2 min on foot from Kiwado Stn.

BY CAR: 40 min from Mine IC (Chugoku Expressway).

YAGUMO HONJIN　八雲本陣

Location: Shinji, Shimane Prefecture.

A former honjin *(official* daimyo's *inn) designated as an important cultural property. Magnificent architectural and interior features in the original sections. A special room was added on for the Taisho emperor (1879–1926, reign 1912–26), who once stayed for lunch. The great highlight of a stay here is the duck meat hot-pot (*kaiyaki*) in winter. Guests each receive a charcoal-lit brazier on which is placed a huge abalone shell. Cook your own duck and copious quantities of crisp vegetables in the shell, seasoning them with the assortment of condiments. The street where Yagumo Honjin stands was a busy highway in the Edo period (1600–1868), though today the town of Shinji is a quiet backwater.*

RATE: From ¥15,000 w/2 meals.　**LANGUAGE:** No English, reservations in Japanese.

☎ 08526–6–0136 Fax: 0852–66–0137

1335 Shinji, Shinji-cho, Yatsuka-gun, Shimane 699–0401

〒699–0401　島根県八束郡宍道町宍道1335

■ **ACCESS**

BY TRAIN: 5 min on foot from Shinji Stn (JR Sanin Main Line).

BY CAR: 1 hr half from Yonago IC (Yonago Expressway).

DOGO-KAN　道後館

Location: Dogo Onsen, Matsuyama, Ehime Prefecture.

None of the conventional mud-colored walls for the Dogo-kan. A flight of fancy of architect

Kisho Kurokawa (1934–), this place was one of the wildest modern inns in Japan when it was built in the 1980s, with alarmingly colorful Japanese-style guest rooms, nouvelle Japanese cuisine, and fabulous rooftop baths.

RATE: From ¥27,000 w/2 meals. **LANGUAGE:** No English, reservations in Japanese.

☎ 089–941–7777 Fax: 089–941–7707
INTERNET: www.mesh.ne.jp/dogo/index.html
7–26 Tako-cho, Matsuyama-shi, Ehime 790–0841
〒790–0841　愛媛県松山市道後多幸町7–26

■ ACCESS
BY TRAIN: 15 min by car from Matsuyama Stn (JR Yosan Line).
BY CAR: 20 min (5 km) from Matsuyama IC (Matsuyama Expressway).

D E S T I N A T I O N
34

KASHII-SO　香椎荘
Location: Yufuin, Oita Prefecture.
The second home of an army commander who distinguished himself in World War II. Although it is not as fashionable as the other Yufuin inns, the old buildings and garden are a picture.

RATE: From ¥12,000 w/2 meals. **LANGUAGE:** No English, reservations in Japanese.

☎ 0977–84–2115 Fax: 0977–84–3299
3015–4 Kawakami, Yufuin-machi, Oita-gun, Oita 879–5102
〒879–5102　大分県大分郡湯布院町川上3015–4

■ ACCESS
BY TRAIN: 5 min by car from Yufuin Stn (JR Kyudai Main Line).
BY CAR: 10 min from Yufuin IC (Oita Expressway).

KAWASEMI-NO-SHO　翡翠之庄
Location: Naga-yu Onsen, Oita Prefecture.
Inn consisting of thatched main building, with tenement-type and detached rooms. Kawasemi looks out over a pine-shrouded dam and has excellent hot spring baths. The fare is simple and may include rice gruel, grilled freshwater fish, free-range eggs, and homemade tofu and miso. Woodworking and pottery workshops are conducted in same compound.

RATE: From ¥13,000 w/2 meals. **LANGUAGE:** English spoken.

☎ 0974–75–2300 Fax: 0974–75–2339
Kutamiga-oka, Nagayu Onsen, Naoiri-machi, Naoiri-gun, Oita 878–0405
〒878–0402　大分県直入郡直入町長湯温泉くたみヶ丘

■ ACCESS
BY TRAIN: 40 min by car from Yufuin Stn (JR Kyudai Main Line).
BY CAR: 40 min from Yufuin IC (Oita Expressway).

MURATA　山荘 無量塔
Location: Yufuin, Oita Prefecture.
Chic contemporary country-style Japanese accommodations, perfect in every detail.

RATE: From ¥40,000 w/2 meals. **LANGUAGE:** No English, reservations in Japanese.

☎ 0977–84–5000 Fax: 0977–84–5001
Kawakami Torikoe, Yufuin-machi, Oita-gun, Oita 879–5102
〒879–5102　大分県大分郡湯布院町川上鳥越

■ ACCESS
BY TRAIN: 5 min by car from Yufuin Stn (JR Kyudai Main Line).
BY CAR: 15 min from Yufuin IC (Oita Expressway).

D E S T I N A T I O N
35

DAIMARU BESSO　だいまる別荘
Location: Futsukaichi Onsen, Fukuoka Prefecture.
Once patronized by Emperor Showa (formerly Emperor Hirohito; 1901–89), this is an inn of peerless taste and exceptional service. It is possible to stay in its highly atmospheric old wooden building (the Taisho-tei, constructed in 1917) for only slightly more than you would pay for a room in the newly renovated hotellike wings (the Showa-tei built in 1970 and the Heian-tei built in 1989) because, as the inn's owner Makoto Yamada said, "We cannot ask a high price these days for rooms in a building that has creaky floorboards." In the new wings I found the rooms in the Heian-tei most appealing, having a mini-Western-style dining room adjoining a beautifully decorated Japanese room. Its high degree of

comfort and professional service make this one of the top inns in this book, but unfortunately its less than alluring location, just outside the Fukuoka metropolis, is a drawback. Nevertheless, inside its walls you are in a different world. The gardens and baths are gorgeous. Nearby is historic Dazaifu, site of an ancient provincial government.

RATE: From ¥18,000 w/2 meals. LANGUAGE: Some English.

☎ 092–924–3939 Fax: 092–924–4126
Futsukaichi Onsen, Musahi, Chikushino-shi, Fukuoka 818–0052
〒818–0052　福岡県筑紫野市武蔵二日市温泉
■ ACCESS
BY TRAIN: 5 min by car from Futsukaichi Stn (JR Kagoshima Main Line, 15 min from Hakata Stn).
BY CAR:　10 min from Dazaifu IC (Kyushu Expressway).

YANAGAWA OHANA　柳川 御花
Location: Yanagawa, Fukuoka Prefecture.
Built in 1697, Ohana started life as the home of the fourth head of the Tachibana Family that ruled this part of Kyushu, but was converted to an inn in 1950. The old wooden building facing the magnificent garden is now only used for private dining, while overnight guests are housed in a multistory hotel, some with tatami rooms. Staying guests eat in the old section. The meals include such delicacies from the Ariake Sea and nearby waterways as mudskipper and steamed eel. A handsome Western-style structure and part of the aforementioned wooden building are open for public viewing, as is a museum of Tachibana artifacts housing armor, Noh costumes and masks, and a palanquin. Worth a peek. Yanagawa is famous for lazy boat trips down willow-lined canals, which were formerly palace moats.

RATE: From ¥15,000 w/2 meals. LANGUAGE: No English, reservations in Japanese.

☎ 0944–73–2189 Fax: 0944–74–0872
1 Shin Hoka-machi, Yanagawa-shi, Fukuoka 832–0069
〒832–0069　福岡県柳川市新外町1
■ ACCESS
BY TRAIN: 10 min by car from Yanagawa Stn (Nishitetsu Omuta Line).
BY CAR:　40 min from Yame IC (Kyushu Expressway).

AKUNE　阿久根
Location: Yanagawa, Fukuoka Prefecture.
A small Yanagawa inn of five rooms, run by a couple. Akune is known for its meals, containing local delicacies, and its intimate accommodations in an old minka building.

RATE: From ¥23,000 w/2 meals. LANGUAGE: No English, reservations in Japanese.

☎ 0944–72–2483 Fax: 0944–72–2483
197 Takahata, Yanagawa-shi, Fukuoka, 832–0826
〒832–0826　福岡県柳川市高畑197
■ ACCESS
BY TRAIN: 8 min on foot from Nishitetsu Yanagawa Stn (Nishitetsu Railway).
BY CAR:　30 min from Yame IC (Kyushu Expressway).

D E S T I N A T I O N
SOUTHERN KYUSHU

IKOI RYOKAN　いこい旅館
Location: Kurokawa Onsen, Kumamoto Prefecture.
Well-appointed hot spring inn with eight baths, including an utase-yu bath, in which the water falls from an overhead bamboo pipe. The food is country fare cooked around a central hearth. Three ryokan in Kurokawa Onsen issue "bath passes" at a reasonable price for people who just want to experience the local baths.

RATE: From ¥13,000 w/2 meals. LANGUAGE: No English, reservations in Japanese.

☎ 0967–44–0552 Fax: 0967–44–0807
Kurokawa Onsen, Minami Oguni-cho, Aso-gun, Kumamoto 869–2400
〒869–2400　熊本県阿蘇郡南小国町黒川温泉
■ ACCESS
BY TRAIN: 2 hrs from Kumamoto Stn (JR Kagoshima Main Line).
BY CAR:　1 hr from Hita IC (Oita Expressway).

SHIGETOMI-SO　重富荘
Location: Kagoshima, Kagoshima Prefecture.
The former second home of the Shimazu lord who ruled the powerful Satsuma Clan at the end of the Edo period (1600–1868). The grand shoin-style rooms have a view of the

smoking Sakurajima volcano. The encircled-cross crest of the Shimazu clan makes its appearance on the interior decor.

RATE: From ¥22,000 w/2 meals. **LANGUAGE:** No English, reservations in Japanese.

☏ 0992–47–3155 Fax: 099–247–0960
31–7 Shimizu-cho, Kagoshima-shi, Kagoshima
〒892–0802　鹿児島県鹿児島市清水町31–7

■ **ACCESS**
BY TRAIN: 15 min by car from Nishi Kagoshima Stn (JR Kagoshima Main Line).
BY CAR:　20 min from Yoshida IC (Kyushu Expressway).

WASURE-NO-SATO GAJOEN
忘れの里 雅叙園
Location: Myoken Onsen, Kagoshima Prefecture.

A renowned contemporary inn, with picturesque thatch buildings, chickens in the yard, and a semi-outdoor stone bath. Wasure offers complete organic meals, and rice cooked over a traditional wood-fired hearth.

RATE: From ¥20,000 w/2 meals. **LANGUAGE:** No English, reservations in Japanese.

☏ 0995–77–2114 Fax: 0995–77–2203
Myoken Onsen, Makizono-cho, Aira-gun, Kagoshima 899–6506
〒899–6506　鹿児島県姶良郡牧園町妙見温泉

■ **ACCESS**
BY TRAIN: 50 min by bus from Kagoshima Stn (JR Kagoshima Main Line).
BY CAR:　15 min from Mizobe IC (Kyushu Expressway).

CLASSIC HOTELS

At the end of the nineteenth century, a series of unique "Western-style" hotels was built for foreign tourists who began to visit Japan in growing numbers. Japanese sensibilities and lovingly sanded wood surfaces infuse many of these old hotels with an ambience only found on these shores. The hotels typically feature an exotic blend of European and Oriental ornamentation: imported European furnishings alongside traditional Japanese decorations and, perhaps, parquet dining rooms with carved pillars and coffered ceilings, where meals such as trout meunière would be served by tuxedoed waiters with the flourish of former times.

NOTE: Unlike the per-person fees of ryokan quoted throughout this book, some of the rates quoted here are for twin rooms for up to two persons.

D E S T I N A T I O N

3

NIKKO KANAYA HOTEL
日光金谷ホテル
Location: Nikko, Tochigi Prefecture.
An elegant old hotel near Toshogu shrine, patronized by many famous guests, including Albert Einstein. The oldest portion was constructed in 1894 and additions were built in 1935. The present dining hall with Toshogu-like carvings dates to the 1964 Tokyo Olympics.

The solid quality of the comfortable old-style rooms, with their large wood-framed windows and coffered wooden ceilings, complements the handsome black-and-white exterior.

RATE: Twin room charge w/o meals from ¥13,000.
LANGUAGE: English spoken.

☏ 0288–54–0001 Fax: 0288–53–2487
1300 Kami Hachiishi-machi, Nikko-shi, Tochigi 321–1401
〒321–1401　栃木県日光市上鉢石町1300

■ **ACCESS**
BY TRAIN: 5 min by car from Nikko Stn (JR or Tobu Line).
BY CAR:　5 min from Nikko IC (Nikko/Utsunomiya Doro).

5

FUJIYA HOTEL　フジヤホテル
Location: Hakone, Kanagawa Prefecture.
A classic Western-style hotel built for foreign travelers at the end of the nineteenth century. Fujiya has both hot spring baths and an indoor swimming pool. Elegant 1920s dining room with a coffered ceiling painted in a wild-plant motif.

RATE: From ¥20,000 w/2 meals. **LANGUAGE:** English spoken.

☎ 0460–2–2211 Fax: 0460–2–2210
359 Miyanoshita, Hakone-machi, Ashigara Shimo-gun, Kanagawa 250–0404
〒250-0404　神奈川県足柄下郡箱根町宮ノ下359
■ **ACCESS**
BY TRAIN: 3 min on foot from Miyanoshita Stn (Hakone Tozan Tetsudo), or 15 min by car from Hakone Yumoto Stn (Hakone Tozan Tetsudo).
BY CAR: 15 min (10 km) via Route 1 from Odawara Nishi IC (Odawara/Atsugi Doro).

6

KAWANA HOTEL　川奈ホテル
Location: Ito, Shizuoka Prefecture.
An ocean-view resort hotel that hosts foreign dignitaries. The grounds also support a well-known, exclusive golf course.

RATE: From ¥28,000 w/2 meals. **LANGUAGE:** English spoken.

☎ 0557–45–1111 Fax: 0557–45–3834
1459 Kawana, Ito-shi, Shizuoka 414–0044
〒414-0044　静岡県伊東市川奈1459
■ **ACCESS**
BY TRAIN: 20 min by car from Ito Stn (Izu Kyuko Line).
BY CAR: 90 min from Atsugi IC (Tomei Expressway).

9

KAMIKOCHI IMPERIAL HOTEL
上高地帝国ホテル
Location: Kamikochi, Nagano Prefecture.
A Swiss chalet–style hotel with an Oriental touch.

This was one of Japan's first Western-style resort hotels. Its presence helped make Kamikochi one of Japan's most patronized summer getaways. The French-style food is of a quality equal to its parent, the Imperial Hotel in Tokyo. Kamikochi is under snow in winter and the hotel is closed from early November to the end of April.

RATE: Twin room charge from ¥27,000 w/o meals.
LANGUAGE: English spoken. **CLOSED:** 11/5–4/26.

☎ 0263–95–2006 (Nov–April, 03–3592–8001)
Fax: 0263–95–2412
Kamikochi, Azumino-mura, Azumino-gun, Nagano 390–1516
〒390-1516　長野県安曇野郡安曇野村上高地
■ **ACCESS**
BY TRAIN: 75 min by bus from Shin Shimajima Stn (Matsumoto Railway).
BY CAR: Leave your car at Sawando Public Parking Lot (*chushajo*; 43 km via Route 158 from Matsumoto IC, Chuo Expressway), and take taxi or bus.

MATSUMOTO HOTEL KAGETSU
松本ホテル花月
Location: Matsumoto, Nagano Prefecture.
Old-world atmosphere (built at the turn of the nineteenth century), with tasteful use of handmade Matsumoto furniture. Both Western and Japanese rooms.

RATE: From ¥7,500 w/2 meals. **LANGUAGE:** English spoken.

☎ 0263–32–0114 Fax: 0263–33–4775
INTERNET: www.mcci.or.jp/www/kagetsu/
4–8–9 Oote, Matsumoto-shi, Nagano 390–0874
〒390-0874　長野県松本市大手4–8–9
■ **ACCESS**
BY TRAIN: 5 min by car from Matsumoto Stn (JR Chuo Main Line).
BY CAR: 15 min from Matsumoto IC (Chuo Expressway).

9 & 11

MAMPEI HOTEL　万平ホテル
Location: Karuizawa, Nagano Prefecture.
An imposing black-and-white building dating to 1936. First opened in 1896 to accommodate foreign guests in this new summer resort town. John Lennon stayed here every summer

*for four years before his death. The guest
rooms have a blend of Western- and Japanese-style interiors.*

RATE: From ¥23,000 w/2 meals. **LANGUAGE:** English spoken.

☎ 0267–42–1234 Fax: 0267–42–7733
INTERNET: www.avisnet.or.jp/ˇmampei
E-MAIL: mampei@avisnet.or.jp
925 Karuizawa, Karuizawa-cho, Saku-gun, Nagano
389–0102
〒389–0102　長野県佐久郡軽井沢町軽井沢925
■ **ACCESS**
BY TRAIN: 5 min by car from Karuizawa Stn (JR Nagano
　　　shinkansen).
BY CAR:　20 min (15 km) from Usui/Karuizawa IC
　　　(Joshin'etsu Expressway).

DESTINATION
16

GAMAGORI PRINCE HOTEL
蒲郡プリンスホテル
Location: Gamagori, Aichi Prefecture.
*Stately Western-style hotel with ubiquitous
Japanese-style roof and entrance built in
1934. On the seafront at the harbor town of
Gamagori in Aichi Prefecture, it was taken
over by the Prince hotel chain at the end of the
1980s. Well cared for, with beautifully tended
lawns and a real teahouse.*

RATE: Twin room charge w/o meals from ¥23,000.
LANGUAGE: English spoken.

☎ 0533–68–1111 Fax: 0533–68–1199
15–1 Takeshima-cho, Gamagori-shi, Aichi 443–0031
〒443–0031　愛知県蒲郡市竹島町15–1
■ **ACCESS**
BY TRAIN: 5 min by car from Gamagori Stn (Tokaido Main
　　　Line).
BY CAR:　15 min (11 km) from Otowa/Gamagori IC
　　　(Tomei Expressway).

DESTINATION
24

NARA HOTEL 奈良ホテル
Location: Nara.
A classic hotel for those who prefer Western-style comfort.

RATE: Twin room charge w/o meals from ¥22,000.
LANGUAGE: English spoken.

☎ 0742–26–3300 Fax: 0742–23–5252
INTERNET: www.hotels.westjr.co.jp/nara/
1096 Takabatake-cho, Nara-shi, Nara 630–8301
〒630–8301　奈良県奈良市高畑町1096
■ **ACCESS**
BY TRAIN: 5 min by car from Nara Stn (Kintetsu Line).
BY CAR:　30 min from Tenri IC (Nishi Meihan Expressway).

ALPHABETICAL LIST OF INNS

Inn	Name in Kanji	Destination	Page
Akune (A)	阿久根	35 Fukuoka Pref.	261
Arai Ryokan	新井旅館	6 Shizuoka Pref.	65
Asaba (A)	あさば	6 Shizuoka Pref.	249
Asada-ya	浅田屋	21 Ishikawa Pref.	160
Asahi (A)	阿さひ	13 Gifu Pref.	253
Asakichi	麻吉	16 Mie Pref.	120
Bizen-ya (A)	びぜんや	15 Gifu Pref.	253
Boguku-so	望嶽荘	10 Nagano Pref.	87
Charoku Bekkan (A)	茶六別館	28 Kyoto	257
Chigasaki-kan	茅ヶ崎館	2 Kanagawa Pref.	43
Chikurin-in Gumpo-en	竹林院群芳園	24 Nara	185
Choju-kan	長寿館 (法師温泉)	4 Gumma Pref.	52
Daimaru Besso (A)	だいまる別荘	35 Fukuoka Pref.	260
Dairo-an	大呂庵	17 Niigata Pref.	131
Dogo-kan (A)	道後館	33 Ehime Pref.	259
Echigo ya	越後屋旅館	10 Nagano Pref.	85
Edosan	江戸三	24 Nara	184
Eiraku-ya	永楽屋	12 Nagano Pref.	99
Fujiya Hotel (CH)	フジヤホテル	5 Kanagawa Pref.	263
Fukiya International Villa	吹屋 国際交流ヴィラ	30 Okayama Pref.	215
Fukuki	福喜	28 Fukui Pref.	207
Fukuzumi-ro	福住楼	5 Kanagawa Pref.	57
Futami-kan	二見館	16 Mie Pref.	122
Gamagori Prince Hotel (CH)	蒲郡プリンスホテル	16 Mie/Aichi Pref.	264
Gemmyo-an	玄妙庵	28 Kyoto	204
Ginrin-so (A)	銀鱗荘	Hokkaido	255
Gohonjin Fuji-ya	御本陣藤屋	11 Nagano Pref.	92
Gora Kansui-ro (A)	強羅環翠楼	5 Kanagawa Pref.	249
Gyokuho-kan (A)	玉峰館	6 Shizuoka Pref.	250
Hakkei-tei	八景亭	23 Shiga Pref.	179
Hana-ya (A)	花屋	11 Nagano Pref.	252
Hana-ya (A)	花屋	Tottori Pref.	257
Hangetsu-an	半月庵	31 Yamaguchi Pref.	221

Hazuki	はづ木	16 Aichi Pref.	123
Hegura (A)	へぐら	22 Ishikawa Pref.	255
Hokumon Yashiki (A)	北門屋敷	32 Yamaguchi Pref.	258
Honke Bankyu Bankyu Ryokan	本家伴久萬久旅館	3 Tochigi Pref.	48
Horai	蓬莱	6 Shizuoka Pref.	64
Ikoi Ryokan (A)	いこい旅館	Kumamoto Pref.	261
Iwa-no-Yu	岩の湯	11 Nagano Pref.	91
Iwaso	岩惣	31 Hiroshima Pref.	219
Juemon	民宿 十右エ門	14 Gifu Pref.	111
Jusen-so (A)	寿仙荘	31 Yamaguchi Pref.	258
Kabuto-ya (A)	兜家	Tama, Tokyo	248
Kaihin-so Kamakura	かいひん荘 鎌倉	2 Kanagawa Pref.	42
Kame-no-I Besso	亀の井別荘	34 Oita Pref.	238
Kami-Goten	上御殿	25 Wakayama Pref.	191
Kamikochi Imperial Hotel (CH)	上高地帝国ホテル	9 Nagano Pref.	263
Kampo-ro	冠峰楼	5 Kanagawa Pref.	59
Kanagu-ya (A)	金具屋	11 Nagano Pref.	252
Kannawa-en	神和苑	34 Oita Pref.	241
Kashii-so (A)	香椎荘	34 Oita Pref.	260
Kawana Hotel (CH)	川奈ホテル	6 Shizuoka Pref.	263
Kawasemi-no-Sho (A)	翡翠之庄	34 Oita Pref.	260
Kaya-no-Ie	萱の家	4 Gumma Pref.	53
Kayo-tei	かよう亭	21 Ishikawa Pref.	162
Keyaki-en (A)	欅苑	17 Niigata Pref.	253
Kiku-no-Yu (A)	菊の湯	9 Nagano Pref.	251
Kikusui-kan (A)	菊水館（大沢温泉）	20 Iwate Pref.	255
Kikusui-ro (A)	菊水楼	24 Nara	256
Kincha-ryo	金茶寮	21 Ishikawa Pref.	159
Kinmata	懐石宿 近又	23 Kyoto	174
Kita Onsen (A)	北温泉	3 Tochigi Pref.	249
Kiun-kaku (A)	起雲閣	6 Shizuoka Pref.	250
Koemon	幸エ門	14 Gifu Pref.	110
Koshi-no-Yu	越之湯	25 Wakayama Pref.	190
Kurashiki	旅館くらしき	29 Okayama Pref.	210
Kuro-yu Onsen	黒湯温泉	20 Akita Pref.	151
Kyo-tei (A)	京亭	Saitama Pref.	248
Le Foret Fukiya (A)	ラフォーレ吹屋	30 Okayama Pref.	258
Magari-ya	民宿 曲がり家	20 Iwate Pref.	155
Mampei Hotel (CH)	万平ホテル	9 & 11 Nagano Pref.	263
Man-tei (A)	万亭	25 Wakayama Pref.	257
Maru-ya (A)	まるや	8 Nagano Pref.	251
Matsuda-ya	松田屋ホテル	32 Yamaguchi Pref.	228
Matsumoto	料理旅館 まつ本	21 Ishikawa Pref.	161
Matsumoto Hotel Kagetsu (CH)	松本ホテル花月	9 Nagano Pref.	251

Matsushiro-ya	松代屋旅館	10 Nagano Pref.	86
Memmen-tei Wata-ya (A)	めんめん亭　綿屋	17 Niigata Pref.	253
Minato-ya	みなとや旅館	8 Nagano Pref.	76
Mitake Sanso (A)	御岳山荘	Tama, Tokyo	248
Miyama-so (A)	美山荘	23 Kyoto	256
Monju-so Shoro-tei	文珠荘　松露亭	28 Kyoto	203
Moto Nakata-tei Kura Yashiki	元仲田邸くらやしき	30 Okayama Pref.	216
Motosaka-ya	元酒屋	8 Nagano Pref.	78
Mukaitaki	向瀧	18 Fukushima Pref.	141
Mukuchi-jima Kadan	六口島花壇	29 Okayama Pref.	211
Murata (A)	山荘　無量塔	34 Oita Pref.	260
Myoga-ya Honkan	明賀屋本館	3 Tochigi Pref.	49
Nagase	長瀬旅館	13 Gifu Pref.	103
Nakamura (A)	なかむら	21 Ishikawa Pref.	255
Nakatani	中谷旅館	11 Nagano Pref.	94
Nanzan-so (A)	南山荘	6 Shizuoka Pref.	250
Nara Hotel (CH)	奈良ホテル	24 Nara	264
Nara-ya	奈良屋旅館	5 Kanagawa Pref.	60
Niki Club (A)	二期倶楽部	3 Tochigi Pref.	249
Nikko Kanaya Hotel (CH)	日光金谷ホテル	3 Tochigi Pref.	262
Nishimura-ya	西村屋	27 Hyogo Pref.	199
Nishin-Goten (A)	鰊御殿	Hokkaido	255
Nishi-ya Ryokan	西屋旅館	19 Yamagata Pref.	146
Noto-ya Ryokan (A)	能登屋旅館	19 Yamagata Pref.	254
Nuno-ya (A)	旅館　ぬのや	9 Nagano Pref.	251
O-an	桜庵	5 Kanagawa Pref.	58
Ohashi-ya	旅籠　大橋屋	16 Aichi Pref.	125
Okasen Ryokan	岡専旅館	15 Gifu Pref.	116
Osaragi-no-Yado (A)	おさらぎの宿	18 Fukushima Pref.	254
Osawa-kan	大沢館	17 Niigata Pref.	134
Osawa Onsen Hotel	大沢温泉ホテル	6 Shizuoka Pref.	67
Rinsen-kaku	御宿　臨仙閣	11 Nagano Pref.	95
Ryugon (A)	龍言	17 Niigata Pref.	254
Saburi	さぶり	23 Kyoto	178
Sakamoto	さか本	22 Ishikawa Pref.	168
Sansui-en (A)	山水園	32 Yamaguchi Pref.	259
Sanyo-so (A)	三養荘	6 Shizuoka Pref.	250
Seiryu-so (A)	清流荘	6 Shizuoka Pref.	251
Seki-tei	石亭	31 Hiroshima Pref.	221
Sekizen-kan Honkan	積善館本館	4 Gumma Pref.	54
Senzai-ro (A)	千歳楼	15 Gifu Pref.	253
Shibukawa Donya	渋川問屋	18 Fukushima Pref.	140
Shigetomi-so (A)	重富荘	Kagoshima Pref	261
Shirakabe-so	白壁荘	6 Shizuoka Pref.	66
Shiraume (A)	白梅	23 Kyoto	256
Shofu-so (A)	松風荘旅館	Tottori Pref.	257
Shoshichi	庄七	14 Toyama Pref.	111

Shozan-kaku	松山閣	23 Kyoto	176
Shukubo Sonsho-in	那智山青岸渡寺	25 Wakayama Pref.	189
Sugimoto	旅館すぎもと	9 Nagano Pref.	81
Suimei-so Wata-ya Besso	水明荘 和多屋別荘	35 Saga Pref.	247
Sumiyoshi-ya	村のホテル住吉屋	12 Nagano Pref.	98
Tachibana	たちばな	6 Shizuoka Pref.	68
Takashima-ya	(高志の宿) 高島屋	17 Niigata Pref.	133
Tamahan (A)	玉半	23 Kyoto	256
Tama-no-Yu	玉の湯	34 Oita Pref.	240
Tamada-ya	玉田屋	16 Aichi Pref.	126
Tateshina Ai (A)	たてしな 藍	9 Nagano Pref.	251
Tawara-ya	俵屋旅館	23 Kyoto	173
Tendo-so	天童荘	19 Yamagata Pref.	145
Teppo (A)	民宿 鉄砲	6 Shizuoka Pref.	250
Tomoe	萩の宿 常茂恵	32 Yamaguchi Pref.	227
Tosen Goshobo	陶泉 御所坊	26 Hyogo Pref.	195
Tsubaki (A)	海石榴	6 Shizuoka Pref.	251
Tsurugata (A)	鶴形	29 Okayama Pref.	258
Tsuru-no-Yu	鶴ノ湯温泉	20 Akita Pref.	153
Tsuru-ya	つるや	28 Kyoto	205
Tsuta Onsen	蔦温泉旅館	20 Aomori Pref.	153
Urushi-no-Yado Yashiki	うるしの宿やしき	22 Ishikawa Pref.	167
Villa Oka-no-Ie	ヴィラ丘の家	7 Yamanashi Pref.	72
Wakana	和可菜	1 Tokyo	38
Wasure-no-Sato Gajo-en (A)	忘れの里 雅叙園	Kagoshima Pref	262
"Welcome Inns" program	——	——	40, 276
Yagumo Honjin (A)	八雲本陣	Matsue, Shimane Pref.	259
Yamakyu (A)	山久	13 Gifu Pref.	252
Yamato-ya Besso	大和屋別荘	33 Ehime Pref.	233
Yanagawa Ohana (A)	柳川 御花	35 Fukuoka Pref.	261
Yatsusan	八ツ三旅館	13 Gifu Pref.	105
Yoshida Sanso	吉田山荘	23 Kyoto	177
Yoyo-kaku	洋々閣	35 Saga Pref.	245
Yudono-an	湯どの庵	19 Yamagata Pref.	147
Yui-no-Ie (A)	YUIの家	32 Yamaguchi Pref.	259
Yume-ya (A)	ゆめや	17 Niigata Pref.	254
Yumoto Choza (A)	湯元長座	13 Gifu Pref.	252
Yunoshima-kan	湯の島館	13 Gifu Pref.	106
Yuto-ya (A)	ゆとうや	27 Hyogo Pref.	257

NOTE: A = Alternative Inn, CH = Classic Hotel.

CHECKLIST OF INNS

Inn	Price	Hot Spring Bathing	Page
Destination 1			
Wakana	From ¥12,000	no	38
"Welcome Inns" in Tokyo	From ¥3,500	no	40, 276
Destination Tama, on the outskirts of Tokyo			
Kabuto-ya (A)	From ¥8,500	no	248
Mitake Sanso (A)	From ¥8,000	no	248
Destination Saitama			
Kyo-tei (A)	From ¥15,000	no	248
Destination 2			
Kaihin-so Kamakura	From ¥20,000	no	42
Chigasaki-kan	From ¥11,000	no	43
Destination 3			
Honke Bankyu Bankyu Ryokan	From ¥18,000	yes	48
Myoga-ya Honkan	From ¥13,000	yes	49
Kita Onsen (A)	From ¥7,500	yes	249
Niki Club (A)	Twin from ¥28,000	yes	249
Nikko Kanaya Hotel (CH)	Twin from ¥13,000	no	262
Destination 4			
Choju-kan	From ¥13,000	yes	52
Kaya-no-Ie	From ¥15,000	yes	53
Sekizen-kan Honkan	From ¥7,500	yes	54
Destination 5			
Fukuzumi-ro	From ¥20,000	yes	57
O-an	From ¥40,000	yes	58
Kampo-ro	From ¥35,000	yes	59
Nara-ya	From ¥25,000	yes	60
Gora Kansui-ro (A)	From ¥25,000	yes	249
Fujiya Hotel (CH)	From ¥20,000	yes	263

Destination 6

Horai	From ¥40,000	yes	64
Arai Ryokan	From ¥23,000	yes	65
Shirakabe-so	From ¥15,000	yes	66
Osawa Onsen Hotel	From ¥23,000	yes	67
Tachibana	From ¥20,000	yes	68
Asaba (A)	From ¥30,000	yes	249
Gyokuho-kan (A)	From ¥25,000	yes	250
Kiun-kaku (A)	From ¥25,000	yes	250
Teppo (A)	From ¥8,500	yes	250
Nanzan-so (A)	From ¥18,000	yes	250
Sanyo-so (A)	From ¥35,000	yes	250
Seiryu-so (A)	From ¥35,000	yes	251
Tsubaki (A)	From ¥37,000	yes	251
Kawana Hotel (CH)	Twin from ¥28,000	no	263

Destination 7

Villa Oka-no-Ie	From ¥8,500	no	72

Destination 8

Minato-ya	From ¥18,000	yes	76
Motosaka-ya	From ¥7,500	no	78
Maru-ya (A)	From ¥22,000	yes	251

Destination 9

Sugimoto	From ¥15,000	yes	81
Kiku-no-Yu (A)	From ¥15,000	yes	251
Nuno-ya (A)	From ¥8,000	no	251
Tateshina Ai (A)	From ¥24,000	yes	251
Matsumoto Hotel Kagetsu (CH)	From ¥14,000	no	251
Kamikochi Imperial Hotel (CH)	Twin from ¥27,000	no	263
Mampei Hotel (CH)	Twin from ¥23,000	no	263

Destination 10

Echigo-ya	From ¥13,000	no	85
Matsushiro-ya	From ¥10,000	no	86
Bogaku-so	From ¥9,000	no	87

Destination 11

Iwa-no-Yu	From ¥19,000	yes	91
Gohonjin Fuji-ya	From ¥9,000	no	92
Nakatani	From ¥15,000	no	94
Rinsen-kaku	From ¥15,000	yes	95
Hana-ya (A)	From ¥15,000	yes	252
Kanagu-ya (A)	From ¥8,000	yes	252
Mampei Hotel (CH)	Twin from ¥23,000	no	263

Destination 12

Sumiyoshi-ya	From ¥18,000	yes	98
Eiraku-ya	From ¥17,000	yes	99

Destination 13

Nagase	From ¥15,000	no	103
Yatsusan	From ¥15,000	yes	105
Yunoshima-kan	From ¥18,000	yes	106
Yamakyu (A)	From ¥7,000	no	252
Yumoto Choza (A)	From ¥16,000	yes	252
Asahi (A)	From ¥9,000	no	253

Destination 14

Koemon	From ¥8,000	no	110
Juemon	From ¥8,000	no	111
Shoshichi	From ¥7,500	no	111

Destination 15

Okasen Ryokan	From ¥7,500	no	116
Bizen-ya (A)	From ¥10,000	no	253
Senzai-ro (A)	From ¥16,000	no	253

Destination 16

Asakichi	From ¥10,000	no	120
Futami-kan	From ¥16,000	no	122
Hazuki	From ¥20,000	yes	123
Ohashi-ya	From ¥8,000	no	125
Tamada-ya	From ¥7,000	no	126
Gamagori Prince Hotel (CH)	Twin from ¥23,000	no	264

Destination 17

Dairo-an	From ¥15,000	no	131
Takashima-ya	From ¥20,000	yes	133
Osawa-kan	From ¥12,000	yes	134
Keyaki-en (A)	From ¥12,000	no	253
Memmen-tei Wata-ya (A)	From ¥16,000	yes	253
Ryugon (A)	From ¥22,000	yes	254
Yume-ya (A)	From ¥30,000	yes	254

Destination 18

Shibukawa Donya	From ¥10,000	no	140
Mukaitaki	From ¥19,000	yes	141
Osaragi-no-Yado (A)	From ¥22,000	yes	254

Destination 19

Tendo-so	From ¥25,000	yes	145
Nishi-ya Ryokan	From ¥8,000	yes	146
Yudono-an	From ¥20,000	yes	147
Noto-ya Ryokan (A)	From ¥12,000	yes	254

Destination 20

Kuro-yu Onsen	From ¥10,000	yes	151
Tsuru-no-Yu	From ¥8,000	yes	153
Tsuta Onsen	From ¥10,000	yes	153

Magari-ya	From ¥9,800	no	155
Kikusui-kan (A)	From ¥6,700	yes	255
Destination Hokkaido			
Ginrin-so (A)	From ¥36,000	yes	255
Nishin-Goten (A)	From ¥10,000	no	255
Destination 21			
Kincha-ryo	From ¥30,000	no	159
Asada-ya	From ¥50,000	no	160
Matsumoto	From ¥25,000	no	161
Kayo-tei	From ¥30,000	yes	162
Nakamura (A)	From ¥5,000	no	255
Destination 22			
Urushi-no-Yado Yashiki	From ¥15,000	yes	167
Sakamoto	From ¥13,000	yes	168
Hegura (A)	From ¥7,000	no	255
Destination 23			
Tawara-ya	From ¥35,000	no	173
Kinmata	From ¥25,000	no	174
Shozan-kaku	From ¥30,000	no	176
Yoshida Sanso	From ¥30,000	no	177
Saburi	From ¥18,500	no	178
Hakkei-tei	From ¥17,000	no	179
Miyama-so (A)	From ¥35,000	no	256
Shiraume (A)	From ¥18,000	no	256
Tamahan (A)	From ¥25,000	no	256
Destination 24			
Edosan	From ¥18,000	no	184
Chikurin-in Gumpo-en	From ¥15,000	no	185
Kikusui-ro (A)	From ¥39,000	no	256
Nara Hotel (CH)	Twin from ¥22,000	no	264
Destination 25			
Shukubo Sonsho-in	From ¥8,000	no	189
Koshi-no-Yu	From ¥18,000	yes	190
Kami-Goten	From ¥15,000	yes	191
Man-tei (A)	From ¥25,000	yes	257
Destination 26			
Tosen Goshobo	From ¥20,000	yes	195
Destination 27			
Nishimura-ya	From ¥28,000	yes	199
Yuto-ya (A)	From ¥18,000	yes	257

Destination 28

Monju-so Shoro-tei	From ¥30,000	no	203
Gemmyo-an	From ¥25,000	no	204
Tsuru-ya	From ¥9,500	no	205
Fukuki	From ¥12,000	no	207
Charoku Bekkan (A)	From ¥20,000	yes	257

Destination Tottori Prefecture

Hana-ya (A)	From ¥13,000	yes	257
Shofu-so (A)	From ¥10,000	no	257

Destination 29

Kurashiki	From ¥20,000	no	210
Mukuchi-jima Kadan	From ¥15,000	no	211
Tsurugata (A)	From ¥15,000	no	258

Destination 30

Fukiya International Villa	From ¥3,000	no	215
Moto Nakata-tei Kura Yashiki	From ¥6,500	no	216
La Foret Fukiya (A)	Twin from ¥5,000	no	258

Destination 31

Iwaso	From ¥21,000	no	219
Seki-tei	From ¥21,000	yes	221
Hangetsu-an	From ¥9,000	no	221
Jusen-so (A)	From ¥16,000	yes	258

Destination 32

Tomoe	From ¥25,000	no	227
Matsuda-ya	From ¥22,000	yes	228
Hokumon Yashiki (A)	From ¥25,000	no	258
Sansui-en (A)	From ¥20,000	yes	259
Yui-no-Ie (A)	From ¥12,000	yes	259

Destination Matsue, Shimane Prefecture

Yagumo Honjin (A)	From ¥15,000	no	259

Destination 33

Yamato-ya Besso	From ¥39,100	yes	233
Dogo-kan (A)	From ¥27,000	yes	259

Destination 34

Kame-no-I Besso	From ¥30,000	yes	238
Tama-no-Yu	From ¥30,000	yes	240
Kannawa-en	From ¥20,000	yes	241
Kashii-so (A)	From ¥12,000	yes	260
Kawasemi-no-Sho (A)	From ¥13,000	yes	260
Murata (A)	From ¥40,000	yes	260

Destination 35

Yoyo-kaku	From ¥17,000	no	245
Suimei-so Wata-ya Besso	From ¥30,000	yes	247
Daimaru Besso (A)	From ¥18,000	yes	260
Yanagawa Ohana (A)	From ¥15,000	no	261
Akune (A)	From ¥23,000	no	261

Destination Southern Kyushu

Ikoi Ryokan (A)	From ¥13,000	yes	261
Shigetomi-so (A)	From ¥22,000	no	261
Wasure-no-Sato Gajo-en (A)	From ¥20,000	yes	262

NOTE: A = Alternative Inn, CH = Classic Hotel.

FAVORITE INNS

Here is a list of personal favorites, which may help those readers needing a quick tip for a good one-off inn experience.

INN	LOCATION	DESTINATION	PAGE
Horai	Atami, Izu Peninsula	6	64
Arai Ryokan	Shuzenji, Izu Peninsula	6	65
Hana-ya (A)	Bessho Onsen, Nagano Prefecture	11	252
Eiraku-ya	Nozawa Onsen, Nagano Prefecture	12	99
Nagase	Takayama, Gifu Prefecture	13	103
Okasen Ryokan	Mino, Gifu Prefecture	15	116
Hazuki	Yuya Onsen, Aichi Prefecture	16	123
Dairo-an	Niitsu, Niigata Prefecture	17	131
Mukaitaki	Aizu Wakamatsu, Fukushima Prefecture	18	141
Tendo-so	Tendo, Yamagata Prefecture	19	145
Kuro-yu Onsen	Nyuto Onsen, Akita Prefecture	20	151
Kikusui-kan	Osawa Onsen, Iwate Prefecture	20	255
Sakamoto	Suzu, Ishikawa Prefecture	22	168
Tawara-ya	Kyoto	23	173
Kinmata	Kyoto	23	174
Shozan-kaku	Kyoto	23	176
Nishimura-ya	Kinosaki Onsen, Hyogo Prefecture	27	199
Monju-so Shoro-tei	Ama-no-Hashidate, Kyoto Prefecture	28	203
Kurashiki	Kurashiki, Okayama Prefecture	29	210
Iwaso	Miyajima, Hiroshima Prefecture	31	219
Matsuda-ya	Yuda Onsen, Yamaguchi Prefecture	32	228
Yagumo Honjin (A)	Shinji, Shimane Prefecture	Matsue	259
Kame-no-I Besso	Yufuin, Oita Prefecture	34	238
Tama-no-Yu	Yufuin, Oita Prefecture	34	240
Yoyo-kaku	Karatsu, Saga Prefecture	35	245
Daimaru Besso (A)	Futsukaichi Onsen, Fukuoka Prefecture	35	260

NOTE: A = Alternative Inn.

RYOKAN-STYLE ACCOMMODATION
IN TOKYO UNDER ¥8,000

On the facing page is a selection of Tokyo ryokan listed with the Welcome Inn Reservation Center supported by the Japan National Tourist Organization (JNTO). The Welcome Inn program has been providing a free reservation service for foreigner-friendly, lower-priced accommodation in Japan since 1991. These include business hotels, pensions, and some ryokan-style accommodations, which, while not necessarily of the same caliber as the selections in this book, are one way to experience tatami rooms and futon.

The prices are for one person, do not include meals, and are based on two people per room. Single occupancy rates are higher. In some cases, three or four people sharing one room may bring down the per-person rates. "W/bath" indicates a room with private toilet and bath; "w/o bath" means the toilet and bath are shared. As a rule of thumb, older, more atmospheric buildings are often of the type that can only provide shared facilities, while places offering private bath and toilet facilities are likely to be newer buildings.

To Make a Reservation

If you can speak Japanese or know someone who can, the Welcome Inn staff suggest making your reservations directly with the inn. Otherwise, make use of the Welcome Inn Reservation Service. This service does not accept reservations by phone. You can make reservations in person by visiting one of the Tourist Information Centers (TIC), or by filling out the official Reservation Request Form and sending it by facsimile to the Welcome Inn Reservation Center in Tokyo. Reservation Request Forms may be found in the pamphlets available at TIC, or on the Japan Travel Updates website, where you can use the e-mail option. Requests from overseas must be made three weeks in advance of departure for Japan, or earlier if you wish to travel in peak domestic seasons. A complete list of Welcome Inns throughout Japan may be found on the Web site. Further information can also be obtained by contacting the overseas JNTO office nearest you.

Contacts

● Welcome Inn Reservation Center (℡ 03–3211–4201, fax 03–3211–9009).

● TIC—Narita (℡ 0476–34–6251), Tokyo (℡ 03–3201–3331), Kyoto (℡ 075–371–5649).

● Japan Travel Updates (www. jnto. go. jp.).

HOMEI-KAN
Location: Bunkyo-ku, Tokyo
¥5,600 w/o bath, 15-min walk from JR Suidobashi Station, ☎ 03–3811–1181.

RYOKAN TSUTA-YA
Location: Bunkyo-ku, Tokyo
¥5,000 w/o bath, 7-min walk from subway Hongo Sanchome Station, ☎ 03–3812–3231.

RYOKAN RYUMEI-KAN HONTEN
Location: Chiyoda-ku, Tokyo
¥7,700 w/bath, 3-min walk from JR Ochanomizu Station, ☎ 03–3251–1135.

HOTEL YAESU-RYUMEI-KAN
Location: Chuo-ku, Tokyo
¥7,700 w/bath, 3-min walk from JR Tokyo Station, ☎ 03–3271–0971.

RYOKAN TOKI
Location: Edogawa, Tokyo
¥4,250 w/bath, ¥4,000 w/o bath, 10-min walk from JR Koiwa Station, ☎ 03–3657–1747.

RYOKAN FUJI
Location: Edogawa, Tokyo
¥4,500–6,000 w/bath, 6-min walk from JR Koiwa Station, ☎ 03–3657–1062.

HOTEL FUKUDA-YA
Location: Meguro-ku, Tokyo
¥5,500–6,000 w/bath, ¥5,000 w/o bath, 15-min walk from JR Shibuya Station, ☎ 03–3467–5833.

SHIN-NAKANO LODGE
Location: Nakano-ku, Tokyo
¥4,500 w/bath, 5-min walk from subway Shin-Nakano Station, ☎ 03–3381–4886.

RYOKAN KANGETSU
Location: Ota-ku, Tokyo
¥4,500 w/o bath, 2-min walk from Tokyu Chidoricho Station, Tokyu Ikegami Line ☎ 03–3751–0007.

RYOKAN SANSUI-SO
Location: Shinagawa, Tokyo
¥4,500 w/bath, ¥3,000 w/o bath, 5-min walk from JR Gotanda Station, ☎ 03–3441–7475.

RYOKAN ASAKUSA SHIGETSU
Location: Taito-ku, Tokyo
¥7,500 w/bath, 3-min walk from subway Asakusa Station, ☎ 03–3843–2345.

KIKU-YA RYOKAN
Location: Taito-ku, Tokyo
¥4,300 w/bath, ¥4,000 w/o bath, 8-min walk from subway Tawaramachi Station, ☎ 03–3841–6404.

SAWANO-YA RYOKAN
Location: Taito-ku, Tokyo
¥4,700 w/bath, ¥4,400 w/o bath, 7-min walk from subway Nezu Station, ☎ 03–3822–2251.

RYOKAN KATSUTARO
Location: Taito-ku, Tokyo
¥4,500 w/bath, ¥4,200 w/o bath, 5-min walk from subway Nezu Station, ☎ 03–3821–9808.

SAKURA RYOKAN
Location: Taito-ku, Tokyo
¥5,300 w/bath, ¥4,800 w/o bath, 5-min walk from subway Iriya Station, ☎ 03–3876–8118.

SUZUKI RYOKAN
Location: Taito-ku, Tokyo
¥6,000 w/bath, 1-min walk from JR or Keisei Nippori Station, ☎ 03–3821–4944.

KURAMAE RYOKAN
Location: Taito-ku, Tokyo
¥5,250 w/o bath, 3-min walk from subway Kuramae Station, ☎ 03–3851–7288.

FAMILY HOTEL KAMOGAWA
Location: Taito-ku, Tokyo
¥7,000 w/bath, ¥5,000 w/o bath, 3-min walk from subway Asakusa Station, ☎ 03–3843–2681.

YAMANAKA RYOKAN
Location: Taito-ku, Tokyo
¥7,000 w/bath, 3-min walk from subway Nezu Station, ☎ 03–3821–4751.

KIMI RYOKAN
Location: Toshima-ku, Tokyo
¥3,500 w/o bath, 7-min walk from JR or subway Ikebukuro Station, ☎ 03–3971–3766.

HELPFUL JAPANESE PHRASES

BOOKING

I'd like to make a booking.
Yoyaku o shitain desu ga.
予約をしたいんですが。

Would you have a room available on [month, day].
[___] gatsu [___] nichi ni heya wa aite imasu ka?
[___]月[___]日に部屋は空いていますか？

How many people?
Nanmei-sama deshō ka?
何名様でしょうか？

How much would you like to pay? We have rooms from ¥15,000.
Go-yosan wa? Ichi-man go-sen-en kara goza-imasu ga. . . .
ご予算は？一万五千円からございますが……

Could we have a room in the old wing, please?
Honkan no heya o onegai shitain desu ga. . . .
本館の部屋をお願いしたいんですが……

We don't mind if the room doesn't have its own bath and toilet.
Basu-toire-tsuki de nakutemo kekkō desu.
バス・トイレ付きでなくてもけっこうです。

We like traditional Japanese architecture.
Nihon no furui tatemono ga suki desu.
日本の古い建物が好きです。

Could we have a room with a nice view?
Keshiki no ii heya o onegai shitain desu ga. . . .
景色のいい部屋をお願いしたいんですが……

Could we have a large room, please?
Ōkii heya o onegai shitain desu ga. . . .
大きい部屋をお願いしたいんですが……

We'd like a room that has its own toilet.
Toire-tsuki no heya o onegai shitain desu ga. . . .
トイレ付きの部屋をお願いしたいんですが……

We'd like a room with its own bath and toilet.
Basu-toire-tsuki no heya o onegai shimasu.
バス・トイレ付きの部屋をお願いします。

It will be more expensive.
Otakaku narimasu ga. . . .
お高くなりますが……

I don't mind if it's more expensive.
Takakutemo kekkō desu.
高くてもけっこうです。

How much more?
Ikura gurai desu ka?
いくらぐらいですか？

In that case, we'll take an ordinary room.
Sore de wa, futsū no heya de kekkō desu.
それでは、普通の部屋でけっこうです。

In that case we'll look elsewhere.
Sore de wa, kekkō desu.
それでは、けっこうです。

Very well, sir/madam.
Kashikomari mashita.
かしこまりました。

May I have your name and telephone number?
O-namae to o-denwa bangō o onegai shimasu.
お名前とお電話番号をお願いします。

What time will you arrive?
Nanji ni otsuki ni narimasu ka?
何時にお着きになりますか？

I'm sorry but we will be late. We will be there about 8 P.M.

Mōshiwakenain desu ga, okuremasu. Hachiji ni narimasu.

申し訳ないんですが、遅れます。八時になります。

I'm sorry but we must cancel our booking for August 8.

Mōshiwakenain desu ga, hachi-gatsu yooka no yoyaku o kyanseru shitain desu ga. . . .

申し訳ないんですが、八月八日の予約をキャンセルしたいんですが……

REGISTERING

Would you like to take a bath first or have your meal?

O-furo o saki ni shimasu ka? O-shokuji o saki ni shimasu ka?

お風呂を先にしますか？ お食事を先にしますか？

What time would you like your meal? (Any time between 6:00 and 7:30 is acceptable.)

O-shokuji wa nanji ni itashimashō ka?

お食事は何時にいたしましょうか？

At 6:00 (7:30), thank you.

Rokuji (Shichiji-han) de onegai shimasu.

六時（七時半）でお願いします。

What time would you like breakfast? (Any time from 7:00 to 8:30 is acceptable.)

Chōshoku wa nanji ni itashimashō ka?

朝食は何時にいたしましょうか？

At 8:00 (8:30), thank you.

Hachiji (Hachiji-han) de onegai shimasu.

八時（八時半）でお願いします。

TIPPING

This is very little. . . . (Said as you pass the maid a tip.)

Sukunai desu ga. . . .

少ないですが……

Are you the lady of the house? (Useful to ask so that you don't make the *faux pas* of handing the tip to the lady of the house instead of one of the maids.)

Okami-san desu ka?

おかみさんですか？

FOOD & DRINK

Where do we eat?

Shokuji wa doko de torun desu ka?

食事はどこでとるんですか？

Can I get you something to drink?

O-nomimono wa ikaga itashimasu ka?

お飲み物はいかがいたしますか？

Some beer, please.

Bīru o kudasai.

ビールをください。

Some sake, please. Warmed.

O-sake o kudasai. O-kan de.

お酒をください。おかんで。

Some sake, please. Cold.

O-sake o kudasai. Hiya de.

お酒をください。ひやで。

Would you mind frying the egg? (Said at breakfast.)

Tamago o yaite itadakemasu ka?

卵を焼いていただけますか？

BATH

Where is the bath?

O-furo wa doko desu ka?

お風呂はどこですか？

Where is the outdoor bath?

Rotemburo wa doko desu ka?

露天風呂はどこですか？

TOILET

Where is the toilet?

O-toire wa doko desu ka?

おトイレはどこですか？

THE BILL

Can we have the bill, please?

O kanjō o onegai shimasu.

お勘定をお願いします。

LEAVING

Could you call me a taxi?

Takushī o yonde itadakemasuka?

タクシーを呼んでいただけますか？

PRICE

¥1,000	*sen-en*	千円
¥2,000	*ni-sen-en*	二千円
¥3,000	*san-zen-en*	三千円
¥4,000	*yon-sen-en*	四千円
¥5,000	*go-sen-en*	五千円
¥6,000	*roku-sen-en*	六千円
¥7,000	*nana-sen-en*	七千円
¥8,000	*hassen-en*	八千円
¥9,000	*kyū-sen-en*	九千円
¥10,000	*ichi-man-en*	一万円
¥20,000	*ni-man-en*	二万円
¥30,000	*san-man-en*	三万円
¥40,000	*yon-man-en*	四万円
¥50,000	*go-man-en*	五万円
¥60,000	*roku-man-en*	六万円

OCCUPANTS

1 person	*hitori*	一人
2 people	*futari*	二人
3 people	*san-nin*	三人
4 people	*yo-nin*	四人
5 people	*go-nin*	五人
6 people	*roku-nin*	六人

MONTH

January	*ichi-gatsu*	一月
February	*ni-gatsu*	二月
March	*san-gatsu*	三月
April	*shi-gatsu*	四月
May	*go-gatsu*	五月
June	*roku-gatsu*	六月
July	*shichi-gatsu*	七月
August	*hachi-gatsu*	八月
September	*ku-gatsu*	九月
October	*jū-gatsu*	十月
November	*jūichi-gatsu*	十一月
December	*jūni-gatsu*	十二月

DAYS OF THE WEEK

Monday	*Getsuyōbi*	月曜日
Tuesday	*Kayōbi*	火曜日
Wednesday	*Suiyōbi*	水曜日
Thursday	*Mokuyōbi*	木曜日
Friday	*Kinyōbi*	金曜日
Saturday	*Doyōbi*	土曜日
Sunday	*Nichiyōbi*	日曜日

DATES

first	*tsuitachi*	一日
second	*futsuka*	二日
third	*mikka*	三日
fourth	*yokka*	四日
fifth	*itsuka*	五日
sixth	*muika*	六日
seventh	*nanoka*	七日
eighth	*yōka*	八日
ninth	*kokonoka*	九日
tenth	*tōka*	十日
eleventh	*jūichi-nichi*	十一日
twelfth	*jūni-nichi*	十二日
thirteenth	*jūsan-nichi*	十三日
fourteenth	*jūyokka*	十四日
fifteenth	*jūgo-nichi*	十五日
sixteenth	*jūroku-nichi*	十六日
seventeenth	*jūshichi-nichi*	十七日
eighteenth	*jūhachi-nichi*	十八日
nineteenth	*jūku-nichi*	十九日
twentieth	*hatsuka*	二十日
twenty-first	*nijūichi-nichi*	二十一日
twenty-second	*nijūni-nichi*	二十二日
twenty-third	*nijūsan-nichi*	二十三日
twenty-fourth	*nijūyokka*	二十四日
twenty-fifth	*nijūgo-nichi*	二十五日
twenty-sixth	*nijūroku-nichi*	二十六日
twenty-seventh	*nijūshichi-nichi*	二十七日
twenty-eigth	*nijūhachi-nichi*	二十八日
twenty-ninth	*nijūku-nichi*	二十九日
thirtieth	*sanjū-nichi*	三十日
thirty-first	*sanjūichi-nichi*	三十一日

TIME

A.M.	*gozen*	午前
P.M.	*gogo*	午後
1:00	*ichi-ji*	一時
2:00	*ni-ji*	二時
3:00	*san-ji*	三時
4:00	*yo-ji*	四時
5:00	*go-ji*	五時
6:00	*roku-ji*	六時
7:00	*shichi-ji*	七時
8:00	*hachi-ji*	八時
9:00	*ku-ji*	九時
10:00	*jū-ji*	十時
11:00	*jūichi-ji*	十一時
12:00	*jūni-ji*	十二時
10 minutes	*juppun*	十分
20 minutes	*nijuppun*	二十分
30 minutes	*sanjuppun* or *han*	三十分／半
40 minutes	*yonjuppun*	四十分
45 minutes	*yonjūgo-fun*	四十五分
50 minutes	*gojuppun*	五十分

GLOSSARY

amerikan "American-style" coffee; a weak brew often served in a larger cup than its counterpart "*burendo kohii*," or blended coffee.

banto the inn's chief attendant/caretaker; in big, established inns he is often the first to greet you at the door and take charge of ushering you inside. Not to be confused with *bento*.

bento a boxed meal. Usually features regional specialties. A train trip is not complete for many Japanese travelers without an *ekiben* (a regional *bento* sold at train stations).

bon See *o-bon*.

buke-yashiki former samurai residence. Most of the extant structures belonged to lower-ranking samurai, the homes of upper-ranked samurai having been mostly destroyed along with the lords' castles at the start of the modern era.

bunraku adult puppet theater that became highly popular in the Edo period (1600–1868) as an entertainment of the townsfolk. Each puppet is operated by three puppeteers.

butsudan a Buddhist family altar, containing a flower vase, incense burner, and *ihai* inscribed with the names of deceased forebears.

chawan-mushi savory egg custard steamed and served in a lidded ceramic cup.

daikon giant radish, or icicle radish. Eaten boiled, as pickles, or grated as a condiment.

daimyo the approximately 250 lords of domains in the Edo period (1600–1868).

daimyo-yashiki *daimyo*'s mansion. Usually situated inside the innermost moat of the castle. Few examples remain.

daiyokujo big bath. *De rigueur* at large inns.

dengaku food, usually skewered, coated in miso paste and grilled. The most common *dengaku* are slabs of *konnyaku*, tofu, and eggplant.

dojo hall for the practice of traditional arts, especially the martial arts; sometimes refers to a whole complex of buildings.

furo bath. Usually referred to as "*o-furo*"; different from *sento*, the public bath. Baths made of cypress are regarded as the ultimate luxury.

fusuma sliding interior doors in traditional Japanese houses. Usually a wooden frame with a paper covering, the paper often decorated with stenciled designs or paintings.

futon Japan's traditional bedding for sleeping on the floor. It consists of one or two floor mattresses and a lighter quilt as a cover. The inn's maids will fold them up in the morning and store them in cupboards and bring them out again at night. At *minshuku* and some cheaper inns, the guest sets out and puts away the bedding. In summer, something known as a *towelket* (towel-blanket) may be used in place of a sheet.

geta footware consisting of a high wooden platform with leather or plastic thong. Good for keeping kimono hems from dragging on muddy roads. Provided by inns for walking in the garden or going out in *yukata*.

Golden Week a holiday-studded week beginning on April 29 and ending on May 5. Being spring, it is a favorite time to travel.

hanare cottages or detached rooms, usually with a separate garden. The most expensive accommodation at the top-class inns.

happi a short, cotton robe worn mainly by festival participants.

hayashi See *o-hayashi*.

hibachi wooden or ceramic brazier.

hinoki cypress wood.

hiraya low slung, single-story structure, usually in *sukiya* style, regarded as the height of architectural elegance.

hito "hidden hot springs." Used to refer to remote springs known only by a few and offering minimal accommodations. Extensive publicity has driven most *hito* well into the public eye.

honjin inn officially designated for accommodation of *daimyo* at stations on the old highways in the Edo period (1600–1868). See *sankin kotai*.

honkan main wing, old wing. Usually the most atmospheric.

hot spring See *onsen*.

inari shrine ubiquitous commoners' shrine set up to pray for prosperity. It is guarded by foxes, who are the messengers of the enshrined rice deity.

irori sunken hearth, originally the place in a farmhouse where the family gathered for food and warmth; now a common feature of country-style inns.

jochu-san maid at an inn. Not to be confused with the *okami*.

Kaga Kaga domain, in what is now Ishikawa Prefecture. Ruled over by the Maeda clan. Famous as richest of all the domains.

kagu furniture.

kamidana literally "god shelf," a Shinto-inspired shelf that used to exist in every home, on which is placed a vase containing sprigs of the sacred *sakaki* tree and some offerings to the gods such as rice and saké.

kasuri Japanese ikat weaving, where the thread is dyed before it is woven, creating interesting uneven edges on patterns.

kazoku-buro private bathing area big enough to be shared by a small family. Common at hot spring inns from the 1920s to 50s, but less prevalent now. See *rotemburo*.

ken prefecture.

kendo art of Japanese swordplay, involving strict spiritual and mental discipline and code of ethics.

Kiso Valley valley of the Kisogawa river in Nagano Prefecture along which several stations of the old Nakasendo highway are being preserved for their historic value. Also famed for its excellent timbers.

kitamae-bune wooden ships that sailed from Hokkaido to Osaka via Chugoku (western Japan) and the Inland Sea; an important method of product distribution in the Edo Period (1600–1868).

kokumin shukusha inexpensive family accommodation built in national parks and resorts by towns and cities using money from public health schemes.

kombu giant kelp; essential ingredient in making Japanese soup stock. Contains natural monosodium glutamate.

konnyaku often translated as "devil's tongue" jelly, this is a starch from the bulb of a type of yam, made into a rubbery jelly and eaten with flavorings such as miso. No flavor, no nutritional value, but lots of fiber.

kotatsu a table with a heating element attached to the underside, over which is laid a thin quilt and then a tabletop. People put their feet under the quilt to keep warm. *Kotatsu* with a foot well are known as *hori-gotatsu*.

koya-dofu   tofu that is freeze-dried for preservation and reconstituted and cooked in soy and other flavorings. Important food in the Buddhist vegetarian diet.

kura   fireproof storehouse for family treasures. Styles differ according to the region. Plaster decorated in elaborate patterns with black or gray tiles is common in Okayama Prefecture; handsome local stone is used in Tochigi Prefecture.

machinami   a street or streets of old houses, now rare. Often preserved as tourist attractions.

matcha   powdered green tea used in the tea ceremony. Also used in other drinks and desserts these days, e.g., *matcha* mousse.

Matsumoto kagu   Matsumoto handmade furniture, including chairs, tables, chests, braziers, and low tables. Quality wood and traditional joinery are used. Developed by Sanshiro Ikeda, a friend of Soetsu Yanagi's, belonging to his *mingei* movement.

matsuri   festival.

meibutsu   a famous product or food of a town or region. Because Japan is so mountainous, every region developed specialties or variations on someone else's specialties, spawning hundreds of *meibutsu* around the country. Part of the enjoyment of a trip to the countryside is to search out the *meibutsu* and if possible the shop or restaurant or craftsman who produces the best.

mingei   folk craft. The word was coined in the 1940s by philosopher and mystic Soetsu Yanagi, who was the first to draw attention to the artistic integrity of the handmade objects of Japan's "unnamed craftsmen." When architecture is described as "*mingei*-style" it means white plaster walls with black pillars and beams. When crafts are described as "*mingei*," they are rustic, but not "naive."

minka   literally "private home," but when discussing Japanese architecture "*minka*" refers to a range of architectural styles of the traditional farmhouse or townhouse.

minshuku   guest houses that provide breakfast and dinner, sometimes in the company of the family. Cheaper than *ryokan*, but without the luxuries.

miso   important condiment in Japanese cuisine, made from steamed soybeans, salt, and malted rice (as a fermenting agent). Up to the Edo period (1600–1868), it was more important than soy sauce, and every household made its own. Each district still has miso of a distinct color and flavor. Kyoto, for example, has a pale, not very salty miso, called *shiro-miso*, while Nagoya has a very dark, almost black miso called *hatcho-miso*.

mochi   round or square cakes of pounded rice served in soup at New Year, or grilled and seasoned with soy sauce.

mompe   simple farmer's pants with drawstring (or elasticized) waistband and ankles, often in blue-and-white *kasuri* or *kasuri* pattern.

Nakasendo   old highway linking Edo (Tokyo) with Kyoto via Nagano. One of the few places where the atmosphere of Edo period (1600–1868) post towns can be experienced.

namako kabe   exterior walls decorated with black and white tiles in geometric patterns, often featured in *kura*, but also a common feature of houses in certain districts, especially Shizuoka, Okayama, and Tochigi prefectures.

noren   split curtain hung outside a shop, restaurant, or inn to show that the establishment is open for business. It bears the shop's name or logo.

o-bon   Japan's All Soul's Day. Spirits of the dead are welcomed back on this day with bonfires, candlelight, and festivities. *O-bon* is August 15 in many regions, but this varies. Famous *o-bon* dancing festivals are held in Tokushima, Shikoku, and Gujo Hachiman in Gifu.

o-furo   See *furo*.

o-hayashi   drum and flute music, sometimes with clappers and stringed instruments, performed to accompany dancing at festivals. The word means to "encourage" or "spur on."

okami   the madam of the inn, she is the artistic director and quality controller, flower arranger, and menu-designer of the best inns; her good taste and attention to detail are vital to the quality of your stay. Not to be confused with the *jochu-san*—maid. The *jochu-san* will usually guide you to your room and serve your meal, but the *okami* will generally make at least one appearance before or during the meal to welcome you personally.

onsen   hot spring. *Onsen* waters are traditionally believed to cure a variety of ailments, but do they really work? Medical opinion is undecided. The benefits may be more psychological than physical. Frequent long soaks in lukewarm water are the most efficacious (overly hot baths are said to be bad for the heart). See also *hito* and *tojiba*.

onsen-gai   town, often gaudy, frequently dowdy, that has grown up around hot spring hotels.

o-shibori   small damp handtowel supplied at mealtime.

penshon   economical accommodation at tourist spots along the lines of European-style bread and breakfast, but with the evening meal also thrown in. The most common variety has pokey rooms with beds and lace curtains, and croissants for breakfast.

ramen   wheat noodles in a broth with a variety of toppings. A common fast food.

ramma   decorative transoms on the top of room-dividing walls in traditional Japanese rooms. Made of slats or carved wood with open work that allows air to flow between rooms.

rotemburo   outdoor bath; not a jacuzzi, but hot spring water fed into natural or manmade rock pools, or wooden baths, exposed to the elements. Quite often mixed bathing, but many inns alternate the hours for male and female bathers. See also *kazoku-buro*.

ryokan   inn, as differentiated from *minshuku*, *penshon*, and hotel.

ryori-ryokan   inn specializing in good food; often operates as a restaurant on the side.

ryotei   high-class traditional Japanese restaurant with private tatami rooms.

samurai   warrior, but after the warring *daimyo* lords were brought under control in the Edo period (1600–1868), samurai became more like public servants. They were among the poorest people, exhorted to live frugal lives according to Zen and Confucian ideals of austerity. Lower-ranked samurai families often engaged in cottage industries on the side to make ends meet.

sankin kotai   In the Edo period (1600–1868) all *daimyo* were required to spend every second year in attendance in Edo, and leave their wives, children, or other relatives behind in the capital as hostages when they returned home. This system ensured good behavior and kept the domains constantly broke and weak. But it also encouraged a lively traffic of people and goods.

sashimi   raw fish (including squid and octopus); the first thing you will be served in almost every formal evening meal. Dip in soy sauce seasoned with *wasabi* (horseradish).

sento   public bath.

soba   buckwheat noodles, a Japanese passion. Comes as *zaru-soba*, a basket of cold noodles with a dipping sauce; as *kake-soba*, noodles in a hot broth, with topping; or as *tempura-soba*, with deep-fried battered prawns on the top.

shibori   See *o-shibori*.

shinkansen   Japan's super express train, the "bullet train."

shoin-zukuri   grand style of architecture

favored by the *daimyo*, featuring a relatively high degree of ornamentation, e.g., murals on the *fusuma* (sliding doors) and elaborately carved transoms.

shoji   sliding screens covered with translucent paper, used on windows or to divide a room from the hall. They take the place of curtains in Japanese architecture.

shugendo   the religion of the mountain ascetics. See *yamabushi*.

shukuba-machi   towns on the old highways where official accommodation was made available for the *daimyo* retinues. See also *sankin kotai*.

shukubo   accommodation attached to temples. Should not be treated like an ordinary inn. Frequently the meal served will be Buddhist vegetarian, served by trainee priests. Some *shukubo* require guests to attend the early morning Buddhist sutra readings.

shunkei-nuri   caramel or toffee-colored lacquerware with a delicate transparency, especially famous in Hida-Takayama. Loved by tea-ceremony practitioners.

sudomari   staying overnight at an inn without meals. Still not a very common option because inns often count on food to make ends meet.

sukiya   the ultimate in elegant architecture. It originally referred to the simple, delicate rooms favored by the tea-ceremony aficionado, but was later combined with some of the ornamental elements of the *shoin-zukuri* style of the warrior class.

tabi   split-toed socks used with Japanese footwear.

tatami   reed floor matting that came to be a standard feature of traditional Japanese architecture from the Edo period (1600–1868). About 1.8 x 0.9 meters, they were originally the size of one man lying flat. Tatami became a standard unit of construction in the Japanese house. Rooms are described by the number of mats they hold. Common room sizes are 4 ½, 6, and 8 mats.

tempura   food (especially vegetables, fish, and prawns) coated in a light batter of flour and water, deep-fried, and then served with a soy-based dipping sauce and grated *daikon* radish as condiment.

tenugui   versatile rectangular cotton cloth, often printed with a design. Used for everything from a headband to a handkerchief or hand towel.

tojiba   hot spring with simple accommodations, where people, mainly the elderly, go for weeks at a time to try and absorb the health benefits of frequent long soaks in hot spring waters. Not as popular as they used to be. See also *hito*.

Tokaido   the most well-traveled highway in the Edo period (1600–1868), linking Edo (Tokyo) with Kyoto.

tokobashira   feature pillar in the *tokonoma*.

tokonoma   alcove; the spiritual focus of a Japanese room, in which is usually displayed flowers, a hanging scroll, and in unfortunate cases, the TV. Don't dump your bags or belongings there.

tororo   a sticky potato, excellent for the health, which is grated and poured over soba noodles or rice.

umeboshi   salty plum. Essential part of the traditional Japanese breakfast. Said to alkalize the system.

unagi   eel, usually served grilled with sweetened sauce. Favorite summer food contains plenty of vitamin A and is said to restore vitality.

urushi   Japanese lacquer, made from the resin of the *urushi* tree. Used originally as a waterproofing for wood. The practice of applying *urushi* eventually led to the development of Japanese lacquerware, a major craft form.

utase-yu   An unusual addition to the hot spring bath, in which hot water is fed through overhead bamboo pipes and cascades down from a height to "massage" the shoulder muscles.

wabi   aesthetic ideal in which beauty is seen in the plain, rustic, old, and decaying. Also known as the "beauty of poverty," in which it is said that "the greatest wealth comes from within" (when we have lost our attachment to material things). The *wabi* ideal was central to the great tea master Sen no Rikyu's tea philosophy. A *"wabi"* teahouse is one made of all natural materials, like a rustic hut.

waka   thirty-one syllable poem turned into an art by the Heian-period (794–1185) aristocracy.

waki-honjin   subsidiary inns for the accommodation of domain officials.

wasabi   horseradish.

washi   Japanese handmade paper. Strong and alkaline.

yakitori   grilled skewered pieces of chicken and vegetables.

yamabushi   mountain ascetics. They combined elements of Shinto, Buddhism, and folk beliefs. They performed ascetics in the mountains to acquire special powers or magic used in healing or exorcisms.

yukata   cotton kimono, supplied by all inns in Japan as a robe to be worn throughout a guest's stay, and even worn as pajamas.

zabuton   square, flat cushions for sitting on in a tatami room.

zazen   sitting meditation of the type practised in Zen.

ACKNOWLEDGMENTS

This book started life as a column in the Mainichi Daily News *called "Inns and Outs," which ran from 1986 to 1988. My interest in the Japanese countryside developed from this. I would especially like to thank Nobuji Itoh, managing editor of the* Mainichi Daily News *from 1989 to 1993, for having faith in an idea developed with Yuko Yokoyama for a publication on Japanese travel and crafts, which evolved into the quarterly* Ichi no Ichi, *from which I learned a great deal more about Japan.*

In 1994 I took 12 wonderful trips to many different parts of Japan for a travel series entitled "Shin'ai Naru Nippon No . . ." in the magazine Nagomi. *Thanks to editor Itsuko Ueda for giving me this opportunity and for her help and companionship.*

Several gems in this book came as a result of tips from friends: thank you to Harumi Nibe for Bogaku-so, Kim Schuefftan and Takagi Shinji for Sakamoto, Stephan Koehler for Okusen, Amy Katoh for Yoyo-kaku, Hiroshi Fukuda for Eiraku-ya, Jacqueline Ruyak for Magari-ya, Chikako Hirata for Kayo-tei, Yuko Yokoyama for Urushi-no-Yado Yashiki, Toda Myosho for Shozan-kaku, Harutaka Ota for Villa Oka-no-Ie, Yukie Iwama for Chigasaki-kan, Itsuko Ueda for Myoga-ya Honkan and Tsuru-ya, and also to Diane Abt and Michael Zielenziger for showing me around the Osawa Onsen Hotel. Yoshie Hayashi and Kimiko Kushiro gave me a much-coveted introduction to Wakana in Tokyo, while textile artist Jun Tomita arranged an interview with Tawara-ya's legendary Toshi Satow. Thank you.

To my traveling companions over sixteen years: parents, husband, flatmates, friends from Australia, whoever would go with me, thank you. Chris Ryan, Toshiko Fukuda, Nobuko Matsushita, and Kosugi sensei deserve a special thank you for their patience in accompanying me on hit-and-miss searches for the perfect inn.

For special insights into the subtleties of Japanese architectural beauty and craftsmanship, I would like to thank Toshiko and Hiroshi Fukuda, who allowed me to live in a Japanese house as beautiful as any of the inns I have seen, and through whose eyes I started to develop a taste for understatement and wit in the things around me.

To Nobuji Itoh, Amy Katoh, Kim Schuefftan, Katharine Markulin, and Rick Kennedy, thank you for your friendship and encouragement throughout this project that sometimes looked like it would never end.

My thanks to Haruna Matsuzaki for filing and compiling lists of inns in the early stages, to Michiko Uchiyama for the never-ending pains taken in contacting the inns and running the tedious final checks, to Micheline Tusenius for working on my wild first draft with courage and professional care and for keeping my chin up when all was grim, to Shigeo Katakura for advice on photographs and illustrations and design work that brought these pages to life, to Kazuhiko Miki for his jacket design, and to Barry Lancet, my editor at Kodansha International, for giving me the chance to do this project, for heading me in the right direction, and for patiently keeping me on the book in spite of distractions and bouts of hopelessness. I am deeply grateful to you all.

PHOTO CREDITS

The author and publisher would like to express their gratitude to the many people, inns, and institutions who graciously contributed photographs to this volume. *For the color pages:* Iwa-no-Yu (page 9), Tawara-ya (page 10), Matsuda-ya (page 12), Takashima-ya (page 13), Horai (page 14), O-an (page 15; 16, top), and Tomoe (16, bottom). *For the black-and-white photographs:* Ben Simmons (page 35), Daisuke Yamaguchi (pages 78, 85, 86, from *Hatago ni Tomaru* published by Shogakukan), Ken Ueda (pages 126, 127, from *Hatago ni Tomaru* published by Shogakukan); the tourist bureaus of Gifu Prefecture, Ishikawa Prefecture, Iwakuni City, Kanagawa Prefecture, Kanazawa City, Kurashiki City, Matsumoto City, Matsuyama City, Nara Prefecture, Shizuoka Prefecture, Takato, Takayama City, Tochigi Prefecture; the inns Arai Ryokan, Asada-ya, Asakichi, Bogaku-so, Chikurin-in Gumpo-en, Choju-kan, Dairo-an, Fujiya Hotel, Fukuzumi-ro, Futami-kan, Gohonjin Fuji-ya, Hazuki, Honke Bankyu Bankyu Ryokan, Horai, Iwa-no-Yu, Iwaso, Kaihin-so Kamakura, Kami-Goten, Kampo-ro, Kaya-no-Ie, Kincha-ryo, Kinmata, Koemon, Kurashiki, Kuro-yu Onsen, Matsuda-ya, Matsumoto, Minato-ya, Monju-so Shoro-tei, Moto Nakata-tei Kura Yashiki, Mukaitaki, Mukuchi-jima Kadan, Nagase, Nakatani, Nara-ya, Nishi-ya Ryokan, O-an, Okasen Ryokan, Osawa-kan, Osawa Onsen Hotel, Rinsen-kaku, Saburi, Sekizen-kan Honkan, Shibukawa Donya, Shirakabe-so, Sugimoto, Sumiyoshi-ya, Tachibana, Takashima-ya, Tama-no-Yu, Tendo-so, Tomoe, Tsuru-no-Yu, Yamato-ya Besso, Yudono-an, Yunoshima-kan. The remaining photographs were taken by the author.

NOTE

Sources that were particularly helpful in my research were the books of Kazuyoshi Miyamoto, especially *Wafu Ryokan Kenchiku no Bi* (The beauty of Japanese-style inn architecture), published by Japan Travel Bureau; *Hatago ni Tomaru* (Staying at old samurai inns) in the Shotor Travel series (Shogakkan); and a supplement on thatch farmhouse inns by *Serai* magazine (Shogakkan).

日本の宿
CLASSIC JAPANESE INNS

1999年5月28日　第1刷発行
2000年4月25日　第2刷発行

著　者　マーガレット・プライス
発行者　野間佐和子
発行所　講談社インターナショナル株式会社
　　　　〒112-8652　東京都文京区音羽1-17-14
　　　　電話：03-3944-6493
印刷所　共同印刷株式会社
製本所　株式会社　国宝社